- THE HAUNT

SPECTERS IN DOORWAYS

THE HISTORY & HAUNTINGS OF UTAH

BY LINDA DUNNING

Dear Paula,
Your are a fellow
traveler on the universal
highway of "empaths!"
Love,
Linda Dunning

- A WHITECHAPEL PRODUCTIONS PRESS PUBLICATION -

For my mother --- Betty McAllister Madsen
Who wanted to write a book herself, But always said that at least she had A daughter who did. I want to also thank my sister Karen Loos and my father B.D. Madsen for all their encouragement and editing work.

Original Cover Artwork Designed by
Michael Schwab, M & S Graphics & Troy Taylor
Visit M & S Graphics at www.msgrfx.com

This Book is Published by

- WHITECHAPEL PRODUCTIONS PRESS -
A Division of the History & Hauntings Book Co.
515 East Third Street - Alton, Illinois -62002
(618) 465-1086 / 1-888-GHOSTLY
Visit us on the Internet at www.historyandhauntings.com

First Edition - July 2003
ISBN: 1-892523-33-7

Printed in the United States of America

"You think the questions asked now are tough.
Wait till the dead rise,
Then think about their questions."

--John McKinley Dunning

TABLE OF CONTENTS

INTRODUCTION - PAGE 6
WELCOME TO HAUNTED UTAH

I. UTAH'S HAUNTED MANSIONS & FARM HOUSES - PAGE 10
BRIGHAM YOUNG'S BEEHIVE & LION HOUSES - BRIGHAM YOUNG'S FOREST FARM HOUSE - GOVERNOR'S MANSIONS - THOMAS KEARN'S MANSION - DAVID KEITH MANSION - ALFRED & ELIZABETH MCCUNE MANSION - THE DEVERAUX MANSION - LESTER & JASMINE FREED HOME - THE ARMSTRONG MANSION - MINER'S MANSION NEAR LIBERTY PARK - WHEELER HISTORIC FARM - HAUNTING LEGENDS IN THE AVENUES - STORIES FROM THE 100 - 200 BLOCK SIDE OF SOUTH TEMPLE, INCLUDING THE LARKIN MORTUARY, GENTILE MILLIONAIRE'S ALTA CLUB & MORE - EVERY BLOOMING THING: THE HANCOCK MANSION

II. UTAH'S HAUNTED HOTELS & BUILDINGS - PAGE 75
THE HOTEL UTAH - SALT LAKE TRIBUNE NEWSPAPER & LAMB'S CAFÉ - CHARLESTON APARTMENTS - ZCMI: ZION'S COOPERATIVE MERCANTILE INSTITUTION - BIGELOW . BEN LOMOND: "THE GRAND DAME OF HOTELS" - HOKEN'S HOLE - SHOOTING STAR SALOON - THAT "OLD HICKS PLACE" - THE PINE HOTEL - THE KIRK HOTEL - HISTORIC LEHI HOTEL BED & BREAKFAST - OGDEN CANYON RESORT GHOSTS

III. UTAH'S HAUNTED HOSPITALS, CHURCHES & MEETINGS PLACES - 132
UTAH VETERAN'S HOSPITAL - STATE HOSPITAL CHILDREN'S PSYCHIATRIC WARD - BUSHNELL V.A. HOSPITAL - INTERMOUNTAIN INDIAN SCHOOL - THE OLD LEHI HOSPITAL - STATE MENTAL HOSPITAL - ST. MARY'S OF THE WASATCH - OLD LDS HOSPITAL : EAST WING HAUNTINGS - THE OLD GRANITE WARD HOUSE - OLD ROCK

CHURCH - HANSEN PLANETARIUM - SALT LAKE CITY PUBLIC LIBRARY - SPRAGUE LIBRARY - CHAPMAN LIBRARY - THE SALT LAKE MASONIC PUBLIC LIBRARY & TEMPLE - TROLLEY SQUARE - UTAH TRANSIT AUTHORITY BUS BARN - TROLLEY BARNS - TERRITORIAL FAIR GROUNDS - LDS TENTH WARD SQUARE -

IV. UTAH'S HAUNTED SCHOOLS, COLLEGES & UNIVERSITIES - PAGE 196

OLD MAIN SPIRITS : SOUTHERN UTAH UNIVERSITY - BRIGHAM YOUNG UNIVERSITY: BYU ACADEMY & ACADEMY SQUARE - WESTMINSTER COLLEGE - MAESER ELEMENTARY - WASATCH ACADEMY - SANPETE ACADEMY & SNOW COLLEGE - HARRINGTON SCHOOL - ROWLAND HALL - ST. MARK'S SCHOOL - ST. ANN'S ORPHANAGE & SCHOOL - JORDAN HIGH SCHOOL - OTHER HAUNTED SCHOOL STORIES, INCLUDING UNION HIGH SCHOOL, CRESCENT MIDDLE SCHOOL, CYPRUS HIGH SCHOOL, TAYLORSVILLE HIGH SCHOOL - ROY HIGH SCHOOL & OTHERS

V. UTAH'S HAUNTED OLD MILLS & FACTORIES - PAGE 272

WEST JORDAN & MIDVALE HISTORIC DISTRICT - GARDNER HISTORIC DISTRICT & OLD MILLS - SHERIDAN HILLS STEEL MINING OFFICE - THE BLACK GOOSE - HAUNTED OLD GRANITE PAPER MILL - BENSON GRIST MILL - CHASE MILL - WOLVERTON MILLS - 200 CO-OPS: THE BRIGHAM CITY MODEL PROGRAM - MERRELL PLANING MILL - BARON WOOLEN MILL - FRANKLIN RICHARDS MILL - WASHINGTON COTTON FACTORY - EPHRAIM CO-OP MERCANTILE & GRANARY - MURRAY SMOKESTACKS - THE STAR FLOUR MILL

BIBLIOGRAPHY - 321
ABOUT THE AUTHOR - 328

INTRODUCTION

My father always said that the reason there were no ghosts in Utah was because there could only be angels and prophets. Ghost hunters and writers visiting the state have found this out. There are several such groups attempting to cover every state in the nation with ghost stories but when they get to Utah and visit the main tourist attractions, they either get puzzled responses or a very polite and sincerely knowing smile. Then there are those few who are somewhat hostile or worse than this, oblivious. One actually has to live here in order to dig a little and find those who would just love to talk about ghosts, and those who don't fear them. In small towns and hamlets across the state there are many quite eager to share their town legends and tales. Stories from the old days are told by both Mormons and Gentiles who still remember the old ways before the 1960s when the push to be "modern" began. While there can be healings, the laying on of hands, dedications and visits from recently departed loved ones, there is still a large faction of Mormons who believe that if something hangs around from the afterlife, it is evil and has to be invited to leave by the Elders.

The underground is alive and well in Utah and has an ever-growing list of ghost hunter societies and avid researchers, although because of the history here, these groups often try to distance themselves from psychics and the like. These healers and visionaries are a little too close for comfort. After all, the entire Salt Lake Valley and Utah Territory, which covered parts of several western states, was founded by a group of people who came from visionary and healer stock. Something that was once celebrated as the ideals of each community has now become suspect due to the great need to be accepted as a worldwide and Christian religion. What has been gained in finances, selective history, LDS church membership, and acceptance of diversity, has been lost in terms of magical thinking, the celebration of the individual and old fashioned, small town community caring. That is something not really very different from what is going on all over our world today.

The whole nation, if not world, in the 1800s was alive with fairies, elves, visions, seers, spirits and things that go bump in the night. Here in Utah, there were the miracle warning voices, the endlessly filling flour bags, the miraculous arrival of the seagulls, the Three Nephites and the wingless giant musclemen angels who helped the handcart pioneers get to the valley. There was a real concrete evil to fight then, often in the woods where people never went at night, or if they did dragon holes and evil spirits awaited them. As for Utahns, the Gadianton Robbers described in the *Book Of Mormon*, might swoop down upon the horses or stagecoaches of the faithful, having lived forever and still being evil of heart. There were also those Danites, a secret society formed during the Missouri phase of Mormon history as a way of defending themselves against the Gentile persecutors. At first seeking blood atonement for wrongs being done to them by Gentiles, the Danites came to Utah too, and continued to carry out blood atonement retributions against those who transgressed within their own religion as well. Blood atonement meaning one had to atone for sinning by dying or being murdered and having one's throat cut so that this blood would spill onto the ground, therefore clearing the way for a "atoned" record in Paradise. Today, much more devastating evils abound, such as World Wars, possible nuclear annihilation, terrorism and those twenty-five or so invisibles who control our nations and world to their own ends.

Mikal Gilmore, whose brother Gary Gilmore was executed by firing squad in Utah, in his book *Shot Through the Heart*, a hauntingly beautiful examination of the author's coming of age in a very unique and different family, put the results of his interesting heritage better than I could. "Between all the Mormons, superstitions, and various Indian tales, Provo (the heart of Mormon country) came to be known as a haunted place. There were stories about ghosts who moved through the hills, and around the farms at night: spirits of men who have lost their land and their lives to the Mormons and their strange, new ways." (p.23.)

Fifty years later, I found Provo to be the most difficult when it came to digging up ghost stories, for most of those who had told them were now gone. All of those absolutely charming campfire tales had become "urban myths" to the younger generation, full of blood and gore and terror. Voices, visions and angels who had once saved the people had been altered by the times that we are living in now. Although Wallace Stegner in his book *Mormon Country*, mentions that in earlier times: "Even when the Mormons built ghosts, they built for the ages." These ghost and angel stories have been replaced by an argument in semantics as to whether the word "holy ghost" was too esoteric and the idea that "holy spirit" might work a little better. It is only within the last decade or so, after a long "spiritual" drought, that the word itself has reappeared in both religions and in those creating new ways to be "spiritual."

Claims of talking to these angels or spirits, which were once celebrated and predicted in Mormon Patriarchal Blessings, are now beyond the psychiatric borders of sanity. They are considered claims of false prophets or misguided souls and the people are gently reminded that if they have such gifts or visions they are to use them only within their own homes and families or immediate communities; there is, after all, only one Prophet with a direct line to God. The LDS Prophet has his counterpart in most other religions, for example the Catholics have their Pope and their Saints and the perpetuators of miracles such as the little children of Lourdes. However, many common folk have come to believe that the afterlife is approachable and that the dead can indeed speak to the living and vice versa. More and more, people are seeing, hearing and feeling spirits. Skeptics say that this is because whenever there is a greater need for such fantasies due to the particular perils of the times, people turn to various distractions and entertainments to relieve their stress. For example, during the Great Depression, movie theaters were packed and entertainers thrived.

The Native Americans who many believe, including many people of the LDS faith, will lead us spiritually out of the quagmire that we have gotten ourselves into, have certain holy tribes scattered throughout the world. There is one such holy people on each continent, for example in Asia, the Tibetans are considered the spiritual leaders of that continent. Near us in North America are the Hopi, who have prophesied that the people of the Fourth World, who continue to stand in one place and defend themselves against all comers, will not find a place in the now-emerging Fifth World. The Fifth World is one full of diversity and world community and understanding, where people of all faiths, nations and nationalities can be approached or welcomed with open arms. Even the spirits will have a place among us, as we will have a place among them. One can see movement towards this Fifth World even in so isolated a culture as the Mormons, with both an encouragement from their Prophet to diversify and a push to learn others languages while proselytizing in other countries. An example of movement towards the Fifth World was when the LDS leaders cautioned their members to step back from missionary zeal when the 2002 Winter Olympics came to Salt Lake City, hopefully engendering a wider interest in their church abroad.

With every change or visit, apparitions and spirits from both the past and present come to visit too. After all, we are a haunted nation, if not a haunted world. This is what ghosts are all about: reminders of whoever we once were, have become, or will be in the future. Ghosts are everywhere, as patterns in walls, echoes in hallways, footsteps in attics or voices coming up from the very lands on which we stand. They are our ancestors and neighbors, whose recordings and interactions come to inform us of what we have forgotten or what we need for the future. They are our muses, and something that we must accept about ourselves as we walk into a future without walls.

This is the first in a series of books about Utah hauntings and mysteries. In this one the reader will visit homes, mansions, farm houses, old mills, schools, churches, hospitals, gathering places, shops, libraries, factories, hotels, saloons and lots of other public buildings where I found ghost stories as well as interesting historical stories. The reader will also be given a bit of my own personal impressions of some of these buildings, having awakened to my own ancestral gifts as an intuitive midway through my life. In the seven years so far that I have been writing and researching these various stories, I found myself becoming much more than a chronicler of ghosts. I became an interviewer, amateur historian and preservationist, as well as a traveler learning more about my home state than one could ever imagine. I discovered small town libraries and museums and had quite a few intuitive experiences within them, while having a great time talking to those older than I and hearing all of their stories.

I found Utah to be one of the most fascinating of places, with its unique, quite wild, and sometimes even violent historical beginnings. I want to especially thank all those small town librarians, genealogists, archivists and museum volunteers whose eyes lit up when I mentioned what I was working on, instead of hurrying me away as though I might somehow harm them. I want to thank the skeptics, owners, managers and back-store storytellers who were thrilled to tell me what they knew, understanding that it was all in fun, or at least necessary to get those "spirit" messages out. I also need to recognize those who will, even after all my research, phone calls, interviews and careful deliberations, find that I have forgotten some important point or aspect of their town story. I may even have made someone's brother his father instead. I did the best I could and hope that the "spirits" think so, too.

In Book Two I will be talking about haunted landscapes such as lake stories and monsters, Bigfoot, UFOs, crop circles, town parks, National Parks, tunnels, regions, town legends and cemeteries, a few modern day tales, and places where accidents or disasters took place. Book Three will be about the haunts in railroad tales, mining and mining town tales, treasure hunting, old forts and camps, old courthouses and jails, and the apparitions of battlegrounds and massacre sites. Book Four will contain stories of mysterious women and men of Utah, stories on the various arts, haunted theaters and opera houses, haunted amusement parks and public parks, spirited dance halls and shrines as well as mystic roots and folktales. Book Five emphasizes silent film star biographies from Utah, but also includes actors, directors and others associated with the industry from earlier eras of film making through the 1950s, as well as a partial film history and brief descriptions of modern day filming and stars here in Utah.

Places, just like people, are born, live out the decades with various changes and have different people inhabiting them. They live their lives and then die, either being torn down or simply forgotten and decaying away. People help birth them, enjoy the community they offer and then mourn their passing when they die. Sometimes residents even build monuments to them or resurrect them in a different form. Places house spirits even after the buildings or lands are changed and gone. Some remain as mere recordings in walls, replays of what once was, while others are just as alive as you or I, yet are somehow trapped and unable to move on to wherever they are supposed to go. This is the cycle of buildings and lands from birth to death, and people are their communities.

So you are welcome to walk among the spirits who inhabit these walls, frames and doorways with images, sensations and voices. Listen to what the spirits have to tell or show you, and let them touch you with their souls. Most of them for good, some of them for ill or even evil, these ghosts and stories are the recordings of history played over and over again for you to see and hear or remain oblivious to. They are the spirits who, if not mere pictures, are trapped where they are, sometimes talking back. We walk through their homes and their time when we visit them. We are their guests and they are our hosts. They haunt us as we haunt them, and in the process, haunt ourselves as well. Enjoy these tales of who we once were as we walked with our own ancestors, and of what we may become in the future.

Linda Dunning

Summer 2003

UTAH'S HAUNTED MANSIONS & FARM HOUSES

BRIGHAM YOUNG'S BEEHIVE & LION HOUSES:

POLYGAMY'S BASTIONS

The Beehive House was constructed in 1854 and the Lion House was constructed in 1856. The Beehive House was the Territorial Governor's mansion until 1855 and it continued to be LDS church president Brigham Young's residence after that, where he entertained visitors from all over the state and country until his death in 1877. The Lion house was the dormitory residence for many of Brigham's wives, twelve of whom lived there with all of their children. LDS church president Lorenzo Snow lived in the Beehive House from 1898 to 1901 and president Joseph Fielding Smith lived there from 1901 to 1918. It was in this house that Smith had his great vision of the afterlife just before his death in 1918. In all, 4 church presidents resided there and 2 of these presidents died in the Beehive House, while Brigham Young died in the Lion House. Both houses were built of adobe and sandstone which was hauled from City Creek Canyon and Brigham Young's brother-in-law was the architect. The beehive on top of the house later became the state emblem for industry and the lion crouching on top of the front portico gave the Lion House its name, as well as Young's well-known nickname "Lion of the Lord." The idea came from a similar one on a home in Vermont where Brigham Young had been born and raised.

For several years after this the homes were maintained by his family and then sold to the LDS church. The Lion House became a home economics center for the Latter

Day Saint University which closed in 1931 and then both residences were used by the Young Women's Mutual Improvement Association. The Lion House became a social center and the Beehive House became a dormitory for young women. Rooms could be rented for wedding receptions and classes were taught on such things as needlepoint, embroidery, art and music, etc. In the 1960's both buildings received major renovations and the Beehive House became an historic site where tours are given, while the Lion House became a restaurant on the main floor called "The Pantry" and a social center on the second floor for wedding receptions, meetings and birthday parties. I have been to "The Pantry" several times with cousins and in a wedding reception or two there.

The Lion House has three floors and several corridors running through the house from north to south. Stairways go up each end of these corridors and in the center of the building a narrow hallway runs eastward to the outside court where the well water used to be. In the basement were two vegetable and fruit cellars and later a pump was placed over the outside well. At the front of the long north side of the basement was what was called the weaving room where several looms of varying sizes were used to make rugs and cloth for clothes and curtains, etc. The looms and spinning wheels were constantly busy in this room, although when the huge harvest of strawberries and peas came in, this room was also used to store them until they could be preserved and bottled, etc. There was a small sitting room beyond this room on the north and still further north, was a milk room for pans and kettles of milk, for churns to make butter, and for cream and cheese to be stored on a stone floor to keep them cool. After this was a small bathroom and then a store room on the northeast corner. The north hallway led to a passageway where the men and boys walked to their own bathroom facilities in the "lower toilet."

On the south side of the basement level in the southwest corner was a long dining room where everyone ate. A long table and a shorter one accommodated up to 70 people at one time if needed. Opening up from this room were several small pantries and the mammoth size kitchen with a huge oven and stove top. The large tin sink and the drainpipe to carry away the dishwater were very novel and expensive ideas in those days. Further north on the south side was the laundry room with benches, wash tubs and a large barrel where the clothes were beaten with a huge wooden pounder. There were great copper boilers; a man always pounded the clothes and carried the wash water. In the southwest corner was a schoolroom with a corner storeroom. The regular schoolhouse was built in 1862 and then the whole room became a store room with places to pop popcorn, and pull and stretch molasses candy on silver hooks attached to the walls.

The main floor consisted of a large parlor in the southwest which was used the most as a prayer room and which also had a piano brought by ox-team across the plains in 1858. Three large glass cupboards were also in this room and they housed all sorts of curiosities and interesting objects locked away from children's prying fingers. Things from Brigham's travels resided there and also many seashells and corals which Brigham liked to collect. It is in this room that Young held sacred prayer circles with those of the faith who visited. All around this large room were red wooden chairs specially made in the cabinet shop and a huge long red velvet sofa. The two doors in this parlor opened up to a small sitting room and a long hallway. There were four more living rooms beyond this room on the west side and on the east side were five living rooms with a small corner closet in each of these rooms. Each living room had a Lady Franklin stove and mantelpieces and at the end of each hall were the staircases which led up to the third floor. There were ten bedrooms on each side of the hall with a dormer in each room. There was also a garret room for storage on this floor.

Twelve wives lived there for a short time until families grew and other homes were built for his other 50 wives. Eleven wives and some 19 daughters and 8 sons lived there when both buildings were at their fullest, and many people were born and died there. The children got to skate and sleigh in the winter time and swim and play games in the big yards in the summer. There was a large wooden font four feet deep which water ran into and out of constantly; this is where they went swimming. There were picnics in the canyons to the east of them and large organs in some of the sitting rooms for musical gatherings. One question often asked concerns how Brigham chose which wife to spend the evening with. This was done by leaving a *Book of Mormon* outside the door of the chosen wife, so that the other wives knew to leave them alone. Sometimes Brigham would leave a bookmark in the book with a certain scripture to be observed before he arrived. The Lion House was not just a dormitory for Brigham Young's wives and children, but a true community all its own where many an event could have been recorded in those walls, and many a haunting could still be taking place today.

The Beehive House is like a typical mansion house with two feet thick walls of sandstone and adobe. It has a wide porch with square columns and the walls in the front hallway are paneled with pine wood, while each room has its own hand carved mantelpiece and fire place. Even the door frames are carved with flower and leaf designs and other designs are carved in the wooden staircase and in the various bedrooms upstairs. Brigham lived in this residence with his second wife Mary Ann Angel and later with another wife Lucy Decker. The west wing was a reception center and office, and the north wing was added in the l890s. On the second story is a veranda and a widow's walk, as well as several bedrooms. One modern improvement has been to stain all of the pine wood throughout the mansion to look like either hardwood or marble. Tours are given every half hour daily now, which precludes any chance to be alone in the building or in the empty restaurant, but I did get a chance to interview a few people there. All either responded by saying that they did not know what I was talking about, smiled sympathetically, or acted like I had asked just about the most ridiculous thing on the planet when I asked if there were any ghosts.

Ghost hunters and writers traveling through Utah, are politely told at the main Mormon historic tourist attractions that such things do not exist. If something mystical or paranormal happened in those buildings from the early days, it was a vision or a dream which brought a vision with it. In later days, one did not talk about such things though if they did it was in terms of angels or Nephites, and nowadays, one gets that "I don't know" pleasant smile or maybe just the hint of angels. I did get the impression though, that many people working at these two historic buildings talk among themselves about feeling the presence of Brigham Young, some of his wives or the later presidents of the LDS church who resided, worked and died there. Knowing the history of polygamy within the LDS church one would have to suppose that not all of those wives were happy about these arrangements.

There are also rumors that Brigham had several underground tunnels constructed not only for safe passage to various important buildings downtown, but also to get to his other wives unobserved, and later to let others hide in them when the law was trying to capture some polygamous husbands. Photos of the tunnels were taken before many of them were covered over, by people being given occasional secret tours. Only a very few remain, maybe three at the most, the others have long ago been sealed off. The tunnels were quite nice and made of brick and not creepy at all as people suppose. They led from the Beehive House and Lion House to the temple and tabernacle and two or three of the first ward houses downtown, like the current Salt Lake Acting Company building. But if one asks about the tunnels, they are myths or unfounded rumors, except to those who know clearly about these tunnels, such as employees at the Lion House who go down to them quite often to get things. These tunnels are used now as storage areas.

On the other hand, women in Brigham Young's household were like royalty too, and perhaps this alone made up for any unpleasantries around the place. They were strong women, powerful women with many talents and abilities, and, with the money they had, they were able to do things of which other women could only dream. They published newspapers, gave speeches, wrote poetry and articles, traveled extensively, became involved in the feminist suffragette movement, were mystics and healers, practiced politics, fostered charities and the arts, helped many women to achieve fame within the arts, taught school, did midwifery, and essentially did what they wanted within the confines of the polygamist life. These were women who would haunt the place by any means, for even after death they are probably still doing whatever they want to do, leaving their mark on these two main houses and others nearby.

Polygamy in those days was not so wonderful for the everyday folk in the state, however. Women in the LDS church have conflicting feelings about it because, although polygamy has long been outlawed, it is still written that women can only be sealed to one man while men can be sealed to several wives for residence in the afterlife. In other words, in our modern day era, a man married five times can be with all five wives in heaven, but a woman married five times has to go through all kinds of things to be sealed to the man of her choice, temple divorces, temple marriages and all the permissions in between. Some women never end up with the one they want before death. When asked about this, women in the LDS church have their stock answer that things are changing or that things look hopeful for the future.

There are stories of wonderful communities of sister wives or aunts who helped each other through every hardship - like the wife who never became Mormon and was leaving her husband when her dear friend wife became very ill. She stayed four more years in the marriage to nurse this woman, watched her die and remained to help raise her children until she just couldn't stand it any longer and ran off. Or there is the story of the woman who made a primitive incubator for her sister wife's twins out of mustard plasters and shoe boxes and then drove them all the way to Salt Lake City to give them the chance to survive. Sister wives did a lot of the healing and midwifery then, besides the cleaning, childrearing, educating, cooking and a lot of the other hard work. They were allowed to have visions and other angelic powers in those early days until this too threatened the church, when one woman visionary in Salt Lake City developed a following and it was revealed that women could no longer do these sorts of things. Many women found the lifestyle wonderful and early visitors to the valley, coming with preconceived notions, often went away much more informed and forgiving.

There are the darker stories like the one told on my mother's side of the family. After an almost-twenty year marriage, my great grandfather, who was the choir director for the town, began bringing home a pretty young thing from choir practice each night. After his first wife, my great grandmother, went to bed, he would rock his future wife on his knee in a handmade rocker, her only good piece of furniture brought across the plains in a wagon. One night after he had left to walk the young woman home, my great grandmother grabbed the rocker and went out in the middle of the night to chop it up for firewood. There are many such stories like the woman who sent for her husband and asked for a new set of dishes, because the other wife had broken all of her new dishes in a fit of jealousy. Elaborate plans were made to get back at someone. One family worked out a strategy whereby the daughter of a man who had forced a woman into a polygamist marriage would be wooed and courted by another man in the wife's family. Then the relative of the woman that supposedly been abused in her polygamist marriage, would desert his new bride just to hurt his wife's father. When the time came for the desertion, the other young man had fallen love with his new wife and refused to desert her.

Wives who threatened to leave their husbands if they took a second wife were often directly counseled by Brigham Young or other church leaders and later changed their minds. A few wives did leave, but then came back to raise their children because they could not stand to be parted from them. Other wives waited until their husbands were jailed for polygamy and then stripped them of all their property, so that when they got out they were penniless and not allowed to come home. In the book *A Mormon Mother : An Autobiography Of Annie Clark Tanner*, it is plain to see that the worst part of life in polygamy was the loneliness. Women were often on their own both emotionally and financially, and they also had to hide their marriages from outsiders or even their own relatives. The financial worries fell on their shoulders because their husbands could not support all of their wives or chose to only support certain favored wives. Often the husbands were simply absent most of the time, especially if the marriage vows had cooled.

On my father's side of the family, even if one was one generation removed from polygamy, the threat of it was still there. Although my great grandmother was a second wife after her husband had been widowed, she came from a family of three wives out in Herriman, Utah. When her husband needed to move into Riverton to be closer to his work in Draper and his new wife refused to move, leaving all her family and friends, he threatened to take a second wife in Riverton and just visit my great grandmother on the weekends. Great grandmother moved immediately to Riverton with her husband. Later when her husband went on two separate missions to Denmark and told his wife to borrow from her two brothers while he was gone, she instead made money selling baked goods, paid off the mortgage on their house and was greeted at the train station with, "How our are finances?" She never forgave her husband for this being the first words out of his mouth when he returned.

Some who never got that far into the religious practice, had even worse things happen to them because they refused the advances of a patriarch who wanted them for a wife. Those who think that Zane Grey's *Riders of the Purple Sage* was just a not-so-well written Western, don't know about the real stories in the valley much more interesting than Grey's. Those who make light of the last scene in the book, when Jane Witherspoon tells Lassiter at least a dozen times to roll that stone, almost comical by today's literary standards, don't realize that it was her last ditch effort for freedom from tyranny as she saw it. She was even willing to live out her life as a primitive locked up in that canyon rather than return to a place where her independence and financial and spiritual power was to be taken from her. Some women chose this lifestyle and were quite content with it, others did not choose it and were never content. .

There are others living in Salt Lake City today who can tell their stories, too. There is the story of two young girls from a Scandinavian country who joined the LDS church in their home country and being the only one from their respective families, were of course "cast out". They came over on one of the boats like so many others of the faithful did, and then made the perilous journey across the plains with only each other for support. When they got to the valley they were penniless and had no skills or education; one solution for such a state, other than immediate marriage to someone, was to indenture themselves for seven years after which they would be free to do whatever they wanted. They were sent together to a farmer in middle Utah; it was soon apparent that he really had only wanted two additional wives and, since they were essentially his slaves, they had no where to go. They both refused to marry him and after a long period of first gentle guidance and discussion, it soon became more urgent on his part. At that point he locked both of them in his potato cellar. The cellar was damp and dark and chilly especially when it rained. The one girl held her best friend in her arms as she died there from pneumonia and it was at this point that the other girl got up the initiative to escape, finally realizing that she too might die there. She made her way to southern Utah where she met a young Gentile miner, got married and had one daughter before her new husband was killed in a mining accident only two years later. She never married again.

While this is rather a dramatic story, one has only to read Maurine Whipple's *The Giant Joshua* to get an accurate and heart wrenching picture of what polygamy life was like for most women of little means. Maurine Whipple planned to write only one book on her own ancestor and that is all she ever did. But she wrote a masterpiece in the early 1940's, strangely forgotten by her own people today, of the sometimes poignant and sometimes tragic lives of women in polygamy back when it was an entirely different thing than it is with today's splinter groups. Reading this book as an outsider to her family, I found that she told me the entire truth of this life, probably not meaning to; I could understand just how terrible it might have been and how wonderful at the same time. The whitewashing of the past hadn't been an issue in those days, and so it is really a wonderful and well rounded portrait of both the good and bad times that such a lifestyle brings to women. Women either loved the sisterhood of it, accepted it because of their children or the wishes of their husbands or both, or did not accept it and lived with it bitterly or in some cases got away from it entirely and even came back for a little revenge by writing and speaking about it.

Then there were the wild ones who ran off to join the theater, like silent movie star John Gilbert's mother, Ida Adair Apperly. She was disowned by her Mormon family in Logan and died a family disgrace, of alcoholism and related diseases at an early age. Her mother, Lydia Mangum, was indentured to a family in Washington City after surviving the Mountain Meadows massacre or so the family history goes. A stolen child without her real name and ancestry, she was never happy in the other household. She married a Mormon man who had other wives. He took her to Logan where she ran away several times while at the same time giving birth to seven children. Eventually she succeeded and disappeared into history. No one knows where she went or what happened to her. Her husband, piled all the children into a wagon and drove around the state pawning his children off on relatives and friends, keeping only the prettiest child, Ida. This is probably why he was so hard on John Gilbert perhaps having adored his daughter a little too much. When Ida died, after years on the road and then returning home to be cared for, fourteen year-old Jack Gilbert (Cecil Pringle) was sent for, attended his mother's funeral and then was put on a train at the Salt Lake Union Station with posters and a make-up kit of his mother's theatrical wanderings. He was given a ten dollar bill and told that he was disowned by the family and was never to return to Utah and he never did.

So, when I was invited to the Beehive House for a special dinner honoring the matriarch of a huge extended LDS family, with black sheep members of course, it was Brigham's portrait I looked at reigning over our dinner. I watched his eyes follow us as we sat together as women at his table and imagined what it must have felt like to live, work and die there - knowing full well that ghosts and apparitions must have free rein there to do as they wish, being ignored as they are by a people with a great need to be "modern." They must have their fun with those of us who visit there, and tell their stories at will to those of us who will listen to them, if we are given the chance and realize their good intentions to teach us. They are good spirits of course, warm and friendly and for the most part proud of who they were and how they lived their lives.

Brigham Young was known for his generosity towards his people and especially towards those many women he either took in as a wife or simply helped to be financially solid and respectable in the community. He loved the arts and was their strong supporter, as well as being a great statesman, businessman and orator. On the other hand, he was plainly a dictator, charismatic and unyielding, as well as fully aware of many "backdoor" activities of his church both for financial gain and to control the people or banish them at will. In short, he was a multifaceted man who could be loyal and loving, while at the same time, controlling and manipulative. What made him stand out as a leader and the Prophet of a church, is that he trully believed in his church and its teachings and was nearly always governed by his faith, mostly for good, occassionally for ill. He was a great man who believed that nearly everything he did was for the best, although sometimes he even mislead himself. However he goes down in history over the ages, he was pretty much a loving husband and father in the ways that he could be within the confines of something that he and Joseph Smith had revealed, the polygamous life.

So why would one even fear to speak to them or see them - the ghosts of the Beehive and Lion houses? Perhaps because it would somehow remind the people of their mystical and magical past, when communities came together and everyone blessed everyone and everyone healed everyone and there was a prevalent belief that magic was alive. Somehow this has come to mean something evil or wrong and we are all to move on and never come back to this life when it is finished. Yet still, loved ones visit us to tell us things are all right either where we are or where they are, and they also warn us of impending dangers along the path. But most of all the leaders of the Mormon faith and I suppose many others, feel that they are perceived as not looking legitimate before the world if they show this side of their past or even present. Although this is not so for the everyday Mormon folk in small towns and communities across the state where the charm of these old-time stories still exists. The irony is that as the people of the world come to the Mormons as converts, they bring with them a rainbow of cultures and beliefs every bit as real as the Mormon magical and mysterious past.

So are there ghosts at the Beehive house? Are there ghosts at the Lion House? Are there ghosts in the many sister wife houses that line the blocks near these two places? Of course there are! It would be like saying that there are no ghosts at the White House or memorials in Washington D.C., or that Europe's cathedrals had nothing haunting them. With all those powerful men and all those powerful women inhabiting the place, how could they have not left something of their former selves behind them? Ghosts are everywhere, and we have only to see or hear them haunting us as we pass by. No impressions needed, they are there!r

BRIGHAM YOUNG'S FOREST FARM HOUSE

THIS IS THE PLACE HERITAGE PARK

EMIGRATION CANYON, SALT LAKE CITY

Brigham Young's farmhouse was moved from its original location several years ago and relocated to the then named Pioneer Trails State Park. The Park houses many old transplanted homes as well as many newly built ones forming a whole pioneer town complete with school house, church, community meeting and social hall, store, blacksmith's shop, various shops and some private homes turned into shops. The farmhouse was the first to be moved long before the town began to form up the hill behind it. Eventually the first original pioneer graveyard, which was located directly across the street from the old Broadway Hotel downtown (now the Palladio apartments), was moved to the Pioneer Trail State Park. The park has now been renamed "This Is The Place Heritage Park" and includes the "This Is The Place"

monument and a pioneer museum and Visitor's Center.

So it is really a patchwork town of both old and new, transplanted and collected antiques and farm equipment. This is what is interesting about such a town, that a haunting or rather several hauntings could travel with the property, for the Forest Farm is another one of the most famously haunted houses in Utah. This brings up a whole theory of hauntings: is it the place or ground itself, or the building which can be moved anywhere - even, it seems, across a body of water - and still carry energy and residue from the past within it? But there have also been actual conversations with those of us in the present, signifying active and interactive ghosts. It is rumored that the staff over the years have kept a running log of all the haunting events there and most of the tour guides will tell you the stories they know if you ask them. The local newspaper has even subtletly hinted at the ghosts there, and as the times change, these invisible and even sometimes visible Utahns have become more acceptable to talk about. Twenty or thirty years ago, people in Utah didn't talk about such things, while fifty years ago and long before this, they did.

Some people seem to agree that it is Brigham's 19th wife, Ann Eliza Webb Young, who is the main spirit in the Farm House. She has been sighted by many people, dressed in her long dark gowns and checking on visitors from the top of the stairs or in a crowd of people even in broad daylight, or staring out of the window as people leave the place, or even just standing by the window for a few seconds while someone else is in the room to see her. One tour guide claimed that while he was giving a tour once, a picture of Ann Eliza's face and shoulders floated out from its frame towards the guide group and then slowly receded back into the photograph as they all watched in astonished disbelief. Apparently Eliza didn't like how the house was laid out anyway and wanted renovations; she especially did not like the stairs to the second floor and was always complaining about them to Brigham.

Ann Eliza was the one who wrote an exposé on polygamy called *Wife No. 19: The Story of a Life in Bondage*, mentioning how Brigham played favorites not only with the gentile actresses traveling to town but with his wife Amelia whom everyone knew he was "silly" for. One of the stories told is of when Brigham, Amelia and Ann Eliza went to a play at the old Salt Lake Theater together. They rode in a carriage and watched Julia Dean Hayne perform in a play. Julia was a young, beautiful and very popular Gentile actress who had a season long engagement at the theater. Brigham fell for her, tried to court her and in fact even had her portrait painted on the side of his carriage. Amelia was the prettiest and favorite of Brigham's wives and after they left the theater, Brigham and Amelia had a big fight right on the steps of the theater, after which Amelia flounced off and drove away in the carriage leaving Brigham and Ann Eliza having to find their own way home. Julia rejected Brigham's advances but was also being courted by a young Gentile officer at Camp Douglas, she married the young officer at the end of her season at the Salt Lake Theatre and moved back east. A year later she died in childbirth and when Brigham heard the news, he had her sealed to him as another wife in the Salt Lake LDS Temple. Amelia Folsom got to design and furnish her own mansion, the Gardo House, where she lived throughout her life.

Ann Eliza was one of only two who divorced Brigham, charging him with neglect, cruelty, and desertion in the 1870s. She asked for a huge alimony and the case dragged on for months in the court where eventually, because of polygamy, Brigham was able to say that he was only legally married to his first wife; Ann Eliza had to settle for a paltry one hundred dollars a month.

One of the most poignant moments in her book is when she first took the train back east and witnessed a single family on the train, noticing how the father deferred to his wife and seemed to value her opinion. How the two parents seemed to be totally involved in the raising of their young and seemed to have a mutual respect for each other. She had never seen such a thing or experienced it within the system in which she had been raised and she found herself weeping at the sight of this "wonder." Life outside the Utah Territory was a real eye opener for Ann Eliza and her somewhat forced marriage to Brigham Young and the polygamous lifestyle became quickly foreign to her. When she returned she spent some time with a reverend and his wife and children and saw the same sorts of things happening within their family. All of these experiences were instrumental in her decision to leave the Prophet.

By this time Ann Eliza had been sent to the Forest Farm, which was a place where according to her account, wives who went against the established order or were out of favor went. At the farm, women had a life of drudgery and hard work from sun up to sun down, and one did not really want to go there according to Ann Eliza. Because Ann Eliza left Brigham she has often been portrayed as a bitter malcontent who tried to browbeat her husband and made up stories against the established order of things. Actually she was a highly intelligent woman who had one marriage behind her when she married into polygamy. She was a very brave woman for her day rising above the circumstances in which she found herself. Her account of her years in the fold is told carefully and with much detail, although one can tell that she did want to inform others about the reality of this life, or at least her reality. She is and was, one of the many fascinating enigmas of her times. LDS historians are still trying to find out what happened to her after she stopped her lecture circuit and disappeared into the history books.

It is therefore no surprise to me that when a local husband and wife team who owned an antique shop completed the initial interior decorations, they felt that both Brigham and some of his wives had assisted them first hand in selecting what would go into the house. She and her husband had bought the house without knowing its history and when they found out they spent fifteen years renovating the farmhouse to the authentic period of Brigham Young's time and then eventually gave it to the Mormon Church. The farmhouse was later traded to the state and then moved to its present location in the park. According to the couple, Brigham had the most to say in dreams, but I would bet that Ann Eliza and a few other wives had a bit to say too. The antique shop owners were convinced however, that it was Brigham Young who directed their every renovation and interior design and since Ann Eliza hated the place perhaps this is true. When one realizes the circumstances of Ann Eliza's last stay in the farmhouse, her spirit trapped there would be a tragedy of Shakespearean proportions.

The antique store owner's wife was a well-known psychic as well, having had many local articles written about her in the newspaper, including a few by Dan Valentine, a well-known newspaper columnist for many years in Salt Lake. She had only become known to the local police department when, on having to take a lie detector test for some witness issue, she sat down in the chair and became very ill and demanded to get up and out of there. One cop became curious at her reaction as she described the last man to have sat in the chair before her. The man happened to be a suspect in a murder case whom they had let go when he passed the polygraph test. So they brought him back in and he eventually confessed to the crime. After that, this same cop began to use her on cases, taking a lot of ribbing from his fellow workers, until he found himself keeping most of it anonymous.

She was always anonymous until over the years a few people broke this trust and printed her name. She worked on the Bundy case like several others and tells of seeing the literal face of evil for a few split seconds in court like a few others have related. Not only psychics but also three law school students in Salt Lake saw this evil face. They had gone to a bar one night with Bundy and when they came out, Bundy stayed a second and was behind them. When the three of them turned around to wait for him, they all saw this horrible devil-like face, but convinced themselves that they had only imagined it in their drunken state. Since this incident, several writers and others involved with the case have described this so-called evil or demon face of the serial killer as well.

One of her most famous local cases was a man who had disappeared from his family, who had called her in desperation to help them locate him. She told the police to go on a certain day, at a certain time, to a certain location up one of the canyons and he would be found. The first time they ignored her specific directions and just searched the canyon but couldn't find him. Finally one man did exactly as she asked, located the car the man was in and found him in a coma. The family called her to the hospital where she spoke to the man in his unconscious state, diagnosed the locations of three tiny blood clots, and then told the family the day of the week and the time of day the man would wake up. The article in the paper shows her sitting next to this man, whose life she literally saved.

After going through mounds of clippings on her lifetime of cases, I find it a little easier to believe in the various happenings at Brigham Young's Farm House. She says that she had a series of dreams that directed her step by step in re-creating the farm as it was exactly in the late 1800s. "She had been in the house six weeks when she saw a man sitting in the front room. She asked him who he was, and the 'impression' came that he was Brigham Young. 'He had his foot up on a stool,...and had a cane in his hand. He seemed about seventy-five years old. I often saw him. I did the restorations on the information he gave me. Brigham Young was my best friend for fifteen years." ("The Ghost of Brigham Young's Nineteenth Wife, " *Ghostly American Places: A Ghostly Guide to America's Most Fascinating Haunted Landmarks*, Wings Books: New York, 1990, p.273.)

This psychic also says Brigham appeared to her as the director of this re-creation, but that occasionally a wife or two had their own things to say. She never saw Brigham at the farmhouse because of course he had several things to attend to even in the afterlife. However, she saw several wives standing between other people or alone while she was inside it and while she was leaving the farm, she also saw them at various windows. She feels that she did her best to satisfy the spirits there in terms of an authentic re-creation down to the last details. When the house was done after several years, the dreams stopped and she never saw Brigham again.

When the couple gave away the house to the LDS Church they had an open house for all of the important leaders of the LDS faith. "Both my husband and I were there. This very good-looking man came up to us and talked to us at length about the house. He was wearing beautiful clothes that dated from about 1880. We didn't know he was a ghost until a newspaper photographer took pictures of my husband and me. We were conversing with the ghost, but he wasn't in the picture." The couple say that at that time there were five spirits in the house: Brigham Young, Ann Eliza, Sarah Decker, Brigham's second wife, John A. Young, Brigham's favorite son, and a man who had killed a man in a robbery nearby and had hid in the house which was at the time, a church. This happened around the turn of the century. (Ibid, p.273.)

As to the staff there, they say that doorknobs rattle, they hear footsteps come up behind them and stop or pass a closed door, and when they open the door there is no one there. A light that looks like a lantern light will appear in the window momentarily and then go out. When people are leaving the place late at night, the most famous ghost woman appears at the window staring at them as they leave. Voices of children playing are also heard, the name of a current staff person is called, and single words or phrases are spoken to someone when no one else is there. The ghosts walk, run, dance, laugh and fool around, former staff members say. A famous sighting was of a figure of a woman in the dining room of the house. Two of the three women present saw her, while the other woman had her back turned. They were giving a birthday party at the time and the apparition was dressed all in black, her hair piled on her head. The ghost was very slight in stature. One of the three women gave a tour and when she returned, the apparition had vanished and the other woman who had seen the ghost, just continued on with the birthday party, afraid to look into the room again.

One of the famous logbook stories involves a guide giving a tour through the house who had stopped in front of a hair wreath design hanging on the wall in the parlor. This incident took place around 1986 and the initial story has been added onto over the years, possibly being the same one as the tale of Ann Eliza's face floating out from its frame for the tour members to see. In this version, the guide had pointed out the wreathe, a Victorian art form of weaving pictures and wreathes of human hair and dried flowers. As the guide pointed out the wreathe it lifted off of the wall about four inches and just hung there for less than a minute and then went back to its place. The whole tour confirmed that they had witnessed this event.

Staff has also smelled chicken soup cooking in the kitchen even though the stove is not hooked up and no one is cooking anything in the room. One day a maintenance person came down from upstairs and wanted to know if they were cooking lunch in the kitchen. Another time they smelled potatoes frying. One woman had been alone in the house all morning and had heard children playing, singing and dancing and making banging and bouncing sounds. She went all over the inside of the house and then all around the outside looking for anything that would account for the sounds that she was hearing, but there was nothing. The forest farmhouse is in an isolated area with a wide and very clear visual field around it. All the noises stopped when she went outside, but when she returned to the house and had been inside a few minutes, all the sounds started up again. She says that they sounded like littler kids as well.

One theory on this phenomenon, which has only been reported after 1989, is that up until the time the basement was flooded and all the pictures in the basement were ruined, no one had ever heard children in the home. When these pictures were ruined ancestors of people who had lived in the home brought in family pictures to replace them. In these Young family pictures are at least three individual pictures of Brigham Young's children in three separate groupings. Before this there were no pictures of any of his children in the home and this is when people began to hear small children playing in the home. Since the 1989 flooding there have been several reports of children either playing in the parlor or upstairs and when staff members checked, no one was there.

One man, who was a retired computer technician and a full-time guide at the farmhouse, was quoted as saying "I definitely have heard children in the farmhouse. The story is that Brigham Young was a smart guy and he had his lovely home in town, and had the intelligence to know that the best place for a teenage party is in your neighbor's house. So when he built this farmhouse, which was four miles southeast of town, that's where he built the ballroom for the kids; that's where the kids would have their parties. And every once in a while their noise has been reported; that's what I heard last March, these kids having a party... These could have been kids anywhere from 12 on up. But they sounded more like littler kids. I looked all over the house, and it was empty." (Ibid, p.270.)

Stories abound at other transplanted park buildings. At the Jewkes-Draper home, where spinning and weaving are demonstrated, children can be heard as if at a party. One evening, when a tour-guide couple was sitting in the house, the front door began to shake and rattle as though someone had a hold of the doorknob. There wasn't anyone outside and the wind wasn't blowing at all that evening. The couple had worked in the house for three years without incident, and the very next night the same thing happened to the woman. Finally she went up to the door and said: "If you want out, all you have to do is ask." She then held the door open for a while and then closed it and it never happened again while they were in the house.

At the Smith home, claims have been made that Mary Fielding Smith has been seen standing in her doorway. Some say she wags her finger angrily and they say that maybe it is because when they moved her home to the park they faced it the wrong way. Footsteps and the sounds of children have been heard in all three homes at the park when no one was around to make these sounds. Mary Fielding Smith's home was originally facing the town and now it faces the mountains. She was married to Hiram Smith, who was Joseph Smith's brother. A standard tale at the park about Mary Fielding Smith's ghost standing in her doorway, no one has ever really seen her apparition, although it makes a good story for the tourists.

Brigham Young's restless spirit haunted the farmhouse before it was moved to the park. Reports of seeing his shadowy figure were quite constant for the last fifteen years before it was moved. Yet when it went to the park, no one saw Brigham any more and Ann Eliza took his place as the premier ghost reigning over her home. Speculation is that Brigham did not like the move and rarely visited there because all whom he had exiled would be there to greet him. The last people that he would want to see would have been at the Forest Farmhouse. However, upon reading her book, I felt that Ann Eliza had her most difficult trials and sorrows at the farmhouse and it is this tragic feeling of being imprisoned, which has left its imprint upon the old homestead not only for her but for others who also felt imprisoned there.

Who knows what ghosts are thinking when they do what they do, though in Ann Eliza's case, she told us in her account of the events leading up to her flight from her homeland. But everyone agrees on one thing, that the farm itself gives off a warm homey atmosphere and that these are friendly spirits, as if they are welcoming the chance to be heard after so many years of obscurity in Brigham's shadow. Although Brigham's nineteenth wife left some of her sorrow behind her, at the time that she made her decision to leave all that she knew and loved so dearly, so that both sorrow and joy can be heard and felt in the creak of a single floorboard or in the deep sigh that an old house can make. Occasionally, the one not so nice robber spirit makes himself known, but this is a rare event in the history of the farmhouse and all in all, these many spirits are simply playful and friendly.

Note: Recently something of a cultural exchange has taken place at the "This Is The Place Heritage Park", at least for the dead. Several hundred yards east of the big statue but still on state land and outside the park's exit gate, sits an unmarked tomb for a people almost annihilated by the westward expansion. It is the newly christened American Indian Burial Repository; a concrete bunker will now hold the remains of those prehistoric Indians still yet to be found. As of now, at the opening ceremonies, 84 sets of remains have been buried there - those whose bones became visible when the floodwaters of the Great Salt Lake receded 14 years ago west of the Skull Valley. Members of the Northwestern Band of the Shoshone claimed ownership of the bones. This site was not their first choice, for they had wanted to leave the bones where they lay, but vandalism and decay made them give in. All of the bones were stored at Utah State University for the last decade.

It took the state years to build the repository. All during that time, the tribe had hoped to have a place more remote on Antelope Island, but it was a state park and they could not be allowed to have a repository there. "This Is The Place Heritage Park" is now privately owned, though it wasn't when the tribe was first asking for a site. The mystery of this strange twist is all but forgotten now, though Governor Norm Bangerter did lobby for the Antelope Island site. In an area already dedicated to the history and heritage of Utah, though one also representing the white takeover of Indian country, these bones have finally been laid to rest in 26 oak coffins. The repository goes two stories underground at the base of the hill just northeast of Hogle Zoo. Any other remains not claimed and needing a burial site will go to this repository. These spirits have wandered aimlessly all of this time, the Indian peoples say, and now they no longer have to. Spirits of their ancestors rest not far from a little pioneer grave within the park, haunted houses and the spirited Forest Farm down the hill. As the years go by and more and more bones are housed there, one wonders what spirits will emerge from such a place to haunt this park even more.

GOVERNOR'S MANSION:

- THOMAS KEARNS MANSION
- DAVID KEITH MANSION

Thomas Kearns was born in Canada in 1862. His parents were Irish Catholics who immigrated to a Nebraska farm and when he was 17 years of age he left the farm to seek his fortunes in the world. He went to the mines in the Black Hills, where one day he accepted the chance to stay in the ring with a traveling wrestler for two minutes to win a 100 dollars. At six foot four inches in height and with a stocky build, he promptly threw the wrestler out of the ring and onto a brass drum in the bandstand. He mailed the money to his mother, who scolded him for doing this, though she kept the money. In South Dakota he weighed cattle that were to be shipped to the east. Then he turned up in Tombstone, Arizona along with thousands of others seeking gold in the mines. He helped a freighter for about 4 years, carrying supplies across the plains and ended up in the Tintic Mining District. Later, he went to Springville where he worked on a supply train and made enough to stake himself, like so many others looking to strike it rich in the mines, though he simply ended up working in the Ontario Mine in Park City. He studied geology and mineralogy and tried his own mining on the side. After about 7 years of hard, grueling labor as a miner, he ended up staking his own claim with his partner David Keith. They discovered an ore vein and went into partnership with three other fellows and purchased the Mayflower Mine. The initial shipment brought in $20,000, of which he spent a goodly sum to purchase his parents a small farm in Nebraska.

One of his partners was a John Judge whose beautiful niece Jennie Judge consented to be his wife. John's original name was McBrehoney, being also of Irish Catholic descent, but he had changed his name to Judge on coming to America. In an interesting side note, Judge had worked 6 days a week in the Silver King Mine seeing his new wife Mary only on Sundays. As a result of this devotion to the mine he died of dust inhalation in 1892, and it was Mary Harney Judge who, through real estate investments, became quite wealthy. Mary built the seven story Judge building for railroad company employees (8th East and 3rd South), endowed Judge Memorial High School which is named after her, and contributed financially to the building of the Cathedral of the Madeleine. It was in this building on the 6th floor in 1985 that Mark Hofmann, the LDS documents forger, pipe bombed and killed collector Steven Christensen because Christiansen had discovered that one of Hofmann's documents was a forgery.

All of the partners then purchased the Silver King Mine in 1892 and soon both David Keith and Thomas Kearns, the principal shareholders, became millionaires. Thomas Kearns was only 28 years old at the time. Kearns was however, a generous and fair employer who never forgot either his church or his mining roots. He was the first one in the area to have an employee's benefit program and soon he was elected alderman for Park City. In 1895, he was a delegate to the constitutional convention and 6 years later he was a U.S. Senator. He kept right on working to better conditions for miners and to improve health and safety for smelters and factory workers. While some criticized him for being a graceless country bumpkin, he fooled everyone and became a socially prominent figure in Washington, D.C.

While Kearns served in Washington, Jennie Kearns, who was also a tireless worker for both her church and community, began work on the Kearns Mansion. She wanted a French Renaissance Chateau and that is what she got. Even to this day all of the doorknobs and other carvings throughout the house have the initials "TK" on them. However, when a kidnapping threat came to her door, she fled to Washington, D.C. with her three children. The Kearns received two mailed threats from a man named Ernest J. Walters who was attempting to extort money from them. He had once been a clothing merchant in Salt Lake City, Ogden and Park City and when caught and arrested he claimed that a "traveling man" had threatened to kill the senator and him if he did not comply. In his two letters, he asked for $5,000 from the senator and threatened to kill him, as well as expose something in his earlier life involving a swindle and a murder. He then addressed a second letter to Jennie Kearns and asked her for $2,500 or she and her children would be killed. Jennie then went to live in Switzerland for a while and enrolled her children in schools there. She left the mansion planning to Carl M. Neuhausen, a prominent local architect who had also designed, among other things, one of the Orpheum Theaters, the Oregon Short line Railroad building, his own Neuhausen House (1265 East 100 South) and of course, the Cathedral of the Madeleine. She returned to Salt Lake City with her children, after the man had been arrested, almost a whole year later.

The oolite stone mansion was completed in 1902 and when President Theodore Roosevelt stayed there in 1903, he commented on the diverse visitors to the home, from a Roman Catholic bishop, an Episcopalian bishop to an LDS apostle with several wives. He was welcomed with American flags draped above doorways on the outside and on every mantelpiece with all sorts of red, white and blue flower arrangements throughout the mansion. He commented in a letter to a friend that he was struck by the queer combination of fanaticism of faiths and the shrewd and materialistic common sense of all who attended the grand state dinner, and also by how just about every belief system and civilization seemed to be represented there. For Kearns had not only invited the cream of Salt Lake society but also his old friends from his mining and freighting days. Even Knute Rockne of Notre Dame fame stayed there, stopping in to visit Tom Jr. after Rockne's team was defeated in 1935 by Stanford.

There are tours of the Kearns Mansion on Tuesday and Thursday afternoons. A description of the mansion's interiors just doesn't do it justice so those who visit have to see it for themselves. Jennie Kearns collected things to furnish her mansion while she was in Europe, so there are all sorts of wonderful objects and furnishings original to the home. There are an all-marble vestibule, iron and bronze grillwork embellishing windows and massive doors, hand carved allegorical scenes on the French oak wooden columns, an amazing stairway, third story dome with hidden lights, a French drawing room, a Moorish parlor, a Flemish oak library, golden oak with Wedgewood frescoes for the family dining room, a marble kitchen and butler's pantry, with 9 fireplaces and 9 turret-corners in the home.

Kearns then went into partnership with David Keith again and purchased *The Salt Lake City Tribune* and in 1911, the Kearns Building was constructed to house the ever-expanding newspaper. It was a ten story skyscraper in its day and has seven striking life-size female figures supporting lanterns on the second story with smaller female heads on either side of each window. It too is on the National Register of Historic places. David Keith also built a downtown building in 1902 (256 South Main) for the Keith-O'Brien Dry Goods store. He owned banks, railroads, mines and was also a member of Utah's constitutional convention. His home on South Temple was built in 1900, though a fire destroyed the upper two floors in 1986.

Keith was a Scotsman from a family of 13 children in Nova Scotia. His parents died when he was 14 and he had to help support the family. At age 21 he was a superintendent for a gold mine when he heard about the gold fields in the United States. He went to Virginia City, Nevada as a miner and then as a pump man, and ended up in Park City, Utah, where he installed a Cornish pump so well that he was made foreman of the Ontario Mine. It was he who discovered the ore vein while building an underground tunnel for the Woodside Mine in the undeveloped Mayflower Mine. In three months they struck it rich and Keith was president of the Silver King Mine with Kearns as vice president. Later when the two of them purchased the newspaper, it was Keith who held the title, though it was Kearns who dominated the operations at The Salt Lake Tribune.

Keith was 15 years older than Kearns and a very inward man, while Kearns was the outgoing and gregarious one. David Keith married twice, had four children and one adopted son. His first wife, Mary Ferguson, had taught school in Park City and was eventually a telephone company manager there for the Rocky Mountain Bell Telephone Company. Some remember her as intelligent, modest and sweet, while others remember her as cold, austere and likely to impose her will upon others. She left Keith for another man and then returned penitent but he would not take her back. She is ignored in all of his biographies and little else is known about her except that she bore him his children. His second wife stayed with him to the end of their lives though in her later years she struggled with a drinking problem. The Keiths did little entertaining and were more private than the Kearns; the tragedy of one of his daughters was probably one of the major explanations for this. Documents found in the 1970s explained why his daughter Margaret had gone into seclusion for the rest of her life, often wearing black dresses and never without a heavy black veil over her face. It seems that she was seduced by his adopted son and gave birth to a child reared in the Midwest by guardians.

In the early years the Keiths did some entertaining despite their daughter Margaret's unexplained withdrawal, but gradually this lessened. Of course neither of the Keiths was comfortable with grand formal dinners and large formal parties and dances anyway, though they did lavish their children with expensive weddings and receptions and were very close friends with the Kearns. The Keiths moved to the Hotel Utah in their later years. Keith died of pneumonia in 1918 and his wife, by then addicted to alcohol, died of a heart ailment in 1919. Margaret continued to live in the family home in virtual seclusion and 24 years later, after her father's and stepmother's deaths, purchased two estates in Beverly Hills and Palos Verdes. She remained heavily veiled at all times, and divided her time between the two estates. Many of the rooms in the estates remained unused and shrouded in dust covers, the windows covered with blankets. And then on April 28, 1934, the doctor was summoned by her servants. He found her note next to where they found her body lying on a divan with a chloroform cloth covering her face. People had imagined, because of not knowing her true story, a scarred and disfigured face behind this veil, but instead the doctor found quite a beautiful one, with graceful and striking features.

The Keith Mansion, just like the Kearns Mansion, has rumors of ghosts, though Ezra Thompson bought the mansion and with his wife Emily raised many children in a happy and warm home. Their son Clyde continued to live in the home as a bachelor after their deaths, until he married. His sister Norinne and her husband moved into the home in 1939. In 1969, this couple leased the home to Terracor who adapted the home for their company headquarters. The carriage house was redesigned for the company's architects and the home remains business offices to this day. I have not had the privilege of entering this house but have read about its interior and sat near it so that my thoughts on the ghosts there are entirely my own.

The mansion has an octagonal rotunda with Gothic archways of polished cherry wood. Passageways open in seven directions from this center and there are original Tiffany chandeliers and newel lamps with a center skylight of frosted white and yellow with touches of ruby and amethyst. There are stained glass windows, ornate beveled glass windows and brilliant lighting throughout the home. It has a ballroom, wine cellar and walk-in icebox, and even the carriage house was equipped with a bowling alley, pigeon coop, shooting gallery and several servants' quarters. The butler's pantry was equipped with an electric warming table; laundry and wet clothes were hung in a special closet where hot air was continuously circulated. There are wrought iron doors, and the whole home sort of looks like a Greek Temple with massive columns and symmetrical wings. It is however, officially called a "Neo-Classical Revival" constructed of limestone.

While David Keith experienced many tragedies in his life, Jennie and Thomas Kearns shared a long and fairly happy life together. They were both outgoing and entertained a lot with large parties and dinners. Jennie Kearns loved children and did much to help them in her own right. She loved to sew, was very witty and charming, and quite a lovely person both inward and out. Neighborhood children played in her yard all the time while treated to homemade cookies, and she had two nieces and a brother who also lived in the home. She became involved in the Ladies Sewing Society which sewed clothing and toys for the orphans at Saint Ann's, which she had endowed with a $50,000 donation, enabling them to build their home and open up their doors. She visited there regularly and provided a lavish Christmas party for the orphans, as well as other financial contributions when they were needed. She and her husband contributed to the building of the Cathedral of the Madeleine, Bishop Scanlon's life long dream, as well as to a school and orphanage fund.

During the Scofield Mine Disaster, when St. Ann's opened its doors to the widows and their now fatherless children, Jennie Kearns was there serving with the rest. The orphans from the disaster found a home there, and many other children lived there temporarily until their widowed mothers got back on their feet, again with the help of St. Ann's and Jennie Kearns. In 1928, she received a papal decoration from Pope Pius XI naming her a Lady of the Holy Sepulcher. She often held lawn parties for the then 150 orphans at Kearns St. Ann's. She practically single-handedly created Kearns St. Ann's Orphan Asylum as it was called then. Her yearly lavish Christmas party for them was truly a thing of wonder. She raised her own four children, and after her sister's death, she raised her sister's three as well. For forty-two years she held the Christmas party at which the children received gifts, played games, went caroling and made holiday decorations. The Kearns *Salt Lake Tribune* began their "Christmas Fund for Orphans" early on to contribute to Jennie Kearn's Christmas party for the children, and eventually it became known as "Sub For Santa," which is still running strong to this day.

Thomas Kearns died tragically on October 18, 1918 when he was struck by a car on South Temple and Main Street. He died 6 months and 2 days after his best friend, David Keith. The family continued to live in their home until 1937 when Jennie Kearns presented it to the state of Utah to be used as the governor's mansion. Altogether, six governors lived in the home: Henry H. Blood, Herbert B. Maw, and J. Bracken Lee in the earlier days and then later, governors Scott M. Matheson, Norman H. Bangerter and our present governor and his family, Governor Michael O. Leavitt. Governor Maw entertained President Truman in the mansion when he made a surprise visit. Later, Maw missed his train headed for some governor's meetings around the country and Truman lent him Air Force One so that he could still get to his meetings on time. Maw was governor for eight years during the World War II years and he and his wife Florence really enjoyed living there with their children from 1941 to 1949.

J. Bracken Lee was the next governor and the first republican to break the long reign of democrats in the Governor's mansion. He and his wife Margaret and their four children reinstated the Christmas for orphans' parties in the mansion. One of the same men who had helped Mrs. Kearns move to California also helped the Lees move into the mansion. He had been raised at St. Ann's Orphanage and related what it felt like to go to the parties every year with Mrs. Kearns. Mrs. Lee had been orphaned at 16 herself and had raised all of her brothers and sisters. She began the parties again with the help of Eugene Jelesnick whose orchestra provided the musical entertainment, and The Story Princess, a local television personality who would tell stories to the children every year. I remember The Story Princess with her long straight black hair and bangs, her wonderful crown and wide petticoat skirts. She was a bit "sweetsie" for me, but still, I watched her every week to hear all the fairy tales. I never understood that it was just a local show, until as an adult I found that nobody outside of Utah knew about her.

Lee was quite the character and a fiery politician too. He didn't believe in paying income taxes, and he did not like the years that they lived in the mansion. It was too cold in winter, too hot in the summer, the shower never worked and it certainly wasn't a safe place to be if an earthquake came with all that glass and marble, he said. The shower to some, especially Lee, was "an instrument of Medieval torture". It had perforated parallel pipes circling the huge shower stall. Thomas Kearns had designed it and it sort of worked like a human car wash. When you turned the handles on, fine jets of water would needle you from every direction. Lee said that he almost drowned in it once and that sometimes only cold water would come and no hot. Several horror movie scenes were filmed in this shower. In one scene, in a movie starring John Carradine, a woman was murdered in the shower. During the Mathesons' term in the mansion, they had the shower dismantled and it was put on exhibit at the State Historical Society, although occasionally they would return it to be used as a fountain at a garden party or two. The shower is currently stored in the basement of the State Historical Society.

The Lees lived in the mansion from 1949 to 1957 and it was during the Lee years that rumors of ghosts leaked out and were quickly stifled because of the prestige of the building. There were footsteps on the main stairway, voices and music in the ballroom and Christmas party noises every year at Christmas time; all of these occurred when no one was there except one or two people late at night. The governors after this did not live in the mansion and in 1957, a new home for the governors was built and the Utah State Historical Society took up residence in the Kearns mansion. Since my brother worked for the Society at the time, I got to see the interior quite often and grew fond of my time there wandering the hallways and exploring on my own. I wish that I had known then what I do now, for I would have taken the opportunity to really absorb the building without anyone bothering me and in total quiet, as it was a public building at that time, and one could come and go there.

However, during one governor's term, there was one successful robbery and one attempted robbery. One burglar climbed the scaffolding on the northwest side and got away with some valuable silver dishes. The dishes never showed up in local pawn shops, so one presumes that the silver was either melted down or kept in a private collection somewhere. In the attempted robbery scenario, the director of the society was alerted by an alarm systems office that the alarm had gone off in the middle of the night. The director went to the mansion to turn the alarm off, got to the second floor, then heard "Stop!", and found a gun sticking in his back. He bolted into his office nearby and the robber took off with nothing from the mansion. In October of 1972, a horror movie was shot in the mansion called *The House of the Seven Corpses*. Scenes were shot mainly on the grand staircase and in the carriage house behind the mansion. All the shooting was done in the evening so as not to be in the way of the employees of the historical society. Two unused rooms on the third floor were made into an apartment suite for filming and the film premiered in Salt Lake City in 1973. This might have been a bit disturbing to the spirits already there.

In 1977, the Utah State Historical Society moved to the Rio Grande Railway Station and the Kearns mansion was once again refurbished for use as the governor's mansion.

The state's first lady, Norma Matheson, can be credited with starting up the whole thing again when her husband was elected in 1976 as the first democratic governor of Utah in a while. She thought that the Kearns mansion was a much more suitable place both to live and entertain visitors than the more modern governor's mansion in which the previous two governors had lived. The restoration and renovations to the mansion cost a lot, but it gave the state a new image among other western governors and encouraged preservation of many other buildings both in Utah and in other states. Both governors Scott M. Matheson and Norman H. Bangerter lived in the mansion. During those years I got to attend two different awards ceremonies, and at one of them, got to shake Mrs. Matheson's hand, who was subbing for her husband at the last minute. Had I known more at the time about Mrs. Matheson, I would have valued that meeting a lot more than I did.

In 1993, on December 15, the now famous fire erupted at the base of the huge Christmas tree in the central hallway, causing major damage in the center of the building. But by this time preservation was a popular issue and people were prepared to keep that fire from spreading through the house. The firefighters even dammed up doorways to other rooms to keep water damage out of them as they carefully put the fire out. The governor and his family moved out and a massive and extremely expensive rehabilitation took place, in the end costing $8 million. Despite many alterations, still to this day the mansion maintains much of its original configuration. Many original fixtures and furnishings were in storage when the fire happened so that much of what is in there now is original to the house. The conservation and renovation of this building received local and national attention because of the care, time and money put into its return to its original condition. The governor and his family moved back in for a short while after the renovation, though rumor has it that his wife was never quite comfortable in it. She was instrumental in it becoming at present a place for state functions, dinners and meetings. She also helped get the Kearns mansion added to the National Historic Register, with tours offered by the Utah Heritage Foundation. Just what would make one uncomfortable in this house, besides its size, age and all those complaints that Governor Lee had? Could it be a few ghosts as well?

Just recently there was a protest over the demolition of the house next to the governor's mansion, after a proposal to turn its grounds into a parking lot. This neighboring house was originally purchased by the state on the premise that a sniper could fire at the governor or his family from it; it had been used for storage for years. The preservationists got wind of the plan and have been fighting it through the media. When the spokesperson of this little protest group asked why the state didn't buy up and demolish all of the old historic homes within a two block area of the mansion, it came out that the governor and his family no longer live there. Who would they, whoever 'they" are, be shooting at anyway? Apparently the family had quietly slipped back to their old home, unbeknownst to the public. When this became known the rumor was that Mrs. Leavitt was uncomfortable in the house. Unfortunately, the state will probably win this one where the other small and not-so-historically-significant house is concerned. Eight million dollars for the rehabilitation of one house and a parking lot of its not-so-attractive neighbor - the irony of our modern-day world!

Anyway, it is not hard to imagine who haunts the Keith mansion with her heavy black veils and eccentricities. I am sure that this house has its tales to tell, while the Kearns home is a little harder to pin down. Though when J. Bracken Lee was governor, the Kearns mansion was rumored to be haunted by a lost child, a little boy who liked to misplace things or put them in odd places where they definitely did not belong, though mostly people could just hear his footsteps around them. Perhaps one of these other governors lost a son or grandson in the house and this is who is there to this day. The more well known story that was told when Lee was governor, was that footsteps were heard on the main grand staircase, even in broad daylight, when the hearer was there alone. At night a person could hear the footsteps following behind him, whether he was going up or down the stairs. Footsteps could also be heard on the floor above when no one was there. But most interesting are the footsteps, music and voices which sometimes come from the upstairs ballroom in the middle of the night - a place where they used to hold dances and parties. It is understandable to me that these stories were told when Lee was governor because he was never discouraged from talking about such things, nor was he a conservative character himself, for "character" he was. His children left their marks on the house as well, roller-skating on the hardwood floors and sliding down the banisters.

But I think there is more to the story, because even fires have a mind of their own. The Christmas fire has always seemed like a rather odd occurrence to me somehow because it was such a tradition from the very beginning of the house, and so many little children enjoyed their visits there. Perhaps one of them lodged a protest for some reason. Or, on the other hand, perhaps the house was lucky to have weathered so many, many years of Christmases with a huge tree going up between the stairs and all that wood without ever catching fire before. These are mansions quite close to each other because of the closeness of their original owners. They are mansions that house spirits and recordings of past and present events. Walking these halls would require a night walk, not something that I am inclined to, nor would be allowed to do in either place.

ALFRED & ELIZABETH MCCUNE MANSION

THE NIGHT RAINBOW

This is the story of a decades long relationship between myself, and an old mansion in the city. It is about the way in which things converge between worlds, or of how time and its histories and futures intermingle. It begins where I once was and the knowing of a place before I ever saw it. A place I dreamed of as a young girl, weaving myself into the fabric of this building and its various histories without the least bit of understanding. In my dreams I wandered there, picking up pieces of various lives and events, never knowing why I did, nor that many of these events were quite real. I thought self-centeredly that I had created these things, which does not surprise me, as my own cultural experience up to that point had taught me that the world was a place to be analyzed, scrutinized and accepted only for what one could touch, see, and explain rationally. It wasn't until I saw it for the first time that I realized that not only was it a real place but one that I had placed in the wrong city. It was instead, right in Salt Lake City where I grew up.

This house, or rather mansion, sits on a high hill close to downtown near the capitol building and it really stands out because of its dark red sandstone color. It was built with influences from the Middle and Far East and just recently I learned that before it was built two other houses were torn down on the hill. Therefore, before all the people who inhabited the mansion after it was built, there were stories of those who lived there before it was built. I had seen the place as a child when we drove by it, had recognized it as the one in my dreams, but had simply dismissed it as part of my rich childhood fantasy world. It was some ten years later that my best girlfriend at the time was looking for a place for her wedding reception. She asked me to go with her to the McCune mansion, which at the time, among other things, was a wedding reception center. I was thrilled to go, as I had always wanted to see the interior of this mansion that I had once dreamed about as a child. Just recently I learned that the mansion had come full circle, once again open as a wedding reception center.

Completely unaware of the gift of sight that my mother had bestowed upon me, I always blamed everything on my vivid imagination. I had put all of this talent into painting a picture or writing a story. So I went with my girlfriend unknowingly, and not expecting at all what happened to me there. As I look back now, I understand that in many ways my previous lack of awareness was a far wiser and certainly safer condition. Watching friends of mine now, who have lived with this so-called gift since birth, I realize it is not an easy path, and certainly one fraught with accusations of craziness and misunderstandings. No one accused me of craziness because I was simply "creating." The journey with this house can also be said to be a journey home for me. A friend of mine in Colorado was once asked how I was doing by another acquaintance. Her reply was that I was still doing all the same things, only now it had a name. Far wiser now, I understand that such gifts are in all of us; we have only to wake up to them, embrace them and work very hard to understand them. However, before I go into my encounters I would like to tell the mansion's story chronologically and begin with its beginnings.

The McCune mansion is a shingle style "bungalow" as the McCunes called it, with red roof tiles imported from Holland and a really dark red brick on a heavy brownstone base. The trim for the house was made from Nugget Sandstone that was quarried either in the Red Butte Canyon area or in Emigration Canyon. The color was very unusual for the period. The brick is a darker red than most, because an iron oxide or mineral rust cements the sand grains together, and also, the more the hematite, the darker the color. The mansion really stands out on a hill in the Marmalade District, as it was once called, near the Utah State Capitol building. The mansion is three stories high with 21 rooms, a conical turret and oval portico with many wrought iron ornaments. It was built in 1901 and designed by C.S. Dallas. It was the first million-dollar home in Utah. The building is on the National Register of Historic places and is a replica of a house Alfred and Elizabeth Ann McCune saw while driving on Riverside Drive in New York City.

Alfred and Elizabeth sent their architect on a two-year tour of both the United States and Europe to study architectural designs, styles and techniques before approving his plans for the mansion. It was considered a "bungalow" because this word meant to the McCunes a place that was simple, comfortable and convenient. There are many imported materials inside as well as carefully crafted and hand-carved walls made from rare South American and European oaks and mahoganies. There are trellises made of Russian mahogany in the interior, as well as Russian leather on some of the walls. Generous amounts of African and Italian marble adorn the house everywhere, and there are silk and brocade walls, some of which are covered with wool tapestries. They collected quite a few cut glass crystal chandeliers, which were hung in the center of every room. There is a large wall mural on the third floor, which is a painted forest scene completed by an artist who lived in the mansion several months, leaving his home in Europe to do this.

Alfred McCune was born in Calcutta, India but came to Utah as a Mormon because his father, Sergeant Matthew McCune, while serving with the Bengal Artillery of the East India Company, had joined a group studying the doctrines of the LDS faith. With India in his background, it was as much Alfred as Lizzie McCune who created such an exotic Asian and East Indian atmosphere in their new home. Elizabeth Ann McCune went by several nicknames including Lizzie, Lizette and Ann and was the real designer of their home. Alfred's large and aristocratic family traveled to various posts and while in Burma were finally converted to the LDS church. Only four brothers survived out of the eight siblings that Alfred had and these four brothers went into the freighting business once they arrived in Nephi, Utah. At the very young age of 21, Alfred contracted to build portions of the Utah Southern Railroad, tried his hand at a timber concern, as well as stock raising, running a mercantile store, and investing in mining interests. His closest brother and partner in these various concerns, died suddenly at the age of 24 and Alfred was devastated by his death. Alfred went on to be one of the largest railroad contractors in the West. He was instrumental in purchasing and operating the trolley cars in Salt Lake City and eventually had so much money that he was able to go into business with the likes of J.P. Morgan, William Randolph Hearst and Cornelius Vanderbilt in purchasing the Cero de Pasco mines in Peru.

Elizabeth Ann Claridge McCune was a brown-haired beauty whose father, Samuel Claridge, had been a grocer for some Mormon customers while in England. He converted his wife, Elizabeth Ann Hopkins Claridge, to Mormonism and they traveled west to Utah. It has always been interesting to me that I have a great grandmother named Ann Elizabeth Hopkins Carpenter and have often wondered if there could be any connection. Elizabeth Ann was a hard worker, kind hearted, fun-loving and never hurtful to anyone. She loved even at a very young age, to do dramatic portrayals with her friends and she was usually the director and writer. She loved to play as much as she worked and had a deep love of music. Her best friend, Brigham Young's most famous daughter, Susa Young Gates, described her as being "Equal to any occasion, she was as much at home on a board seat across a wagon box covering the dusty plains of Idaho or Mexico, sweetening every difficulty with a smile and cheering all discouraged hearts with her unfailing golden outlook on life - as she was in a palace sleeping car." ("Elizabeth Ann Claridge McCune: At Home On the Hill," by Carol Ann Van Wagner, *Women Worth Their Salt*, edited by Colleen Whitley, Utah State University Press: Logan, Utah, 1996, p.97.)

At fifteen Lizzie trained to be a telegraph operator and made friends easily. In 1867, Brigham Young visited her parent's home in Nephi and called her father on a mission to Nevada. Her father took his second wife, Lizzie and her brother with him. On their journey, they had to unhitch their wagon bed and attach it to heavy log chains to haul it up a particularly steep hill. The wagon tongue gave way, rolled down past Elizabeth, catching her skirts in the wagon wheel. Instead of plummeting to the bottom of the hill to her death, with her skirts all entangled in the wheel, the wheel simply tore off all her clothes and rolled on past her. Her father was quoted as saying at the time that she didn't need to worry about standing there half naked because he had had a prophetic dream in which he saw her in her own future wearing much better clothing. Some people think that he should have prophesized that she would have better homes to live in too, as Elizabeth McCune's greatest and most remembered accomplishment, is her home, the McCune Mansion.

Soon after the Clarridge family returned to Nephi, a nineteen year old newly-arrived Alfred W. McCune bought an acre of land to farm in Nephi but soon ended up in the freighting business instead. Alfred and Lizette must have become acquainted in Nephi. In 1871, Lizette went to St. George to be a telegraph operator and there met and became best friends with Susa Young Gates. Elizabeth Ann kept contact with Alfred all during this time. They eventually married and remained in Nephi until after their first child was born. Lizette's second son, Harry Bertrand, was only two months old when he died. Their first eight children were born in Nephi. Frank Claridge died there at five years of age. In 1888, the McCunes moved to Salt Lake City and lived in a home near the Union Pacific Depot. Their ninth child was born in 1891, and Elizabeth continued to take on LDS church callings while Alfred made money. A list of the nine children's names might help to solve some of the mysteries that came up later on. Their names were: Alfred William Jr., Harry Bertrand, Earl Vivian, Raymond, Sarah Fay, Lottie Jacketta, Frank Claridge, Matthew Marcus and Elizabeth Claridge. Harry, Frank, one older brother and another of the nine died young.

Alfred took his whole family on a year long trip to Europe in 1897 and leased an elegant residence at the seashore in East Bourn outside of London. In 1889, the family moved back to Salt Lake City and leased the Gardo House, also known as "Amelia's Palace." This mansion was probably the most ornate in all of the city and Brigham Young had originally built it for his favorite wife Amelia Folsom. It is a sad comment on the times that this palace was torn down and that one can only get a flavor of it by visiting the Daughters of the Pioneers Museum where a small-scale model of it is on display with photos of the interiors. It was at this time that the family began building the McCune Mansion. Susa Young Gates and Lizzie McCune began attending the International Congress of Women during this time, as well as completing many LDS church callings. They were also able to visit church missions all over the world. Lizzie was also a patron of the National Council of Women of the United States, which had been founded in 1881. Both organizations worked to promote "womankind" and worked for women's rights. At the same time that Susa and Lizzie had an audience with Queen Victoria at Windsor Castle, Alfred made an unsuccessful attempt to become one of Utah's United States Senators.

Elizabeth was in charge of the construction of the mansion, during which time, Alfred took his family on a second trip to Peru to investigate his investments there. Elizabeth became very ill from altitude sickness and a special train had to be engaged to carry her down off the mountain where the mines were. Once in their new mansion, Elizabeth received another honor when she was named a trustee of the Utah State Agricultural College in Logan, Utah. She served in this capacity for the next ten years while touring the United States to inspect various Home Economics Departments at other colleges as part of her duties as a trustee. She was on the General Board of her church's women's auxiliary association, the Relief Society, as well. For nineteen years, the McCune's lived in their red brick mansion on the hill. It has often been noted that Alfred's bedroom faced the Capitol building which was being built at the time, and that this allowed him to keep an eye on the political comings and goings of the day. Elizabeth's bedroom faced the LDS Temple, reflecting her devotion to her church and her strong faith.

In 1920 the family moved to Hollywood, California where they lived for three years. The McCunes donated their mansion to the LDS church to be used preferably for a women's building, perhaps housing the Primary Children's Association, Young Women's Mutual Improvement Association and Relief Society headquarters for the LDS church. Elizabeth was in failing health at this time and alone a lot of the time while her husband traveled on business, so they sold their home in Hollywood and returned home. Alfred and Elizabeth took rooms at the Hotel Utah intending to build another much smaller home in City Creek Canyon. Elizabeth was supervising this construction but took ill soon after. When it was evident that Lizzie was dying, the remaining children were cabled and all of them came home to be by their mother's bedside. A grand funeral was held in the Assembly Hall on Temple Square in Salt Lake City. Both Alfred's oldest son and Elizabeth died within a year of each other in 1923 and 1924. Alfred went to France grieving the loss of both his son and wife, where he passed away in Cannes in 1927. His body was buried next to his wife's in Nephi, Utah.

Some interesting and unusual things happened even when the McCunes lived in their mansion. A granddaughter remembered an armed robbery while she was staying there. Her grandmother told her to stay in bed because gunshots could be heard downstairs. The robbers got away with some silverware but were apprehended later. One time Alfred McCune was sitting down to his breakfast, when a shot penetrated the east window of the room. The bullet missed Mr. McCune and lodged itself in the dark mahogany wallboard of the breakfast room. The assailant missed his target by quite a wide margin. In July of 1917, Lizzie's closest friends were invited to a weekend retreat, which became an annual event after that. Husbands were only allowed to enter the house once during the weekend and this was for the Fourth of July dinner. When all the female guests arrived, they were presented with a simple gingham gown, which was what they were to wear for the entire weekend. Not even the married children of the host were let in the house that weekend. Guests were allowed to select their own bedroom and bathroom. One of the guests even wrote a poem about "the house that Elizabeth built." (Ibid, p.98.)

The house was not used exclusively for LDS women. For many years it housed the McCune School of Music and Art from the old LDS University. Then it was used for the BYU Extension Services and various private concerns such as wedding receptions and other social events. Finally a couple bought the mansion essentially to save it from deterioration and began making extensive renovations while using it as a private residence. After they sold it, it sat idle for several years, though various organizations rented it out for one-time functions and some movie and television productions were filmed there, such as an episode for *Touched By An Angel* and the movie about a serial killer *Absence of Good* with Adam Baldwin. Recently, one of these functions fit the mansion beautifully. It was a one-woman play on Emily Dickinson performed at the mansion by the Emily Company. "The Belle of Amherst" was performed in the drawing room of the mansion. It is a play which has been often called a love affair with language. The actress performing as Emily Dickinson wore her long brown hair in a bun and a long white gown, echoing Elizabeth McCune's visage and her love of home and hearth. Even during these performances, some odd things were reported by those involved in the production.

I was worried by the "for sale" sign though, having seen how the city, the LDS church and individual developers have found it more convenient to tear down prime commercial properties for financial gain or to gain space. It was therefore a wonderful surprise to see the full-page ad in *Salt Lake City Magazine* just a few months ago, proclaiming the re-opening of the mansion as a wedding reception place once again. A member of the same family trying to maintain control of the *Salt Lake Tribune* newspaper had purchased the mansion just to save it. The hauntings at the McCune Mansion are legendary even during the time that the McCunes lived there. One of the most famous stories and a favorite to re-tell, involves several congressional strategists who were meeting in the dining room one evening a few years ago. The talk had turned to ghosts prowling about the mansion. The finance chairman, a very vocal skeptic, said something about how all these people were pulling his leg. Not five minutes later, a huge and very heavy dining room chair, with wood carved legs, started moving towards the fireplace with no one in or near it. It moved quite a distance while several witnesses watched it, and those who happened to be facing the other way, could hear it moving across the floor from the next room. The finance chairman completely lost his cool!

While the McCunes lived there they had a special small room constructed inside the grand staircase, which a few musicians could enter from a tiny door and sit within to play for the guests. In this way, beautiful music could be heard all over the house but none of the guests could figure out just from where it was coming. It was a bit uncomfortable for the musicians but they were richly compensated for their discomfort. However, it was reported on more than one occasion that music could be heard coming from the staircase when no musicians were in the room. Years after the McCunes had moved away, people in the building would still report hearing live drawing-room music coming from the house when no one was in it. There was also an organ inside the home that could be heard playing when no one was around. When the mansion was the McCune School of Music and Art, quite a few live musicians could probably be heard practicing.

Doors have locked that don't have locks on them and lights have flickered. There are several cold spots about the place and once the elevator was installed it began running by itself with no one in it and no one pushing any buttons. Wedding arrangements laid out the night before would be re-arranged the next morning when employees returned. The couple renovating the house to live in heard voices in the home and doors would open without anyone coming in. On more than one occasion they would drive away late at night having securely locked the place and turned off all the lights. They would look in their rearview mirror and see lights coming on and going off all over the mansion. "Through the years, there have been a few stories of unexplained events, voices and unfamiliar people that suddenly appear and then vanish." A man in a black cape has been seen watching various people when they are alone there. Doors and windows left either locked or unlocked are opened or locked the next morning. ("New Look for Landmark," by Hilary Groutage Smith, *The Salt Lake Tribune*, Thursday, November 15, 2000, D.)

One story the present owner tells happened at the time of the first Christmas that he and his extended family spent together in the mansion. "He sent his teen-aged daughters upstairs to turn the lights off in the ballroom. 'Finally they came downstairs and said that I had to go up there and do it,' he said. So he did. But no matter which switch he flipped, a bank of four lights stayed on. It was Christmas Eve so he left the lights on and went home. The next day he returned, determined to figure out how to turn off the bank of lights, but he couldn't. 'I was so frustrated that finally I just said right out loud: 'Mr. McCune. You win.' The lights flickered but stayed on. Several days later, an electrician discovered the switch used to turn the lights off. It was in a room two floors below. 'Why would he do that?' I have no idea, but it wasn't scary,' McCarthey said. 'We figured it was just because it had been 79 years since a family had had Christmas in there and he was glad someone finally was.'" (Ibid, D.)

My first experience with the McCune Mansion was when I went with my friend to check it out as a possible site for her wedding reception. I was twenty-one. We were given the grand tour and I was able to stay behind in the ballroom on the third floor for quite some time while my friend went on the tour alone. When I first saw it, I just couldn't leave it, for it was the very ballroom from my dreams as a child. I recognized it, though I had thought that it was in another town to the north. It was rather like my experience at the Notre Dame Cathedral in Paris where I became so lost in the layers of energy and emotions left behind in the place that I literally forgot where I was and almost missed my tour bus as I pounded on the back door as it pulled out of the parking lot. In the ballroom however, I had plenty of time and just sat there enjoying its splendor, totally unaware of my intuitive ability. Huge mirrors, balconies and alcoves of the most exquisite woods and little pillars surrounded by seats and mirrors surrounded me. I had a strong feeling of having been there before and at the same time I was aware of a presence in the room. I didn't see her, but in my mind's eye I could have described her perfectly. Long medium brown hair, slender build, above average height, gliding gracefully from mirror to mirror, dressed in a long white nightgown that seemed to propel her from mirror to mirror.

This experience so affected me that I went home and launched into a second gothic and ghostly science fiction romance novel, which while a pretty bad early attempt at writing, had many elements I was thoroughly convinced I had made up. It was years before I realized that I really didn't know which parts had been from intuition and which had been from my imagination. There were two parallel stories going on in the novel and the few who read it said it made no sense to them at all. It was about the woman in the mirrors who lived as an essence on the vibrational waves and was traveling throughout the universe trying to locate a time and place where she had had a physical body and had first been in love. She was sad and mournful and spoke in a stream of consciousness style readers found too difficult to follow. The other parallel story was about a junior high school girl who enlists the help of her nerdy scientific genius boyfriend to get rid of a ghost the girl has seen in the mirrors of an old deserted mansion. The woman ghost follows her home and can be seen in the mirrors there. They have to enlist the help of a teacher who is a history buff and his friend, an archeologist, when the ghostly apparition abducts the girl through a vortex or portal door found in a huge old well in the backyard of the mansion. It is made of brick and the girl is enticed down to it and swept into the well. The boy has to go in after her and when the movie "Poltergeist" came out I was crestfallen to see parts of my novel on the screen. The men pull the boy and then the girl out of the well, after the novel describes the other world where the boy has a few adventures. None of them realize that the apparition and the girl have changed places and that this was the place to which the woman in the mirrors had been trying to return. The young boy is the apparition's first love and she is back in a physical body again, happy to be mortal. The junior high girl becomes the apparition and is happy to travel the waves for eons.

On to this story, I stuck an ending that made no sense then. An old grandmother, who turns out to be the girl as an old woman waiting to die, has her granddaughter in the attic of the mansion. She is putting out a collection of snow globes at Christmas time all around the fireplace. Then she picks out one particular snow globe with a young couple skating on an icy pond in the snow and dressed in turn-of-the-century clothes. The grandmother seems to remember something and while holding the snow globe, she begins telling her granddaughter about the well and how it is a portal of some kind, for she remembers when a young teenage boy and girl were skating on a pond nearby and fell into the well and were never seen again. It was an incident from her childhood it seems. Men went to search for the couple's bodies but nothing was ever found. Then the grandmother tells her granddaughter that several people have been lost down that well over time and that a rabbit falling from the sky is always a warning of the next event. She tells her that is why the well has been capped and covered over - to prevent any others from falling down into the portal. She warns the granddaughter to stay away from it.

The book was eventually entitled *The Night Rainbow* in honor of the universal stream from which we gather such information. It sat on a shelf for years with only a half dozen people attempting to read it; none of them ever finished it. I went on to other writings and tucked it away, never remembering that the girl's name was Ginny

Ann or that the other characters might have had names of real people: Dr. Henry Michaels, Dr. Clinton Richey, Walter and T. Willie the dog. Siri was the apparition's name and Serac was the man she searched for.

My friend decided on the Lion House for her wedding reception instead. I served at her wedding there and had a few strange experiences, with doors blowing shut suddenly or lights flickering. It is also odd that all these years later I learned that Susa and Lizzie spent a lot of time in the Lion House when it was the Home Economics Center for the old LDS University from 1918 to 1931. The Beehive House was a girl's dormitory for the LDS University then. I all but forgot the ballroom and the mansion for almost twenty years.

Then there I was, at the McCune Mansion again. Another wedding reception was underway, only this time, through another odd set of circumstances, I was actually attending the reception. I was a special education teacher at the time, and to make some extra money, I was spending two nights a week doing parent training for foster parents who had severely multi-handicapped children in their homes. A former student of mine from the pre-school where I had taught was in one of these homes and I had become friends with the foster parent. The child's mother had been a good acquaintance of mine for twenty years. Out of the blue, the foster mom called me and asked me to do her a favor. It seems that the child's mother's other daughter was getting married and they wanted the little girl to attend. The foster mom couldn't do it and wondered if I would take her. I bought a long skirt, drove across town and picked up my little charge and proceeded to the McCune Mansion to attend the gala occasion as "governess" to my little "Adele." However, she was neither Adele nor Helen Keller, having the intelligence of a two year old and not able to be potty trained. Her mother had wanted her to be included in the festivities but she also needed constant attention. So together we climbed the many stairs to the third floor ballroom where the wedding and reception was to take place.

The foster mom had really dressed the little ten year old up and while she understood very little of what was going on, she did feel the excitement of the event and was on her best behavior, actually quite prim and proper for the whole evening. Most people stared at us, a few approached us and one of her brothers came to play with her for a while. The mother came up to see her, but the rest of the family ignored us. It was quite the party with a rock band. A myriad of the woman's children were there, from the most conservative of BYU professor to the most outlandish wild child. Each of the woman's children had chosen his or her own path in the world and the diversity was incredible. As the night wore on and I drifted off towards one of the corner alcoves, I saw a young man dressed in an outfit that just didn't fit with the rest of the people. On the other hand, the diversity of costumes made the place quite colorful and I just dismissed what I had seen. However, I had the strange sensation that the young man wasn't really there, that he was like a cardboard outline standing in among the real human beings around him. He had on a sort of Sherlock Holmes jacket of light tweed and when I searched for him later, he was nowhere to be found. Now I know that I had seen my second "ghost" at the McCune Mansion but was unaware of it at the time.

The mysteries of this house became just that, unsolved mysteries. Had a few other things not come my way, I would just have filed these mysteries in my "fool's file" of experiences that are never answered. This McCune Mansion wedding experience was like the time I stepped over an old foundation at Fort Hays in Kansas, not realizing that it was the old hospital. I became very ill all of a sudden. Two young men appeared in beds lying side by side. One was writing his sweetheart in St. Louis and the other was dying. Soon they were both dead, having died of one of the fort's epidemics. The two men told me that they had been separated and that the one young man's letters still existed in his sweetheart's attic. The curator asked me to drive over and check out the old cemetery by the fort on my way out. We went there and I felt nothing at all. As we drove away, I finally had time to read the pamphlet on the history of the fort and found that about 60 years after the fort had been abandoned, all the graves had been moved to another cemetery in another town. At that moment, I knew why the two had been separated. They had been buried side by side in the old cemetery but when they were moved, they were buried far away from each other. The information was of no use to anyone, yet it was a confirmation to be put into my own private file.

I expected the mansion's mysteries to remain so. I was working on these books, doing my research and ran across Jack Goodman's book, *As You Pass By*, which is a collection of his various columns in *The Salt Lake Tribune* on architecture and history. The McCune Mansion was in it, and it was here for the first time that I learned of the Virginia Tanner Modern Dance School, which was conducted in the ballroom for many years. Others knew this from firsthand experience having taken dance from her, but I knew nothing about it. The sentence that caught my eye, however, was the one that mentioned how Virginia Tanner had insisted that her little girls all wear something called Ginny gowns, which were long white nightgowns much like Wendy's in Peter Pan. Many of her students had gone on to dance for famous companies or to teach modern dance at local universities. Friends asked me why I didn't research this some more. Perhaps they thought I would find out about a particular woman or student and be able to identify my ghost. Having done intuitive readings for a while, I now know that what I think of as minimal, or remain somewhat "Pollyanna" about, almost inevitably turns out to be much more important than I had thought when talking to the person. I would rather not know the tragedies, if I can help it. With the loss of so many children and other tragedies that occurred there, it is better to let the ghosts have their say.

The latest information for me came out of an article about the new owner of the mansion, Phil McCarthey. He said that the mansion, after being a family home, living quarters for renters and owners, an LDS music school, dance studio, reception center, art gallery, office space and a wedding reception facility, was purchased in 1999 just to preserve it. The Salt Lake City tornado had even by passed the mansion, toppling some trees and one of its chimneys, and yet still, it remained. He didn't want another generation to go by with no one remembering its former glory days as a home. It had taken an extensive overhauling with new wiring, more parking space, new air-conditioning, heating and even a ramp and new elevator. He added a bronze boar to greet guests where the carriages used to park, and created a new tradition - rubbing its snout for good luck upon entering the home. He also talked about his fascination with the stately dining room where many a heated political discussion probably took place.

The startling paragraph in the article though was this one, "Outside the front driveway, workers unearthed what looks like a giant, deep, stone-filled well. But the mansion always has had running water, so there would be no need for a well. No one knows where the mysterious structure came from. After it was discovered, McCarthey installed some lights in the walls, placed a safety grate at ground level and built up the sides so people can sit and enjoy a spectacular view of the city." (Ibid, D.) Perhaps there was once a gazebo there, just as in my story. Psychics often become confused at the directions within a vision, putting the well in the backyard rather than the front. Or the well might have belonged to one of the two original houses built at the bottom of the hill, making the well located in the backyard. Though the most startling to me was the idea that with the discovery of the well, what I had imagined as a portal, was really just what I had seen. It was the scene of at least one or more terrible accident, like someone falling into the well and drowning, or the memory of such an accident elsewhere on an icy pond.

What is imagined and what is real now? I can never know, though pieces of the puzzle continue to emerge regarding the mysteries of this mansion and the land upon which it was built. I only know that I have some sort of affinity to this house and the ballroom within it. I now expect more rendezvous to come while thinking of what Elizabeth McCune's architect had to say about the house itself, and especially the ballroom. "The chambers are dreams of beauty. The principal one belonging to Mrs. McCune is furnished in a white enamel and is pink brocade and white lace. Mr. McCune's room is oval in plan and designed for a den as for a chamber of rest....There are six other private and guest rooms on this floor and it would be difficult to decide which is of the greater merit." "Going up to the ballroom one enters at once into the vision of a fairyland. There are four great alcoves, while the mirrored walls on every side reflect vistas innumerable. The artificial marble called sageola, which forms most of the furnishings of this ballroom, required importation of a German from his fatherland, and he was eight months in making this, practically unknown composition." (*Women Worth Their Salt*, Ibid, p.95 & 98.)

THE DEVEREAUX MANSION

Former CHART HOUSE---SALT LAKE CITY

In 1855, William C. Staines, a Mormon convert from England who crossed the plains with one of the first groups, began building his dream house. It is probably one of the most elegant mansions in the city, though the once lovely gardens are minuscule today. Staines was a horticulturist who built his house square in the middle of his property so that the real showpiece would be the gardens that surrounded it. He was also Brigham Young's chief architect and horticulture consultant on all of the projects he planned. The Devereaux was like an English Gothic cottage, though much bigger than most and was surrounded by orchards as well. The cottage was completed in 1857 and Staines had President Young, Kimball, Wells and several members of the Council of the Twelve Apostles to his open house party. The new territorial governor took up residence there the following year when many people fled their homes in fear of Johnston's army. The Staines sold their home to William Jennings in 1866 and by the time he was through expanding the property he owned over five ten-acre city blocks.

Jennings built a general merchandising store downtown called the Eagle Emporium and five years later sold it to the LDS church: it became America's first department store, Zion's Cooperative Mercantile Institute - Z.C.M.I. Jennings made vast improvements on the Devereaux mansion and its grounds. He put up a three-story addition to the west side of the building, put on a mansard roof with Gothic elements to it and bought even more land around for a total of approximately five acres. On these lands, to the orchards already there, he added stylized formal gardens and a fountain. In 1876, Jennings traveled to England and purchased all sorts of furnishings for the home. He picked up exquisite silver, crystal, china and some hand carved furniture pieces, which he shipped or brought back with him. He also had a well-stocked wine cellar and put up additional buildings on the grounds. In 1877, he added an east wing, so that much of the original house is no longer apparent. The house became much more of a Second Empire dwelling and lost most of its Gothic elements.

Jennings was the one to name it Devereaux after an English country estate that his mother's family owned. He put in the magnificent gardens and fountains with a tall hedge that had beautiful ornamental iron gates at each corner directly opposite the central entrance to the home. The garden was in symmetrical lines, divided into quadrants and connected by broad gravel driveways. Jennings also added a carriage house, hothouses, vineyards, stables and a kitchen garden. Behind the front parlor was a big ballroom, with French doors at the north opening into the garden. Across the hall from the parlor was a big library and behind that was the dining room with kitchen scullery, storeroom and pantry. The second floor had three master bedrooms, six smaller bedrooms and a nursery. The attic was a trunk room that his boys made into a billiard room and the other side was servant's quarters.

He kept a full time gardener, maids and a cook as well. Many distinguished guests stayed in the Devereaux while visiting the west - such people as the Japanese ambassador, governor of Canada, General Sherman who was Secretary of State at that time, and two American Presidents - Hayes and Grant. Many distinguished people from abroad visited there and it was not unheard of to have over 300 visitors there at one time; no one ever went home without having had a meal or at least light snacks at the Devereaux. Everyone went away commenting how cordially they were treated, with a warmth and hospitality unrivaled in the area.

Jennings continued to stockpile his investments and wealth, being prominent in the development of the railroad in the area. He even had the railroad lay a temporary track for his daughter's wedding, so that she and her new husband could walk directly from their wedding reception in the mansion's ballroom onto a train coach waiting to take them to their new home ten miles away. Jennings was mayor of Salt Lake City in 1882 and wanted to run for territorial governor, but he became ill after his first term as mayor and died in 1886. His widow, Priscilla Paul, stayed in the mansion until her death in the early 1890s. Their eldest son and his family lived in the mansion until 1903.

The Jennings sold it in 1904 and it became something called The Keeley Institute. It was a private clinic for drug and alcohol rehabilitation until 1918. In editor Kate B. Carter's series *Hearth Throbs from the West*, from the Utah Daughters of the Pioneers, written in the 1930's and 40's, I found one reference to the Institute in volume one, 1939, pp. 329-330. Carter took this information from an article in a much earlier magazine *Utah As It Is*. "Devereaux house, with its cozy accommodations and elegant appointments, makes an ideal home for so praiseworthy an institution as the Keeley and as the treatment it affords has been before the public since 1880, counting those it has cured by the thousands, it is worthy of every encouragement. As there are hundreds of people who need the treatment there given, many of them unable to incur the necessary expense, it is intended to appeal to the legislature for the passage of a law which will secure to those unable to pay for the same, treatment necessary to save them from absolute ruin and make of them self-respecting citizens.... The Keeley Institute treats drunkenness as a disease and cures it, and those who have any knowledge of its results need no assurance of its safety to the system, its administration being equally salutary and effective whether applied in infancy, youth or old age."

In 1918, a contractor named Coan, whose first name was unavailable in records, bought the home and remodeled it into a private residence with several rental apartments as well. He and his family lived in the home for 30 years and of course many people passed through its doors during this time as renters. In 1929, the Coan family moved out and he used the house as a used mining equipment business, but the Great Depression forced him to sell his business and move his family back into the mansion. In the late 1930s Coan was able to make some improvements and purchase the home. But they had to sell off much of the land that surrounded it. The Coans moved for the last time in the early 1950s.

The mansion then began to be used for private business. The orchards disappeared and in their place were scrap metal and heavy equipment and the house became very run down and severely in need of repair. In the late 1950s there was a lot of interest in renovating the Devereaux House but nothing was done until almost twenty years later when the National Register of Historic Places put it on their register in 1971. Eight years later the State of Utah bought the Devereaux House for $750,000, but then funds for the renovations had to be raised in order to really preserve the building. Renovation was financed by a mix of public and private funds; the state, the city and the Triad Center all contributed funding.

By 1981 the area was called Devereaux Plaza and contained an ice rink, amphitheater and beautiful landscaping around the mansion. Architectural historians dug up the old foundations, garden paths and artifacts to determine how to make the mansion as close to its former glory as possible. Old photographs were studied as well as letters and diaries, and even the paint was carefully removed to determine the original paints and color schemes. Former residents were also interviewed to gather whatever information was available about the mansion. By doing this they were able to re-create the Devereaux to the original look it had between 1876 and 1880.

Once it was fully restored, it stood empty until in 1992, when The Chart House restaurant chain picked it up. Throughout the house were dining areas sprinkled with large glass cases holding large wooden models of sailing ships, which is a trademark of The Chart House restaurants. We were told when we dined there that some of the furniture and things that belong to the house were already there and had been restored, but this seems a bit strange. The rest was gathered from period pieces and used to re-furnish the home to its original splendor. It really is a gorgeous house with extremely high ceilings and almost oversized finely carved and very elegant wood grained doorways. Wood graining took the place of hardwoods that were scarce in the valley at that time. The appearance of hardwoods is given by painting the wood and then putting several layers of varnish over it. But the wood carving in the rooms and on the staircases is outstanding. We were lucky to have dined at the Devereaux House when we did, just to get a chance to see the interior of the place.

But the Devereaux House also has its rumor of a ghost. The employees of the restaurant alluded to this generally, but privately had their various specific stories to tell. There are lights going on and off when no one is there, doors shutting on their own, footsteps and voices. And of course only those employees "into that stuff" had actually seen things at night or reported the most common occurrence - things being moved about and transported to odd places, or sometimes never even found. Sometimes staff found on first opening up the place, that things laid out the day before were now repositioned for them. The rumor is that it is the ghost of a little girl who likes to do poltergeist sorts of things, and that she lives upstairs where most of the activity takes place. Tricking people and playing with their minds and memories, she comes downstairs only to make things disappear and then they are found in other unlikely places in the house.

The assistant manager of The Chart House was quoted as saying that some of the previous tenants never left the place. " We think it's the spirit of a child, someone who had to stay upstairs when parties were held downstairs, and who was mischievous to get attention, ... More than half the crew has had something odd occur to them in the restaurant and it always happens upstairs. Food servers walking into the study frequently lose their equilibrium. Order tickets placed at the wait station mysteriously disappear only to be found wedged between the bookcases of an old armoire, the only original piece of furniture in the house." ("Ghost Stories? Experiences with Spirits" by Christopher Smith, *The Salt Lake Tribune*, October 31, 1992.) Cutlery will be found laying neatly in an odd place, when it was in the drawer or on a table only moments before. But all who have worked there agree that something, perhaps spirits, often climb the back stairs of the old Devereaux House late at night.

After dining there and taking a walk about, back when The Chart House was there, I wrote down my own impressions of the place. Active areas were the second floor west bedroom, kitchen area and basement (if it is still there). There was a young man who lived in the second floor west side of the house from a later period than the little girl. The young man may have committed suicide there, possibly when it was a rehabilitation center. His route is to come downstairs to check things out in the kitchen and then all around. The third floor room on the east has a window where people see things at night, possibly a light, or even a shadow outline in the day. The little girl likes to move things around. She has blonde curls and is maybe three or four years old. She probably died at that age. The feeling was that these ghosts like a lot of the people who come there, but a few they don't like and these are the ones they pick on. All the little girl wants to do is play. My feeling was that the young man was a patient of the Keeley Institute and the little girl was someone from the Coan family period.

There is a third young man who has dark brown hair and wears a turn-of-the-century suit, indicating he was a fancy dresser. He seems to come from the earlier period of the original "glory days" of the mansion and had traveled a lot before coming there. He went on a long ocean voyage possibly through the Panama Canal but only thought of the Devereaux house. He came back to marry a girl and she had married someone else. He may have committed suicide somewhere else but returns here to where the girl either lived or visited several times.

Perhaps someone out there can research further and find out if any of these impressions have a basis in fact. Alas, on my last visit to the Devereaux, the place was empty. The arts festival, which used to be held with the Devereaux right in the middle of the festivities, had moved to the fair grounds and now to the Gallivan Plaza a few blocks away. The old Union Pacific Railroad Station down the street became part of the Gateway project; the Devereaux ended up on the other side of things. Unlike the renovated Rio Grande station just down the street, the Union Pacific Station is not as ornate. The huge main terminal room has one thing to boast of - some magnificent paintings telling the story of the pioneers coming to Utah. There are ghosts there too, but this is another story being reserved for a separate volume. The beautiful plaza that the city spent so much money on is quite deserted except for those who wander down to eat their lunch or enjoy the little park. The Devereaux looks a little forlorn sitting in the middle of the plaza, for all of its trees, lawns, gardens and fountain. I guess we were lucky to get a chance to see the inside of it when we did. Perhaps The Chart House found the place not lucrative enough or in a poor location for business. Or just maybe the owners were plagued a bit by those dwellers who didn't want them there. I wonder what the next occupants will bring with them? Or what the apparitions and ghosts will have to tell or show them when they arrive and get a little added bonus to their business.

The Union Pacific Depot will now house two businesses - a restaurant and The House of the Blues, a chain of nightclubs owned by Dan Ackroyd of Saturday Night Live fame, named for a movie he and his partner John Belushi made together called *The Blues Brothers*. The House of the Blues may bring one more apparition to the place with Dan Ackroyd sometimes performing in remembrance of John Belushi.

During the 2002 Winter Olympics, the Devereaux was first used as an art gallery where colorful, life-size buffalo were on display. They were decorated with every color of the rainbow, and the bright colors were really something unusual to see within the old mansion's walls. But the local Chamber of Commerce had an even brighter idea for its use, opening its doors as a venue to host corporate parties. Approximately 70 parties were held there at a cost of five to ten thousand dollars each. Other activity conducted at the Devereaux House included attempts to help rural areas attract high-tech businesses, and to assist the launching of ethnic and women-owned businesses. Economic developers were assigned to rural communities to help locate high-tech companies in the area. Parties were arranged, providing places for minority or women-owned businesses to socialize with these major corporations.

After the Olympic games, the Devereaux House went back to being quiet and still, except for its occasional ghostly antics. Who knows what the next adventure will be for this grand historical setting? It seems the city values the thousands of dollars they invested in her renovation, as they keep finding ways to keep her alive!

LESTER & JASMINE FREED HOME

BRIGHAM STREET, SOUTH TEMPLE

The Freed Furniture Company was located on Third South and would later become the Victory Theater. Lester and his father had opened the store together when they came to Utah in 1890. He and his father did everything in the store at first, but then Lester began to branch out. In 1922, he sold the store and began his own finance company, became director of a bank and also began to have mining interests. He was very outgoing and gregarious with a quick wit and a charming way with words. He belonged to a dozen clubs: Alta, Commercial, Rotary, Shriners, Elks, and several country clubs. And everyone thought that he would never get married. But Jasmine Young, whose father was a nephew of Brigham Young, lived with her folks on a large farm in Red Butte Hollow. This was out in the country then and it was quite a miracle that they managed to meet each other at all.

Both of them were handsome and outgoing people and one of the most popular couples of their day. In 1910 they built their house on South Temple. It had nine large rooms with long wide windows and lots of sun. It had a sleeping porch on pillars that went out over the front entrance on the east side and really let the cool breezes in especially in the evening. We called it the captain's room when we lived there because it had thin strips of wood paneling halfway up and then total windows all the way around. The upstairs bathroom still had the original tile and old claw bathtub and of course at that time it was divided up into apartments. There were four single rooms down the hall, our apartment with three bedrooms in the front upstairs, two large apartments on the main floor and an apartment in the basement. And one could go half way up the stairs and then be able to climb over a window seat and out onto the roof which was our private sunbathing place overlooking the school playground.

The family lived there 38 years. It was a rather plain house; the Freeds were more concerned with a good and happy life than a fancy facade. They had four boys who really got to be what boys should be in a warm family life. Sometimes their mother would load everyone up in the car, after a rough day of playing and before wash time, and go for a drive. The basement had a laundry room, cook and chauffeur quarters and small stage with footlights where the children could put on their own plays. But when I lived there those nine rooms had been doubled if not tripled by all of the additions and room divisions. That's why when I read the other day that it is now back to a private residence, I was surprised. I wondered if they totally remodeled or just kept a lot of the extra kitchens and such. But they certainly did one very wonderful thing and that was to paint the house a pale yellow after years of an ugly green.

Lester and Jasmine owned many automobiles because Lester was just crazy about them. Some people said that they had more cars than anyone else in Salt Lake. On one trip they drove to New York, loaded their car on a ship, sailed through the Panama canal, came back to San Francisco and then drove home. There are still many Freed businesses, and many relatives still important in society and cultural circles to this day. Lester Freed died at 62 and the family left the house in 1948. Perhaps that was when it was divided up into apartments or maybe this was done a little later. I only know that my two roommates and I lived there for the last years of the sixties and the first years of the seventies. The story would end here if not for so many events which I am sure contributed to the odd feeling in the house and perhaps even affected things that happened there.

I can remember that certain areas of the house had more of a dark feeling; my bedroom was one of them. Many a night I would wake up with the feeling of someone leaning over me, sort of neutrally checking me out, perhaps seeing if I was okay. Our bathroom was in the middle of the apartment with the kitchen, then the three bedrooms and the living room surrounded them. Jennie had the captain's room over the front porch, which I had wanted but was finally pressured to give up. Sandy had one of the single rooms meant to be its own one-room apartment, but the door opened up into our apartment and so we talked the landlord into letting us have it as the third bedroom. The bathroom and kitchen never felt good to me either, but especially my room and the bathroom. All the other rooms were light and airy with lots of windows and I often thought that my bedroom had been intended to be a walk-in closet.

All the walls were that horrid pale green and there was even an upright piano in the living room painted green to match the apartment. It is the events in the house that made it a haunted one. Downstairs there were three bachelors from southern Utah, not college kids but guys who had come up to the big city looking for adventure. In the apartment under us was a young married couple with a baby. In the basement was a young man with a ponytail and a German shepherd dog. Down the hall from us were a young sailor, a strange actress, and a little European cabinetmaker who had survived the holocaust in World War II, losing most of his family in the process.

The cabinetmaker was always very nice to us and he rode his bicycle to work every day. One time we left cookies at the door of everyone in the house and no one responded except for him. He came up to our door in tears, thanked us profusely and when he quit living there he gave each of us beautiful silhouette pictures which he had made and let us draw straws for the only two remaining inlaid wooden jewelry boxes he had left, and of course I lost. It was only later that we learned the cabinetmaker had pulled a knife on the young sailor in the shared bathroom because he wanted to use it first and he had even held it at the sailor's throat. We learned that actually he had just been released from the Veteran's Hospital psychiatric ward and the real reason he had left his apartment was that he had had another breakdown.

The young couple below my bedroom fought a lot. I would lay there on many a night and listen to them yell and scream at each other though I never heard the sounds of anything physical. It was awful to hear it night after night, and the little baby would scream and scream and no one would come for it. During the day all was quiet but the moment the man came home it would start up again. One night, one other guy and I were home and the wife came running out of her apartment pounding on our doors, screaming and yelling hysterically. Her baby had stopped breathing. The police and the ambulance came and I will never forget the paramedic rushing out of the house to the ambulance with this little baby, its arms limp and hanging almost straight out from its body. The couple moved out immediately afterward but I know the baby died in the home because I found the obituary in the paper. I have always felt that she died from the atmosphere in the place, compounded by her parents constant fighting.

Then the pony-tailed guy had a tragedy strike him. He and his girlfriend lived in the basement. One day I walked home from the college to find a tiny crowd gathered out in front of the house. His German shepherd dog had somehow gotten loose and had been struck by a car. They slid the dog onto a big flat board to try and take him somewhere to get help but then he just died right there in front of us all. The landlord told us that he thought it strange that this guy had rented the apartment because the basement area had always been rented to a young single girl ever since he could remember. He even said that he had been told that this was the way it had been long before he owned the building when the home was first divided into apartments. We asked him why and he told us that there was a bad energy in it, which had caused several tragedies to happen there always with young girls. We of course did not believe him and figured that he was just trying to scare us. Then he told us an awful story about our house that at the time we semi-believed but it frightened us anyway.

Later we found out that it was a true story so far as the suicide, though all the gory details that the landlord told us could have been added on later. I don't suppose the landlord ever told any of this to anyone who was looking to rent this apartment however. A young girl had rented the basement apartment several years ago, he said. She was a dance major at the college. Her boyfriend jilted her and she was very depressed. Anyway, she killed herself in the bathroom of the apartment, leaving her hair dryer running and the bathroom door was shut. It was a week or more before anyone investigated or looked for her. Her body had disintegrated somewhat because of the hair dryer being on. The investigators had to carry her body out in several plastic bag containers and the place was really a mess. As I think about it now, I often wonder about the landlord's state of mind as well.

I had only been in the basement apartment once and only for a few minutes while I talked to the renter's girlfriend. But I well remember the feeling and didn't want to go there again, though I did wonder if the children's stage was still there somewhere in this apartment. I talked to both of them outside after that. I got a chance to go back there several years later when I had moved back to Salt Lake after ten years in Colorado. I just walked right in the front door like I was visiting someone, walked up the stairs and climbed onto the roof over the playground. It was such a lovely place to be in spring and summer. The huge lilac bushes were still there then and fortunately in bloom; the smell was incredible.

I can remember thinking about the Freeds and how they must have put so much warmth and love into their home. But afterwards, dozens of people had passed through the various apartments and at least two people that I knew about had died there. Hauntings are often an accumulation of lives lived in a place - the more people, the more energy. Then if there is tragedy it is heightened. The walls talk and the floors creak, and shadows come by you in the dark. And yet the feeling of the house was not one of malevolence at all, but rather one of great sadnesses, of losses deep and mournful, of memories that must cling to those who surrounded the tragedies even today. It is not something to fear, but rather something to grieve for and gain comfort from. At the time it was a house that needed healing from those spirits who live on within it.

Recently I went by the Freed house that is now a private residence. I stopped and studied it for a while from the outside. It is back to how the Freeds must have had it and really has a very warm feeling with window box flowers, a new roof, pale yellow clapboard walls and white trim. It looks nothing like it did when we lived there, and though the porch roof still looks over the playground, the old school across the street is gone and a new one stands in its place. The underground walkway seems to still be in use and the playground across the street is still there. I can go back in my mind to when I spent hours out on that roof enjoying the summer trees and evening breezes. I can think how life and the passage of time changes things. No one would know today what went on there then, and the house as a whole is back to what it should have been all along - a warm house, full of laughter and family - though residue, and sometimes even active residue, does remain.

ARMSTRONG MANSION

BRIGHAM STREET -- SALT LAKE CITY

In September of 1865, William Wright Armstrong was born in Darlington, Wisconsin. He lost his mother at a very young age and the family then moved to Kansas where he spent his school years. He got his law degree at the University of Wisconsin and then married Eva Lees of Irving, Kansas. Eventually they had one son only, named Sherman. There are many mysteries about why they then moved west in 1890 and settled in Nephi. Armstrong never practiced law and nothing can be found in the records to answer this mystery either. Instead he became a cashier in a bank there and did some investing, so that soon he had interests in hardware and gas companies and also a bank.

They moved to Salt Lake in 1903 and soon Armstrong had holdings in several banks all over the west. William was president of the National Copper Bank and quite active in his political and civic life. The Armstrongs both had quite the social life; Mr. Armstrong was a member of the clubs at the university, in commercial concerns, and even the Alta Club, which was considered the premiere rich man's club in Salt Lake City. Armstrong also belonged to the Masons and had many political interests as well. He was elected to the State Senate in 1917 and he helped with many tasks during the Great War. He was director of the State Food and Fuel Administration, chairman of the Victory Loan Drive and a member of the State Council of Defense.

The Armstrong mansion was built in 1911 and 1912 and was designed by Richard K.A. Kletting in the Neoclassic style. It has a Palladian plan with a classical portico supported by several columns that also features French doors and a second story balcony. When I lived in the area it was not the most attractive of houses on South Temple or "Brigham Street" as it was then called. But it was a sturdy one with an unusual two-story portico and side entrance. To me it looked like an old-fashioned bank itself in those days and was a dull gray color. It was fitting for a banker and his family to have lived in it from 1912 to 1933. With its four great columns in the front, it looked like a building that one would find in the nation's capitol or as the facade for a Greek temple. It was no surprise to me that the same man who designed our state capitol building also designed Armstrong's home. The fact that the entrance is not in the center of the columns is quite odd to me, but on the other hand, makes it all the more unusual a house. The guesthouse in the back seemed more like a carriage house then.

You have to remember that when I lived on South Temple, a lot of the old mansions there were sort of run down and divided into apartments for college students. The park up the street was not quiet and deserted like it seems to be now, but a mini version of Haight Ashbury. West of the park was where all the artists, musicians and writers lived who played for the symphony, displayed in galleries downtown or were writing their great American novels. We aspiring artists from the college got to hang out with 'the real thing" by attending parties there. Now there has obviously been a resurgent interest in renovating and restoring many of these houses to their former glory days and of course the prices are out of this world. It is really nice to see many of them returned to their majestic splendor with beautiful gardens to match.

The local legend about the Armstrong house is that someone who lived there, either in the Armstrong family or more possibly after they left in 1933, committed a murder and got away with it.

The story goes that a married man caught his wife with her young lover and shot him. The lover fell backward out the window and bled to death on the lawn. This has never been substantiated I guess, nor maybe can it be. But people who have lived in the house over the years have had all the ghostly occurrences of a typical haunting, especially footsteps racing towards a particular window in the house. It is a private residence so one can't ask about it, though I guess police records could be checked to verify the story's truth.

My intuition says that a murder did happen there, but not in the way the legend depicts it. It has somehow to do with Armstrong's son or young friend, and then there was a second occurrence much later when others occupied the house. The son was protected by money and influence and seems indeed to have "gotten away with it," whatever "it" was. I don't know which incident involved murder. I just know that both were quite negative incidents and that there are two entities appearing in windows rather than one. Whenever I passed this house on my block in those days - several years of college in the seventies - I did feel something that put me off, but never guessed what it was.

Now the Armstrong house is quite a beautiful place with an almost luminescent coat of white paint and black shutters all around. The cottage in the back has been made into a guesthouse I think and the gardens that surround the house are quite regal. You can tell that someone really took an interest in reviving it to its former beauty and perhaps even improved upon it. One would never know what might have taken place there many, many years ago. But isn't that the irony of such things - how a home, any home, even a gorgeous mansion home, can contain such secrets and keep them. The layers of a dwelling just fascinate me. An architect can study the structure of a building, an archeologist can study foundations and artifacts from decades before, and an historian can research the facts and interesting stories about such a place, but it is the intuitive who feels the house in layers, views it in the mind's eye and listens to its breathing.

A MINER'S MANSION HOUSE NEAR LIBERTY PARK

SALT LAKE CITY

This is a house that my brother has owned for years, and so I have been there often for many family gatherings on holidays. I also used it as a base at various junctures in the long slide my mother took towards her eventual release from pain, as it is near her nursing home. In both the happy times and not so happy times, we all gathered in a house which my brother had jokingly once said he bought for its 12 foot high ceilings which made him feel smaller than his 6 foot 7 inch frame. The house was built by a miner who had gotten rich from the Tintic Mine, but who for some reason had never moved into it. It was purchased by a doctor and his family, then owned by a series of families, then was broken up into apartments for a while, and eventually was turned into a single family dwelling again. My brother made many wonderful renovations in the house and simultaneously, went through several different lives himself. I think now that he is retiring and moving away, he will be very sad to leave the place, even though it is like most old mansion houses, a real handful to maintain.

My favorite part of the house is the sun or plant room, which my brother built off the kitchen out of redwood and then used old glass-paned doors stained a redwood color to form a huge covering of windowpanes. It lets in a lot of light and is quite cool in summer and quite warm in the winter. It is full of plants and the ribbons he and his wife win every year at the State Fair for things they cook and plants they grow. The main floor has a huge living room - originally two rooms, dining room, entryway, kitchen and small bath. The upstairs has two bedrooms, a bath and a big den or family room. The den has a closet where a small ladder is built into the wall to climb through the cold drafts to an attic room with a dormer window. This closet is the heart of the house to me, or the cold spot that people talk about in houses. The basement has one cement floor laundry room, a series of very low-ceilinged rooms with dirt floors, and a huge octopus heater with arms that go every which way. Various guests and visitors have reported seeing or sensing things in the house. My brother and his wife have lived there quite comfortably and have the gift of walking right through such things without it bothering them. They love it dearly and I am sure that my brother has put his very heart into the place, even researching its history as much as he has been able.

When I visited the house I was always being drawn to the upstairs closet area. In fact one day it was a sort of joke, because my brother came home and asked his wife where I was and she told him matter-of-factly that I was upstairs sitting in the den closet. To me the hot spots in the house are the basement, bathroom behind the kitchen and of course the den room upstairs. One time many years ago my brother told me that the only thing he had ever noticed was that sometimes when he was working in his den at his desk all alone, it would feel as if a little old lady had come up behind him and laid down a batch of fresh cookies in front of him. The aroma was enchanting. At one point their cleaning lady told them that a little old man and a little old woman lived in the basement and that only the old woman would come upstairs sometimes to spend time in the kitchen. But when they arranged for me to meet the cleaning lady, telling her that I had some intuitive abilities, she quit her job shortly after that. They did not think that there was a connection but I regretted missing the opportunity to meet her.

Two friends that stayed overnight saw a shadowy figure more than once in the den upstairs, and once one of them actually saw a little round woman appear in front of the closet door momentarily. When I was there I felt there were two people, this round woman, and a young soldier in the northwest corner of the den. Once I did an intuitive reading for the sister of my brother's wife who was visiting from back east. We sat in the downstairs living room and I was having a real difficult time getting started. At first I thought it was my brother's sister-in-law blocking me, but then I became conscious of a huge roar of sound in my head like the static on a radio that is not quite on a station. I could not get through the fog and haze to where this woman was across from me. It was my first experience with this because I usually did my readings in my own home or outside. The noise continued every time I tried to concentrate on the lady. I was just about to suggest that we go outside when an idea came to me. I said in my head, "Could you please stop all the noise. I am trying to do a reading for this lady. She is only here for a few days and might not have an opportunity again to visit here. So could you please stop?" Abruptly, all the static and noise stopped. It happened so suddenly that it scared me; it took all I had to go on and do the reading. I have had this happen since in other places, with other people and have found that this always works, if you are polite or in some cases, firm about it.

When my brother was renovating the main floor bathroom behind the kitchen and tore out the back wall of the bathtub, he found a giant walk-in closet there. He closed it so fast that my sister-in-law didn't get a chance to check it out thoroughly. One night when they had invited all of the family to dinner for a little respite after a long day at the hospital, I asked my sister-in-law if I could go sit in the bathroom and write down my impressions about the hidden closet. She was interested in my doing this and very interested in old houses in general. So while the family was busy in after dinner conversation, I slipped out with a yellow note pad and spent some time in the bathroom. In the middle of my contemplations a startling vision came to me. Nowadays I know that when one asks a literal question, one gets a literal answer. It is just that most of us never listen in the first place and when we do, we most often don't expect something literal. I had asked the spirit in the house what it was that she needed or if there was anyway that I could help her with.

In the vision, I saw a little old lady with white hair and a bun on the back of her neck wearing a long, to-her-knees, see-through shimmering, almost glowing white apron, though the top part of it was a solid green. She wore a gray dress with little pink flowers on it and she was climbing up and down the stairs that used to be between the kitchen and the bath in which I was sitting (once a bedroom). The printed words "Millennium Closet" kept appearing before me as the woman climbed up and down the stairs busily stocking the closet my brother had uncovered with jars of fruit and canned goods from the basement. Each time her breathing became more labored and finally she could not climb the stairs any longer and her breathing stopped. At the end I asked her if there was anything I could do for her. The answer came back that I was to bring her son back to her and that his sisters were the only ones who could do it. I supposed that he had either left the house angry, never to return, or that he had died in some war, accident or perhaps a suicide, and could not return.

I vaguely remembered my brother telling me that once a lady had parked in front of their house for a long enough time for them to notice, and he had asked her what she wanted. It turned out that the house had once been her family home and that she had grown up there. She was the one to tell them about the back stairs that were no longer there and that the bathroom behind the kitchen had once been a bedroom. When I thought about this, it came to me that if I ever found my brother's visitor, I would then know who the woman was lying in bed in that converted bedroom, on the main floor, too sick to stay upstairs any more. My intuition said that it was the visitor's mother in the bedroom, that both of her parents had died in the house, and that at least one of them had "sugar diabetes" as they called it in those days, just as my mother had. That was the crazy intuitive connection then, I thought - those sugary jars of fruit that the woman was hoarding for the millennium.

My mother had really craved sugar in her last years and ate a lot of fruit. My grandmother always supplied my mother with extra long white aprons that she made for her. So I thought that perhaps I was either seeing my short grandmother or a symbol of the death angel that visits just before someone dies. A friend told me that I would see the colors in the vision-woman's dress at my mother's funeral and this part did come true. The gray with pink flowers was everywhere I looked in the funeral home carpet where we dressed my mother, the inside of her coffin, the pink rosebushes she was buried near, and the last minute change in gravestones which fell upon me, never the decision maker in my family. I chose a granite background of gray, copper and black speckles, with engraved pink roses. The material of the dress seemed to be everywhere.

I felt that the woman who had parked out in front of the house was somehow the key to the young man who had left. I also felt that the son had nothing to do with my family but was someone who had either been killed in a war or estranged from his family because of a war. Perhaps he had only been in contact with his sisters or they knew something that his mother did not. After my mother died I realized that this vision was something exclusive to the house and separate from anything concerning my mother's journey, though at the same time parallel to it. Mormons saved up for the disasters or hard times that would come just before the second coming of Christ and in this house the path to this storage lay from the basement shelves to an old bedroom closet behind the kitchen where all the activity had probably been. More than one old person had died there I thought. But the words "Millennium Closet" had me baffled as in Mormon and many other Christian theologies; the Millennium represented the thousand years of peace before the end of the world, as we know it. It is a time when all saving of souls could be completed and the dead will walk among the living.

Because I see symbols from other's belief systems, I often have difficulty interpreting them correctly. So it was not until my aunt's funeral when I saw her in her Temple garments that I noticed the green and white apron she was wearing with the Masonic and Mormon symbols on it. These are called endowment clothes and have secret meanings. One also wears them to go into the afterlife to meet loved ones in the Celestial Kingdom which is the highest kingdom where of course everyone wants to go, though there are two lesser kingdoms for those who do not make it there. The apron's symbolic nature did not dawn on me for a long time afterwards. I had seen the spiritual version of this in my vision because it was glowing and shimmering.

Several years later, when my brother was at our house, he read this story. He told me that I had not gotten the story right about this ghost in their house. The two visitors who saw the old lady were right, and he had also seen this ghost. This was a new story to me. It seems that one year he was refinishing the wood floors upstairs. As he was working on the den floor, he suddenly looked up and saw a very small round older lady with white hair and a bun at the back of her neck looking at him from in front of the closet door. He looked at her again and realized that her feet were about a foot off the floor so that she was floating in front of him. She then promptly disappeared; he had attributed this delusion to having worked too long in an enclosed area with the fumes from refinishing the floor. He read my story and thought I should get it straight, while at the same time, startled that I was describing this very woman in my vision from a few years before. Once again I had not believed that what I was seeing was real and had thought it symbolic, when actually it was a real image of the ghost of the house, showing me her mission and search for what it was that kept her bound there.

Almost four years after my own mother had died, I got the message. I had asked the woman in my brother's house what she needed and she had answered for her son to come back to her. It had never occurred to me that he had left her religiously. That perhaps he had either died in a war having left his religion before this, or gone to war and come back having left his religion. The woman wore her spiritual apron and she was waiting for the Millennium to come so that she then would have time to save her son's soul. So all that she could do was to continue to stock up her storage for the bad times before the second coming while waiting for the Millennium which would then bring her son back to her when the dead rose and everyone had a chance to be saved. This was her religion and her beliefs and her spirit was held there because of this son who had not come back yet. As to why spirits are held in places when the answer to their problems are actually located elsewhere or are even in a different time frame, is a mystery that people have been trying to answer for centuries.

My brother and his wife have put a coin they found in the foundation in a little frame in the kitchen and they also have part of a little porcelain doll they found under the house. One day I felt that if they walked into the backyard and dug around the roots of a big old tree there, they would find a little box of treasures - nothing monetarily valuable though, just little things like people put in a time capsule, or what a child would collect and bury in a box. Of course they have never done this and I could be entirely wrong as well. Perhaps they might even be things that belonged to the long lost son. They both are very comfortable in their house and my brother's heart is there after so many years and lives and renovations. But I could never live in such a house because too many echoes of people linger there, too many voices talk in the stillness of the night, and too many dreams and memories are in the walls. I would be haunted by them as I slept - or perhaps did not sleep. Every sound and light would tell me stories that perhaps I would or would not want to hear.

As for the old woman in my brother's home, she loves the owners dearly and will be just as sad to see them go, as they will be. And while my brother, ever the scientist, asks me if I just make this stuff up, actually the pieces of each puzzle fall around me over time and things often make more sense now than they used too. I don't have to make anything up, the pictures just come and sooner or later make an esoteric sense that many would never perceive or ponder. Though for myself, I now know what it is that the spirit of the house is waiting for, why it was my brother she appeared too, and just how directly she had answered my question when I asked her what it was that she wanted. My brother representing to her, her own lost son, and a search which will go on for the new owners and beyond, because the son has probably long departed this earth wandering in another world where whatever he did is done. There is no "apron" for him at present, though his mother just might get her wish. Some say that we all go to the Heaven that we believe in, and if this is so, she will.

WHEELER HISTORIC FARM

GRAND LADY OF SOUTH COTTONWOOD

The land in this area was first claimed in 1864. A man named William Goodall Young, who was related to Brigham Young and a man of means, moved there with his second wife Martha and their five children in 1870. Builders Ole Hansen and Olaus Johnson Nordstrand made major improvements on this land and built an adobe house

with a pitched roof which had a dining room, parlor, kitchen, washroom and 4 bedrooms along the west side of the rectangular building. The Youngs never really owned the property and were much like squatters until in 1884 Elizabeth Cooper Pixton bought the property. In 1886 Henry J. Wheeler and his new bride of just 3 years, Sariah Pixton Wheeler, moved into the adobe dwelling where at least 5 families had lived at one time or another.

Sariah had been married before to a William Lee Dykes and had one son named William Leo. This was at the time when polygamy was going out of favor with the Mormon Church and about the same time as the manifesto discouraging the practice. Because of so much pressure from the outside, especially from the United States government, arrests and imprisonments of both men and women had been happening steadily. In 1882 William Lee Dykes married Emily Platts and they had their first child in 1883. Sariah and William Lee Dykes were married in 1883; Sariah divorced him on the grounds of abandonment in 1885 after having had one child, William Leo. It is hard to say if this was polygamy; though the man was married to two wives, it was only a matter of about two years and Sariah did call it abandonment. Anyway, Sariah and Henry J. Wheeler Sr. were married in 1886 and moved onto the farm in 1887.

In 1898 they tore the original adobe brick house down and used the bricks to start building their Victorian style farmhouse. Sariah was the sole architect and designer and directed the entire building project herself. She also had 6 more children: May Lisadore in 1888, April Elise in 1890, Henry Jr. in 1892, Leona in 1895 and two more daughters born by 1906 - Cilma and then Ann. The farmhouse has a dining room, pantry, kitchen, two parlors, 3 bedrooms upstairs and a large bathroom and closet. The 4 middle girls slept cross-wise in one bed, while the two boys had the smaller bedroom, the oldest girl had a room to herself, and the baby slept in a cradle next to her mother in the master bedroom. In the master bedroom there is a painting of Mrs. Wheeler's mother holding her as a baby; this was painted while her father was away, so that when he came home, he could see what she had looked like.

There are four chimneys with two fireplaces upstairs and downstairs. There are some carved wood doorframes with round domes, as well as a larger dome on the bottom of the staircase that supposedly represented the state beehive. This is said to be the only contribution that Mr. Wheeler made to the house's interior. Most of the original furniture was stored in the more recently built barn that burned down in 1973, so a lot of the furnishings one sees today are period pieces donated by various people. But the bathroom, kitchen and pantry have some of their original furnishings. Indoor plumbing came to the Wheeler house but Mr. Wheeler thought it an impropriety to use it, so only guests were allowed to use it. There is an outhouse in the back, a granary and fruit cellar built around 1870, the original barn built in 1910, and the remains of the second barn which burned down in 1973. There is also a root cellar built in the 1870s or earlier, a garage built in 1904 and a guest house built in 1934, all of which are right behind the main farm house.

The John P. Calhoon mansion in Murray was built in 1900 in a style similar to the Wheeler Farm house, though it is a much larger home. Sariah did put her heart and soul into designing her own home; it was also good enough that someone else, perhaps a trained architect, recognized her talents and perhaps "lifted" a few ideas from her.

In 1912, Henry Sr. and Henry Jr. began the Rose Bud Dairy farm together. The dairy ran until 1933 as a retail marketer and then began selling wholesale only. Joseph Ramoselli, recently from Italy, began a truck farm just south of Wheeler farm in 1930 on the same property. The dairy was sold in 1943 when Henry Wheeler Sr. passed away and left no will. The Sterling Furniture Company purchased it and a family called the Siddoways ran the farm until 1947. Then the Richard Madsens, who owned the furniture company, moved in for a while, but eventually a series of tenants lived there until 1969 when the property was sold to the county. In 1974 the farm was put on the Utah Registry of Historic Places and in 1976 it was placed on the National Registry of Historic Places. By 1979 the restoration of all of the main buildings was complete and Sariah's house had been restored to her original plans.

By 1998, when the 100th year centennial took place at the Wheeler Historic Farm, a new barn stood there, a huge recreational barn stood not far away for all sorts of social gatherings and dances, and many other buildings had been added to the property. The farm also housed a host of farm animals to visit and enjoy. Wheeler Farm offers tours of the cellars and main house, birthday party facilities, historic craft classes, and seasonal activities, such as the Haunted Woods - a pumpkin patch at Halloween, where you pick your own pumpkin and then paint or carve it. People have weddings there, family reunions, dances, and various other social gatherings. When I worked with multi-handicapped preschoolers, it was a yearly field trip for us. There are a blacksmith shop, a gift shop and various other things to do there, especially for very young children. Though I would venture to guess that many older children enjoy the Haunted Woods show, too. This past year's show for example was called "Crime and Punishment" and featured the "bloody beer barrel murders" supposedly based on actual murder cases in Utah!

I took a house tour near Halloween because people at Wheeler are a bit shy of talking about any ghosts seen around there at any other time of year. I have learned over the years that the winter months are always the most active months for ghosts and the Wheeler Farm is no exception. The lights at the old farm often do not work right; they will either not come on or will not go off. The doors are left unlocked and then later found to be locked, or if left open, they are found shut tightly the next morning. If left tightly shut, they are swung wide open the next day on carpeting on which they should get stuck! The other thing that happens quite often is that the doors suddenly slam shut when there is no wind to cause it. And they seem to slam right while a tour is going on or when more than one person is in the house. However, no one has ever heard footsteps or voices or sounds of any kind.

Most startling however, is the fact that more than once, a ghost has been sighted there. She is always seen late at night, just before closing by only one person, so her presence cannot be verified as yet. She is described as a woman with pale skin and black hair swept up in a bun, dressed in a long dress, floating above the floor towards where the Wheeler boys used to sleep upstairs. The assumption is that she is Mrs. Wheeler checking up on her children in the middle of the night. It is always during the winter months that this happens. However, with so many people having lived there it would be hard to tell who she is. The designer of the house, though, might have the most rights and investments to be the one doing this.

Mr. Wheeler died at the farm in 1943. Mrs. Wheeler died in 1928 and I could not find a reference as to just where she passed on. Intuition tells me that she did die there: this would make her the most likely candidate for such a haunting. I imagine that Mr. Wheeler would be found somewhere out on the farm surveying his fields or cows late at night in the middle of winter because he probably expired out there in the open air, not in the house. My impressions are that the two Wheeler sons who slept in the room right by the top of the steep and narrow stairs, liked to stand up there against the railing and look down. I think at least one of them took a tumble that required some healing time. The woman walking the hallway upstairs is checking on them from time to time. One of the boys spent some time in that room due to an illness and had to be nursed for quite a while. These are my impressions of the first layer or dwellers of the house.

The second layer, or those who dwelled in the house after the Wheelers, is quite scattered and could be any who lived there after. My impressions of this layer follow:

- One family had an oldest son who did not get along with his father and left the house angry, never to return. He left this anger behind him and this is why the doors slam sometimes. When he left after having words with his father, he slammed several on his way out more than once.

- Someone's daughter was forced to marry, and she cried a lot in the upstairs room. It was probably a forced marriage because of an unanticipated pregnancy and she was extremely unhappy before the marriage and during it. In my head, I could hear her crying herself to sleep in the upstairs front bedroom on the north side. I wonder if perhaps people there hear her tears upon occasion, but dismiss it as their imaginations or the wind.

- I also felt that there were footsteps sometimes walking across the upstairs hallway but no one reported this to me.

Wheeler Farm had a tragedy just a few years ago. A small boy was killed when two other slightly older boys shot off their play guns and startled the horses pulling the hay wagon, which ran over the boy. It was a very sad sequence of events and really affected people. The hayrides were suspended for a very longtime. Some groups even canceled their yearly reservations because they just couldn't handle going there and being reminded of this event. .

Those who have not been to Wheeler Historic Farm should indeed go there and enjoy the things offered especially for young children. It is a wonderful place especially in the fall; there is even a small museum on the second floor balcony of the larger barn. Researchers on the farm's history have done an excellent job gathering all the information they can and will soon publish a history of the farm for all to enjoy. As for me, visits to such places are fun and taxing at the same time. Houses, especially very old and very loved ones, can carry a lot in their walls. One house can "call me" and then at another site, I never see or hear a thing. Each one is entirely different, and it is only the connections which sometimes haunt me. The north side of Wheeler farm is full of ghostly activity, while the larger rooms on the west side hold only a sort of enchantment or charm for history buffs.

HAUNTING LEGENDS IN THE AVENUES

SUMMER HOMES OF THE FAMOUS

One summer several years ago I met a man claiming to be a parapsychologist. He was in town for a while doing some private investigations that were not intended to be very well known, regarding a haunting of a famous movie star's summer home. I can only relate this story from memory; I did my best to see if there was a Claudette Colbert - Utah connection in the thirties or forties but I could find nothing. Perhaps he had the wrong movie star, though the only hometown star that I can think of with dark hair (what I remember for sure was the color of her hair) is Loretta Young who left Salt Lake at three years of age and to my knowledge never returned to the Salt Lake area. There is Linda Darnell who came here for the opening of "Brigham Young" and might secretly have fallen in love with the place; this is all I can think of. None of these three in their autobiographies - or even their biographers - ever made mention of a summer home here or that of any relatives. While my short-term memory is getting a bit rocky, my long term is not. It's Claudette Colbert who sticks in my mind.

The home the parapsychologist was investigating was supposed to be a big secret anyway, and whoever the famous star was, she is probably dead by now. Anyway, the people who managed the home for her at the time called in a parapsychologist; he was quite old when I met him. They had been having all sorts of "haunting" problems and needed some help. To the west of the main living room was a little plant room with lots of windows and a window seat. Houseguests were reporting seeing a shadowy or misty shape standing in the corner of this little room. At night a few had actually seen what seemed to be a young girl standing there. Of course all the usual other sorts of phenomena were taking place. Doors would lock and not open or open by themselves. Things were taken and then appeared in other odd locations about the house. Lights would go out, or on and off by themselves, and footsteps could be heard.

The managers had called the parapsychologist because they just couldn't take it any more, but loved the house and didn't want to move. The investigator went directly to the little plant room and then on out the doors to the small garden beyond this almost immediately. He told them that this was the center of the activity and that something dreadful had happened there. He said the awful occurrence was why the spirit everyone was seeing never left this area, and that they had to find out what had happened. On the other side of the little garden was a gardener's tool shed, so they searched it thoroughly but found nothing. He advised them that he wanted them to dig up the garden but they refused to spoil it. He was discharged without the people in the house finding the answers that they wanted.

A year or two later he got a call from the owners. They had decided to put an addition on the house and had torn down the little plant room, digging down to the foundation to add on a much larger room. In doing so they had discovered human bones near the foundation in the garden. They called in the police and it was determined that they were the bones of a young woman. They put two and two together and remembered that a young woman they had engaged as a maid had suddenly just disappeared one day without giving her notice. At the time, they had thought nothing of it, or of the fact that the chauffeur, who had been working for them only a short time, had quit within a few days after the young woman disappeared.

Most interesting was the fact that someone who had seen the spirit remembered she had appeared to him as if in some sort of uniform of black and white colors. The police never solved the murder, but in the minds of the house owners, it had been solved. The parapsychologist left town and I never saw him again. Perhaps this is just all a made up tale, though I have read that there is a house on "I" Street that is haunted. The tale about this house is entirely different from that of the "I" Street house however, so perhaps they are two separate houses. Of course in this case I cannot substantiate anything because the exact place has not been identified. However, recently an article appeared in the paper about an archive museum on the history of skiing in Utah that some people want to start here. It would have meant nothing to me except that along with the article was a picture of Claudette Colbert who apparently came quite often to the Alta resort to ski in the 1940s.

The tale about the house on "I" Street is that when the house was being built, the carpenter building it had to stop because he was going to have to declare bankruptcy. This carpenter was married, but knew that the house would sit empty for a while, so he brought his mistress there thinking that they would never be discovered. But the boyfriend of the mistress had followed them there and he shot his girlfriend there. Nothing is said about the carpenter but his mistress apparently died there on the spot. She is the one who haunts the house and the family who lived there in the sixties just accepted her being there.

I don't know if the same family lives there now, and the way the avenues are, perhaps the house has even become several apartments now. Maybe there is a connection between the two stories and maybe not. Stories can change so rapidly passing through the hands of so many over the years. When I looked at the book *The Avenues of Salt Lake City* by Karl T. Haglund and Philip F. Notarianni (Utah State Historical Society, 1980), I did find a few interesting stories about a house or two, though I found no connections for either story. There were at least four houses built by carpenters for themselves. One man died in his garden only two years after moving into his new house. Another house was the one built for Alfred McCune and his wife but she never was able to move into it and died at the Hotel Utah after two months of confinement there. Overwhelmed by grief, McCune went abroad and died there, never moving into the house himself.

Most interesting is another house on "I" Street where Governor Spry and his wife Mary lived beginning in 1911. Joe Hill had been sentenced to death during Spry's term, and even though President Woodrow Wilson and others had sent pleas for leniency, Governor Spry refused to intervene in the case. In December of 1915, the night before Joe Hill's execution, two men attempted to blow up the house but were caught by the police. The very next year, even though Joe Hill had been executed, the "unionists" tried once again to blow up the house with the whole family in it but the building survived this attack. Governor Spry's term of office ended in 1917, and by 1921, the family had sold the house and moved to Washington, D.C.

The Avenues I am sure have many more stories to tell than just the ones highlighted in the books I mentioned, or the ones that cannot be substantiated in any way. Houses leave their layered impressions for us to research and interpret the best we can. Even as a child, I thought that I saw more in them than senses could substantiate. We used to drive by houses when I was a child and I would look in the open front windows and wonder about what it would be like to live in that home rather than my own. Not that I wasn't happy where I was, just curious about how other people lived their lives. I would make up stories about them and their lives, though now I know that some of this was not made up but rather intuitive impressions and really quite true. Nowadays, I can say that I honestly don't know what I am seeing, just that I do see, and a lot is substantiated in one way or another along the way.

STORIES OF THE 100 - 200 BLOCK SIDE OF SOUTH TEMPLE

- FORMER KING'S ROW FORMAL WEAR – GINGISS FORMAL WEAR – 242 EAST
- FRANK AND MARY ELLEN HAGENBARTH – LARKIN MORTUARY – 260 EAST
- THE GENTILE MILLIONAIRE'S ALTA CLUB – 100 EAST

Nothing much is known about the history of the mansion now housing a formal wear store, except that the address 242 East South Temple, indicates a possible old Brigham Street address if the building is that old. Also, just two blocks west of King's Row Formal Wear was the Gardo House and across the street from that is the still standing Alta Club at 100 East South Temple and then the Eagle Gate Apartments at 109 East South Temple. The Larkin Mortuary is located on the other side of King's Row at 260 East South Temple. King's Row could always have been a store and may have had a family living above it like people did in those days, though it is obvious that a new and very wide front was put on an old home and almost completely hides it. The whole building looks newer than this with a store on either side and then next to one of them, the mortuary. All of this is guess work and I will have to put down my own impressions after mentioning all of the phenomena going on at the King's Row store. I do feel strongly that the ground itself has another history and that a family home was there before it became the King's Row Formal Wear store. But what this history is can only be speculation.

A previous manager reported several events in the building. One morning early before the store was to open, he was working upstairs when the fan on a box on the floor threw itself with a mighty force into the door several feet away right in front of him. Another time he was rummaging around upstairs, looking for some papers that he desperately needed. He could not find them and questioned each employee endlessly trying to locate them. Two weeks later, he found the papers right where he had left them on a counter stacked neatly as though they had never been lost. Another morning he came in early and unlocked the front door, put the lights on and then went to turn off the alarm system. He heard footsteps upstairs and went to investigate but found nothing. Then he came back downstairs, got the cash register ready and went downstairs to turn the boiler on. He heard footsteps above him on the first floor. He ran back up the stairs but found nothing just as his two employees walked in the front door, making it certain that no one had been in the building the whole time. He had several other similar experiences over time and became a bit frightened by it all.

Other employees have reported similar experiences whenever they were alone in the building, including one employee who claimed to have the footsteps follow him about but right behind him. Others have reported seeing dark shadowy figures dart about among the clothing and in corners and absolutely no one likes to spend time alone either upstairs or downstairs. I could speculate that with the mortuary so close perhaps this has something to do with it, because it was creepy when my sister and I dressed my mother there. It can be a bit unnerving to think of all the lost and fallen spirits who have passed through their doors over the years. Another idea would be that someone remained behind on that spot of land or in another more ancient building, walking the floors of a place no longer around. Perhaps it is a person who never left King's Row or the mansion before it and did away with themselves there or loved the place so much that they couldn't leave. Someone other than I would have to tell more about the history of the place and those who lived and worked in it over the years to understand why more than one person, and in fact a whole set of people, still occupy the place.

Down the block is the now famous Larkin Mortuary which was once the home of Frank Joseph Hagenbarth and his wife Mary Ellen. Frank was a graduate of Notre Dame and then was a vice-president for a while. He was a top student, and while there, he received several awards for elocution, knowledge of Catholic church history, and for musical and dramatic performances. He graduated with a degree in Commerce in 1887 and returned to his home in Idaho to work for the Salmon River Mining and Smelting Company. He went into the sheep livestock business with his stepfather in Salmon, Idaho and they did very well. With his brother, he incorporated and became vice-president of the Wood Livestock Company. Soon they had land in Idaho and Montana which eventually encompassed 16 ranches and 750,000 acres. Frank became president of the National Livestock Association and was one of the best informed experts in the country on every aspect of the wool business. In 1902 he, his brother, stepfather and one other man, bought a ranch in Mexico which grew into a second livestock industry involving cattle. They eventually had 35,000 head of cattle on 2,465,000 acres of land. In 1908 he became president of both companies.

During World War I, Hagenbarth was chairman of the livestock section of the Agricultural Advisory Commission under Herbert Hoover and in 1929, he was on the board of directors of the National Wool Marketing Corporation. He also became the president of the National Wool Growers Association and held many other positions on the boards of banks, insurance companies, and mining companies. In 1897, he married Mary Ellen Browne of Melrose, Montana. Her father was a general. She was beautiful and accomplished and had studied art in many private schools. They had four children. They purchased their home on South Temple from Thomas Woodbury and lived there until 1914, when a fire destroyed the home. They then had the entire foundation removed and built an entirely new house on the property, though they shared carriage and stable accommodations with the people across the street. These neighbors, the J. D. Woods family had a new mansion which was just across the street and a little up the block at 307 East South Temple. There was no room to build a carriage house on the Wood's property. So the Hagenbarths shared a huge carriage house that was large enough to accommodate 15 vehicles for both of these families.

The Hagenbarths wanted to live part of the year at a hunting lodge near Sheridan, Wyoming. Mary Ellen, who went by the name of May, was deeply involved in planning this lodge at the time of her death in 1924. After her death the lodge was completed and christened the Mary Ellen Lodge, and her family spent many happy hours there on holidays and vacations. Frank was a member of the Alta Club down the street and did belong to the commercial clubs for wealthy men like himself. He died in 1934 and their residence had already been sold to the Larkin Funeral Directors in 1925. While the house has had a few additions and adaptations, it is essentially the same structure on the outside. The funeral directors have kept the interior of the home in beautiful condition with beautiful cherrywood-like paneling, gorgeous carpets, stained glass windows and various fixtures in keeping with the era of the original home. Larkin Mortuaries have several facilities throughout the valley now and this building is considered the original home for their mortuary business.

I have been inside this mortuary twice, once for my grandmother's viewing, and a second time when my sister and I went to dress my mother for her funeral. The first time I was a little girl and was simply awed by the grandeur and beauty of the place. The second time, I was conscious of the fact that there were people standing around, or one might say, lurking, in the shadows. It was during the day when hardly anyone was there, and dressing one's mother was not as usual a practice as it used to be. But we knew that this had been her wish and I was also very conscious of a dream that I had had earlier about the place though I had not known just where her body was to be taken. Some men came and took her from her apartment where I had kissed her still-warm body on the forehead. A catholic nun came in and offered to say some prayers. My sister arrived from California with the dress for her to wear and we went in the front door together where I looked down and saw the very pattern of material that I had seen in my dream about my mother. It was a deep maroon with little pink roses in it and my sister and I walked together down the stairs to a little waiting room where our mother lay in her slip on a low table. Her bruised body showed all the needle pokes and scarring of her skin disease and the big red sores on her swollen legs which they had wrapped in plastic to her knees.

We walked in together and my sister burst into tears because she had not seen our mother in the last few weeks of her life and was jolted at the sight of her lifeless body. I held my older sister and then when she calmed down we dressed our mother together, wondering about whether she should wear the shoes that we had brought her or not. My sister said that shoes had always been important to her and so we put them on. When the assistant came back we told him that we wanted to have her hair and makeup redone as it looked nothing like her. So they sent a woman in to set her hair again and dried it while we re did our mother's make-up. Then we sat on the couch together while the woman finished up and reminisced about our mother.

Interestingly, we asked the woman if this was usual for us to be reminiscing about our mother and actually laughing now and then as we remembered things. She said that it was not only unusual but very delightful to her, as most of the time people stood about and cried and sometimes even got into arguments right there in the dressing room over the relative's dead body. She told us that we could stay there as long as we wanted and we did. I can remember my sister and I joking a bit because we wondered if the people who had put her in place knew that what was on her legs was highly contagious. We even went exploring a little bit around the floor because it was such a beautiful place and just the style our mother would have loved, French Provincial.

Death takes a long time to sink in, and the death of a mother takes even longer. Someone once said that when your father dies you miss and mourn him, but when your mother dies, a piece of you dies too. Being an intuitive person, I was very conscious of death within the entire building. I did not pay attention to it like I normally would have because this time it was our mother who lay there waiting to be buried underneath the ground after people had viewed her for the last time. We were both still recovering from the fact that the dress she had worn at my brother's wedding was the one she had pointed to in my photo album book and had asked me to bury her in it. That dress was now on its way to some Deseret Industries store . I had made trips around the city to various Deseret stores looking for it, while my sister hunted for one that looked as much like it as possible. I think that our mother would have been pleased with our choice, just as she would have been angry with us if either of us had spent too much time mourning her or visiting her grave. She would have wrinkled up her nose and said, "What a waste of valuable time."

Even through this haze, I was very conscious of those others standing about in the shadows or in corners who weren't really there, but were in my mind's eye. Now, because of my mother and her own unconscious gift, I could see them. I doubt that I would ever visualize the ghosts of the people who actually lived in the mansion when it was a mansion. For over the casket of my mother, were the many layers of those who had been dressed here, being readied for their departures to various points and beyond. It was rather like being in an old railroad station, only smaller and less busy, and the images of those who stood about were only bits and pieces, snatches of emotions. These were needs that no one was ever going to fulfill in such a place, because they were invisible and from another time. Yet there they were watching us, watching our Mom. I tried for a long time to look around the corner and see our mother. Friends told me to stop looking so hard and just wait, and that she would come and see me when she was ready and she did, almost a year later in an oval picture frame, in her sweats and jewelry, happy and younger and thinner. She was telling me in one image all that I needed to know.

Like any funeral home, I suppose that many a spirit or residue image hangs out in the building. Perhaps even my mother might still be there, though I think not. She had no need to, as all her projects would have called her away. It is interesting to note that within a block of each other there once was a funeral parlor, formal wear and a flower shop. Young men and women used to get their tuxedos in one shop, their corsages at another and do everything right there in those two blocks along east South

Temple to get ready for the high school proms. The only thing missing to complete life's pageantry was a hospital for births. For quite close to this was the old Alta Club where older men of means ruled the gentile side of the city for many years, and there are ghosts there too.

Established in 1883 by prominent gentile businessmen in the city, the Alta Club was named after the Alta Mining District and barred Mormons from being members. There was bar, slot machines and high-stakes poker games. Lots of dark wood and an Italian Renaissance style made this men's club quite luxurious when it was completed in 1897. It was formally opened on June I, 1898 and was designed by one of the city's premier architects, Frederick Albert Hale. In 1909 the east wing was added to the building and the main entrance went from the State Street side to the South Temple side of the building. There are high ornate ceilings, oak interiors and fireplaces, crystal chandeliers, marble sinks and even some stained glass windows inside. Carpeted hallways are lined with large oil paintings with elegant meeting rooms, parlors, dining areas and even third floor hotel rooms which hadn't been used for over forty years because a guest fell asleep in his room and left a cigarette burning which almost burned the entire club down.

Most prominent to everyone who passes the place is the high sign that proclaims "Guest Entrance" on the west side. It used to be called the "Ladies Entrance" before a court battle brought the sign down and leads directly to the second-story dining room which was the only area where women could go as guests climbing up their own private set of stairs. Though to this day there are still fewer women members than men, back when the issue was a hot one, those first women members had to things to say. One was that men resisted the change until they began realizing that their own daughters could not join if they wanted too and the second were the older women who remembered attending parties there and saying such things as "I'll never forget being dropped off at the side entrance for women, while the men in the wedding party were taken around to the front door. That had a profound effect on me." ("Female Alta Club Members Agree: Fewer Barriers Good for Everyone", by Paul Rolly, *The Salt Lake Tribune*, May 31, 1993, A1.)

I remember one incident concerning my own mother and father. My father who was not a member of the Alta Club on principal (they did not allow women or blacks into their club then) and could relate to how if women felt this way, then blacks had been dealing with this for a very long time before this. He had been invited to some sort of occasion there and arrived with another couple at the front entrance. As all the other women separated from their men and took the "Ladies Entrance" to the west, my mother and the other woman looked at each other with a mutual agreement glance and walked right through the main entrance ignoring the sign. It was the late seventies with the feminist movement in full swing, and my father, who did not belong to the University Club either for the same reasons, went in with them through the main entrance.

As other women began ignoring the sign, a new one soon appeared entitled "Guest Entrance." Though the true story is that a city judge threatened to take away the club's beer license in 1987 which then forced the club members to vote to allow women members into their club. The irony of this being that when the third floor apartments were operating, some ladies of the evening had free access to the rooms upstairs to visit various mining magnates and bankers staying there. There was even a small battle over the women's restrooms, the upstairs one being called "The Powder Room" and the downstairs one being called "Women." They were changed to "Ladies" and then back to "Women" several times until they finally decided on "Ladies."

One great story about the place is when Thomas Kearns, David Keith and Thomas Bransford played poker in the card room for three days straight, day and night. Entire fortunes were won and lost over and over again, though it was Thomas Kearns who came out of the game the big loser with plenty to spare. One can imagine the ghosts of these three men playing there still, and enjoying every minute of it.

During Prohibition the club got more revenue from alcohol than they did their members and negotiated for the alcohol with bootleggers at the Hotel Utah down the street. Members went to the Hotel and had the bootleggers drink a sample of their products in front of them. Then they would wait an hour and if nothing happened to the bootlegger they would place an order. A mysterious white coat hanging in a coat closet at the Utah Hotel acted as the transfer point where bottles were garnered daily from its pockets. The Alta Club also had their slot machine revenues up through World War II "...when whirring machines, their facades featuring cherries, bells, bars and similar esoteric signs, provided considerable revenue to the Alta Club treasury. Alas, the slot machines vanished long ago." ("S.L.'S Venerable Alta Club Keeps Changing", by Jack Goodman, *The Salt Lake Tribune*, November 14, 1993, D2.)

Recently the Alta Club began renovations and refurbished the third floor rooms to make them available once again to those who wish to stay overnight. They also had the main lobby restored, new lighting installed and added a few other amenities as well as a new board room. Next in their plans is a chemical scrubbing of the Montana limestone exterior to wash off a century of dirt and grime. During the Olympics the Alta Club was rented out as the "France House" hospitality headquarters. While some members were upset about renting out the building, and rightly so, since they now have permanent champagne stains on the ceilings and heavier tobacco smells than usual; others felt that this was a new turn for the club in becoming an international club welcoming of diversity. Club revenue from the bar tab alone while the French stayed there was enough to quiet any grumbling from club members.

Renovations often bring out ghosts and spirits, or make them go and hide until the renovators are all done and then they appear after decades of quiet. A few new spirits have been added as well since the Olympics. So it will be interesting to see what the ghosts in this place do or don't do in the next few years in this 119-year old building.

EVERY BLOOMING THING

- THE HANCOCK MANSION

Every Blooming Thing is located at 444 South and 700 East and is now a flower shop. But for many years it was the home of a woman named Mary Hollister Hancock who lived in Salt Lake City from the age of 7 to the age of 92. Pam March has been restoring the home since 1977 and runs a floral shop there. She has had several psychics and even some ghost hunters in her shop and has had a bit of media attention for Hollister's ghost in the home. March says that Hollister must have chosen to stay close to what she loved the most, her home. As March has worked on the restoration over time, she has found that Hollister likes to oversee everything that she is doing. For example, as March attempted to get into the bathroom one day, she found that both doors on either side were locked from the inside with hook and eye latches. She had to climb out on to the roof and into the little bathroom window to unlock the bathroom doors. This particular sort of thing has happened more than once since the flower shop has been there. Once a lot of the restoration had taken place, Hollister didn't seem to be worried so much and she became friendlier. There was an arsonist fire and while there was a little damage to the house and the wood floors had to be replaced on the main floor, some of the lead glass windows blew out. While fixing this damage, the owner could hear footsteps going from window to window over and over again, probably checking the locks or inspecting the work as it progressed.

Even new employees will ask if the place is haunted because of sounds or feelings that they experience. It is usually a sensation or feeling of something being within the building. For example, while going downstairs, staff members sense something passing them going the other way. Employees say that when things are hectic around the place, the energy is more "frenetic" too. March says she had always been a skeptic and never believed in any such things until within a few days in her new business when the house let her know that it was already occupied. She has grown into it, simply accepting this presence after 25 years of growing more intimate with Hollister. She calls Hollister, her "guardian angel" and enjoys the many visitors who sense Hollister's presence. Customers are always giving her just a little more information about her resident spirit, as well as other spirits who might linger in the house. For example, several people have reported hearing little children laughing and giggling in the toy room upstairs that was once Hollister's bedroom and library.

Mary Hollister Hancock's ancestry in Utah goes back to a group of Michigan man who came out to stake their claims in Park City in 1873. Her great-uncle Edward P. Ferry came west to a mining camp in Park City because of his asthma, and his brother, Hollister's grandfather, Col. William Montague Ferry, soon joined him there. Edward P. Ferry was the entrepreneur though, and in his lifetime pioneered the Flagstaff Mining Company, developed the Woodside Mine, built the Anchor Mining Company and consolidated Union Mining claims into the Crescent Mining Company, while Col. William Ferry helped oversee many of these endeavors. Eventually the Ferry Brothers owned a large part of the Silver King Mines as well. A little later Edward Ferry decided to build both the old Miner's lodge in Park City and the old Miner's Hospital. The Colonel and his wife, Jenny Hollister Ferry, helped to decorate and furnish several of the rooms in both buildings.

Rossie Hill in Park City was named after Rossie, Michigan and most of these Michigan men owned homes there. Eventually both Edward Ferry and Col. Ferry's families built winter homes in Salt Lake City on "Billionaires Row." Maps of the area in the Avenues of Salt Lake City show that Edward P. Ferry lived somewhere between "D" and "E" Streets. One of Edward P. Ferry's sons lived very near at 474 East South Temple from 1904 to 1911. However, just two years later, this lawyer son, Edward N. Ferry, put a bullet in his brain when he was only forty years of age. There was never any public explanation for this. It is unclear whether Col. "Mont" and his wife Jeanette Ferry lived. They may have lived in the Avenues or not far from where their daughter, Kate Harwood Hancock and her husband George Hancock built the mansion home on 7th East. However, the Colonel and his wife by this time owned the entire Fourth South block on 7th East and it is known that there were at least three homes built on this block. So one could speculate that the Colonel and his wife lived part-time in one of these other homes on this now entirely commercial block and the rest of the time in Park City. Kate and her husband George came to Utah in 1890 and their mansion was completed by 1897, which means that Holl was seven when they moved out west and fourteen when they actually moved into the mansion. Only the Hancock mansion remains now, sandwiched in between Fendalls Ice Cream and other business buildings on the block. The flower shop Every Blooming Thing cannot be seen until one is almost directly in front of it. This astonishing old mansion catches one's attention immediately with its ornate and romantic looking Victorian style.

Jeanette Hollister Ferry had six children, but only two of them survived past the early years, both were daughters. One daughter lived most of her life in Redlands, California with her husband and family. Jenny Hollister Ferry is well known to historians on the Westminster College campus in Salt Lake City and her life story has been sadly neglected, although a current archivist at the college is working to remedy this. Jeanette Ferry was the driving force behind the survival of the College and also the leader of the Presbyterian women who took on the task of building up the school. Colonel Ferry, who was at one time the mayor of Salt Lake City, owned the acres where Westminster College stands today. Jenny invited a small group of powerhouse Gentiles to her daughter's 7th East home or perhaps her own home located on the same block. The purpose of the meeting was to convince Colonel Ferry to donate 22 acres for Sheldon Jackson College that was eventually renamed Westminster College. The Colonel was undecided as the group departed, but Jenny winked and told them all they would have their land for sure.

Not only did the College get the land but also eventually Converse, Foster Hall and Ferry Hall came into being. Converse was the administration building for many years, Ferry Hall was the girl's dormitory and later, Foster Hall was built for a boy's dormitory. Ferry Hall was torn down in the late 1970s to make way for the Gore Business Building. It was named after Jenny who was on the Board of Trustees of the College for her entire lifetime. Her daughter Kate served as well and then Kate's daughter, Mary Hollister Hancock, continued this tradition, serving on the Board of Trustees for her lifetime too. Interestingly, Ferry Hall had a famous ghost or even ghosts, which occupied that building for as long as the Hall stood. It was rumored to be a young man who had accidentally fallen to his death from the top of the fire escape ladder when a group of young men went on a panty raid. He was seen either at the end of hallways or as a face floating outside the window where the accident took place. It was also rumored that a woman important to the Hall had been seen there over the years, possibly Jeanette Hollister Hancock, or Mary Hollister Hancock, or perhaps a housemother for the girls who lived in the dormitory. Even to this day, although Ferry Hall is long gone, some ghostly activity has been reported in the Gore Business Building anyway. It seems the elevator likes to run by itself when no one is in it pushing the buttons and people in the building have reported seeing shadows wanderin. More about these ghosts are written in the story on Westminster College.

One great story about Mary Hollister Hancock, who chose to go by the name Hollister or "Holl" instead of Mary, is when someone in her family donated two love seats to the women's dormitory. Hollister's comment on this was that, "I think they're doing quite enough of that without us providing the furniture to perform it on." Hollister never married and devoted herself to her work for Westminster College as a member of the board and took this task very seriously. She was also a member of the P.E.O. Sisterhood, which was originally a sorority, although later it became a society dedicated to promoting educational opportunities for women with scholarships, grants and loan programs. In Hollister's obituary for February 21, 1976, it states that she was cremated and buried in Grand Haven, Michigan, that she was born July 1, 1883 in Luddington, Michigan, and that besides the P.E.O. Sisterhood, she also belonged to the Spirit of Liberty Chapter, and the Daughters of the American Revolution.

According to Pam March, Hollister became quite a character over the years. Holl was a small woman and a very independent one. She lived to be 92 years of age, all alone in her later years. She spent only one week at St. Joseph's Villa before she passed away and had managed to maintain herself after a series of strokes in the Hancock home for quite awhile. But when she fell and broke her hip while living on the main floor, she had to leave her beloved home. So it is no surprise that she would have returned to the place she so loved as a "guardian angel." She left the mansion house to her neighbors, the Fendalls, because of their many kindnesses to her because she was the only surviving child of the Hancock's. The Fendalls used to bring over sandwiches and soups to her when she could not fend for herself in the later part of her life. She willed all of her furniture and collections to the Emersons who were old family friends, who in turn donated some of this furniture to Ferry Hall on the Westminster College campus. The house stood empty and forlorn for two years, the beautiful gardens overgrown and weeds all around it, looking very much like a haunted house in jeopardy of being torn down on such a now busy street in a commercial district.

When asked why she leased the house, March, who was living in Ogden at the time and had just gone through a divorce, says that she was always visiting friends in Salt Lake City. On more than one occasion she would stop and look at the mansion, feeling drawn to it and probably formulating her plans for a flower shop. Twenty-five years later, her shop, Every Blooming Thing, is not only a very successful and community oriented business, but also the reason that the Hancock mansion survived intact without all the interior and exterior changes that have taken place in many other mansions. All the original California redwood staircases and ornate fireplaces are still as they were and the layout of the building is still essentially the same. There are two parlors and the one to the North was once the dining room with tiles of the full figures of Romeo and Juliet on either side of the fireplace. The Southern sitting room has tiled faces of Romeo and Juliet on either side of that fireplace with a "Danish" stag on the center tile. This parlor was used for entertaining in the wintertime with parties and games. There are five working fireplaces in the mansion and the intricate inlaid wood floors are spectacular, although they are not original to the home. The fire made them buckle up and they had to be replaced with exact duplicates of the originals. Pam put some of the original wood squares across her counter top, over which customers who come into the shop do their business with the flower shop. Besides the lead glass windows there is a large stained-glass window on the main floor that is of a very rare type of process that includes amethyst and gold in the design. This process is well known by glassmakers in the city. Almost everything is original to the home and even a few pieces of original furniture remain.

Hollister's bedroom is at the top of the curved staircase. The owner has made this into a children's toy room in the area where Hollister had her library. There is a smaller bedroom to the southeast of Hollister's room that she used as a sewing room. Across the hall to the west are several smaller rooms, which were servant's quarters. The old bathroom with the claw bathtub is where employees are often locked out and have to let themselves in through the window. The back stairway leads up to the attic room and down to the kitchen, although it is now blocked off partway with a second stairway leading to a half basement from the kitchen as well. The owner took the old stove out recently and the employees use this area to make floral arrangements. There is a cold storage area as well as a huge walk in refrigerator where at one point the owner was locked inside the refrigerator and no keys were available because it never needed to be locked. Staff members had to take the hinges off the door to get the owner out. This incident was also blamed on Hollister. Before knowing about the other Hancock children, the owner insisted that Hollister was an only child and that no other children could have been there, even though customers often report hearing children laughing and giggling in the library.

Today, three big cats live in the home, a black one, a tan one and a black and white and tan one. They each have their own oversized and handled woven basket as a bed to sleep in. The Double Parlor French Victorian home is only one of very few in Salt Lake City and little of its original large gardens remain although a few of the small side gardens are still there. A pear tree over 100 years old still thrives in the backyard of the home and the iris bulbs are also purported to be over 100 years old. Examining the wooden tulips over each wooden door frame in the house makes one feel that beyond the popularity of flowers in Victorian designs, perhaps Kate Harwood Hancock and her daughter Mary, loved flowers and gardens dearly. This may also be another reason why Hollister likes what has been done with her house, with its evolution into a flower shop.

Apparently Hollister even saw fit to visit at one point, as Pam March's premier ghost story can attest to. About 20 years ago, March was alone in the shop when an old lady came dressed all in black with a beautiful enamel chopstick in her hair and carrying a silver tipped cane in her hand. The old woman seemed to know where everything was in the house and claimed that she could identify every antique in the house and any other valuables that the family retained. Pam assumed that she was a close friend of the family but was so busy at the time and somewhat startled by the woman's sudden revelations, so that she didn't try to keep up the conversation. The woman wandered around the store and then turned and said that Hollister was quite pleased with what Pam had done with the house. She then went out the front door. Pam suddenly realized what a wealth of information the old lady would probably have for her and ran after her. When Pam got out on the porch she looked both ways but the lady was gone, so quickly that it was practically impossible for her to disappear so fast. A year or so later, Pam was at a function at Westminster College and happened to be looking at the portrait paintings hanging in Ferry Hall. She noticed a familiar face and walked over to view it more closely. It was a little lady with white hair, dressed all in black, and with an enamel chopstick in her hair, holding a silver tipped cane. Pam look down at the little plaque and read the name, Hollister Hancock.

Pam March says she wants everyone to understand that Hollister or "Holl" is a guardian angel that adds to the warmth of her flower shop community of friends and employees. Hollister seems pleased with what has been done with her home, and animals and little children seem to be much more aware of her presence, as one day a little two-year-old pointed to the empty stairway and then asked, "Who is that lady in white?" Pam's three cats also acknowledge the presence of Hollister by mysteriously appearing in the rooms when Hollister seems to be present, often when no one knew where any of the cats were just before this. Hollister will also rearrange things to her liking all about the shop overnight, as well as help the owners to locate things, even some things not known about. For example, one day an antique shop owner called to let them know that they had an engraving press that belonged to Hollister and they wanted to return it to the house. The Emersons on the other hand, could not find certain items when they went through the house and assumed that Hollister had given these items to someone. She had willed her little gray Dodge two-door sedan from the 1950s to the owner of the service station on the corner who had taken care of the car for her over the years.

Ghost hunters and psychics who visit the shop as its notoriety grows, have left their thoughts and some suggestions behind. All agree on the little children that can be heard talking and giggling in the toy room. Others have agreed on a tall, thin older man standing in the south front bedroom upstairs who is somehow connected to the Civil War. The spirit is a dignified but stern individual who only occasionally visits, but to whom Hollister is quite attached. Speculation is that this was her grandfather, the Colonel. Because Kate or Katie Harwood, Hollister's mother, died in the house, it is possible that her spirit is also there, although none of the psychics whom I talked to felt her presence in the home. All three generations of women, Jeannette, Katie, and Hollister, spent a great deal of time in the home and all three women were known for their quiet leadership abilities, compassionate and caring personalities, outspokenness, kindnesses to others, and their community organizing skills. They were women who were very spiritual and who would certainly make visits if at all possible.

Most interestingly, Kate Harwood Hancock was the mother of four children. Apparently, she gave birth to three other children one of whom lived to be at least eight or nine years old, possibly a boy. It is very possible that these three children followed Holl, in "spirit" at least, to play with her when she was growing up, if not in the flesh. Either the family while still living in Michigan had lost these three children, who then followed the family out west in "spirit," or Hollister did actually play with some of her brothers and sisters before they passed away in the Hancock house. Perhaps they were all three babies dying very young, or perhaps at least one of them survived long enough for Holl to have a brother or sister to play with, perhaps even more than one. I am still waiting to find out which of these scenarios it might be, although it is more likely that the children died before the family moved out west and are probably all buried in Michigan. However, if Hollister was fourteen when she moved into the house and was not the youngest child, then there must have been others there for a while, even as infants.

All who have worked there through the years agree on one thing though, that the Hancock mansion always feels warm and friendly even when the hairs on their arms or on the back of their necks stand on end to signal that Hollister is around. My own intuitive impressions about Hollister, is that she absolutely loved ice cream and her nieces and nephews. However, she had a low tolerance for children in general, loved her privacy and antiques and especially her collection of miniature teacups and dishes. She liked gardens but had no interest in working in them herself. When I first saw a portrait of Hollister's mother, it bothered me that Hollister did not look like her mother. Then I read the article about her grandmother and was startled to realize that Hollister probably looked a great deal more like her grandmother and not her mother. I felt that Jenny was a small woman, whereas Kate was a larger and taller woman and Hollister was like her grandmother. It was Jenny's face that I had seen on Hollister's face in my mind's eye, only with a more modern hairstyle. On talking to another Emerson family member who remembered Hollister and her mother, I found out that Kate Hollister was almost a foot taller than her daughter, Holl.

The only thing known about Hollister is that she had a great love of her life who was a man who either killed himself, or jilted her, and that this experience made her decide to stay single the rest of her life. As I talked to inner circle friends they seemed to agree on the speculation that this man was one of the Emersons named Ralph, who went away to college at M.I.T. before World War II and was expected to come back and marry Hollister, whom everyone assumed he had been courting. Instead he married another woman from Boston that he met while in College back east and brought his new wife back out west. Hollister became good friends with his wife and family through the years and this is probably the reason that the Emersons got left all the furniture in the Hancock house after she died. Hollister was outspoken and told it like it was most of the time. She was prim and proper to a fault well as having an inherited wit. She always cooked and had catered the traditional Thanksgiving dinner for the whole family every year and at Christmas time; she always baked fruitcakes and chutney as Christmas gifts. She considered herself a gourmet cook and loved to listen to her old player piano.

There are a few other interesting facts about both the Ferry and Hancock families, although I'm still fitting the pieces of this puzzle together. Jeanette Hollister Ferry went to live near her other daughter in Redlands, California where the Ferry's maintained a third home. She died at the age of 89, immediately after making a few addresses and speeches while leaving a few gifts of money, furniture and "articles of practical value" to Westminster College. Immediately upon returning home to Redlands, she passed away. Until the day she died, she was President of the Women's Board of Westminster College and Correspondent Secretary of the Presbyterian Synodical Society of Utah. Kate Harwood Hancock rushed to her mother's bedside and joined her sister, Mary M.F.Allen in vigil. Jeanette Hollister Ferry had been born in

Romeo, Michigan in 1828. Her father was a government surveyor in Missouri and Arkansas. She entered a College Academy at 13 years of age and finished her studies in Rochester, New York. She taught French and was a fine scholar when she met Col. Montague Ferry and married him in 1851. While all four of her other children died in their early years, Mrs. Ferry lived a happy married life. The Colonel began in the Civil War as a private and rose to the rank of Colonel becoming a member of a General McPherson's staff. Mont and Jenny held court where they lived in Park City, providing what came to be called a "Rest House" for the Gentile educational and religious workers in the Utah territory. Jenny's father had been a Colonel in the War in 1812 and she was a member of the Daughters of the American Revolution. William Montague Ferry and Jeanette Hollister Ferry lived in Grand Haven, Michigan on a family lot on the hillside of Lake Forest before moving to Park City, Utah. Jenny's two daughters accompanied her body back to where her husband had been buried years before.

Kate Harwood Hancock lived on ten years past the death of her own husband and that of her three children and passed away in her 7th East home on March 1st, 1940. She was 83 years old. She was born in Ferrysburg, Michigan in 1856 and married George R. Hancock of Winchester, Michigan in 1882. They lived in Ludington, Michigan, before moving from Grand Haven, Michigan to Salt Lake City in 1890 and they finished their mansion in 1897. It was Kate who decorated her fireplace with Romeo and Juliet tiles. She was also a strong, powerful woman and besides being on the College Board, belonged to the Ladies Literary Club, was Treasurer and served on the Board of the National Federation of Women's Clubs. She was described as being a cultured and very wise woman with a keen mind and natural leadership skills. She was poised, generous and kind, with a great sense of humor. She had to spend her last year bedridden, becoming both blind and deaf. It was Hollister who cared for her in this last period of her life and then lived on alone in the house.

Having gone through a similar caring for an ailing mother becoming both blind and deaf and unable to get about for several years, I can understand that doing this entirely alone would have taken a very strong caring woman who had to have the patience of a saint. Or perhaps she did not have the patience of a saint and had had to suffer a little discord from time to time, unless of course a servant remained behind, although this is unlikely. Little else is known about Hollister Hancock's life, although one can assume that she was well read and a well-educated woman just a like her mother and grandmother. She was probably just as outspoken as they were, with a quick wit and a great sense of humor. Living on her own as long as she did, she probably got somewhat finicky and particular, if not also a bit peculiar. Apparently her spirit is the soul of this home, and she has no desire to leave it. She is quite content to continue to guard it while keeping everything in its proper place.

Pam March has created such a beautiful atmosphere and has kept the home so graciously preserved that she perhaps does not give herself enough credit for being as intuitive as she is. More importantly, is the fact that Every Blooming Thing carries on a traditional family atmosphere in this once family home. March has been the guiding force for many a weary traveler or employee looking for a place to belong if only for a short while. One year Pam received a letter from a former employee who stated in the letter that the Hancock mansion reminded him of the famous poem by Edgar Guest about the "house by the side of the road." This was at a time in his life when he needed a lot of support and had been provided with respite or a place of safety by working for Pam at the Hancock mansion. He also stated that her community of workers, bosses and customers, had been his "house by the side of the road." When one first comes upon the Hancock mansion, dwarfed as it is between high business buildings, it really is a surprise to walk inside and be transported to another time and place. With a warm, homey atmosphere, so many gorgeous stained glass window hangings, and an old world atmosphere of one of Salt Lake City's few Victorian "Painted Ladies," is it any wonder that this place has become a "house by the side of the road" for many?

Several years ago the staff got the idea to use the money they spent on an elaborate Christmas party each year in another way. In the spirit of giving, they sent the Deseret String Band to a senior citizen's center to entertain the people there, sent the money they would have spent on food to the Utah Food Bank, sent the magician to Primary Children's Hospital to entertain the children, and sent their Santa Clause to another rest home to give the gifts they had purchased. They then sent a letter to their own patrons and invited them to visit the shop to enjoy the beneficial rewards of their traditional Christmas Party. They told them that now all of their valued customers and patrons could come into the shop to enjoy the spirit of giving together.

There are many warm and friendly spirits in this flower shop, and these include the three lost children, Kate and her husband George, possibly one or both of the grandparents, a servant or two, and of course Hollister, who reigns supreme over her home. This had been a happy home full of laughter and many family community gatherings, even though in the later years the children who visited the home were constantly in trouble for going through the drawers in the upstairs rooms. Pam March, finding the house as she did and being drawn to it as she was, provided an opportunity for the house to continue on in a life of its own. The tradition of community and carrying continues, and is ever present and this is why Hollister is so pleased with what has been done with the house. The Emersons say that had they inherited the house as well as the furniture, they would probably have sold this prime commercial property and the mansion would have been long gone by now. They think that Hollister had an intuitive sense about this, and that Pam March was probably attracted to the place just to open her flower shop Every Blooming Thing.

- CHAPTER TWO -

UTAH'S HAUNTED HOTELS & BUILDINGS

THE HOTEL UTAH

UTAH'S CLASSY LADY, THE GRAND DAME OF HOTELS

(This piece is taken entirely from the colorful book by Leonard Arrington and Heidi S. Swinton, *The Hotel: Utah's Classy Lady*, 1911 - 1986, published for the 75th anniversary of the Hotel Utah by The Westin Hotels: Salt Lake City, Utah, 1986.)

Before the hotel, several one and two story buildings were built on the corner of South Temple and Main Street: a tithing office, a bishop's store house and a printing plant for the Desert News. President Joseph Fielding Smith of the LDS church met with various community leaders of other faiths to discuss the construction of a large hotel, which would promote peace, unity and cooperation between the various factions in the valley. The proposed site for the grand hotel had also once been the location for the church mint with currency personally signed by Brigham Young. Both the printing building and the three story Desert Store with a 12 foot Spanish wall surrounding them both, had to be razed to make way for the new hotel. There was a public outcry over the loss of yet another landmark building but to no avail, as plans for the hotel went forward. The visionaries and the preservationists were at odds once more.

In 1909 construction on the large hotel began. The frame of the ten-story structure was of steel and concrete while the outside would be of white glazed brick and enameled terra cotta. Horse drawn wagons were used to excavate the basement of the hotel, though two bombings halted construction along the way. The American Bridge Company which had furnished the steel for the building was having problems with a labor strike at the time and the Industrial Workers of the World got involved as well, a more radical group with various smaller and even more radical splinter groups. The head of the Jones Construction Company, the subcontractor for the steel frame of the Hotel Utah, was also under attack for running an open shop with both union and non-union men. In December of that year Mr. Jones, his brother and brother-in-law were attacked on the streets of Salt Lake City. Richard Jones was slashed with a knife while his brother-in-law fired shots at the men who then fled. Three weeks later the first bomb went off at the construction site at 3 o'clock in the morning, but there was very little damage.

The second explosion scared many a citizen because it occurred on the date that Haley's Comet would be most visible in the night sky over Salt Lake City. In 1910, such an event still filled people with all sorts of unreasonable fears, such as a huge ball of flame cracking the earth like a meteorite, or deadly gases spreading across the earth killing everything in their path, or the earth passing through the tail of the comet with massive devastation. People actually hid in caves or stayed under the water when the comet was at its height in view in the night sky. Even scientists were not sure then just what might happen. So when the second explosion took place, many residents were awake and looking at the night sky. The terrible explosion sent some people running into the streets where they were quickly assured that it was not the comet but another sabotage at the Hotel Utah site. Again, no substantial damage was done and construction continued while the perpetrators were apprehended soon after.

On June 8, 1911, the grand opening of the hotel took place on a summer evening with all of the cream of Salt Lake Society in attendance. The lobby was framed by twelve massive gray marble pillars, had walls of pink marble, green carpeting, velvet and brocade chairs, and four large brass and crystal chandeliers. There were also a presidential suite, ladies parlor, mezzanine, the Grand Ballroom, the Empire dining room, the Starlight Gardens, Sky Room and 300 hotel suites. The hotel was located in a place that was once the highest point in the city and so needed no address. All who lived there would know it for the beehive on its top. The hotel was also called "The Grand Dame" or 'The White Palace," but more often "The Classy Lady." The Hotel Utah survived two world wars and many a decade of strange and unusual events, while hosting nearly every President of the United States since its dedication and hundreds of other celebrity guests and travelers.

Long before anything at all stood on this spot, Emmeline B. Wells, editor and woman suffragette, had camped in her wagon on what was to become the site of the hotel. I guess the hotel could consider her its first guest before real rooms were available. One of the first famous visitors was William Howard Taft who weighed 300 pounds and stood 5 foot 10 inches tall. When he visited the hotel in October of 1911, he needed a special bathtub. He praised the hotel's restaurant for their fine food; for $2.15 he ate the following breakfast: toast, rolls, coffee, eggs, creamed potatoes, crescent rolls, bacon and eggs, peaches, cantaloupe and a sirloin steak. The hotel's most infamous resident was the Greek godfather Leonidas Skliris who lived in and operated his businesses from the hotel. He ran a protection racket, getting Greek workers and establishments to pay monthly fees, as well as providing strikebreakers for the mines from mainland Greece. Once he did this in a dispute with Crete, testing Cretan loyalties to the labor unions. During this dispute, his assistant was gunned down and Skliris narrowly missed the same fate. This incident contributed to his demise as a crime lord. There was another mining magnate, Daniel Jackling, who stayed there as well, though his practices were much more legitimate.

During World War I, attendance at the hotel dropped by 50 percent and some of the staff were let go while whole portions of the hotel had to be shut down. Though, strangely, a few of the very wealthy wives of prisoners of war staying at Camp Douglas took up residence at the hotel while waiting for their husbands to be released. After the war, the nineteen twenties brought in a new breed of guest, including Carrie Chapman, Edgar Guest, Herbert Hoover, Jack Dempsey, Florenz Ziegfeld, Mary Pickford, Charlie Chaplin, William Jennings Bryan and Duke Ellington. Will Rogers was refused service in the Empire room because he had no suit and tie, and had to borrow them from the front desk.

In the thirties, famous orchestras and jazz bands entertained celebrities and important dignitaries. Governor Henry Blood stayed there in the thirties until by the generosity of Jennie Kearns, her house was donated to the state for a governor's mansion in 1936 and he moved in there. During World War II, hotel business nearly doubled with the influx of troops. Nehru of India stayed there during this time, as well as Olivia de Haviland, Fred Astaire, Arthur Rubinstein, Wendell Wilkie, Eleanor Roosevelt and President Truman.

In the fifties and sixties, celebrities of all sorts stayed at the hotel: Jimmy Stewart, Johnny Miller, Lowell Thomas, Katherine Hepburn, Bob Hope, Henry Fonda, Ella Fitzgerald, Helen Hayes, John Glenn, Beverly Sills, Isaac Stern, Clare Booth Luce, Van Cliburn, Liberace, Danny Kaye, Dinah Shore, Bing Crosby, Arnold Palmer, Jack Benny, Robert Kennedy, and William Holden. LBJ slept in the hotel in August of 1969 in an extra long king-sized bed ordered especially for him. When he left, the head bellman, who had carried his bags, bought the bed. During the sixties many rock and roll bands spent a few days there while giving concerts. Stevie Nicks and Fleetwood Mac stayed there several times because Stevie had grown up in Utah, graduating from Judge Memorial High School; she still has many ties to Utah to this day.

LDS Church President Spencer W. Kimball and wife, as well as President David O. McKay and wife, lived there several years and entertained presidents, kings, queens, business and education leaders and ecclesiastical leaders from many faiths. Right from the hotel's beginnings, many wealthy and famous local people retired at the hotel long before there were senior citizen apartment complexes. I know the McCunes retired there and the Kearns also, as well as the Silver Queen from Park City, Suzanne Bransford Emery Holmes Delitch Engalitcheff, and many others too numerous to list. There were many long-term and some short-term residents who actually passed away right at the hotel. It was also common practice, especially in the early years, to live at the hotel while your new home or mansion was being built; the McCunes did, along with various people waiting for their turn in the Gardo House. Of all the lost buildings in our city, I think the loss of the Gardo House is the most tragic. The Gardo House must have been the largest and most ornate of any home in the city and had an amazing history.

Probably from its beginnings, blacks were not allowed to stay at the hotel. This was of course how it was everywhere, though the LDS faith stood out because of its idea then that black men could not hold the priesthood in their church. A revelation some years later changed all that. Many of the employees at Hotel Utah were, however, black. Just before the civil rights movement and even during it, several black entertainers were denied access to the hotel, which garnered it and the LDS Church some negative publicity. Among those denied a room were Ella Fitzgerald and Harry Belafonte. To my knowledge Mr. Belafonte did not ever stay at the hotel, but Ella Fitzgerald did. I have often wondered just where Duke Ellington and his band stayed while his orchestra performed there for extended periods.

Marian Andersen came to Utah twice. Both in 1948 and 1960, she was given a room at the Hotel Utah but with the stipulation that she use the freight elevator at the rear of the building rather than the front entrance. Towards the end of the sixties, things in the entire country began to change considerably; by the seventies, with the LDS Church revelation and national changes, hotel policies had changed.

I remember these times because my father, a professor at the university, and his friends always got around this discrimination by having visiting dignitaries and students who were black stay in their homes and eat meals with their families. It was a fascinating time for me, because we never knew who would be staying with us and what interesting things would be talked about at the dinner table. I especially remember a student from Africa who had tribal scars all over his face and who wore long colorful robes and told us children the most wonderful folk tales.

In the seventies, the hotel underwent many elegant expansions and renovations while hosting celebrities and the making of a few Hollywood movies, such as "Harry In Your Pocket" with James Coburn and Walter Pidgeon. In the eighties this tradition continued with visits from such celebrities as Cliff Robertson, Ed Asner, Raymond Burr, Peter Vidmar, and return visits from Henry Fonda, Jimmy Stewart and Danny Kaye. Some of the royalty who stayed at the hotel included Denmark's Queen Margrethe II and Norway's Princess Sonja.

In August of 1987, the LDS church, which owned the building by then, decided to close the hotel, giving as the official reason that convention business and local interest in the building had waned. However, insiders knew that shots had been fired from the roof of the Hotel Utah at the church administration building across the street, and that alcohol and patron behavior were a growing problem for the image and safety of the center of the LDS church's worldwide organization. Rather than tear it down, they decided to preserve it and turn it into an LDS meeting house, office building and community meeting hall. The hotel's colorful history was changed once more. It was reopened in 1993 as a National Historic Site.

The LDS church did an excellent job of preserving the Hotel's great beauty and splendor, though its colorful history would have been lost but for a great book produced by Leonard J. Arrington and Heidi K. Swinton. The book was written for the then Hotel Weston's 75th anniversary, and was called *The Hotel*. The church put in new marble floors in the lobby, cleaned and polished the marble columns, brass banisters, ceilings and even the original art-glass skylight. A chapel on the mezzanine preserves the ornate ceiling of what was once the LaFayette Ballroom. New additions to the building seem to blend in with the décor - such as a bronze statue of Joseph Smith, which is a copy of a much older version, new chandeliers, and a Quebecois organ. There is a new theater for visitors with a film about the church's history taken from the diaries of one of Brigham Young's wives, Mary Elizabeth Rollins Lightner. The roof garden restaurant and the cafe are still being used, but minus the coffee and alcohol. There is a Family Search Center with 130 computer workstations for working on genealogy.

Besides the "ghosts" of those who stayed there, both famous and infamous, in the hotel's long history, there were legendary employees as well. Joseph Rimensberger, wooed away from the Waldorf-Astoria in New York, was the first pastry chef for the Hotel Utah. He was from Lucerne, Switzerland and was noted for his two-foot-high sugar sculptures of local landmarks, such as the LDS Temple and tabernacle. Clint Jackson worked his way up from busboy in 1918 making $40 plus meals, to head waiter in the Sky Room, 51 years later. Louis Torres worked 50 years as the hotel's butcher; he carved for four chefs and five managers and did about 180 tons of butchering per year. Pleasance "Jackie" Furse Skinner was the manager of the cafeteria for 25 years. Jackie was already famous before she came on board, having been a much-photographed welder on the Liberty Ship Oregon during World War II. All 12 of her brothers and sisters were in the armed forces or in defense work during the war. She also wrote a column for The Desert News on housekeeping problems called "Pleasance Surprises." Bill Morris was a hat checker for 30 years at the hotel and memorized the faces of his customers. They never needed a number or stub to claim their hat. He made it into "Ripley's Believe It Or Not" by returning, from memory, over 400 hats to their rightful owners.

In 1938, local talent show host, Eugene Jelesnik, had an orchestra called the New York Continental Orchestra and was booked in the hotel for a 17 month contract. He met his future wife who was a hotel guest, settled in Salt Lake, and gave free Sunday night concerts in the hotel lobby. In the twenties, the hotel had been famous for washing its money. An elderly gentleman who is unnamed, ran a money laundry in the basement. He poured each day's coins into a pig trough filled with a chemical solution and then sorted the coins out for redistribution the next day. The paper money was put in a box each day and exchanged at the bank for brand new currency each evening. So it is no surprise to me and even a bit ironic, that many years later, a hotel employee, the night kitchen cleaner, was arrested for criminal money laundering and counterfeiting. He was arrested for passing counterfeit coins and when the police went to his room they found coin molds and a metal ashtray sitting on a hot plate being used as a melting pot. He had been melting down the hotel's silver cutlery and minting his own coins.

Uncle Roscoe (Grover) spent the dinner hour in the 1950s at the Hotel Utah Coffee Shop drawing pictures of children dining with their parents. He had designed the menus and liked to autograph them, as well as to draw animals and creatures on them for the children. He had his own local television show "Playtime Party," where his creation "Tubby the Goldfish" was a favorite of his young audiences. Before this he had been a broadcaster and had trained other radio broadcasters at New York University. On his show he had children's performing groups and birthday kids for whom he drew a special picture. One boy complained that his special picture was supposed to be a surprise so Uncle Roscoe drew him a beautifully wrapped gift box never to be opened, ever!

Then there are the unusual occurrences such as the radio marathon in 1957 which broke the world's radio broadcasting record. Ray Briem of KLUB radio station raised $7,653 for Hungarian refugees by broadcasting for 150 hours straight. It was a long week with over 500 spectators watching him. He was in a glass booth in the lobby when a fuse burned out in his microphone and the sound went dead. He simply picked up a soldering iron with which he had come supplied, and welded the fuse in place while munching on a cheese sandwich. The music played on.

Another even more strange happening is representative of many other stories that we will never know concerning the everyday average permanent residents at the hotel. It seems that a 1940s Cadillac sat in the hotel garage for a little over twenty years in the same parking stall where it had been left after a Christmas shopping spree. The woman who owned the car returned to her apartment to find her husband dead of a heart attack. She never returned to the car to take the packages out, though sometimes she would ask the bellman to set up a chair by the car so that she could sit by the car and stare at the packages inside. The woman died in 1981 and the bank handling her affairs opened the car to find the wrapped packages but no gifts inside them. She had apparently been sneaking down on her own, or perhaps someone else who had known about them had been sneaking into the car, and replacing the gifts with bogus packages.

There are the usual objects missing or gone on a world tour, such as a bar of soap and shampoo bottle, or a pillowcase and towel or two. Bigger things have been taken. The hotel's large sized flag showed up at the Salt Lake Attorney's office in May of 1985, wrapped in a plastic bag. A typewritten note confessed to stealing two flags 15 years before, from both the Hotel Utah and the State Capitol building. The hotel sent someone down to get their flag but before he got there, a woman came in and claimed the flag apparently for the hotel; both flag and woman were never seen again. Stranger still is the story of the Australian pilot using a Hotel Utah towel issued to him in a prisoner of war camp in Germany. Later, he wrote the hotel and thanked them for this little touch of normalcy that had come across the sea as part of a donation to the Red Cross.

There are also the "ghosts" of starlings and peregrine falcons who chose to take up famous residence at the hotel. In the 1960s, a mass of starlings took up residence on the roof, scratching and squawking. The hotel tried poison, bright lights, scarecrows and electrified wires, but the starlings stayed on. Finally the manager hired a psychologist who came up with the idea of using recordings of starlings in distress to fool the birds into thinking that the place was dangerous, so they then would fly away. Speakers were installed on one side of the roof as a test and the intermittent sounds played. The starlings flew to the other side of the roof. Soon speakers were installed on both sides and sure enough the starlings flew away. The peregrine falcons, I remember myself. There was a series of articles about the pair's residence at the hotel and a peregrine watch all across the valley. They were named Ebenezer and Florence and returned each year for three years in 1984, '85 and '86. They nestled in the center ledge at the top near the Beehive. Recently only about 40 of these still endangered but growing population of birds have been sighted in Utah.

These are a few of the recognized "ghosts" of the Hotel Utah. Employees, guests, animals and objects - all of them contribute to the life and legends of a grand old hotel. But I have mixed feelings. On one hand, I am glad that she was not torn down to make way for something new and that parts of her are still accessible to me. On the other hand, I wish she was still a hotel and that I could still enter her doors, have one of her famous hard rolls in the Empire Room, or stroll the rooftop gardens with a cup of coffee in my hand, or perhaps dance in the Grand LaFayette ballroom, or talk to employees and guests. Still, she was saved. Her ghosts, who loved their homes with a passion or some of whom experienced some sad tragedy within her walls, don't acknowledge barriers or restrictions. They still walk her halls and rooms, moving about for those of us able to see, feel or hear them.

SALT LAKE TRIBUNE NEWSPAPER BUILDING & LAMB'S CAFE

The *Salt Lake Tribune* began as a reaction to the Mormon dominated newspaper business in Salt Lake City. Four Gentiles joined forces to publish the *Utah Magazine* in 1868, after which their paper, *The Deseret News*, urged the LDS readership to boycott this magazine. Two years later, these four Gentiles, William H. Shearman, Edward W. Tullidge, Elias T. Harrison and William S. Godbe, added a newspaper to their publishing entitled the *Mormon Tribune*. Almost immediately, they stopped publishing the magazine and put all of their efforts into what they said was their intention to oppose the "priestly authority" in town. In June of 1870 they dropped the "Mormon" from the title, and by the following year they had added quite a bit to the title: *Salt Lake Daily Tribune and Utah Mining Gazette*. Soon after this they shortened the title to *The Salt Lake Tribune* and it became a small weekly paper only meant to irritate the powers that be. In 1880, three men from Kansas bought the paper and began to turn it into a real and thriving daily newspaper.

However, these men too, continued to promote the conflicts between the Mormons and the Gentiles in the city, hoping to sell more papers. Mormon publications at the time called these other publications "the border ruffians" and the Gentile publications began calling *The Deseret News* the "Granny" paper. In those days the number one thing to write about in Salt Lake City was polygamy. Attacks on this practice were almost daily in *The Salt Lake Tribune*, with a current editor from Nevada named C.C. Goodwin. The editor of *The Deseret News*, Charles W. Penrose, began to be nicknamed "Granny's Imp" by the *Tribune*. Both editors were good men who were well respected in their community and both of these men built up their little local papers into widely circulated, prestigious and well written papers. Goodwin eventually helped to buy the *Tribune* and stayed involved with its production until 1901 when an unidentified buyer came into the picture. Though soon everyone came to know who this man was, Thomas Kearns.

David Keith and Thomas Kearns had both made fortunes from their various mine holdings and both of them being Catholics, they had become powerful Gentiles in the city. They had mutually decided to take over the *Tribune* and build it into an even better newspaper than it was at the time. Thomas Kearns, who was a U. S. Senator from Utah by then, wrote editorials, contributed financially and put some memorable quotes in the paper, but it was Keith who mainly ran the paper. Keith always said that it took "a great mine to run a newspaper." They added an evening paper called *The Salt Lake Telegram*, which was delivered for several years, but then gave up their ownership in 1920, only to regain ownership ten years later. They continued to own the paper even when the *Telegram* was discontinued. In 1919, Kearns passed away and the Keith family took over total ownership of the paper. The Keith's owned the paper until the modern-day squabbles of only a few years ago. Thomas Kearns's secretary, J. F. Fitzpatrick became the publisher of the paper in 1924 and was often called "Mr. Tribune." *The Trib*, as it is often called now, continued to increase in circulation and in fact surpassed *The Deseret News* circulation during the next few decades. In 1952, the two newspapers merged their advertising, production, circulation, and business departments while maintaining separate editorial control. The Kearns-Tribune Corporation had holdings in publishing companies, cable television, and other non-media enterprises. ("*The Salt Lake Tribune*," by Sherilyn Cox Bennion, from *Utah History Encyclopedia*, edited by Kent Powell, University of Utah Press, pp. 485-486.)

When a giant corporation from Denver did a major takeover of both papers just a few years ago, the thin line between the two papers began to blur. This was disastrous for the staff and readership of *The Salt Lake Tribune*. What was actually going on only insiders really knew, though articles did appear almost every day in the *Tribune* regarding this soap opera of major proportions. A major happening was that the management of *The Deseret News*, being the smaller paper now, wanted it to be delivered in the mornings, hoping to increase its circulation and compete more openly with the *Tribune*. One does have to wonder just how two very different papers with very different readership, reflecting a huge division in our fair city, ended up being run by the same corporation. It is well known among the readership, that while the *Tribune* provides its readers with a link to the outside world and operates like any other major city newspaper, *The Deseret News* provides their mostly Mormon readership with the Mormon version of the news. I never believed this myself until I began scouring *The Deseret News*, just as I had the *Tribune*, for articles on subjects relating to my books and slowly became aware of the lack of news within it, at least for someone like me! Disgruntled subscribers of the *Tribune* watched as suddenly articles about the Mormons became more prevalent in a thinly veiled attempt to narrow the gap between the two communities, which then took away from more interesting outside articles on what was happening in the world at large. Happily, this one-sided view of things began to change and *The Tribune* slowly began to be its old self once again.

Many of the staff on both papers were concerned about what was happening and agreed that the merging of the two papers would be a disaster for both of them because as we now have two opposing views in the valley, in the near future we could only have one, thus curtailing our freedom of speech. *The Deseret News* staff says that they like having its religious constituents and enjoy the rivalry, which stirs things up. The Keith family, in honor of their late grandfather who loved the *Tribune* with all of his heart, banded together and is now engaged in a court battle to reinstate the family as the true owners of the paper. They realized too late, it seems, just what would happen in the valley and one of the siblings, none of whom live here anymore, rallied the others into joining in to try and retrieve the paper before anymore damage is done. They have waited at least two years to go into battle with the big corporation, trying to regain ownership of the paper and the type of publishing that their ancestor relished. Even after reading all of the articles on this battle, one comes away somewhat confused by it all, wondering just why ownership slipped away in the first place with both groups accusing the other of underhandedness. Those of us reading the *Tribune* are holding our breath, hoping for a favorable outcome and joking that if we lose the one newspaper in town that brings us news from the "outside," we will have to start subscribing to *USA Today*, which is only second best because we would not get any of our local news this way.

As for me, if I want to find out what the LDS church is doing, I read *The Deseret News*, and if I want to find out what is happening in the world, I read *The Salt Lake Tribune*. My favorite column in the *Tribune* was Jack Goodman's architectural and historical musings and drawings, so I took it as a sign, that he retired just about the time that all of this mess was in full swing. It was also a sign that the history of our state is not of much importance anymore, though Will Bagley is still allowed his "History Matters" column on Sundays and Tom Wharton has his byways column. Of late, those articles that I hunted for, which had all but disappeared for a while and were replaced with Mormon missionary stories and the like, mysteriously returned. I can only surmise that I was not the only one complaining. Like most people, I would love to see the gulf between Mormons and Gentiles reduced; although on the other hand, not at the expense of getting my daily news about the world. Lets hope that after this big trial is over, we still have two newspapers with two voices like we did during the 2002 Winter Olympics in Salt Lake. A few mavericks on the staff of both papers can still write about what they want to, so that we can read about the paranormal as well. I can then get on with the "publishing ghosts" behind me!

At 165 South Main Street is a five story commercial building called The Herald. Founded in 1870, the original pro-Democratic newspaper called *The Salt Lake Herald* was housed there. While this newspaper changed hands several times in the next few years, the newspaper was housed in this building, which was built in 1905. The paper ceased publication in 1920 and the building was used for other purposes until the original owners of *The Salt Lake Tribune* took over again and built the much larger *Tribune* building that is still in existence today. In other words, this haunted building was the original home of the variously named *Salt Lake Tribune* until 1930. The building managed to survive periods when such places were being razed and it is quite an ornate one with elaborate metal cornices and lions in friezes. Below the lions at ground level is a place called Lamb's Café, which has been there since 1939. The whole building is on the National Register of Historic Places along with stories over the years of a bit of haunted activity. With a history of such rivalry between the *Tribune* and the *Deseret News*, is it any wonder? Both the building itself and the café are purported to be haunted, as reported by those who work there or those who visit the quite famous and "in" café, which covers the whole first floor.

George P. Lamb was a Greek immigrant who opened a little restaurant in Logan, Utah called Lamb's Grill Café. He opened his restaurant on George Washington's birthday in 1919. The governor of the state, George H. Dern even gave Mr. Lamb a picture of George Washington to commemorate the opening of the café. This café remained open until 1939 and was so successful that Mr. Lamb was persuaded to move his café to Salt Lake City. He opened his new restaurant on the ground floor of the old Herald building.

"The restaurant has remained unchanged since 1939. The booths, tables, wainscot, back bar, counters, counter stools, light fixtures and steam table...came from a restaurant previously located on Main Street, known as Gunn's Café. Mr. Lamb from Vienna imported one notable exception, the chairs on the main dining room in the 1920s. Ted J. Speros...joined Mr. Lamb in 1941 and the two men worked as partners for 32 years and built Lamb's into a veritable downtown institution." ("Lamb's since 1919 'Utah's Oldest, Most Famous Restaurant' Welcome to Lamb's Restaurant," restaurant menu pamphlet.)

Lamb's Café has been nationally recognized for years now, earning awards from United Airline's 'Excellence in Dining' program, the United States Trout Farmer's Association, the Coffee Brewing Institute, *Town and Country* Magazine, *The Orange County Register*, and *Salt Lake Magazine*. But more than this, Lamb's has always been the place where important business deals are consummated or where one takes visitors from out of town for a "quaint excursion." Deals are made over lunch and important papers are signed there. Important locals and even visiting celebrities and dignitaries are wined and dined at Lamb's. If one asks about the ghosts, they are a bit downplayed, though those of us who have lived here all our lives can remember hearing about them by word of mouth. Although many people seem to know about their existence, little has been done in the way of researching any words written down in the past about these ghosts. As I looked into this, I found very little as well. However, there were some people willing to talk about their experiences both in the Herald Building and inside the café downstairs. Former employees and even a few current ones would enjoy knowing even more because it would add to the mystique of the place, although owners are often slightly more conservative in their views of this sort of thing.

One cannot "beat city hall" as they say, or any of our own history as a city. Ghosts exist and are talked about long before and after owners or employees come and go. They are a part of any city and its history, making all of us, every generation, have what we term "colorful pasts." Custodians and those who work in the Herald Building have talked over the years about the usual ghostly encounters in terms of doors being locked when they should be open or lights flickering or turning off or on when they shouldn't be. The employees have also mentioned cold spots and strange drafts in the middle of a warm summer day, although no one claims to have seen an actual apparition. In Lamb's Café there is definitely one ghost at least. People have seen him since the seventies after Mr. Lamb passed away, standing on the stairs that lead up to the offices above the restaurant that look down on it as in the old speak-easy days or in old gambling casinos. The apparition is said to be Mr. Lamb still overseeing his restaurant from the stairs, and various customers and employees have actually seen his full apparition standing there in his old fashioned clothes, both in the evening and in broad daylight. He has also been seen from the window up above, in a place where a window is no longer located! Upon occasion, a customer or employee has simply seen him standing somewhere in the café mingling with the clientele.

Other things mentioned within the café itself are that the lights and the calculators seem to like to run themselves. They turn on and off at will, or in the case of the calculators in the building, they like to add or subtract numbers that no one put in them, sometimes making it so that bills will have to be rung up several times or re-done several times because the figures that were entered are completely wrong, with witnesses having seen them being entered correctly. In one incident the present owner had some difficulty with the electric bill when somehow it was overpaid due to this mis-figuring. Another time he was way over-billed but just paid it anyway, although many people wondered if the lights had been going on by themselves or other electrical equipment had been operating on its own when no one was in the building. People have come in the morning only to find strings of lights left on all night when they were sure that they had been turned off. Equipment in the kitchen will sometimes turn on by itself, though everyone always does a double take about it. Employees do agree that the light problems have gone on for years and similar incidents took place when former employees worked there.

Shadows in doorways, lights flickering and a few strangely misplaced items certainly indicate hauntings in the café. Besides Mr. Lamb who is seen looking out from the office upstairs or from the middle of the stairway leading to these offices, there may be residual energies about, which produce images and smells and sounds. Although Lamb has been identified over the years and is said to be haunting the place to this day, there are no reports of interactive ghosts and spirits at the café. Some long time customers however, are who led me to the place to investigate the building because they felt that something was going on there. Employees felt this way too but were either reluctant to say anything or couldn't go beyond the usual rumors that such things produce. So perhaps there are customers out there who have their own stories to tell about the old newspaper building and the café that it has housed for so many years.

CHARLESTON APARTMENTS

JUST BELOW UNIVERSITY OF UTAH CAMPUS

Most of this information is taken from an article entitled "*Charleston Phenomenon: Rich history, diverse community make high-rise a Salt Lake City landmark*," by Patty Hentz, *The Salt Lake Tribune*, July 28, 2001. And I love the title, thinking the author is probably some college student who took an interest in writing about it. Maybe not, as she barely mentions its affiliations with the college, for there are no really official ones except for its location along 13th East just below campus. However, when I went to school at the University of Utah, many of the employees on campus lived at the

Charleston, especially librarians of the older single variety. I was a work-study employee at the Marriot Library in the evenings for the five years that I was enrolled at the U. I remember the old flavor of the Charleston and how elegant it was with all the of the things offered by big hotels then. One of my co-workers lived there; she had cerebral palsy and the building had all the things she needed for her disability, plus it was within walking distance of her work. We became friends because we were both writers and as a young person she had had quite a bit published. Another old library employee tells me that she has passed on. I visited her at the place on a few occasions and felt as if I were going for tea in a British hotel.

I also remember our Black art professor from San Francisco who couldn't get a room at the Charleston and had to go across the street to the other old and not-so-elegant high rise which was senior apartments. They gave him an apartment in the late nineteen-sixties when no one else would. Over the years I suppose that the Charleston has become senior apartments because of all the long term renters. These residents often meet on the roof for an evening "rooftop soiree" to watch the sunset with a great view of the whole valley before them. The 12 story 130-unit apartment all white high rise was built in 1950, and at the time it was considered earthquake and even bomb proof because of its two foot thick cement walls and frame. It was also one of the most expensive apartment complexes of its kind between Denver and San Francisco. The apartments are all spacious and sunny with an architecture old enough to make it quaint and charming. The Charleston at one time had a coffee shop, a gas station in the basement and a hair salon, along with a front lobby that some insist looks like an old cruise ship's lobby. The hazards of pumping gas under this huge building brought the demise of the gas station though the ethyl pump is still there, and the coffee chop was never able to make enough money to keep afloat. The hair salon is still operating because many older women residents like its convenience. A diverse population of attorneys, taxi cab drivers, priests, and LDS missionaries are in residence. Several short-term apartments are available for visiting professors, foreign students, medical residents or for people needing to be near relatives who are in the area hospitals. Actors and actresses in town to perform at the University theaters also enjoy the Charleston's services.

It has been owned by three generations of Eliasons. The now-retired Ellie Schenk, who had been the housekeeper there since coming from Germany in 1952, now lives at the Charleston, paying a rent that is a secret to everyone but the owners. In 1975, Bud Eliason Jr. gave controlling interests to his two sons, Dan and Eric, who now manage the place while remembering running around it when they were youngsters. One son had been operating it for 25 years until the other one gave up a job as sheriff in Alta,

Utah and returned to help out. There is a resident ghost and a lot of interesting little stories about the place as well. A golfer resident who invented a stroke-perfecting device, practiced in a spot under a mural painted over one of the parking spaces on the wall. He practiced his stroke right out in the parking lot and in the painting is a scene of a golfer on a heavenly fairway teeing off towards the mountain range in the distance. Another resident who passed away had his ashes sitting in his favorite chair in the lobby for quite a while before his widow finally showed up to claim them. Oma Wagstaff lived at the Charleston for half a century and just recently passed away. She was the longest resident still on a month-to-month rental agreement.

Another resident kept getting tuna fish cans stolen from her apartment. The only entry was through a little milk delivery door, and some think that only dwarves or little people could get in to steal the cans. This reminds me of the pudding thieves a friend of mine had to worry about. The solution to this puzzle was little kids left alone in another apartment during the day. They never made off with anything else - only pudding. Perhaps the thief was a child, or someone on a fixed income needing some protein at the end of the month, or even a raccoon? "We had one fire in one apartment, but it never spread..... We had one person jump off the roof. We had one robbery, when they came in and stole the entire safe. We had two secretaries who stole, and we fired them .... There was a guy camping on the roof. Built a campfire .... they had to evict two tenants. One was growing tomatoes in the bathtub, the other was growing marijuana in the tub .... The most embarrassing moment came when Frank Lloyd Wright, in town for some hoity-toity lecture, refused to stay in the Charieston's llth floor penthouse. He said, 'This place is abominable,' Sid says. 'l think it was the cowboy furniture.' 'Dan and l have these dreams,' Eric says, 'that we find secret passageways that connect rooms that look like Roman palaces. Or there's a mysterious tenant who's always one step ahead of us." ([bid, p.A6).

Like so many other landlords, they held 20 furnished units for the 2002 Winter Olympics, but did not charge any more than their regular rates. The landlords always hold the other 10 of their short-term units for actors coming into the valley. The proprietors say that the hardest problem is that many of the residents are old now and don't seem to have any relatives visit them. Papers pile up at front doors and it is they who too often discover residents they are quite fond of who have gone to their rest. Sometimes the owners learn of such deaths in the newspaper. The elderly tenants say that the Eliasons are pretty good substitutes for a family. I think about my co-worker who lived in the building, about tea and crumpets, sharing our writing, and enjoying her company because we had worked together. She was a good teacher for a young person like me then, and I learned a lot from her.

Ghosts apparently abound at the Charleston, which is why knowing the history of a place is so important. Such apparitions might include a roof jumper, a few old tenants who get their wish to die at home, and all those other energies which like to hang around such a place. The resident ghost, or should I say the neighborhood ghost seems to like to walk up and down the street and into the hotel lobby dressed in a black top hat with a black cape and cane. He has been sighted ever since the high rise opened in the neighborhood and can be seen around the hallways inside the Charleston. Karen Molen, the beautician at the Charleston for the last 19 years says that she is not the only one to have seen him, though she admits that she saw him more often in her younger days at the salon and only senses him now. Customers at the salon however, say that they have seen him recently in the middle of summer, walking by the window in black cape and top hat. Speculation holds that he is from the turn of the century, perhaps an actor or professor on his way to the University. Or he could be an old Mormon bishop on his way to church or to visit members of his ward. Perhaps he may be a more modern day version of a ghost who just happens to dress this way.

I wonder if he couldn't be "Charlie," the campus freaked out druggie and protesting intellectual who used to ride all over campus on his bicycle with a flag on a pole on the back of it and a black cape and top hat. He was seen in the hot summertime back in the sixties and early seventies. He had a beard and old fashioned spectacles, though under the cape he often had on some sort of rainbow outfit indicative of the times. He could either be dead having returned to some of his favorite areas on or near campus or be a real ghost, or he could be in his late fifties, stilled in time as a residual image as a sixties person and still running around in this sort of outfit. Or perhaps he may be living as a hermit with his various mental imaginings and only coming out in the evenings to roam about, though it is more likely that he like the rest of us and has completely changed from those days and is living out his life quietly somewhere else. Maybe this is my active imagination and nothing more, because he could just as easily be a wall street banker in a suit and tie now.

The neighborhood residents might be able to set me straight on this, for if the ghost has been sighted before the Charleston was built, he really is an original resident, roaming the streets in ghostly form. The black cape and top hat would certainly be indicative of those early times, perhaps a stately or even prominent citizen taking a morning constitutional with cane in hand. He could be someone who lived in the area and took a daily walk past the Charleston before it was actually there. I have a feeling that other people in the neighborhood have seen or heard a few things that they don't want to admit or took no notice of, because ghost sightings make one suspect even in this day and age and Universities are notorious for strange events and "character" residents not found elsewhere. Just a quick walk into the lobby assures me that there is more than one ghost at the Charleston with so many "character" residents having now passed on. Ghosts can come in layers or decades and may or may not be aware of their other ghostly neighbors, though the experts say that they always are and often interact with each other just like any " live" community would. So that when the residents of the Charleston gather for their summer get together's on its rooftop overlooking the city, they just might have a few community members among them that aren't really there.

ZION'S COOPERATIVE MERCANTILE INSTITUTION - ZCMI

SALT LAKE CITY

The first store of some 146 cooperative branches in the Utah Territory was built in 1868 by the LDS church to cultivate self-sufficiency as well as to have a way to boycott Gentile merchants. The store on South Temple is the oldest site of a chain of department stores in the United States. The "People's Store" was formed because Brigham Young could see that with the coming of the railroad, the territory would need an organization of community-owned home manufacturing stores to provide goods and services at the lowest costs, whose profits would be divided among the people to help all of the residents of Utah. Though ZCMI was never a true cooperative itself, as a result of its formation, a regional system of local cooperatives sprang up all over the territory.

For several years all of the various stores or departments were housed in their own buildings. For example, the shoe factory or "Big Boot" put out 83,000 pairs of shoes yearly and the clothing store manufactured its own line of clothing, including the popular "Mountaineer" overalls. By 1876, it was decided to house all of these various departments under one roof, the three-story brick building that stands on Main Street today. In 1880 another wing was added making the store almost a block long. The faces of ZCMI have changed a lot over the years but it is still there, now housed within a huge mail, and since 1961, modern ZCMI stores are in malls around the state. Although the LDS church at the time only owned 51 percent of the stock and it was a publicly owned store, ZCMI still has very strong ties to the church.

The facade that existed in 1876 was retained in the present store and it is made of cast iron. In 1874 the Mormon all-seeing eye came down from the Z.C.M.I. building. It was a symbol similar to a Masonic symbol meaning Mormon unity, with church members only trading, bartering or selling with other church members. This symbol was no longer to adorn church buildings and businesses. Most of these stores also had signs in them which said: "Holiness To The Lord." These were also removed when LDS leaders thought them no longer appropriate. For many decades there had been a sort of unwritten rivalry between the Gentile stores in the valley and the ZCMI cooperatives. But there came a time when this was not to the advantage of both the Mormons and the Gentiles and a separate store system was no longer necessary.

The old ZCMI building has a new look now and has entrances on both South Temple and State and Main Streets because it is a mall called the Z.C.M.I. Center. There is even a special small museum called the Social Hall Heritage Museum which was created and mainly funded by ZCMI when the foundation of the old Social Hall was discovered as an underground walkway was dug across State Street. The foundations were excavated, archeologists did their work, and then ZCMI agreed to put these early footings under glass with several other artifacts and information exhibits in its own little corner of the store.

The old ZCMI downtown had numerous cafes and restaurants over the years, though now the modern world seems to inhabit the main food court downstairs and misses out on the down-home folksiness and more relaxed atmosphere of most other eating places around. In homage to its own interesting and varied history, the store now displays old photos and memory boxes all about the store of what the store was like in the old days. The miniature display cases house books and items or artifacts for the curious to browse through and the huge poster photographs give one a feel for what it must have been like then. Even the center poles of the old original store are displayed in places, made of pine and having held up this section for decades, but probably with many changes and reinforcements over the years.

I would guess that there are probably many ghosts wandering its premises at night that we will never know about, downplayed as they are. The most famous ghost of ZCMI worked in one of its numerous cafes and restaurants up through the 1950s. She is the ghost of the old Equestrian Restaurant which is now gone perhaps to a new name in the same old restaurant or not there anymore, as no one seemed to know exactly where this restaurant might have been in the store when I asked about it. Someone will know when it opened and closed or adopted a new name. Ghost stories are so much better when you know these things. I hate to be left hanging, because then the layers of history make little sense. Knowing the progression of things can often explain them. This woman deserves more attention for her good cooking as well.

Apparently she was the cook in this downtown store cafe for many years and was known for her excellent cuisine. Exactly what floor the old restaurant was on is still a mystery to all the clerks to whom I talked. The story goes that this cook has never stopped serving customers and that the customers or regulars are still coming to the restaurant. One can smell the great aromas, hear the chatter of voices and laughter and the clinking of glasses and plates and silverware mainly at night when the store is more silent. This cook loved her job and after she passed away a few years back, she kept right on serving her delicious meals. Through the years her regular customers who were mostly women, have come back to dine and haunt the area to this day.

Talking to a few old-timers, I was able to discover that the Equestrian Restaurant was the fanciest and biggest one in the store and that it was located on the first floor of ZCMI. Many of them remembered the wonderful cook and the great dishes that she prepared. When the new mall was built, the restaurant disappeared never to return. It would be nice to give credit where credit is due. Such a fine cook ought to have a name and some recognition for being given a chance very few of us get - the opportunity to continue cooking beyond the grave, and with her own eternal customers included.

Note: On October 16th, 1999, it was announced that the ZCMI store was to be sold to the May Department Stores chain for $52 million in stock and an acquired debt of $48 million. It continued to operate in many of the same ways but was no longer the oldest mercantile store in Utah. I am hopeful that someone will take over to establish a museum in the store either somewhere in the new May building or at a place nearby. The buyer of the store gained a real bargain as ZCMI had been operating at $14 million in losses in just the previous 18 months alone. The 51 percent stock owned by the church would be better spent on various LDS missions around the world, church officials said. It was a bittersweet sale not only for the owners but for thousands of loyal customers who now know that the ZCMI title has disappeared forever. It was a real icon in Utah; and some have wept at their memories of visiting the store as children. Would the new May store be open on Sunday people asked? Will the store offer the same items, like free samples, LDS merchandise, candy windows, angel trees and the spring flower show? People who visited the Tiffan Room to dine shared memories with each other and wondered if the place would still have a homey atmosphere. Some people said that former lifelong employees would be turning over in their graves. Other people came into the store crying because it had been their "home" store for years.

I guess whoever said, "change is good" had better rethink the quote. The Zions Co-operative Mercantile Institutions were one of the last bastions of Utah history. I hope that the store's facade is not changed. In the end, it was the Gentile merchants who came out ahead. Meier & Frank department stores have changed the name of the original store after two years, remodeled the buildings, and horror of horrors, have opened on Sundays! The change for many citizens of Utah was so traumatic and allegorical that right after it happened the local and annual production of "Saturday's Voyeur", a takeoff many years ago on the LDS film "Saturday's Warrior", decided to use this theme in their play that year. The Salt Lake Acting Company's political and cultural satire play, while running for many years, always has a new bent to its production and that year the mannequins at the old Z.C.M.I. store coped with the changes going from Mormon bosses to Jewish ones. And since even the old Twilight Zones highlighted mannequins as ghostly echoes of our society's changes, everyone had a grand time at this particular play poking fun at our state and its oddities.

Only time will tell, in this case, if the ghosts or mannequins of the old store will appear in the new one. And the same goes for the ghost of the Equestrian who apparently still wanders the downtown store, spending most of her time in the area where the old kitchen used to be and cooking up delicious smells and invisible foods for her ghostly customers. As the old customers left this world a few of them returned to her restaurant, making this area of the store a "spirited" reunion of sorts. She was such a good cook that nowadays she is gathering customers as she goes.

BIGELOW / BEN LOMOND

"THE GRAND DAME OF HOTELS"

This hotel in downtown Ogden has had half a dozen names over the years: The White House, the Reed Hotel, the Bigelow Hotel, Ben Lomond Hotel, Raddison Suite Hotel and finally its present double title, the Bigelow/Ben Lomond. In 1868 there was a small hotel on this corner in Ogden called The White House, which was owned by H.C. Bigelow. This building was torn down and the Reed Hotel was built in its place in 1891 by E.A. Reed who contracted to build it at 2510 Washington Boulevard, several blocks straight up from the Union railroad Station and the notorious 25th Street of red light, gambling dens and prohibition fame. The hotel was built in what is called the Richardson Romanesque style with a big clock tower. It was five stories tall. On the northwest corner of this same intersection sat the gorgeous Broom Hotel built in 1882. A donkey engine pulled two trolley cars on tracks up the street to take passengers from the Union Station to both of these hotels.

Right next to the Reed Hotel in the same block was the first Browning Fire Arms plant and south of this was the old Orpheum Theatre built in 1890 and known as the Grand Opera House where such notables as Sarah Bernhardt and Oscar Wilde performed. It was a rectangular building with five stories above ground but in the very center were arched balconies on every floor leading to a grand Russian style turret that towered above the city. All of these fine buildings are gone now with the wave of razings and downtown "improvements" which reached their peak in the seventies and eighties. Somehow the Bigelow/Ben Lomond survived all this, along with some of the buildings on 25th Street, the Union Station and the Egyptian Theatre, which has haunted stories of its own to tell. Salt Lake City faired better with keeping some of its structures but Ogden lost most of its old city to "progress."

Part of this hotel was torn down in 1926 after it was sold to A.P. Bigelow, an ancestor of H. C. Bigelow. From 1926 to 1930, Mr. Bigelow completely renovated and rebuilt the hotel for 1.5 million dollars, incorporating the lower level into his new plans. The Bigelow Hotel opened in 1930 with eleven stories above ground and two stories below ground. Right after its completion, Bigelow lost all of his assets and had to leave town in a hurry. The hotel stood for three years until the new owners named it the Ben Lomond Hotel for Ben Lomond Peak just behind it to the north in 1933. A large group of Scottish immigrants had come into the valley after Brigham Young bought out Miles Goodyear, a Gentile trader who had settled in the valley long before anyone else. Trapper Goodyear moved on to California where he made a second fortune before dying at a young age. The Ben Lomond became a major hotel facility and accommodated people through two World Wars as well as many conventions such as the National Livestock shows that were so popular in the 1930s.

From the thirties to the seventies, the building continued to operate as a hotel but began to become somewhat run down. In 1974, Weber County bought the facility and used it to house administrative offices. In 1983, Dan Cook bought the place and converted the 112 suites that it has today into a world-class hotel with the help of the Raddison Hotel Corporation. The interiors of the rooms were completely modernized for a goodly sum of 7 million dollars, while the lobby and hallways and elevators remained as they had been in earlier times. In 1995 the hotel was registered as one of the historic hotels of America by the National Trust for Historic Preservation and nicknamed the "Grand Dame of Hotels." Recently the hotel was returned to its two original names as a hotel and is no longer affiliated with the Raddison Hotel Corporation. The new hotel manager runs it as a family affair and offers wedding receptions as well.

The hotel offers several dining areas, a gift shop which sadly closed recently, 122 spacious and very modern rooms, a breakfast buffet, massage therapist, chiropractor, hair salon, fitness center,10 meeting rooms, and has two large ballrooms with much of the original sculpting intact. The old atmosphere blends with the new quite nicely and the manager of the last few years has spent his spare time collecting copies of old original newspapers, photographs, clippings and objects found during the renovations or related to various periods in the hotel's history. Several parts of the lobby have framed pictures and display cases as well as the original shoeshine stand, where a man has run his own shoeshine business for the last twelve years. The people who work there are down home and friendly with a care and concern that one does not find in a large hotel chain. Many of the stories, ghostly and otherwise, revolve around the ongoing up-keep, renovations and improvements, in which the people are constantly involved.

What I liked about the manager was the ease with which he told us about all aspects of the hotel equally, considering its ghosts as a part of its history just as the underground tunnels are part of the hotel's history. Some speculate that the tunnels once led downtown to the train station and red light district, although Mr. Budge says that he has been unable to confirm this. In one of the articles on the wall, he was quoted as saying that rumors of ghosts gave the hotel a certain ambience, which enhanced the historical significance of the place. He said that he thought it was kind of neat to have these otherworldly stories to add to his ever-growing collection of historical photos and documents about the hotel. He could see the significance of collecting any and all that he could about the place and it was obvious that he really cares above and beyond the collecting of the usual dollar. The real stories are as good as the fantasy ones and though there is a wealth of tragedy to draw from and several ghosts besides the premier one that people seem to know about. Recently a program on the Travel Channel featuring Donnie Osmond as its narrator made the Bigelow/Ben Lomond one of its stops expressly to talk about the spirits in the place.

A funny story connected to the place which has caused a lot of ghostly rumors in the Crystal Ballroom where the wedding receptions are held, is about the two women who spent six months flat on their backs on scaffolding just a few inches away from the very ornate ceiling. They were local artists hired to restore the checkered ceiling with about 12 inch chess pieces all around the edge of the room, all of them little cherubs, vases and knights. They painted the ceiling white with touches of maroon, which makes the whole ballroom quite a spectacular sight. They individually painted the cherub figures as well as the large cherub faces and shoulders with wings, which come out in the four directions from each chandelier in the room. On either end of the room facing each other on the north and south, the artists managed to leave their signatures on these two particular cherub faces. To the south is "hot lips" with a maroon line running around the cherub's mouth and to the north is a mustached and goateed cherub "artisan." Employees at the hotel talk about feeling as if the many faces and eyes follow them about, or that they feel dizzy in the room, standing in specific areas where the cold spots make them shiver or a strange energy which seems to pass right through their bodies where these cold spots are.

The room itself is quite active and we felt a bit eerie standing in it. The original colors must have been quite spectacular with lime green, gold gild and black trim, even though one half of the room's ceiling is covered over. Painters working in the room during this time had a very odd experience indeed. They looked up to see an old lady standing in the hallway in front of the ballroom. She said that she was looking for the nightclub that the painters knew was no longer accessible nor in use in the basement. In fact it hadn't been in use for decades and was closed off to the public. They went out to help her and explained to her that the nightclub was no longer in use. She then asked them to help her get to the lobby, which they did, and then she promptly disappeared right before their eyes. On another occasion several people were in the ballroom talking about the angels on the ceiling, when suddenly these same angels appeared to move with cold spots and flashes of light accompanying this movement. One woman in the party reported that she felt as if she had either walked through a force or had been walked through by a force, feeling it to be of a masculine nature.

The hotel at one time had another nickname, the "Suicide Hotel," because of supposedly several individuals who jumped off the roof of the place or from the original restaurant on the top floor. Some were successful and others, not so. In actual truth there has been one known double suicide when two brothers, possibly twins, jumped from the restaurant in one version and off the building when it was being re-built in the other. Then there are two other rumored deaths that have never been actually confirmed in the hotel suites. There are two reported murders in the hotel, one in RM 1106 where a husband murdered his wife and then a second one in which a prostitute was murdered by her male client. No room number was indicated in the last case. Incidents in 1106 have included a housekeeper being pushed into the bathtub there by unseen hands while working alone. In another incident she felt invisible hands on her shoulders as she worked in the room. The story behind the first murder is that the husband was trying to inherit his wife's money. Her son, returning from overseas, was so grief stricken upon learning of his mother's murder that he returned to the scene of the crime and committed suicide in the same room. However the name Eccles has somehow become confused with both this ghost and the premier ghost at the hotel. Either there are two Mrs. Eccles, or one of the apparitions has a different name. It is really possible that all three stories are one and the same.

The night manager who died there was the result of a botched robbery attempt. In 1976, a fifteen year old boy named Johnny Perez stabbed the sixty five year old night clerk, Henry Topping Jr., forty-four times to make sure that he had killed him. Perez got away with $370 from the till and was soon captured. Perez was tried as an adult, but did not receive the death penalty and was given life in prison instead. There was no mention of his ever having been paroled, which means that he is still possibly at the state penitentiary or perhaps has been transferred to another facility. He would be over forty years old today. Henry Topping is said to hang out around the main desk. No one has actually seen his apparition, only felt him around. Some strange things have happened around the front desk such as the phone cord lifting by itself at least eight inches in height perpendicular to the desk and then just suddenly dropping, or the office door can be unlocked from the outside but when you turn the handle it refuses to open. People in the front office will hear music outside in the foyer, especially Christmas music that shouldn't being playing at all, especially when it isn't Christmas time. When they open the door and step out to the main desk the music will stop immediately. This will happen over and over again with the music starting and stopping all night long, every time the office door is closed and then opened.

Some strange things have happened in other rooms as well, or at least rumored to have happened, such as what occurs in RM 608, when bills for movies are printed when no one is occupying the room. People try and explain the phantom phone caller from RM 1106 who calls from the eleventh floor, which is now considered the top floor because the 12th floor is closed off and used for storage. Infrequently, someone will call the front desk on the guest room phone, but then no one can be heard on the other end of the line from this room. At the time no one is registered there. The room is always empty when employees investigate the calls. In several of the restrooms, papers can be heard shuffling or being moved around, when no one is in the room except one person to witness these noises. Sometimes several people just outside have heard the ghostly sounds. On several occasions the night manager has gone up with a card to open a door, inserted it and had the light turn green, only to have the door refuse to budge at all. Once a janitor checked a room and joked that a force of some kind had appeared directly in front of him and did not seem to want him to enter the room. Lights floating down through corridors can be seen at the end of the halls but then disappear as soon as a person starts walking towards them.

Most interesting is the tunnel beneath the whole building, which in the early days some speculate connected the train station and red light houses, opium and gambling dens to the hotel. Later, during the Prohibition era, this tunnel is rumored to have housed a fancy bar underground but none of the staff likes to go down there, especially alone. There have been several incidents of orbs or lights or mists floating at the end of the various narrow passageways between the older hotel and the newer one. The tunnel where it has been closed off to the street looks as if it were well ventilated with a big vent right over its entrance. These mazes are used as storage areas now, but when the painters were down in this area, they saw a light begin to form at the end of the tunnel into the shape of a person and it scared them so much that they left for the day. One of the painters left for good. Since the city of Ogden has been investigating opening up some of these tunnels around 25th Street, some people have speculated on just how far the tunnel under the Ben Lomond might go, or if it will be found to connect to a whole system of underground passages in the area. The city is interested in the tourist dollars that tours of these tunnels might bring in like they have in other cities.

There are older citizens who remember being in the tunnels, swearing that they do indeed connect from the early days of the railroad to the hidden speakeasies and bars when liquor and gambling were prohibited. In renovating some of the shops along 25th Street and Electric Alley, which was the main crib row for prostitutes, shop owners have found some interesting things such as a vial of unopened opium or old unopened liquor bottles, and an old broken roulette wheel. Older citizens have visited the hotel and in their stories have given the manager some new information about his hotel. One such octogenarian who was 103 years old told about taking a girlfriend in his younger days on a date there and going to a movie in the old movie theater in the basement of the hotel. There was no evidence of this movie theater having ever existed until the old fellow told the manager to check for the old floor tile in the basement. When workers chipped away at a tiny portion down by the old tunnel they found a portion of the old checkered and tiled floor described perfectly by the old man.

Employees at the hotel say that the tunnel runs the length of the hotel and then is closed off in front of the hotel aimed towards 25th Street. The temperature underground is always at least fifteen degrees cooler than outside with numerous vents leading to the street. Yet the tunnel itself is usually five to ten degrees cooler than the rest of the basement. One time an employee went down the tunnel to check on the sounds that others said they were hearing. He was surprised to confront a white misty presence floating way down from where he was. At first he froze, but as the mist formed into a milky white color and started to drift towards him, he said he turned and ran as fast as he could up to the first floor never looking behind him. We were taken on a tour of the narrow hallways after a previous visit where the employee left us alone to find our own way and we turned right around and went back up the stairs because the feeling was so eerie. This time we were with several other people with intuitive abilities and got together afterwards to compare what all of us had seen, sensed, and heard. Mr. Budge confirmed that there was indeed an old bar down there which had paintings on the walls or pictures from both World Wars in it, though he has not found any photos to confirm this.

Ghost Hunter groups have had their own annual Halloween event in the area where the tunnel leads out to the street and have had the usual things happen, faulty equipment, lights going out and a few EVP recordings as well. Ghostly orbs, electrical difficulties with equipment and phrases found on tapes, have been reported but never posted on the Web. Ghost hunter groups however, are convinced that the Bigelow-Ben Lomond Historic Hotel is one of the main haunted places in Ogden. Tape players and cameras stop working in the tunnel and basement and then return to normal once the visitors reach the surface. Their lights will flicker or go out entirely even with brand new batteries in them and then return to normal when the surface is reached. Some of the hunters have filmed ecto-mists and orbs of light floating around and the voices on tape have some of the usual phrases that they come across like "Help me...." or "Get out...". With more and more investigative groups popping up especially in northern Utah, they will surely make the Ben Lomond one of their stops. Interestingly, the ghost hunters who have ventured up to the 12th floor have found that every time they want to leave the elevator refuses to take them down right away. They have to wait quite some time before it will finally allow them to descend.

One of the most intriguing stories about the hotel concerns a night auditor who was training a senior employee one night. They had stayed quite late. They began hearing sounds of a wild party going on upstairs at three o'clock in the morning. They looked out from the office to see quite a few women arriving from their rooms with number tags on their dresses. Though the tags seemed a bit odd, they didn't think much about it as the hotel is always having wedding parties and receptions late into the night. Then all of a sudden they heard this huge rumble and came running back out of their office just in time to experience "A wind came down the main stairs turned to its left, shook the leaves on a tree at the bottom of the landing, proceeded north and around the lobby turning every chandelier as it passed them, went around the two ladies witnessing the phenomena (but didn't blow their hair) and continued south setting off a sensor locked in a closed room (the sensor was three feet inside the locked wrought iron gate), went down the steps and threw open the double doors leading out of the hotel."

"The ladies were so scared that they called security, who was making rounds on the next floor up. He said he heard and saw nothing but would come check it out. They had him look around and see if windows were open or something but he found nothing, he also tried to open the doors as quickly as the 'wind' did but was unable to give the same amount of force required to match what had just happened." Amazingly, there were no wild parties or wedding receptions going on that night, inside or outside the hotel ("Haunted Hotel Offers More Than A Great Rate," (http://powow.com/ghostmag/aug01/page5.html.)

The premier ghost at the hotel is rumored to be a Mrs. Eccles; this is a very prominent and important name in Ogden and there are two very different versions of her story. In addition there is rumored a little girl with no attached history sometimes seen at the end of hallways and the story of the murdered night manager, the two brothers who jumped to their deaths early on in the hotel's history, and of course the prostitute murdered by her pimp in some other room in the hotel. The two rather confusing stories about Mrs. Eccles involve either two separate and definite hauntings or one story with two very different versions that have developed over time. It is just that only one of them can be called Mrs. Eccles and the other one probably has a different name altogether. Perhaps neither of them is an Eccles, and the woman's real name has yet to be revealed. The manager is trying right now to find a letter, which would indicate the woman's real name. He feels that there is only one story and not two and that the two stories have somehow over time become separate versions of the same events. However, both stories are interesting and equally plausible. Mr. Budge felt that while he knew of no other murders or deaths at the hotel, it was entirely possible for there to be some that he did not know about, especially deaths from natural causes.

When I talked to the manager I pretty much figured out my own theory. I think the Mrs. Eccles story is the one, which concerns the woman who was murdered by her husband in RM 1106 because he wanted her inheritance. Her son, returning from overseas some time after this event, was unable to live on without her and returned to the same hotel room and killed himself there also. It is this apparition which is seen appearing at the end of guest's bed in this room and then when seen by the guest, immediately disappears. There have been at least three sightings of this nature in RM 1106, though no one seems to know in what decade this incident took place. However, I have a feeling that it was a much earlier event than the second story, which took place during World War II. Having read several accounts of the first story, I think that this was Mrs. Eccles or a woman with some other name. The manager concedes that more than one murder or suicide could have taken place when the hotel was younger and the rooms were quite a bit smaller, so that the hotel accommodated many more guests than it does now. The ratio would be about three rooms to every one room now and the room numbers would have been entirely different. Thus RM 1106 is being blamed for everything that happened at the hotel!

While the current manager could not remember the name of the woman whose story I am about to tell, he could remember people who would have known her real name and it was not "Mrs. Eccles." Ironically, with the name Eccles being pretty prominent, this makes the name itself rather suspect for any one of the stories about the hotel. Mrs. "X" as I shall call her for purposes of clarity, is the only fully formed and solid apparition to have ever been sighted at the hotel on more than one occasion over the decades since she first appeared. The story is that she came to the hotel in the 1940s to help care for her severely wounded son who was in a hospital in Ogden. Another version concludes that she was simply staying on the twelfth or eleventh floor to wait for her only son's return from the war where he had been severely wounded. In any event she stayed at the hotel for quite some time, either visiting her son or the train station daily. Eventually her son died, either at the hospital or returned to her in a body bag at the station. She went home, but was so grief stricken after the death of her only son, that either at home or upon returning to her same suite at the hotel, she killed herself. Others say that she lived out her life and died of old age forever grieving the lost of her only son. Either way, her spirit then returned to the hotel where she has been haunting it ever since.

Her perfume can be smelled on the fifth floor and on the twelfth floor in the hallways as well as when the elevator doors first open to these two floors. Quite often her perfume will simply permeate the elevator itself as one is riding in it, although we found the north one which we took down to be the one that smelled like perfume. People have sensed her around or smelled her presence over the years but others have actually seen her dressed in a 1940s suit and hat walking down a corridor, especially on the fifth floor. She comes around the corner of the hallway and walks towards them, disappearing just after she has passed them, although a few claims have been made that she walks right through them. Her perfume is said to have the scent of lilacs or lavender and she is never seen in the rooms, only in the hallways and corridors. The manager says that he personally believes that Mrs. "X" probably returned to the hotel later, after her own death elsewhere of natural causes, because this was where she was able to spend the last days with her son. This event is supposed to have taken place in RM 1106 also.

My own impressions are that the phantom caller is a gentleman who stayed at the hotel quite often and was very meticulous in his personal habits and routines expecting a lot out of the hotel employees. Perhaps he was the husband who wanted his wife's inheritance. The little girl is a trickster spirit and may not be a little girl at all. Mr. Topping hangs around the front desk and does all these little strange things that happen there. The two brothers have not been reported anywhere in the hotel but this may be because the area where the restaurant once was, is closed off to the public now on the top floor of the building. The actual existence of the restaurant on the twelfth floor is suspect too, because while no one seems to know about it, though historical accounts mention its existence several times. Nothing is ever said about the murdered prostitute and this could even be a third version of the same Mrs. Eccles story, although one would like to imagine that there are even more spirits inhabiting the hotel. The murdered Mrs. Eccles is much more likely to be the apparition motivated to appear at the end of guest's beds at the hotel. Guests, who have stayed in this room, say that while the room gets cold they feel warmth and friendliness rather than hostility. There could be one or two other such spirits whose stories we don't even know as yet. In addition to the active areas of the quite scary basement and convoluted closed off doors, hallways and exits both in the back of the building and all over the basement, there are specific rooms where something is reported to have happened. In the basement was something once called the Pine Room Bar with pictures of German and American soldiers in it, though no one has really figured out where the bar might have been located exactly. Then there are the 11th, 12th and 5th floor corridors, as well as the Crystal Ballroom, the Oakroom and the lobby. The 12th floor elevator sometimes won't let people back down and the elevator will often stop at the 5th floor when the button for it has not been pushed. The guest rooms themselves have all been totally remodeled and modernized, while the areas mentioned have retained their original materials and décor.

It is also my opinion that another spirit hangs around the shoeshine stand in the lobby, leaning against the wall and staring somewhat menacingly at passers bye. There is a gentleman shoe shiner who has worked there twelve years during the weekdays. He is wheelchair-bound and owns his own business at the hotel. Down from him is the place where one year ago a gift shop was located and I received several leads for other ghost stories from the woman who managed it. It is now a law office, making me feel as though I had seen a ghost too! In the Oak Room to the north of the building where weddings are performed, and other such events, one can see the original ornately inlaid faces and figures that are oriental in design. It was here that one employee felt a sharp breeze, a lowering in temperature and when walking around the corner into the Oak Room came face to face with an entity, which made eye contact with her, and then promptly disappeared. Perhaps the apparition is still enjoying the solitariness of the once open sitting room from long ago.

More than anything though, the woman whose name is not Mrs. Eccles and who came to wait for her son, is a symbol of a time in history that many still remember with great sadness. Ogden's Union Station is full of such memories and spirits of its own, because it was the place where young men departed and returned, alive, wounded or dead from two World Wars, the Korean conflict, the Vietnam War and the Gulf War. It is a place where these young men walked up and down a street with a very bad reputation, looking for a good time if only for the day. The main part of 25th Street extends from the train station and to the Ben Lomond Hotel, and would have provided the fulfillment of every desire for a young man who could be thinking that he could did die tomorrow, which many young men did. While the rest of the "restless spirits" at the Ben Lomond may never have their stories fully explained, they may always suffer from their lives being added onto. In some cases, these incidents could be trivialized by the sensationalism of the events surrounding them, like story of a mother waiting for her only son's return, or even his impending death.

This apparition deserves to have her story and her son's story told accurately and well, as the two of them although of separate generations, represent an era, an aroma and an atmosphere of a time when many, many people were separated from each other and waited patiently and sometimes not so patiently, to hear from each other. It was a time when many suffered losses and traumas and had an inner strength that future generations might not somehow muster, because they had not experienced all that this particular generation did. Back then, no one really knew what the future might bring or if they would ever see each other again. Many people did not.

HOKEN'S HOLE - SHOOTING STAR SALOON

HUNTSVILLE, UTAH

Hoken Olsen was the original proprietor of Utah's only continuously operating bar. The bar has been operating since 1879 in Huntsville which is in the Ogden Valley on "the loop" or "the balloon" as it is sometimes called being the only road through the canyon which then forms a little loop through three small towns, Huntsville, Liberty and Eden and back out to the main road back down the canyon. The Shooting Star Saloon is on the main street in Huntsville and just outside of town up in the mountains nearby, on private land, is the ruins of a once huge and prosperous mining town called La Plata. The history of La Plata contributes to the history of this haunted bar. There were actually four mining towns all having lived short durations, surrounding the town of Huntsville and some of the old foundations can still be seen of three of them, though two of them are way up in the mountains and the other is now covered over by the Pine View Reservoir.

La Plata's ore was discovered in the late 1890s by a sheepherder named P.O. Johnson in a place called Ant Flats, a bowl-like depression in a Beaver River mountain meadow at around 10,000 feet. He followed his sheep under James Peak to the head of the Little Beaver River and picked up a rock for his dog to chase but noticed that it was unusually heavy. He walked over and chipped a piece of what is called galena from a big boulder near where he had found the rock and took this to his foreman, W.H. Ney. Ney recognized it to be silver-lead galena and took it into an assayer in Logan who gave its value to be 400 ounces of silver to the ton. Just before winter Johnson and Ney registered the claim in the Paradise Mining District at the head of Bear Gulch and dubbed the place The Sundown. Investors and speculators came out of the woodwork especially from Ogden City. Tom Harrison, an experienced miner in Park City and Eureka arrived, along with an H.C. Wardleigh, Joseph Farr, Gid R. Propper and C.K. Westover.

By spring more silver was found and people began arriving from all over. In the first month over 1,500 people showed up at the East Fork of the Bear River and the town meaning "silver" in Spanish sprang up with the discovery of the ore, its name being proposed by Tom Harrison. Newspapers reported 100 men a day passing through Ogden headed for the silver to be found at the top of Ogden Canyon, as well as an average of a thousand or more visitors to the area on a daily basis. They traveled up Ogden Canyon to Huntsville and then through Middle Fork Canyon to La Plata on horseback or in wagons. Both counties petitioned to build roads to the town but it was

Cache County that had the first road built by September of 1891 and Weber County's came along in October of the same year. Tents and cabins sprang up all over the place and what with the constant blasting and mining machinery, the whole valley became anything but peaceful. Johnson did not like all the noise and bustling and sold his half of the claim for $600.00 dollars. Probably the biggest mistake he ever made in his lifetime.

Salt Lake and Park City miners soon took over the area making the place an official boomtown and some have estimated that the population reached as high as 5,000 at one point in the town's short history. They laid out the streets and graded the roads for such names as Harrison, La Plata, Logan and Washington. Before the first winter, there were several dry goods stores, sawmills, grocery and butcher shops, a post office, a bank, a newspaper named *The Courier*, three rooming houses, four restaurants and eight saloons. Over seventy buildings built of logs and with sod roofs, sprang up in the town that was surrounded by many mines such as the Silver King, Red Jacket, La Plata, Lead King, Sundown, Sunrise, Yellow Jacket, New State, Lucretta, Mountain Boy and Queen of the Hills. There was a town marshal, a jail, and even a stagecoach line to both Ogden and Logan with a special stage just so that the miners could visit the red light district in Ogden. The local newspapers wrote quite often about the growing number of "vagabonds, rascals, speculators and other loathsome people" who showed up daily at the diggings and in town. Miners also put up off-color signs to warn away the Chinese and Italians who might try to come and work at the mines, though this never worked and a wide diversity of people came to La Plata to mine. (*Some Dreams Die Hard* by George A. Thompson, Dream Garden Press, 1982, p.177.)

Cache County license rates for LA Plata included $40 for a meat market, $20 for a lunch counter, $40 for a boarding house and $800 for a saloon. By 1892, most of the places were controlled by large companies rather than individuals. Miners were hired to work below ground for $3 a day and above ground for $2.50 a day. A miner could live in La Plata for about $12 a day and each paid 10 cents for a loaf of bread and a lot less for beef than in Salt Lake City. The cities of Logan and Ogden competed not only for the silver prices and lead prices, but also for the supply orders for all of these businesses and miners. Both cities did rather well during the boom, though most of the shipments went to Logan rather than Ogden City.

At 10,000 feet winters were harsh with from 25 degrees to below zero temperatures and snow storms piled up sometimes as much as 15 feet deep. Women and children did not stay for the winter months, though there were a very few hearty women who did. So that in the winter time the men would gather in Dan Ensign's bar to fortify themselves with "anti-freeze." They spent their time telling stories, gambling, drinking, reading and sleeping, while the women and children made themselves comfortable in Huntsville or other settlements nearby. One would suppose that some of these men also spent their time in Hoken's place when they went into town for supplies or to visit their families if they had one. In the spring of 1892, even more prospectors arrived finding all of the best claims already being staked out. Giant boulders of high grade ore were found everywhere at first, and all of this ore on the surface produced astounding amounts such as one 15 ton boulder which melted down, produced 12 tons of bullion. La Plata became what many called the world's only silver placer camp and the only large mining strike in Northern Utah's history. Ore was hauled over the divide to Beaver Canyon by wagon and then down Logan Canyon or Ogden Canyon following what is now Highway 39 and then eventually loaded in Salt Lake City onto the Utah Central Railroad.

It was soon discovered that La Plata's silver veins ran only about 50 feet deep and once the surface was mined, there was very little left of the silver. By the end of 1891, no major ore vein had been found and miners were only able to extract clay soils and 80% lead with some other materials but no silver. The smaller lodes soon were exhausted and the larger mine's values dropped. The lower altitude mines began to take on water and in one final last ditch effort, the new owners of the Sundown ran a190 foot tunnel directly under the original strike but found nothing. 250 tons of ore sent to the Salt Lake valley smelters only produced 10 ounces of silver per ton, though the rest contained lead which the miners were now working for. Unfortunately the lead prices dropped also and the miners were faced with almost no income.

In 1893 president elect Grover Cleveland convinced Congress to repeal the Sherman Silver Purchase Act, which had kept the price of silver high for quite some time. The price then dramatically dropped from a dollar an ounce to only twenty-five cents an ounce. It was called the "Crime of '93" and caused silver mining and production to pretty much cease. La Plata became a dead town overnight and by 1893, few people remained in the town with nearly all of the mines out of operation. By 1894, the town was boarded up and only a few individual diehards remained for perhaps the next ten years. In three years the La Plata mines had produced over $3 million worth of silver. Most of the town crumbled into dust except for a few foundations and some of the buildings, though as late as 1970, quite a few log cabin structures remained.

The town is located in a canyon just off of old Highway 242 and is fenced off and privately owned, which has helped some of these old buildings remain untouched. The two roads that led directly to La Plata can still be seen, the road to Logan following the Little Bear River and the Ogden City road going over Wolf Creek Pass. The three smaller communities or mining towns were located in various parts of the Ogden Valley. Mineral Point was on a high ridge overlooking Porcupine Reservoir. Porcupine or Baxter City is under the Pine View Reservoir and Mound City was just across the Weber County line. As late as the 1980s, people reported having seen ruins of some of the cabins at both of these other sites. What has saved them is the fact that one has to hike or ski quite a distance to reach either one of them. Apparently old rusted machinery, mine shafts, and a few cabins; still exist where La Plata once stood in all of her glory.

Ghosts in these areas have been reported by those brave enough and wise enough to find these old mining towns, however, the chances of finding such things in La Plata are dim due to it being on private and closely guarded property. Winds and chills might send one into a suggestion of ghosts and spirits and certainly there is one individual who might haunt the path between La Plata and Huntsville, in the form of a former Prophet of the LDS church, David O. McKay. His extended family lived in Huntsville and the young Prophet was the mail rider between La Plata and Huntsville for those few years. "I'd saddle up in Huntsville, get the mail from our post office, and head up the canyon and over the hills to the flat. Sometimes I had a light load, other times my saddlebags were filled. I made the trip three times a week and enjoyed it, except in the snow." (*Weber County History* by Richard W. Sadler and Richard C. Roberts, Weber County Commission, 2000, p.45.)

Besides the Valley House mansion and the two McKay homes, which probably have ghosts of their own, the Shooting Star Saloon is still the oldest known structure in the area. Hoken Olsen and his family were there long before the mining towns and even a lot of the settlers in the valley. Hoken operated the saloon from 1879 to 1930 and originally it was the only store in town as well as a saloon. The store offered confectionaries, supplies and liquor in a valley settled by Mormons. It became the local men's social club where they gathered together to have a bit of conversation, play cards or pool and have a beer or whiskey. Also in the early days there were bars on the windows and the early settlers used it as a gathering place if there were rumors of Indian trouble. Eventually the Mormon settlers built their churches and schools and had other places to gather, but this old saloon retained its gentile quality and sort of represents the independent attitude of most of the Huntsville residents even today.

The homemade still in the basement was also in continuous operation until it was dismantled in 1947, even during the Prohibition era, probably because it was a small operation and everyone knew about it. The still simply got bypassed by the local law enforcement officials during this era, as no one ever had trouble with them at the bar. Some claim that they can still hear that old still running in the basement even though it is long gone. After building the store and saloon with his son and letting his son run it after him, Hoken and his son sold it in 1930. The saloon then had a series of owners, including an ex-madam from Nevada and got rather run down until the Posniens bought it and made it what it is today. Locals are divided about its reputation over the years. Some see it as a real dive where all the local motorcycle clubs like to hang out when they are on the road, while others see it as a last bastion, a temporary retreat for gentiles in the world of Zion. Still others, and probably the largest group of followers, have made it an "in" place for nature lovers and ski adventurers traveling through the area.

John Posnien and his wife are the present owners who purchased the bar in 1989 and eventually catapulted it into national fame around the country with their famous "Shooting Star Burger" and "Stuffed Dog On The Wall." While the bar continues to have a total small town atmosphere and has no web sites of its own, there are at least 38 known web sites that refer to this "must visit while in town" bar. Travel magazines, ski magazines, nature magazines and other outdoor travel magazines, all recommend a visit to the Shooting Star. And during the recent 2002 Winter Olympic Games in Salt Lake City and nearby Ogden and Snow Basin, they were able to add a lot more foreign visitors to their guest books. Since a lot of foreign teams trained at the tiny Nordic Valley Ski Resort in nearby Eden, the Shooting Star was a favorite gathering place. And of course the Shooting Star is probably one of a few places or even the only place open on Sunday until midnight in Huntsville.

Besides the various strange things hanging on the walls in the old bar, such as an old boot, an elk head, an antelope head, an old broom, old beer signs and dozen of business cards and dollar bills on the ceiling; there is a giant head of a St. Bernard.

This St. Bernard made it into roadside.America.com in the Pet Cemetery section, called "The Dog." However the entire story is not here, as it is in Tom Wharton's article which appeared in *The Salt Lake Tribune* on January 21, 2001, entitled "Aged Bar Lures Burger Lovers to Huntsville." "Each trinket has a story. The St. Bernard weighed almost 300 pounds when it roamed West Yellowstone, Montana in the 1950s. It was the town pet. Kids once rode on its back. When it died, the sad owner had a taxidermist stuff its head on a grizzly bear mount. (Its head was too big for anything the taxidermist had but this, and it ended up stretching it a bit so that the dog looks sort of mean, which it wasn't, but it is sort of grumpy looking with a cigarette in its mouth.) His wife would not let it in the house. Once, while visiting Ogden Valley and the Shooting Star, he ran up a tab he could not pay. So he pulled the stuffed St. Bernard head from his truck to pay the rest. The animal has become, more or less, the bar's mascot." Its rear end has also been mounted on the wall with a false mouth inserted, which makes it look like it is snarling.

Another tradition at the bar involves putting dollar bills on the ceiling. This tradition started when beer cost a quarter several decades ago. A guy nick named Whiskey Joe wanted to make certain that he always had good credit, drunk or sober, so he pinned a dollar on the ceiling above the bar and this 1901 dollar bill can still be seen today. Whiskey Joe, whose real name everyone seems to have forgotten, grew up in the saloon drinking sodas and watching the men play pool. When World War II came along, he was a young man and went off to war with everyone else. Huntsville has always been reputed to have the most men enlisted in that war per capita than any other city in the United States. When Whiskey Joe returned, the saloon wasn't selling his kind of beer and he decided to boycott the place for a while. Eventually the beer came back and so did Joe, and that is when he put his antique dollar on the ceiling.

Soon others followed his example, only they had a more solemn reason to put dollar bills up there. The ceiling slowly became a war memorial for those friends and buddies killed in World War II and especially those who did not come back from the town of Huntsville. About 15 dollar bills were on the ceiling in remembrance of these men. People would write their names on them or put a quote or saying or even a brief letter to the friend who had died. This practice went on for about a decade after World War II, but then this tradition was all but forgotten and the lonely little dollar bills stayed where they were, as a remembrance of a time long past.

About twelve years ago someone did more than just notice these dollar bills. They left a dollar bill of their own with their signature on it and asked an employee if they would put it on the ceiling with the others. No one really remembers who this fellow was, though one might guess that he knew the story, was perhaps a veteran himself, or just intuitively was intrigued by all the other dollar bills on that ceiling. Anyway, he started the tradition up again, though few who leave their dollars know what the original intent was. There are so many dollar bills now with signatures or initials on them, that the entire ceiling is almost covered now. The stack of bills sits on the old cash register all week and then every Sunday employees take the time to put them up. There are a few business and even credit cards up there too. And like a Jack London bar in California where people leave poems and sayings on napkins on the walls, the dollar bills add to the feeling of both camaraderie and community at the Shooting Star

Saloon. Just as the guest books do with signatures from all over the globe included there: Mongolia, England, Australia, Panama and now so many from Olympians as well.

USA Today declared the Shooting Star Burger the best in the west in 1991 and their signature menu is well known all over the country. The owners claim that combining the polish sausage and hamburger was one of those accidents that happen in the late sixties when some sausages which had been sitting in an old crock pot for days and had to be used or thrown out, gave the cook the idea of putting them in with the burgers. The cook today claims that this old story is not true and that it is a carefully balanced and created recipe that has to be done just right for it to work. However one of the owners proudest acquisitions, which they, the cooks, waitresses and bar tender agree on, is an old jukebox filled with 45-rpms which plays constantly in the place. All the old cowboy tunes play with the likes of Tex Ritter, Marty Robbins, Porter Wagoner, Gene Autry and Johnny Horton. It also plays music from many other eras, though none of a recent variety of course. And it is set to play its tunes randomly, though one can request a favorite simply by putting in the correct change and pushing a certain button.

However there are other things that this jukebox does that cannot be explained. The bar tender and others claim that this jukebox likes to play just the right song for just the right occasion or mood of the person who pushes the button. In other words it plays requests of its own even though the person might have asked for something else, or it even just plays a tune appropriate to what is happening in a person's life just as they walk in the door or maybe when they have settled down and are ready to listen to the tune being played. On many an occasion the tune has been one meant to warn or comfort or communicate something to the person who is listening. One evening it was the bar tender, who has been there for seventeen years, who got a message herself. It was close to closing time and she was really down and thinking of quitting her job. They had turned everything off for the night, including the jukebox. Suddenly it just came on by itself and began playing "Gray skies are going to clear up, put on a happy face...."

Another woman came in right after visiting her father's grave and her father's favorite tune came on the jukebox all by itself. It was one of those old Kingston Trio songs about Bill (her father) being taken in the hurry up wagon. Once it kept playing "The Anniversary Waltz" every few songs, all day long. A man who did not live there but came into the bar quite often, loved to select that song and get people to dance with him to it. By the end of the day people who knew him were beginning to wonder if he was all right. They found out later that on that very day that the jukebox had been playing the song, the man had fallen from his roof and badly injured himself. He is an older man and the bar tender said that just lately that song has been playing a lot and she has begun to wonder if something else has happened. Suffice to say, the old jukebox starts and stops when it wants to, plays whatever song it wants to when it wants to, and has even upon occasion played while not being plugged in.

Then there are the baskets in the kitchen. They have a mind of their own too. It seems that for decades the cooks have been serving their burgers in various kinds of little baskets with fries or chips, etc. These containers are stacked up in the kitchen in about the same place all the time. Yet through tenures of several owners and many an employee they just decide to take flight whenever they feel it. The baskets will just fly off the counter or table and go sailing about the kitchen either individually or in a stack. Whole stacks of these baskets will just suddenly fly off and begin hurling themselves every which way and then land on the floor in a scattered mess. Asking about the ghosts at the bar can be scary too. One day a couple from the East came in and the woman asked if there were any ghosts in the bar. Above the bar, centered near the ceiling is a small ornately framed picture of Hoken Olsen and his family and friends. It is always noticeable right off because the whole bar is dark and yet the light colored frame and picture look almost as if it had a halo around it. The picture hangs on a cup hook and when the woman asked about ghosts it suddenly flew off all by its self and landed face down at the woman's feet. This was enough to scare the couple right out of the bar.

While not much in the way of dimming lights or closing or opening windows and doors has been noticed - and who would in a bar anyway - employees do not like to be left alone in the place, especially at closing time. Because some of them feel that old Hoken and his wife are haunting the place to this day. Besides the mists and shadows noticed around the place from time to time, but only by those sensitive to such things, a full apparition was spotted by two employees one day. The bartender and one young guy were the last there to close up. The bartender was in the kitchen cleaning up and the young guy was out in the bar when suddenly he shouted back to the kitchen, "I thought you said everybody was gone!" The bartender rushed out just in time to see what the kid was seeing, a woman seated in one of the booths with a long brownish wool dress which buttoned to the top of her neck. She had dark brown hair pulled into a bun and a little pair of spectacles on her nose that she was looking over. She did not move but just sat there staring straight ahead to the other side of the booth. It was then that she simply vanished right before their eyes. It scared the young man so much that he quickly left, however, the bartender who says that she is used to the eeriness of the saloon, remained to close up. She was sure that she had just seen Hoken's wife because the woman looked a lot like her portrait above the bar.

More than the ghosts there, however, the people who work in this bar pride themselves in having visitors from all over the world and are constantly building a community spirit about the place. One of the best stories about this is when a man from New Zealand came in and was talking about how the place felt like the taverns at home and how comfortable he was there, when to his great surprise he found out that some people from his hometown in New Zealand were already seated at the bar. He was traveling alone, there were no conventions and only about 50 people lived in this little place in New Zealand. The odds against meeting in this little bar in Huntsville were enormous.

THAT "OLD HICKS PLACE"

THE OLD COLE HOTEL, KANAB & GLENDALE

Kane county is the gateway to many different National Parks and recreation areas. Among them are the Kaibab Plateau and forests, Glen Canyon and Lake Powell, the Kaiparowits Plateau, Hole-in-The-Rock where Mormon pioneers chipped a hole through which to lower their wagons one by one, the Escalante Grand Staircase or Terrace Plateaus as they were once called, and of course Bryce, Zion and the Grand Canyon. The Paiutes believed that Bryce Canyon was formed because of the "Legend People" who could shape shift and take on the forms of various animals. These "Legends" did something mighty bad enough that Coyote turned them all to stone. They even had the paint on their faces long before they became the stone people. The Grand Canyon in Navajo myth was formed by the sea rising up to such a height that it carved out a giant chasm. Or it may have been that a brave chief lost his wife on their marriage day and was allowed by the Gods to go to the spirit world to visit his wife. He could tell no one what his route was upon returning, and the Gods turned this route into a huge canyon filled with water at the bottom.

There are many stories of spirits who haunt the various canyons in this area, long before any white men came. We will only visit Glendale and Kanab, because this is where my mother's ancestors settled and the stories are hers. The spirits are everywhere in this rough and difficult country to travel through, even to this day. Spirits jump into people's cars as they are traveling through, or walk up behind them on a twilight trail, brushing past a shoulder as they walk on by. Or they whisper in a hiker's ear and send the wind down through a certain place to warn, or even sometimes to heal. Indian spirits are not the only ones appearing in these places some say, for there may be spirits from the days when Spanish and Mexican explorers and miners, and trappers and mountain men were roving the region. A myriad of haunted canyons exist where campers have seen ghosts and have talked about them for years. These vagrant wanderers are everywhere in this land of my mother's childhood, the place where she was happiest and forever stilled in time by her own memories.

My mother was born in a log cabin, the Stewart's house in Glendale in 1917. Her parents had been taking care of a ranch north of there and moved into town just in time for the baby. Soon after this they moved into Kanab and began renting rooms. My mother's grandmother, Eleanor Jackson Adams McAllister, was considered the town's best cook, having run a boardinghouse for years in Kanab, and my mother's mother, Ethel Carpenter McAllister, felt that she was a good cook, too. A small rivalry soon developed between the two. In 1920 my grandparents moved into a house of their own directly through the block from Eleanor's boardinghouse. The boardinghouse survived for many years.

Eleanor Jackson Adams McAllister or Aunt Nell, was one very strong pioneer woman, who had had to cut up her father's underwear to make a layette for her unexpected twin. She bore eight children and ran several businesses in town including an ice cream parlor for a while. William James Frazier McAllister, though he was greatly loved in the community and held many offices in town, really did just two things well - beekeeping and directing the church choir. So Eleanor was the one who had to figure out ways to support them all, and she did. William married a second wife in his later years, a singer in the choir. After choir practice, he would court her by bringing her home, sitting her on his knee and rocking in a handmade rocker which was Aunt Nell's only good piece of furniture . After several nights of listening to the rocker creak, Eleanor sneaked down one evening, took the chair out and chopped it up for firewood. Aunt Angie lived in her own house on the edge of town because Eleanor refused to live with her.

Eleanor must have been quite a pretty woman from her picture and she is listed as a hotel keeper and milliner in the *The History of Kane County* by Adonis Findlay Robinson published in 1970 by the DUP, p. 525 "....a very prominent woman. She took many parts in dramatic and musical production. She was an energetic business woman with great ability. She was a seamstress and had a dressmaking shop. She also ran a hotel for many years. She had the first ice cream parlor in town." William James Frazier McAllister was born Aug. 16, 1845, at Pottsville, Delaware, the son of Richard W. and Elizabeth Eleanor Bell McAllister. He crossed the plains when he was 18 years old, driving an ox team for a family whose father had died. He freighted ammunition during the Civil War. He helped colonize St. George. He led the choir in Kanab for 43 years, was an active church worker and assisted in musical productions in Kanab for many years. He had two wives, Eleanor Jackson Adams and Angeline Brown and was the father of 16 children. He spent his last years in American Fork where he was honored by the community on his 93rd birthday." In his later years with his wide brimmed straw hats and his waist length white beard, great grandpa always looked like one of the three Nephites to me.

Long before tourism and the movies came to "Little Hollywood," miners, financiers, and drummers peddling their wares were the main traffic through Kanab. They needed a place to stay and good food and my great grandmother took them in to her home to make extra money. Word soon spread about her excellent cooking and finicky housekeeping and her small home gradually became a boardinghouse. Two mining engineers came through quite often and they soon offered to buy her a building suitable for a hotel and set her up in business as the proprietor. The biggest home in town was up for sale, and it then became the Cole Hotel which my great grandmother eventually purchased and ran but still with some financial assistance from these men. After many years she grew tired of it and there were some differences of opinion and she moved down the block but continued to manage the place from there.

My mother goes on in her own writings to tell of things that were a way of life then and of how Kanab became a place for the European royalty and wealthy to stay when visiting the grand sights of nature. Movies were being filmed there as early as 1922, and later, the town of Paria was born as a movie set. My mother tells of how hard the women had to work in those days and how her father became nine different county servants all at the same time. Besides the county clerk, county treasurer, county recorder, assessor, janitor, and dogcatcher, her father was the county jailer and occasionally a deputy as well. He had to go with the sheriff sometimes for a raid on a still or to catch a poacher or two. Mom had fond memories of playing in the jail cells and sharing with her father fresh-made clabber milk, or running out with all the neighbors to take advantage of a particularly icy day when they could fill the ice house with ice close to home rather than further out of town.

Glendale, which is less than ten miles from Kanab, had originally been called Berryville. Joseph and Robert Berry returned home from a short journey to find that only a few days before, their families had been murdered by Paiute Indians on what is now called Berry's Knoll. This was in 1865 and for a while the settlement was on very shaky ground with several abandonments until it was finally safe again to settle

Berryville. In 1869 some members of John Wesley Powell's expedition were also killed near the Grand Canyon; the Black Hawk War was going on then. It was 1871 when the town was finally named Glendale. Levi Stewart was asked to settle Kanab by Brigham Young in 1876. Mills and irrigation companies were soon thriving, though in 1890, floods just about ruined the town. By 1894, the town had its first doctor and my great grandmother was thinking about how much she enjoyed the ice cream at Halliday's Ice Cream Parlor and Millinery. She was the only woman on the town council at the time.

Later, such famous people as John Wesley Harding, Buffalo Bill Cody, Zane Grey, the queen and king of Sweden and lords and ladies of British royalty came through. Emerson Hough, a famous writer and photographer at the time, took a picture of my mother because she was the most beautiful little girl he had ever seen. Still later, the movies came to town with such celebrities as John Wayne, Clark Gable, Henry Fonda, Barbara Stanwyck, Claudette Colbert, Gary Cooper, Robert Taylor, Joel McCrea and Maureen O'Hara. My favorite movie from the peak years of Hollywood in Kanab is *Westward the Women* where hundreds of extras, mostly women from Kanab, got to play in a film about and for women. It is one of the few Hollywood films of that era that is really heartwrenchingly real where pioneer women were concerned. Over the years films have continued to be made near Kanab.

Many years before my mother passed away, my mother and father and I made a trip to Kanab for a visit. Calculating this by my graduation from high school it would have to have been at least 30 years ago. Mom left the town of her heart when she was in fifth grade, skipping to junior high, which was quite tough she said but worth it, when they arrived in Salt Lake City. She was never to return except for occasional visits soon after the move, and then a rare trip down to the area after that. I can remember her saying that once you have left a small town it was like you had died. You no longer existed there and therefore you became invisible to everyone. When you came back to visit it was like you had come back to life again and never left. People who knew you just a little asked you when you got back and not how long you were going to stay. People who knew you better wondered if you planned to stay. We visited relatives, found the old home in Glendale, but not the one in Kanab and went to the cemeteries in both Glendale and Kanab, though the one in Glendale was sadly overgrown and neglected at the time.

Then we went to look for the old hotel. It was still standing but just barely. An old hermit seemed to live in it with typical things like stacks of newspapers everywhere, junk piled up in the yard, trees and shrubs so overgrown that they hid the entire giant house. But to me it was magnificent. It was the kind of house a painter of landscapes dreams of finding somewhere out in the country, though this was only a couple of streets off the main drag between two very nicely cared-for houses. We talked with the neighbor next door who had lived there all his life. His house was the only other one with three stories but still not as huge as great grandmother's old boardinghouse. He told us how he used to put a board across from his third story room and crawl across to the other boy's room in the old hotel. He also told us how sad he was to see the place so run down and that the old man who lived there wouldn't come out and talk to us because he never talked to anyone. He was the same old man that he had played with as a boy.

So we took the mystery of this house away with us, wondering who he was and if he was a relative. Years later - my mother was by then a semi-invalid - my husband and I took his parents, who were visiting from Indiana, to the Grand Canyon. We went to Kanab and Glendale because I wanted to; this was about 1985. The people of Glendale had cleaned up their cemetery and it was beautiful now with lovely flowers and shrubs around it. I found all of my ancestors this time and took pictures. We went to where the old hotel was and there it still stood, in even worse disrepair but still holding on. I took a dozen pictures of it from all angles and went home and painted a watercolor of it, though my mother had seen one by Sheepherder Sam first (his last name was Jensen I believe). He was an artist and cartoonist - columnist for the *Salt Lake Tribune* and had painted a not very good oil painting of my great grandmother's hotel. My mother had seen it on exhibit somewhere and had purchased it for $300, a goodly sum then.

When the second issue of the *Utah Preservation* magazine came out from the Utah State Historical Society in 1998, I turned the pages (p.41-42) and found a small article with a very nice picture of the restored Cole Hotel in Kanab and I wished that my mother could have been there to see it; just maybe she was. The article said that in 1998 the Hotel Highway had not survived the years in Kanab, "but an even older hotel in Kanab has survived. Located just off the main road, the Cole Hotel has reemerged from years of neglect under the careful nurturing of Arthur and Alice Brown. The Browns who live in California, have spent the last several years restoring the long neglected structure as a part-time residence."

"The Italianate style 'hotel' was actually constructed as a home in 1884 for polygamist William D. Johnson and his four wives. The twelve bedroom house, the largest in town at the time, was converted into Kanab's first hotel around 1889. Turn-of-the-century proprietor Mrs. Eleanor A. McAllister is noted in local histories as 'a very considerate and hospitable hostess who served splendid meals.' Another history of Kane county states that an Alfred Young purchased the home from a Mr. Neagle, though it was built by W.D. Johnson. Mr. Young ran the home as a hotel with 15 rooms available. A Mr. Cole bought the hotel, named it the Cole Hotel and hired Mrs. McAllister as the proprietor. Later she purchased the building, ran it several years, sold it and opened another smaller hotel two blocks north of Center street. She served splendid meals and her hotel was very popular and she continued to run a thriving hotel business for many more years until ill health forced her to give it up."

As I looked at the wonderful photograph of the restored hotel, it felt as if something had come full circle. The two big trees in front were chopped off and gone and the house was painted white with a soft gold and maroon trim and muted green or gray railings. There was some lattice work and the yard had been completely changed with flower gardens and the like. It had a porch and two balconies and large long windows. I wished that I could walk through it just once as it is now, just as I had wished to do this when it looked so like a haunted mansion. Both ways were fine with me, because it was a part of me and my history, just as it was a part of my mother and her history.

I remember what my mother had written about this house and the old north bedroom where lots of events had taken place. She told how she and her sister had made up plays to perform for the adults and how she had taken ice up to her dying great grandfather when it was her turn. She also recorded how she had been there when her uncle leaned over the bed and pronounced his grandfather dead. Only a year later my mother's little brother was born in that same room too. She talks about how much she loved that house and the time they spent there before they had a house of their own. She remembered how the house smelled of "spicy, tempting aromas" the "old north bedroom" where she and her friends produced plays, and where she stayed when she was being punished for something. These were some of the best times she had, enjoying her imagination and its great companionship. She also enjoyed helping her grandmother with the cooking downstairs, or perhaps cheerfully hindering it. She was especially remembered riding out with her grandfather to help him on his bee farm, his long white beard hanging to his waist and his big straw hat shading his face. She also enjoyed a walk into town to visit her father at the jailhouse. Or going down with her little red wagon to the ice house to haul a huge block of ice home for the ice box. She remembers how much she missed that life, that small town time that was no more.

These are the kind of ghosts and spirits that every house keeps, especially one with so many layers and people passing through it. Besides Mr. Johnson and all his wives and children, and the owners after that and all their hotel guests, there were my great grandmother's guests who came for the food alone and all the others who ate and slept there as they passed through when it was her hotel. Lastly there was the hermit, whose name I just recently found out, "old Hicks", who lived there after that for quite a while - another of the ghosts of this once famous hotel. Ghosts go to places that they loved just as often as they stay somewhere because of a tragedy. People just like to pay attention more to those places where a tragedy occurred. What I believe is that a part of my mother is there even to this day - the part of her that is still a child, basking in her memories of a time and place now changed forever. She is probably in that north bedroom visiting from time to time, to think up another play or waiting for a few others to join her who remember their childhoods there as well. It is one of her haunts that I can only attempt to feel, while she herself wanders there totally at ease in her own memories.

This past summer I went to Kanab again, determined to find out more about the old hotel. Everyone in town calls it "the old Hicks place" and had never heard of the Cole Hotel. The Hicks it seems bought the place after it was sold as a hotel and it stayed in their family even during World War II when the place was changed into rentals. The last remaining Hicks to remain living there was the old bachelor Sy Hicks, one of the town characters and tolerated war veterans, having been "shell shocked" in World War I. He liked to jump out of the bushes and scare little children walking by or poke people hard with his cane. In the last years of his life he lived in the chicken coop in the backyard. He would walk up and down the streets and sit down and take little cat naps wherever he was at the time. The town would make him grand marshal of the parade every year just to get a chance to clean him up a bit. He loved to tell passersby things like, "Don't go upstairs I have my dead wife up there," just to frighten them. Sy was strongly built, wore coveralls and white shirts in his younger days but now had a broad brimmed hat and white beard and glasses. He apparently became stranger and stranger as he grew older and he lived into his nineties. His story reminds me of my husband's war veteran character in his home town, who inherited the family farm and lived there all alone, spray painting the whole place in bright patterns of acrylics. He never took a bath either, was always covered in coal dust, and built trenches all over his own back yard so that he could take his old guns out whenever there was a thunder storm and shoot at the sky.

Apparently Sy kept living in the home after his mother died and when he passed on, the home was repossessed by the bank and just sat there empty for a time. Everyone in town thought that at long last this big eyesore would be razed just like its neighboring house had been years before. But then, enter the Browns from Carlsbad, California. As luck would have it, they were there working on their house. They let us in and I made a new friend named Alice. Two and half hours later we had to leave and just couldn't stay any longer. This is how the story goes according to Alice Brown. A con artist came through southern California selling lots around Kanab to unsuspecting marks. He would sell them the land, they would come out and see how desolate it was and then they would sell it back to him at a good profit for him. However, a few stubborn people didn't do that and actually came out and bought or built houses in the area. Alice says that she almost left her husband over this affair, but he brought her out, took her on a whirlwind tour of all the beautiful National Canyons and Parks. They ended up in Kanab and she decided that it was okay for a summer home.

Mrs. Brown is an antique and western history buff who fell in love with the west while reading Zane Grey's books. She and her husband bought a trailer and lived in it in the summer while her husband built a house. Then they went looking for an older home to renovate and they found one. When they went to buy it, they found it had just been sold the day before. They drove around and around the town looking at the old houses and one day her husband said that they had better buy something or people would think that they were crazy. Alice had made friends with a little old lady in town who used to bring her sacks of apples and pies; she and then the real estate woman suggested that they consider the old Hicks place. Then people though they WERE crazy, she said. They went into the house and walked about through all of the mess in little narrow passageways with cobwebs and dust everywhere. Alice has a balance problem that helps her ascertain if a foundation is solid and stable or not. Her husband asked what she thought and she said that she was not getting dizzy or anything and that meant that the foundation was good. They bought the house, sold their other one in town, and began their work. Eleven years later they are almost done. At our visit, they just had the two front rooms left to renovate and other little projects on the first floor. The house became their love and their hobby and their joy. Her husband took care of building projects and she decorated and collected the antiques and memorabilia to put in it. The townspeople really do not understand their obsession, Alice says.

Rumor has it that John Wesley Harding, Buffalo Bill and Zane Grey lived in the Cole Hotel for a while. So Alice made a wonderful Zane Grey room complete with a collection of his writings and things that he would have loved. She and her husband also filled in the entire attic with other rooms that are just amazing. They are a little miffed at a relative of mine who, before they bought the place, went in and took out all the original antiques in the house and stored them in various places about his property. He won't sell them any of things that they would like to have to put back in the house. So Alice obtained pictures, talked to people and tried to duplicate things like the big hutch in the kitchen. The two owners would also like to get hold of a hotel register if such a thing exists or still exists, to try and prove who stayed there and when. The place is just so lovely that it could be a museum rather than a bed and breakfast . They have Jensen's pen and ink drawing of the old house, and we discussed that I had the oil painting. We also noted that Sheepherder Sam wrote at least one article about the Cole Hotel, if not more, for the *Salt Lake Tribune* in the 60s. Jack Goodman also later wrote another article about the hotel.

Alice sent me the records about ownership and I sent her my mother's writings about Kanab and the old hotel, and a copy of the Preservation magazine with an article on the hotel that they didn't know about. We talked about the antique books and everything else she had in the house, as well as taking a very long and wonderful tour. Apparently they get interrupted quite often when they are at the place, because many other people want to visit the house too. All the Johnson ancestors come; all the Hicks ancestors come. All of the people who had ancestors who stayed in the house at one time or another like to visit, as well as those who stayed during WW II, or honeymooned there. Many, many people, it seems, have attachments to this house and its memories, not necessarily just those living in Kanab. Now the house has a mythology too, with famous people staying there and other things that can entice tourists into town. We spent some time trying to figure out just where the old north bedroom might have been, as the original house was quite a bit smaller and much has been added and changed inside the house over the years. Finally, we decided that it was located where two bathrooms are now. What had been a little room at the top of the original little narrow stairs, and really too little for a room, the renovators had put in one bathroom off a bedroom and another off the hallway in front of it. Joined together it made sense that an old person who was dying would be put to bed right at the top of the stairs so people could easily bring things straight up from the kitchen.

Finally, we sat down at the kitchen table and talked a while. Alice really opened up when she found out that I was also there to "intuit" the house, as well as to write a piece about it for this book. She writes children's books when she can get the time, sometimes getting up in the middle of the night to jot her ideas down. She is also an intuitive person, I believe. It was not her balance alone that made her dizzy in places, but also what she felt in them. This house had felt warm, friendly and welcoming the minute that she stepped into it. She asked if I was going to see what I could identify using my intuition right then, and I said that I was way too tired. However, I told her I would sit down at home, concentrate on the house, and then put my impressions down once I had written about the rest of my visit. She asked if I would send her a copy of the impressions I felt when I did do this, and I agreed.

Then she told me a story she had heard about Sy Hicks which seemed to have been confirmed by an old letter found in the chicken coop out back where Sy took to living in his later days. She asked if I would concentrate on the story and write down my impressions of the situation. Both of us are romantics at heart and would love to have the story be true. The story goes that old Sy, once young Sy, let a woman in town into his house because she was trying to hide from her abusive husband. No one knows how long she stayed there, but eventually she went to another town and divorced her husband and never came back. People were never allowed in Sy's house the story goes and so she must have been quite privileged, or Sy was fond of her or perhaps owed her a debt. Besides, says Alice, if you want a ghost story, Sy would provide the material for it. We only stay here a few weeks each summer; perhaps someone staying here all the time would have more intuitive experiences. Still, Alice said, the usual ghostly activities do not seem to take place, even with so interesting a character as the old hermit Sy as a former resident.

I told her that I would try to concentrate on this as well. I am sure that all of this story was meant to be. The Browns were supposed to be there and let me in. I was suppose to go at that time to meet Alice. I think we just might have some more things happen to us in the future too. I intend to leave the oil painting to the house. I asked Alice what they thought they would do with the place when they couldn't take care of it anymore and they had completed the renovations. She said that they would either leave it to their children or sell it as a bed and breakfast. I think that her kids would probably do the same thing, unless there is just one of them who is really interested in moving in and running it. But the children are from California and used to that way of life; it would take someone special to run it. One thing is sure now, the house won't be torn down. It is now one of the grandest houses in Kanab, and certainly of value to someone with the heart to live in a small town and to open its doors either to their own family or to others who would really appreciate staying where once Zane Grey stayed. The early history of the place would entice them to own it.

Note: Jack Goodman wrote a little article on my great grandmother's boardinghouse entitled "Handsome Hostelry in Kanab," *The Salt Lake Tribune*, Sunday February 25, 2001. This is what the short piece had to say:

"Life in Kanab in southernmost Utah was hard for the first permanent settlers who arrived in 1870, but one of them, William Derby Johnson, became fairly prosperous. Johnson and his wife, the former Lucy Annie Salisbury, built the (one and one half) story frame house,...in 1884. It sits at 54 N. Main, what was the heart of the growing town.

The 'cross-wing' house eventually was too small as Johnson, a polygamist who became bishop of Kanab in 1877, married Lucy Elizabeth Brown, Charlotte Prescoft Cram and Mary Agnes Riggs. To accommodate his wives and his nine children, Johnson had a new two-story, 14-room Italianate house built.

All went well until a missive arrived from Apostle Erastus Snow advising a prompt move to the Mormon colony in Chihauhua, Mexico. The family left town a day after being questioned on polygamy matters by federal marshals. George Neagle, who had two wives, bought the house for $150. He later moved to Mexico also, and new owner, Alfred Douglas Young converted the house to a hotel.

He sold the property to Thomas E. Cole, who hired Eleanor McAllister to run it.

Among her guests, local reports say, was author Zane Grey. Art and Alice Brown own the hotel today and have restored both structures. They have applied to the National Park Service for inclusion on the National Register of Historic Places."

Alice sent me an old rusty nail from the original house and told me that she and her husband, while not having any ghostly experiences themselves had had others mention just a very few things. It seems that the new light fixtures flicker and dim, the water turns off by itself occasionally, and the people next door have also seen a few odd things. Her guess is that while they were renovating, everyone was happy. But once things neared completion, the spirits residing decided to quit being so absolutely quiet. With so many wives and children, renters, an old hermit with his rumored "dead" wife upstairs, plus a few rumored celebrity ghosts, and all those antiques with energies of their own, both old and new spirits could abound. The Browns haven't the heart to let go of their hobby and summer home just yet. They are just about done with everything but have so much of their heart and soul invested in the place that they want to enjoy it for a long time to come. One can expect that the ghosts in the place will too.

THE PINE HOTEL

MOORE'S OLD PINE INN, MARYSVALE

This hotel is considered the oldest hotel in Utah, built in 1882 and has that date painted on the front building. Marysvale is in Piute County on the old highway 89. It has about 380 citizens at present and was once a mining town near gold, silver and uranium mines. Similar to the old Cole Hotel in Kanab, rumors are that both Butch Cassidy, who was born nearby in Circleville, and Zane Grey, who spent time there while writing *Riders of the Purple Sage*, stayed there at one time or another. Butch would have been only 14 years old when the hotel opened, but this doesn't mean that he didn't stay there later on. Zane Grey probably stayed several places in the area while working on his not-so-favorable book about the Mormon authoritarian polygamy life, *Riders of the Purple Sage*. I for one just loved all of his books as a kid. However, when I read *The Giant Joshua* by Maurine Whipple, about her own great grandmother in the St. George area, this whole way of living became much clearer, because it was told from the woman's point of view, and told beautifully. I asked my mother once why this woman had never written another book since she was such a wonderful writer. My mother knew her, and said, "She always wanted to write a book about her great grandmother and so she did. I guess that's all she had in her to write."

In 1919, this is what some travelers had to say about staying at The Grand Hotel in Marysvale, a hotel that does not exist anymore: "As we were coming out of the Marysvale Canyon of the Sevier River, about five miles north of Marysvale, we experienced engine trouble that brought our car to a dead stop ... after a wait of an hour ... a keen looking, athletic young fellow came along and quickly diagnosed the trouble, and towed us into Marysvale. He would accept nothing for his service, for, he said quietly, 'It is a courtesy of the road.'"

"As it was getting dark, we all put up at the Grand Hotel ... The hotel accommodations at Marysvale could be improved. At the time of our visit the house was crowded. We were assigned three in a room, with two beds and two towels for three persons. The dinner was beans and pork, steak, potatoes, bread and butter, pear preserves, cake. For breakfast we had the saltiest bacon we have ever tasted. The landlord came to us at the table and said the breakfast would only cost fifty cents, as he was unable to serve eggs." ("Hotels Revisited: Retracing a 1919 Utah Road Trip," by Roger Roper, *Utah Preservation*, Volume 2, p.39.)

Old photos of the Pine Hotel show the large house and one small addition to the south of it in 1912. It was built in the middle of a forest of ponderosa pines and the saplings planted there are over a hundred feet tall now. A fire in 1920 damaged the second story section, so that the roof and upper windows had to be redone and modified. Other than this the hotel is essentially the same as it was then, but with a few smaller buildings added on. The Moores live in the little home next door to the hotel on the south side. Katie and Randy Moore left their careers in Davis County and took a chance. It seems that Randy's grandparents live in Marysvale and this is how they first caught sight of the Pine Hotel. His grandmother moved from Pleasant Grove to teach in a one room schoolhouse in Angle, Utah in the 1920s. When she first was teaching, she stayed at the Pine Hotel.

The place at the time they purchased it, was failing apart and had not had a hotel guest since the late 1960s when Interstate 15 was completed and took away a lot of the traffic through town. They bought the place in 1994 and began their work on it. It needed everything - rewiring, replumbing, lots of renovating and repair work. Most of the original furnishings were there and these too needed a lot of work. The Moore's children were all grown up and gone, and the Moores thought that this venture, though risky, would give them the change that they needed to live the quiet country life. They kept a scrapbook of their renovation work and when finished painted the entire place a pale yellow. There is a main building that is like an old home and several cottages around it with a little cottage down front by the road which entices people to visit, just as it did us, as we didn't know a thing about the place when we passed it on the highway.

The Moores had many adventures during the renovation process, like having 20 wheelbarrows of soot fall in the dining room when they first discovered that there was only one chimney for both the dining and living rooms, when they thought there were two. One escapade involved climbing 35 foot ladders to finish the outside of the buildings. They even found New York Times newspapers from 1882 still glued to the rafters. The Moores feel that they became rehab experts by the time that they were finished. Friends and family helped along the way, after they first sought the advice of a preservation architect, Kim Hyatt. "We would fall into bed exhausted at night,' Katie recalls, 'but wake up in the morning ready to get going again. That was a sign we were doing the right thing." (ibid, p.41.)

After 15 months of work, they opened their Inn in October of 1995. "We figured it would take a few years to reach the level of business we started getting in the first full year." (ibid, p.41.) With the Paiute ATV trail opening up in the forest land nearby, Marysvale is back on the map. There are a few antique shops, a river running business, a renovated rug weaving business, a sculptor's studio, metal workers, ranches,and campgrounds and cabins now. The Moore's Old Pine Inn also has its share of ghosts, which the Moores don't mind talking about. As I read the article on the various experiences of their guests and employees, I had a strong vision of a woman proprietor in a white blouse with puffy long sleeves and tight-fitting tan or gray long skirt. Her medium brown hair was pulled up in a bun or some style of the day and she was slim and wiry. In fact I dreamed about her because I had stopped writing about the place in the middle of the article late at night and had retired. She said in the dream that she was not the only one there, but the most likely or strongest apparition for people to spot. Apparently she cooked the meals and was probably the wife of an owner, who really loved the place and did not want to leave. She was outspoken and tough and rather gruff, and did a lot of the work herself, therefore feeling that she still owns the place. This talkative dream woman told me to come back for a visit and I would get more about her and the three others who make their presences known only occasionally.

Onc of the Moores' guests was a psychic who was asked by a guest if she had ever done an exorcism. When she said that she had, a door to one of the rooms slammed and bolted shut, though no one had a key to the room. When the same woman said that she would never do an exorcism unless she was invited to, the door unlocked by itself. The same psychic came back later to stay in the room that had locked itself. This time she said that a mysterious woman approached her in the night and asked her what in the hell she was trying to prove and then promptly disappeared never to return, at least to this woman. Another guest waited in the hall all night hoping to get a picture of a ghost. Mrs. Moore's two year old grandson once pointed at a blank place in the hall and said that he did not like the lady standing there, though no one else saw anything. (Some of this information was taken from an article which appeared in *The Salt Lake Tribune* on Saturday, July 8, 2000 written by Tom Wharton, "Ghosts Help Bring a Town Back to Life.")

Another guest saw a group of young women using the porch swing and wondered if the building could ever have been used as a brothel. No one else of course saw these women, but the idea of it once being a brothel is quite plausible, especially when all the surrounding mines were open and Marysvale was a boom town. Perhaps the woman the psychic saw was a madam, but I think not. I think the young girls on the porch had been visitors there, one of those imprints that buildings experience. Then someone intuitive enough happens to see the rerunning of this tape or imprinting on the building. As for the three occasional visitors my dream woman described, I see two men and one other woman, all people who were somehow involved in running the place and not guests at all. One is a younger man, perhaps a son who somehow did not live to adulthood. the other man worked about the place all the time, an owner or handyman. The other woman is from a different, more modern era altogether. She could have been a guest, but if so, she was there quite often to visit. All of them, however, have one major thing in common - they really loved the place and guard and protect it to this day.

Although the Moores have never seen anything, they feel that all the ghosts are friendly ones and like what they have done with the place. They are absolutely right about this. Marysvale has very little history written about it, but I did find some in the Utah State Historical Society's *History of Piute County* by Linda King Newell and the Piute County Commission, published in 1999, with reference to the Pine Hotel as well. The first setters came to live in the area in 1864 and built a small fort near where the hotel now stands to protect themselves from the Indians during the Black Hawk War. These first settlers abandoned the fort when two people were killed by Indians. Then, in 1869, a couple of prospectors found, among other things, waterfalls, gold and the remains of a possible Spanish mine which then began the Bullion Canyon gold rush nearby. This old abandoned arrasta or Mexican rasta was used to mine ore and was the most effective way then to remove the gold. It is constructed of stone like a circular barrel with a pole as a shaft in the center, which is then attached to two stones and drawn around and around by mules or horses. It grinds the quartz to powder, and the gold, being the heaviest, settles to the bottom.

Marysvale was also the end of the line for the Denver and Rio Grand Railroad, so it became during this period both a railroad and mining town. Kimberly was just up the road apiece high in the Tushar Mountains at the head of Mill Creek Canyon. This was where the miners worked, though many of them lived in Marysvale. The Annie Laurie Gold Mine became central to the Gold Mountain Mining District, and Peter Kimberly from Chicago established the town. Lower Kimberly contained the businesses and Upper Kimberly contained many homes and shacks. The boom period was from 1901 to 1908 and a stage ran up to the area daily. About 500 people lived in the place. There were many brothels, several murders and Butch Cassidy hung out there during this time. By 1932, 50 families remained in town working the mill. The last vein to be discovered ran out in 1938. By 1942, the town was basically deserted. The skeletal structure of the Annie Laurie Mill once stood at the end of the canyon road as late as the late 1970s, though now I am told it is a pile of rubble.

On the other side of Marysvale was the town of Alunite which came into being because of a Marysvale prospector who discovered potash ore of alunite in 1910. Up Cottonwood Canyon ten miles southwest of Marysvale, more potassium aluminum sulphate ore was found than, it is said, in any other place in the entire nation. Some of the mines were the Florence, Kenyon, Lucky Boy and Mohawk and the first shipment of this ore to Marysvale 5 miles away was 28 tons of potash. The Alunite Company built up around this canyon mine, so that about 100 people lived in the town at its peak and up through World War I. By 1930, potash extraction became too expensive and the mine town was torn down almost overnight. Beyond a few foundations, all that remains is where the Deer Trail Mine once operated.

One can now guess, having read all this, that Marysvale and the old Pine Hotel might really have a few ghosts about. People who mined there and people who passed through the area on vacation after the mines were long abandoned may have experienced some ghostly visits. For me, besides the woman who seems to be dressed from an earlier time, everything else haunting the place is associated with the 1920s. Why, I don't know. Perhaps some day I will stay there and get my own immediate and more specific impressions of the place. I have found over the years that simply concentrating on a place can give one quite a few intuitive impressions. The ghosts at the Pine Hotel have been sensed and even seen upon occasion by many a visitor over the years, so one can speculate that they will be heard from in the future.

KIRK HOTEL

TOOELE, UTAH

Tooele is the largest city in the county and though it is really called Tooele City, the "city" part was dropped by just about everyone a long time ago. Its name came from the word "tuilla" which Captain Howard Stansbury dubbed the whole valley on his 1850 survey maps. One theory holds that the original Indians in the valley were called the "Tooelians" by the early pioneers, while another says that the word 'tuilia" is the Spanish word for the bullrush plants found all around the area. Even in 1847, herders grazed their cattle in the long grass in the area. Ezra Taft Benson helped settle the valley by ordering that a sawmill and a gristmill be built at Big Creek Canyon. The Benson Gristmill still stands today and has been renovated and made into a state historical area where summer musicals, tours and other exhibits are presented. The town incorporated in 1853 and it covered nine square miles. Rumors of buried gold still persist in the area.

In 1943, the U.S. government bought land 5 miles south of the city and thus began the Tooele Army Depot which became one of the Army's largest supply centers in the west. In 1993 it was put on the Department of Defense's list of closures, but while its future is at risk, it still remains open as a source of controversy for its destruction of chemicals once intended for chemical warfare. Tooele City became an agricultural center for the valley and farming was increased by the building of a dam for more water for the west country. Grazing herds and mining were the most important commodities back in the old days. Besides the sheep and cattle, a smelter was operated from 1903 to 1972. Orrin Porter Rockwell had a ranch nearby in Skull Valley as well. The old ghost town of Mercur still has some mining going on where residents of Tooele commute to mine. Because of the army depot, the economy in the city was greatly enhanced and new schools and businesses boomed. The Tooele *Transcript Bulletin* is the oldest continuous business in the city having been founded in 1894. The Tooele Valley Railroad Museum is open to visitors, and many an old lineman or fireman who worked hauling from the mines will tell you a tale or two if you visit the town. Today Tooele is mainly a "bedroom community", and many people commute from Salt Lake City to work at the army depot.

Tooele, because of the gold rush, had to accommodate a lot of miners or smelter workers and so the city eventually had four hotels. One of these, the Kirk Hotel, was built and operated as a boardinghouse hotel ever since. A mining magnate, Phil Kirk, built the hotel and then lost it one year later in the stock market crash of 1929 when the bank took it over. In 1930, Millie Jones acquired the property from the bank because her 200-room boardinghouse in Bingham Canyon had burned to the ground. She operated the 100-room hotel for many years, becoming a prominent businesswoman in town. During those decades the hotel had a ballroom on the top floor, a restaurant near the lobby with a beer bar and a pool hall in the basement. When his mother could no longer run the hotel, her son Garth Sr. took over management of the hotel but by the 1960s the hotel had fallen upon hard times with rooms going for $3 a night. By then, the hotel had developed quite a seedy reputation.

Who really saved the hotel was a grandson of Millie's. Millie's son, who was getting along in years, called his son in Southern California where he was living in 1972 and said that if his son wanted any inheritance he had better come home and take the hotel over, otherwise the father was going to sell it. The son found a partner and they managed to generate more money and began to renovate the place bit by bit. He tore out the tiny bathroom-less rooms and converted the inside of it to 40 modem apartments spread over three floors. He found historic door frames from old hospitals and from the City and County building in Salt Lake City and is building a conference center next door. He also wants to turn the third floor apartments into a weekly bed and breakfast business, and says that if there are any ghosts it doesn't bother him at all because all of them are friendly.

Tenants describe a different story of all sorts of paranormal activity and so do the ghost busters who have visited the place. One of the co-owners who lives in one of the apartments reported that while walking down a hallway, her good sized dog Kaboo was suddenly seized by an unseen force and hurled two feet into a wall. Another tenant reported that she often hears piano music though no one in the building owns a piano. She insists she can also hear the clicking of pool balls or the clinking of glasses. There is no bar any longer nor is there a pool table, and the old piano has been gutted to use as a liquor cabinet. Another tenant has the habit of setting out a potted tomato plant every evening in front of a long sealed doorway in her apartment, though practically every morning she finds it knocked over. If she places the plant anywhere else away from the old door, the plant stays upright. There are also the usual doors left open and found closed or vice versa, as well as lights that flicker and objects that seem to move when no one is around.

In fact there is so much activity reported by tenants at the hotel, that the owners, Allison Jacobsen and Garth Jones, decided to bring in some ghost busters. Michele Buck, head of the Tooele-based Paranormal Ghost Research and Investigative Services, staked out the potted plant apartment for several hours on a Saturday night and then walked about the hallways with video cameras and electronic field detectors. Buck immediately said that the hotel had a lot going on, and while she did not hear glasses or pool balls clinking, she did hear the piano music and a woman singing an old-fashioned love song. A motion detector in front of the apartment's sealed door went off repeatedly and doors could be heard shutting even though no one was in the area. The video film showed various orbs throughout the building, which ghost hunters say are balls of energy that just might be the spirits of people long gone from the earth. Also, an"ecto-mist" or long wisp of smoke-like substance followed Buck upstairs as recoded on the film.

Ghost hunters say that these mists are a collection of souls often seen in graveyards. Michele Buck came to the same conclusion as the tenants and owners, that while there are many spirits, they are friendly and warm with nothing negative or evil present.

HISTORIC LEHI HOTEL BED & BREAKFAST

- SMITH SCHOOL

This old adobe square boxed building is the oldest standing hotel between Salt Lake City and Denver. Right next to it is a little two-room adobe schoolhouse called the Smith School, which was built in 1865. This old school has now been made into additional rooms for hotel guests. There is a newer brick addition to the old original hotel behind it. The Millers are the present owners of this entire block and complex, which include the hotel, school, and the foundations of a blacksmith and wagon shop, which were all once included inside the walls of the old Lehi Fort.

Joseph Johnson Smith began operating a blacksmithing wagon shop on this site in 1853. From 1865 to 1886, John Woodhouse converted the building to a general store using surplus supplies and materials from the nearby army post of Camp Floyd. He also sold these surplus supplies and materials from his store. In 1887, Joseph Johnson Smith built the hotel for one of his plural wives, Sarah Ann Lilliard Smith. In addition to managing the hotel, Sarah Ann Smith kept making improvements to the place by first adding a cafe in 1891. That same year a saloon was added. The first year the saloon was in operation a robbery occurred. Someone came into the hotel during the night and took the hotel guest's watches, pocketknives, and all the shoes that they could carry while guests were sleeping. Eventually Sarah Ann added a cigar and candy shop and a dentist's office. Drummers used to display and sell their wares from the two front rooms of the hotel. There is a low window on the east side of the building through which the actual business was conducted.

The building ran as a hotel and eating-house until 1926. It was considered the finest example of a hotel in the territory and eventually became convenient to the railroad. In 1929, Mary "Mame" Alice Smith Thomas purchased the building in which to raise her family. When all of her children were grown, she lived on the there alone, occasionally renting rooms out for extra income. The building continued to be a family home until 1960. From 1960 to 1997, the history of the building is sparse. It either sat empty or was used for various other things, while managing not to be torn down.

Coral and Dimple Miller purchased the property along with the Lyall and Audrey Thomas family in 1997 to preserve their ancestor's dwelling. They spent long hours researching the history of the place as well as restoring the original portion of the building as accurately as possible. They built a glass window into the floor so that visitors could see a part of the foundation of the old blacksmith shop as well as the remains of an old pioneer well. Upstairs in a little guest sitting room are many articles on the history of Lehi and the surrounding area as well as old newspapers from World War II.

Today the hotel is open for guests at a very reasonable rate, and the owners also offer private parties, catered banquets, etc. Ghost hunters have visited this tiny hotel more than once. A large party of ghost hunting enthusiasts from a local community class recently invaded it late in the evening. And the hotel does have all the signs of at least one or more hauntings. When we went there in broad daylight, it was easy to feel the usual signs of ghostly occupation. The loud static in our ears and the oppressive pressure on our chests making it difficult to breathe, are always indicators to sensitives. Ghost hunters who go there come back with reports of extreme changes in temperature and electromagnetic energies registering on their equipment.

As to who these other invisible guests are, is anyone's guess. Perhaps it is Sarah Ann working on her hotel, an early guest or two, or even a drummer selling his wares. Or perhaps it is "Mame" Thomas and some of her children, or a renter who liked the place and wanted to stay. Whatever happened between the 1960s and the 1990s would also contribute to those uninvited guests at the hotel, perhaps a transient, vandals or anyone else who attempted to use the building for something during those years. Although I am sure that everyone would just love to think that some famous Danite like Orrin Porter Rockwell is occupying the place, although Rockwell died before it was a hotel, he had his wife Christina did live in a place just outside Fort Lehi where the hotel now stands. Rockwell married Christina after his wife Mary Ann Neff died leaving him with several small children and rode out every day to his hotel at the point of the mountain. The Rockwells lived in Salt Lake City after leaving Lehi, but when Porter Rockwell died, Christina returned with her family to Lehi and had one more child born two months after Rockwell passed away.

In the '50s and '60s, a widow lady and her sister lived in the old hotel on the main floor. She was probably a Smunin relation, as the Smunins, Wilsons and Thomas's had all owned the hotel at one time or another. This widow woman had some sort of rare skin condition, which required her to put cornstarch on it everyday. This in turn made her skin very white. The little kids who lived in town were often afraid to go to her house because she looked so scary with white skin and hair woven into a bun on the top of her head. She lived there for about 15 years, and when she passed away the hotel became a storage facility except for a brief period of time when the Wilson's operated a woodshop on the main floor. Carl Miller, a retired schoolteacher and avid town historian, bought the place on a handshake and turned it into a bed and breakfast hotel.

Those who work there or manage and own the hotel say that they haven't really noticed any strange phenomena around the place, although employees do not like to go to the attic or the cellar because the hair stands up on the back of their necks. They say they can feel a presence there that makes them uncomfortable. The ghost hunters, having visited the various rooms in the hotel, say that they can feel several spirits around the place, especially a woman in the Century Bride room who was badly hurt. The various rooms of the hotel have been named for specific parts of Lehi's history, such as the Pony Express, Stage Coach, Porter Rockwell, Sugar Room, Israel and David Evans room, Smunin - Thomas - Wilson Room, Joseph Johnson's Smith Room,

Century Bride Room, etc.

My own impressions of the place included the possibility that something more than trash lies buried in the old pioneer well. I also felt the blacksmith's presence from time the time or that the guests can occasionally hear some of the sounds from the original blacksmith shop, although they probably don't notice it and dismiss it as just the creaks and groans that an old building makes in the middle of the night. Either Sarah Ann or Mame, or both of them, like to keep things tidy around the place from time to time. The two-room Smith school to the east of the old hotel seemed to also be active, although I could not go inside and no impressions came to me from outside the building. The old schoolhouse has been made into some of the living quarters of the owners and is also an area where they offer banquets. My most interesting impression was one of some sort of gun battle down the street outside a store or saloon, which brought the wounded party to the front parlor of Sarah Ann's hotel for rest and recuperation. If anyone knows any history that would account for this impression I would be interested to know the details of such an incident.

What I asked Carl Miller what prompted him to buy the place and turn it into a bed and breakfast, he said it was the fact that the land there had three different very important layers of history. Where would one find an old hotel built over the foundation of a fort and an old general mercantile store? Fort Lehi was 16 square blocks with four blocks running in each direction and the walls 8 to 12 feet high. In order to live in the fort each family had to build four rods on the outside wall and a rod equaled 16 feet. There were entrances to the fort on all four sides that eventually had to be closed up. The old blacksmith shop and the old pioneer well were located on the corner where the hotel now stands. These buildings were torn down to make way for Woodhouse's General Mercantile store, which is the second part of the land's history. Then these buildings were torn down and the hotel was built where the store once stood, making the third layer of history. To me there are five layers of history altogether, what with the time when individual families lived in the place, the storage facility it became, and then its return to a hotel bed and breakfast.

The ninth room in the hotel is called the Mystery Room because of an old sign they found concerning the general merchandise store, which they had to fit together like puzzle pieces and still cannot figure out exactly what the sign said. In each of the rooms they have photos and documents, supporting why they chose these particular names from Lehi's history. They also have a 10th room called the President's Room, because at least four U.S. Presidents either passed through the area by train or stopped to give a speech there: Harrison, Taft, Franklin D.Roosevelt and Richard M. Nixon. The hotel serves both supper and breakfast with the room price, according to Miller, to provide the same way meals were served to train passengers who came through town many years ago. The owners like to carry on the tradition of serving a good meal as part of the hotel stay.

During the 2002 Winter Olympics, the editor of a national sports magazine from Holland stayed in the hotel and featured a lead article about the hotel in his magazine when he went back home. The President of the Bulgarian biathlon team spent a night there was some of his team members and quite a few other foreign visitors have found their way there as well. Some people come to the hotel on a feeling says Carl. They look for a hotel on the main drag and then decide to drive into town because none of the places feel right. They end up at the old historic Lehi hotel. Some of them say that they feel like they have come home. And quite a few of the descendants of the several families who at one time owned the hotel, store, or were pioneers in the original fort, come to the hotel for annual reunions or banquets, etc. They have even had the descendants of Orrin Porter Rockwell dine at the hotel, some of whom believe that the gift of prophecy has been passed down through the family. Brigham Young was supposed to have blessed Rockwell with both the gift of prophecy and a protection from death as long as he kept his hair long.

When the Millers were restoring the hotel, they wanted to restore the "widow's watch" as well. This is a flat area on the roof with a door and stairs that open to a platform walkway surrounded by a little fence. Popular among architects of the day the "widow's watch" was really just for show. However there is a history to it, in that wives who saw their husbands off to work on the railroad or in the mines, often became widows. With a railing around the flat roof, the wife could walk up-and-down waiting for her husband to return, or knowing that he was dead; she could walk about in the area having remembrances about her lost husband. Suffice to say, the historic Lehi Hotel, while just a plain square adobe building with a little two-room adobe schoolhouse attached to it, offers a lot of history with a hint of both angels and ghosts, all in one. And Carl Miller can take you on an historic jaunt about the area if you are a Porter Rockwell fan.

OGDEN CANYON RESORT GHOSTS
- THE GRAY CLIFF LODGE

The Gray Cliff Lodge Restaurant was originally the Thomas D. Dee family summer home in Ogden Canyon. At one time this whole canyon was a resort area for the cream of Ogden society and there were several big hot springs resorts in the canyon as well as a number of family camps, many of which still exist today. While the largest resort hotel called The Hermitage no longer exists today, the old Ogden sanitarium at the mouth of the canyon, now called The Rainbow Gardens, is still going strong. The Idlewild was another lodge which today is privately owned by a local corporation and is used for company retreats. Some of the other hot springs locations in the canyon are now covered over by the Pine View Reservoir. Each of these places had a few ghost stories but not like those at the Gray Cliff Lodge.

In the early days there was a toll road up through the canyon and the narrow passageway before this road had been pretty much impassable. Before the road, the canyon had a fascinating history, full of early explorers, trappers, miners and settlers, especially in the Ogden Valley. Most important to our story here is the fact that long before any white men came to the canyon or its valley high above Ogden City, there was what is called the Indian Trail. This trail was used as a passageway to the valley, a place to store lodge poles to be harvested the following year, as they were stripped and pushed down between pine trees to cure. The trail was also a way to get to the various hot springs all up and down the canyon. It was a mystical place even then to those who sought the warm waters and their various cures for ailments and diseases.

While there is a very romanticized story of how the canyon was formed, the truth is that many early Northern Shoshone died in those waters after the white man came bringing various fevers and epidemics for which the native people sought to cure themselves in the hot springs. Instead these waters killed them, for while the Shoshone had found these hot springs a wonderful cure in the past for various aches and pains, the warm water aggravated these fevers, causing many to die. No one seems to know how the formation of the canyon story came about. No one is aware of whether this story came to be made up by promoters and locals, or really is a legend told through the oral traditions of the Northern Shoshone people. But it is no matter, for it is a charming story that those who live in Ogden Canyon cherish and tell with great fondness and passion. The tale does represent this entire era of the canyon in a way, because it forewarns one of what was to come later or perhaps had already occurred.

Dark Flower's people were camped near the present town of Huntsville in the Ogden Valley. She had met Twin Feather and they had fallen in love. One day Twin Feather decided to hunt for some small game for winter storage. After he left, Dark Flower became ill with a fever and her family took her down to the hot springs seeking a cure. When Twin Feather returned from his hunting he heard of his love's illness and took the narrow and steep passageway down the canyon along what came to be known as the Indian Trail. He was in such a hurry that he took quite a few chances and short cuts and made a mistake in judgment, falling off a steep cliff, which cost him his life. Soon after, Dark Flower died of her fever bathing in the hot springs waters. The people moved their camp down the canyon for winter and the following spring as they were preparing to climb the trail up to their summer camp in the high mountain valley, they noticed the profile of Dark Flower at the top of the steep and narrow canyon walls. The following spring when they found Twin Feather's body and gave him a proper Shoshone burial, they again noticed that the profile of the canyon walls had changed slightly to include Twin Feather's profile as well. They rest together as silhouettes along the ridge as the sun comes up over them casting just a very few hours of sunlight down through the dark canyon.

This canyon was considered full of spirits long before any white men or women came through it. Winslow's Grove was the first camping, boating and picnicking spot, and then came the Idlewild, a resort restaurant and lodge before it became privately owned. The Idlewild is a miniature version of the old original lodge at Yellowstone National Park with antler staircases and stone foundations. If there are ghosts at the Idlewild no one would know it because it is tightly secured and carefully watched.

There was a long period of time between when it was a lodge, privately owned by two prominent families in the city of Ogden, and when it became a dance and restaurant place again. After this the Thiokol Corporation took it over and now uses it for company meetings and retreats.

Further down the canyon where the old Hermitage Resort's amusement park once stood, the rather new Alaskan Bed and Breakfast Inn has reported a few odd occurrences. At the peak of this resort's life, foreign dignitaries, some Senators and even a few Presidents traveled up first by carriage and then by train to this famous resort to vacation. A man named Billy Wilson had a family camp up the canyon and got the idea to build this huge resort in 1905. Tragedies associated with the hauntings are the deaths of two of his young children who drowned in the river, which ran by the sawmill he had built on the property before the resort took its place. The resort accommodated 600 guests and the amusement park down below it had a merry-go-round, outside bar around an old tree, camping and picnicking areas, boating, horseback riding, dance hall and tennis courts. When Billy Wilson died in 1918, the resort went through a series of owners and made the newspapers during the Prohibition era for having the biggest moonshine distillery operation in the county. On January 4, 1939, an explosion rocked the hotel in the middle of the night. No one was present when the huge fire started; it burned the resort to the ground, causing speculation that some sort of retribution might have been going on.

Guests and employees at the Alaskan know that their bed and breakfast is built over where the amusement park was and they say that a few guests have reported the presence of little children about, as it was a place where children looked forward to going all week long. There have been instances of lights going on and off when no one is around and a few phone calls being made from empty guest rooms. Fire alarms have gone off when no one was around and when they weren't supposed to, also doors have been observed opening or shutting right in front of a guest or employee. Although the activity is mild, it has been enough to intrigue a few ghost hunters to stop by and investigate the place.

The Ogden Canyon Resort at the mouth of the canyon was originally a very ornate Victorian structure that many know little about because it soon burned to the ground and was replaced by a second building called the Ogden Canyon Sanitarium built in 1904. By 1906, a local train company had extended its line to run directly to the resort. In 1919 a huge addition was built and it became the Ogden Canyon Natural Salt Mineral Springs with a café, dance hall and hotel. It burned down and was rebuilt entirely out of brick and opened in 1928 as the El Monte Springs resort. This resort had two outdoor swimming pools and one indoor. There were private mineral baths, a hotel, dining room, and a grand ballroom. It offered wrestling matches, gaming, marathon dances, nightclub entertainment and winter sports including a tobogganing hill, ski lessons, ice-skating, and a ski jumping hill. In 1932 the resort shut down and the Ogden city "cowboy" mayor purchased it and reopened it as The Rainbow Gardens. He really promoted it just as he did his city and got many famous entertainers to come to the resort both as guests and as performers in the 1940s and 50s.

Many changes have taken place over the years since this time as his family has continued to own the resort. The indoor pool became a sunken garden shop; the outdoor pools shut down; the porch where once tuberculosis patients gazed down at the river and where later resort guests dined is now a series of shops along with the grand ballroom. A bowling alley was added and then later became offices with Utah Book Nook booths in front of it in an area called the Planet Rainbow. Plans are in the works to make the bowling alley into another café to complement the fancy Greenery Restaurant that is now in the front of the building. What is most interesting though is the fact that the beginning of the Indian Trail is directly behind the building just above where the two old outdoor swimming pools and the mineral baths were once located in the hills above the resort. Many believe that Indian spirits visit this area from time to time as they walk up and down the old trail.

Ghost stories at the old resort involve the Indian Trail area and the bowling alley area which is just in front of and slightly to the west of where the old swimming pools were located. The old porch overlooking the river in the far-east area of the building has also been reported to be haunted, by visitors who feel an oppressive heaviness on their chests and find that they have difficulty breathing. Visitors and employees have reported this feeling out on the porch where once those tuberculosis patients were trying to breathe while rejuvenating themselves in the warm sunlight. When the pools were still in operation, more than one teenage group sneaking into the pools at night to go for a midnight swim, found themselves confronted with misty ghosts rising from the steamy baths behind them.

The resident ghosts however are located in the bowling alley where many visitors and employees have reported hearing the voices of several children speaking at once in some language that no one understands. Psychics visiting this area have had to leave the room because the feeling was so overpowering. One time the Rainbow managers hired a set of temporary employees to help with the inventory. None of these employees had ever been there before and had no previous experiences or knowledge of the resort. As they worked they heard little children's voices coming from the walls and went to their employers and asked them where these little children were, speaking in some foreign language. Many who work there assume that they are Indian children perhaps playing in an ancient camp by the hot springs while some of their parents bathe to cure their various ailments and aches and pains. Others think that they could be from a later era when so many children swam in the pools nearby, though no one seems to understand what the voices are saying.

The best ghost stories in the entire canyon however, belong to the Gray Cliff Lodge Restaurant. Thomas Duncombe Dee was a native of South Wales and was sixteen years old when his parents converted to Mormonism and came across the plains in 1860. His future wife, Annie Taylor, when only eight years old, traveled west across the plains with her family in the very same year. The Taylors and the Dees were distant relations. Annie and Thomas married in 1871. They lived in a two-room adobe house in the city of Ogden where Annie had their first four children. Mr. Dee used his carpentry and business skills to invest in several ventures, which soon made him a very wealthy man. They moved to an elegant home on Washington Boulevard in Ogden and Mrs. Dee had four more children there. Dee became a valued member of the Ogden community, serving in many city and civic capacities, while Annie Taylor Dee became very interested in health care. The Dees lost one of their sons at the age of twenty-one because there were no hospital facilities available and an emergency appendectomy failed when performed on the family dining room table. In 1905, her husband went to assess some water works and slipped and fell into the nearby river. He died of pneumonia at only sixty-one years of age.

Convinced that both her husband and her boy could have been saved with more adequate hospital facilities available, Annie Dee founded a hospital in 1910 with her daughter Maude Dee Porter as president and secretary of the Dee Memorial Hospital. In 1914, the hospital was in financial difficulties and was considering closing its doors, so Annie went to Apostle and future Prophet of the LDS Church, David O. McKay, and begged for help. Ownership of the hospital was transferred to the LDS Church and remained under its direction for the next sixty years. In the 1960s the old original hospital was demolished and fifteen blocks south of this the new McKay-Dee Hospital was constructed. What began as a 100-patient hospital is today the biggest and best in the city of Ogden.

Annie Taylor Dee built the family summer home in Ogden Canyon in 1912. The main dining room was originally the family gathering room. Three studio apartments on either side of this provided privacy for each of her six daughters and their families. The youngest son was single and had his own room upstairs next to his mother's quarters. The family used the summer residence as a way for caring for their mother and some say that Annie used it as a way of keeping the family together, although this was not always successful and some of the children quit visiting as they had in the early days. Grandchildren spent their summers on the long sleeping porch built especially for them and there is still a painting signed in 1917, hanging in the front entrance painted by a student at Weber State College as a way of paying for his keep.

The family continued to spend their summers there until 1932 when they sold the house to Ed Greenwell and his wife Toby. Toby was a good cook and Ed was a great entertainer, so while they lived in the center section of the house and rented the side apartments as a boarding house, they began to host special parties in the place. They would push all the furniture to the walls and host anniversary and other special events parties in the lodge. In 1945 they moved to a house next door to the lodge and opened the Gray Cliff as a restaurant. They put in the bar to the west of the building and it certainly has that forties or fifties flair to it, including an old jukebox. They sold the place in 1965 to Neal and Louis Sniggs, whose son and his wife run it today. They serve a Sunday Brunch as well as an evening meal which is excellent, opening their restaurant at 5:00 p.m. and running until 10:00 p.m. each evening during the week giving any ghosts in the place plenty of time to themselves.

Most people call the premier ghost at the restaurant, Mr. Spargo. Apparently he was the owner of Spargo Realty, which still exists down 12th Street where the canyon comes out into the city. Two stories are told of his demise, although I tend to believe the less romantic one. One story is that Spargo was either driving down the canyon after visiting the bar and restaurant or going up to do so, and was killed in a car accident. In the other version he died right in the restaurant of a heart attack after enjoying a good meal. In either case, he chose to stay where he had enjoyed himself, playing cards, drinking and relaxing with friends. A lifetime bachelor, rumor has it that the only woman he ever loved was murdered and he enjoyed listening to certain jukebox tunes, which reminded him of her. This story is further enhanced by what happened to the repair shop owner when the restaurant owners sent the jukebox to him to try and get it repaired so that it would play properly. No one had any sightings of Mr. Spargo in the bar or restaurant during this time and when the shop owner returned the jukebox he reported that he had had several unusual incidents while he had the jukebox stored in his shop. He had four false fire alarms go off when this had never happened before. Several times he couldn't get out of the front door of his shop even though he knew the door was unlocked. He said it was as if a force of some kind had wanted him to stay inside and get the thing fixed and returned as soon as possible. Once the jukebox was returned to the Gray Cliff, these incidents never happened again at the repair shop, and the sightings of Mr. Spargo returned to the Lodge.

People who work in the restaurant have figured out that Mr. Spargo loves music in general, because it isn't just the jukebox that he hangs around but also the old piano. One day during the winter months, the owner's son came in unexpectedly at about two in the afternoon through the back door, which was not the normal way that employees entered the restaurant. He heard piano music playing and went back to where the piano was to see if someone had broken in. Instead he stood face to face with Mr. Spargo who had a look on his face like "what are you doing here at this hour". When Spargo stood up and made eye contact with the son, Mr. Spargo simply walked away into nothingness. There have been many, many sightings of this full apparition and he is always described in the same manner, wearing what appears to be a fifties suit with a hat.

Another time, during the month of September, a slow time at the restaurant, a couple came in and waited patiently on the porch for a seat right by the fireplace. Once they were seated they mentioned that while they had waited on the porch they had seen a man sitting in the bar all alone. The waitress knew that no one could possibly be in the bar and a bus boy ran immediately to the room and there was no one there. The owners sat up alone late one night playing cards and relaxing in the restaurant when suddenly they saw a man walking out of the bar across from them and when they went over to investigate no one was there. Guests have reported seeing the apparition on several occasions and those of an intuitive nature have always described Mr. Spargo in the same clothes and with the same description. People who have never been there before and are not even from the area will come in and say such things as "Young lady, do you know you have a ghost here?," and then proceed to describe Spargo perfectly even though he can't be seen.

There have been several sightings of this solid full apparition ghost, and the employees say that the ghost also has several likes and dislikes. For example, he doesn't like men for some reason and prefers the ladies. If a male customer comes in and is loud and boisterous, especially about not believing in ghosts or making fun of such things, more often than not, a glass or two will fly off a shelf or cans will pop in the kitchen. People also sense Mr. Spargo or at least some presence watching them in the bathroom, which would make just about anyone uncomfortable. The dishes, cans and glasses lost over the years, amount to a sizable quantity. In fact, when I first heard about the restaurant, it was this story that everyone knew. It was famous for glasses especially, launching themselves off shelves and hurling themselves at particular individuals or just doing this for show. For decades this show had been the case at both the lodge and the restaurant where tomato cans in particular can explode or simply drop off the shelves in rows.

Psychics who have visited the place have found that there are at least two entities and many of the employees agree on this fact, though they don't agree on what the second entity is like. Intuitive people claim that these two forces work in tandem to freeze people to one spot, keeping them from leaving the place. However, long time employees at the restaurant say that they have a theory regarding who the second ghost is. She is not sighted as often but a very few times people have seen her more as a white light in the center room, though one waitress said that she actually saw the ghost floating a few feet from the ground and looking quite a bit like an angel with long blonde hair and a beautiful face and figure. I thought this ghost suspect until the theory or story was explained to me and then I too wondered if maybe this might be true.

It seems that a bus boy, who had worked there for several years, had met a young woman with whom he was very much in love. She was a beautiful and stunning young woman with natural long blonde hair past her waist and blues eyes and slim figure. They got married, and because he worked at the restaurant, they wanted to find a place to live nearby. Eventually he was able to rent the house directly in front of the restaurant to be close to his work. Soon they had two small children and were very happy. Only a few years into the marriage his beautiful wife was killed in a car accident near the dam farther up the canyon and her husband, deeply grieving, quit his job at the restaurant and moved away. Employees at the restaurant believe that this is the explanation for their second ghost. They believe that the man's wife returns to where she had been so happy and that she not only visits his work but gazes adoringly at the house where their family lived together. However, no one has reported any activity in the home across the way. Perhaps it is just more romantic for her to be where many people gather of an evening for a good meal and pleasant conversation. Or perhaps as some believe, where there is already activity of a ghostly nature, a portal forms where more such activity can follow.

On the several occasions when I have visited, nothing has happened inside the place but plenty has happened as I view in my mind what seem to be still pictures from the past taken from outside the Lodge. I have seen people playing billiards or pool inside the bar area and a young blonde woman dressed in twenties or thirties style clothing leaning against a non-existent porch rail outside of this bar in the front. I have also seen a lone man sitting at the bar but only in my mind's eye. These mind's eye pictures appear to be all a jumble, as they are from different layers of the history of the house, although I too could see a man coming down from upstairs, which I assumed was the youngest son of the Dees or perhaps a later lodger. I felt, however, that all I saw was warm and loving, a family portrait of the house as it once was when the original family stayed there. Perhaps a later layer over this exists of those who visited the bar or were lodgers in the place.

I wonder now if perhaps I was seeing a daughter or granddaughter of Annie Dee or Mr. Spargo's girlfriend who might have visited the place with him, at least in "spirit." The house has not only the two entities described, but also residue of many former decades and residents within it. Most touching to me is the thought that both ghosts have a love story or at least what might be called a tragic lost love. One is about an older man remembering the one love of his life and pining away for her by listening to jukebox tunes and or playing old piano pieces. The other is a more tangible story of a young man who lost his beautiful wife due to a tragedy in the canyon. Even if none of these ghost stories are real, enough people have had enough sightings or what they think were sightings, to make a visit to the Gray Cliff an interesting one.

The last time we were there, a gentleman who felt that he was not getting quite enough attention and certainly challenging the house ghost with his boisterous nature, managed to get out of the restaurant without a glass hurtling or two. As he and his wife passed our table after an evening of ghost talk on our part, he said, "The 'Ghost and Mrs. Muir' bid you adieu." The best part about this was that he actually knew what that movie was and perhaps had even seen it. Most people nowadays have never even heard of this film, nor would they make the connection to the ghost of the Gray Cliff Lodge, whose very name proclaims a place of a romantic nature and two love stories instead of only one.

- CHAPTER THREE -

UTAH'S HAUNTED HOSPITALS, CHURCHES & MEETING PLACES

UTAH VETERANS' HOSPITAL

STATE HOSPITAL CHILDREN'S PSYCHIATRIC WARD
SALT LAKE CITY

In 1930, the state of Utah made a plea for a Veteran's hospital in Salt Lake City to provide a place for war veterans to go for medical and psychiatric help as well as to help relieve the unemployment problems during the Great Depression by putting men to work on such projects. The United States government allocated $400,000 for this public works project and $18,000 was spent to purchase two blocks of land in the avenues. The style decided on was similar to a Victorian mansion and it was the style for most VA hospitals being built at the time. Several other smaller structures were built around the grounds though only one such structure is still standing today, possibly a garage or maintenance building. The building was dedicated on the morning of Independence Day 1932 by Governor George H. Dern. Oliver J. Hunter, a World War I veteran, was the first patient admitted to the facility the very next day. For 30 years, veterans from the Spanish-American War, two world wars and the Korean "police action" received treatment and care there.

In 1960, plans were announced for the building of a research facility at what would be called the Fort Douglas Hospital. The problem was discussed regarding the difficulty and expense of having then to run two separate VA hospitals. The new facility was to be a $200,000 research building that would accommodate medical and surgical research laboratories. The military decided that it would be quite inefficient to operate two separate facilities, and that they would save roughly $100,000 a year by consolidating the two hospitals. In February of 1962, the patients were moved to the new facility. At that time only 130 medical and surgical patients had to be moved from the old VA hospital because the sudden drop in tuberculosis patients, which was a hospital specialty, had decreased the number of patients there dramatically. Also, most of the psychiatric patients had already been moved to a new psychiatric facility in California. The old hospital continued to house laboratories and various research facilities in conjunction with the new VA hospital for about a year after the move.

In July of the following year, the old Veterans' hospital was turned over to the General Services Administration for disposal. The GSA officially declared it surplus in July of 1963, although it was still occupied by experimental laboratories run by the Salt Lake City Health Department which had leased the building in April of 1962. After a year of discussing possible Federal uses, the buildings and grounds were on the auction block. Several groups were interested in acquiring these 27 acres at the time. First, the Salt Lake City health department discussed purchasing it but then decided that it was an inconvenient location and too expensive for them. Then the University of Utah wanted it for research space because at the time the University was using old World War II surplus buildings on campus and the old Veterans' Hospital was still a sturdy and nice looking building. None of these or a dozen other proposals were finalized.

The Utah Public Welfare Commission finally obtained the building. The commissioners proposed to use it for several things: to house the staff of the Second District Juvenile Court, as office space for 60 employees of the commission, to provide quarters for 140 employees of the Salt Lake County Welfare Department, plus a few other state agencies and also for a division of the Utah State Hospital with a special section for children. The State Welfare Department occupied the old Veteran's Hospital for many years; I can remember going there in the early eighties to visit students of mine in the psychiatric facility when I worked at Developmental Disabilities (DDI), a preschool for children with all sorts of handicaps and problems which drew its population from the entire valley. One of my fellow teachers from DDI who continued to work for there, says that she was still making visits to the State Hospital's children's section in the mid 80s. Sometime during this period, the facility was purchased by the LDS church and became the Brigham Young University Extension School.

Before discussing the 'fight" in 1978, I need to pause and explain the difference between the old Primary Children's Hospital and the old VA Hospital. Many people, even today, confuse the two and their locations. One reason is that they were located so closely together. The other reason for the confusion may be attributed to the rather typical, historical and yet very subtle 'feud" between the LDS church and the State as represented by the military "occupation" years and years ago. In the beginning it was not subtle at all, but nowadays remnants of these harsh feelings seem to linger on the part of a few citizens, in the form of ignoring any military presence in Utah. These two buildings may still be symbolic of this whole rivalry. Both hospitals were located on 12th Avenue only a few blocks apart with Primary Children's a little to the west of the VA hospital. I remember spending a great deal of time there when our little charges grew ill and sometimes had to make multiple hospital teaching or testing visits or just visits when the family needed someone to hold their hands. It was a huge building which is entirely gone; the area is now covered by new houses.

Primary Children's Hospital housed patients for 38 years; it was built in 1952 after having been housed in a home on North Temple since 1922. When funds were needed to build the new hospital by the Primary Association of the LDS Church, 120,158 red bricks were purchased by children all over the state for 10 or 20 cents each. One thousand children helped build the hospital and the corner stone was moved to the new Primary Children's Hospital when it was completed next to the University of Utah Hospital in 1990. The old building was completely demolished and it is still somewhat a mystery that in the tiny park dedicated to both hospitals in front of the old VA hospital, there is a second corner stone of the Primary Children's Hospital. Perhaps it was moved again or the reporter telling this story was mistaken or there are two corner stones, one in each place? Maybe it is a replica or not a cornerstone at all? Upon reading the two plaques a visitor can be confused as to which hospital was which. A tourist to the area would be even more confused if trying to locate the place.

In 1978, several articles appeared in the local newspaper illustrating the great debate over whether to make the old VA hospital a national historic site. The LDS church, which by now owned the building and grounds, was opposed to making it an historic site. Brigham Young University Extension School was holding classes there at the time but had decided to move to a more convenient location and the church had the building and grounds up for sale. Becoming an historic site would ruin most chances at a big sale by LDS leaders. The old Salt Lake Theatre comes to mind here, with the telephone company getting the property from the Church and razing the entire building, but not without a fight from the Daughters of the Utah Pioneers. This time it was the Utah State Historical Society and the LDS church which squared off. Perhaps there was just a little of that "revenge is sweet" involved after the early pioneers had had to watch the military overseeing and occupying a location in their town. In the end it was probably just a plain and simple need for money and priorities that dominated this fight.

The Church's attorney requested a hearing to fight the proposal in which he stated that the site had no historic value, that it was an undistinguished example of many early 20th century Veterans Administration Hospitals and was less than 50 years old. The City Commission voted with the LDS Church, though it was recommended that a study take place to determine if the building might be eligible for the National Register of Historic Sites sometime in the future, if the property's new owners were to ask for inclusion on the register. Obviously this never took place, as the old VA Hospital is now surrounded by very exclusive and expensive homes, although they are built in a style to resemble the hospital. Perhaps this feature is due to a building code or just something that the particular building companies conceived as an attractive alternative. There is a rumor that the builders at one time intended to turn the buildings into condominiums. People are still living in apartments in one part of the structures, but the building is run down and sadly in need of major repairs. It is ironic to see it sitting there on the hill in this very fancy area, like a huge ghetto that is supposed to be the area's focal point.

At least someone still owns the place and is using it which is a thin protection from being demolished. When I talked to neighbors around the place, asking them if it was haunted, they looked at me strangely and said they had moved there from out of town and knew nothing about the place. A few began telling me a few of the usual ghost stories like lights going on and off when no one was there, children laughing, and screams in the middle of the night. With it being occupied however, all of these things may be explainable. A group interested in the building must have bought the lot right in front of the hospital, because it has been turned into a little park with lawn, a flagpole and little red brick stairs leading up to it on either side. A single sidewalk leads up the hill and then is fenced off completely around the whole structure, probably to protect it from vandals. Perhaps the added features have been funded by a few of those who lost the fight back in 1978 to make it an historic site. Or maybe some concerned citizens in their zeal to tell about both of the hospitals forgot to place a plaque telling the interesting history of the VA Hospital. The Primary Children's plaque is quite interesting but information about the hospital on it seems to be rather thin. Still, the memorial does show some concern about the future welfare of this grand old building.

A final note might be that while I was sitting in this tiny alcove of grass and flowers, listening to the slight breeze stirring the flag and its ropes against the pole, I was getting rather strong impressions of the building and its former occupants. My first thought was that the condominiums may never be built, for the feeling of the land itself is curious. There is an overwhelming sadness which engulfs it and permeates the land around. It housed not only the anger, guilt, psychological and physical pain of several generations of young men sent off to war, but also carries the mental and emotional anguish of many juveniles and young children who passed through its doors to dwell there for months at a time. Such a place would somehow knock at the doors of its tenants like the waves of a dark sea, though most of the occupants would never know why they were feeling what they were feeling or perhaps not understand what might be caused by other more present and living things. It is a general "static" that tells one that the building is still occupied by its own memories. The roar of it increases as one tunes in, indicating its magnitude and force, while the duration tells one just how long the noise will go on. As I sat there, the sound was continuous and increased until I no longer paid attention because I wanted to focus on individuals in the building. But it is the land itself which will not allow occupation. If developers do renovate and build condominiums, even on empty land, owners should be prepared for some ghostly difficulties.

As I sat down to write my notes, now concentrating on the voices and images that I was receiving, I was overcome with a feeling so strong that my eyes began to tear up and could not stop this terrible depression for several minutes. Such suffering came from this place that it seemed overwhelming. There have been times in my various travels to historic places where I was taken by surprise because I did not know the exact history of the place or a certain location before I arrived. For example, one would expect such feelings of suffering and death at the site of the Gettysburg battlegrounds and I certainly had them, but not upon entering what appeared to be an old bank building and then finding out much later that the building was used as a hospital for many years. So I am not always forewarned about a building and am sometimes taken by surprise, though I am never prone to dramatics when this does happen.

I asked about active spots in the old VA building and was told that the third floor on the west end where the old children's unit was located, the east side of the basement floor, and the garage or maintenance building behind the hospital were the most active. A maintenance man seemed to occupy this building occasionally, while in the main building these particular pictures came to me: one little boy and two little girls doing trickster stuff in the building, and five veterans still lingering there, one of whom was a burn victim who had died a terrible death. The sadness, oppressiveness and loneliness of those who had stayed there long term were also overwhelming. These were the few men who did not recover and were hidden away, living their lives in isolation and loneliness, the war having either physically or more likely emotionally stilled them in time forever.

There were three good buddies who now traveled about the hospital together doing various pranks as they had when they were there to boost the morale of others. Their spirits were possibly still alive somewhere else but a part of them had remained in the building. The most prominent image contained the written words "Angel of Mercy". This was a woman in a white uniform, white hat and long white cotton veil down the back of it, sort of like what nurses wore in World War I or perhaps what nuns and Red Cross volunteers wore then, though the building was built in 1930. Someone may be able to set me straight on this because in the 30s and 40s, somebody may have worn this type of outfit and the angel of mercy phrase refers to an order or group of people? This person was all in white and had apparently dedicated her life to this hospital and is still to this day making her rounds there. Her footsteps can be heard as she visits patients no longer there. She opens and shuts doors, and she sometimes raffles doorknobs to make sure things are locked up tight and secure. She was a haven of light among those miserable in spirit and can be heard running to a patient who has cried out in the night. Maybe she only worked at night, but she was there when someone was in great pain and walked the halls, spreading her mercy and love to those less likely to receive it. Apparently even her light can be seen upon occasion in the wards. She was definitely unafraid of hugging anyone, no matter how terrible the disease or how violent the patient.

By the end of these visions I was shaking and tears rolled down my cheeks and my friend was concerned about me. The bane of the intuitive is the disbelief which would have made many chuckle at my supposed "performance." However, no one was filming me, no one had told me a thing about what to expect ahead of time, and no one was prompting me to feel what I felt. Nor can I confirm any of what I experienced that afternoon. I will take the chance that many intuitives do and be a target for anyone's disbelief, for I felt what I felt, saw what I saw and don't, at my age, have the least bit of worry about being considered balmy. I just feel sorry for those who cannot see or hear or at least be attuned to the music playing in our heads when we listen for its melodies. One theme throughout my visions was the phrase: "You want to hug them but you cannot. They call out for hugs in the night but you cannot give them." Either the nature of their illnesses denied them touch or their emotional traumas hid this ability. I got the impression that those who came for short term illnesses or rehabilitations never came back. By the 40s, the Bushnell Hospital in Brigham City had been built and all of the rehab patients went there. A few, a very few stayed long term, and it was my impression that some from the Spanish-American War onward, lived their entire lives there, hidden away until the hospital shut down. Some of them did not want to let their families know that they were still alive due to the horrendous nature of their physical or mental injuries. Those who remained in a coma long term were lost to their families anyway. They are the ones there now. Their breathing, child-like sounds, and cries in the night, can still be heard.

It is also said that when the old Primary Children's Hospital shut down and was awaiting demolishment, little children could be heard crying out in the night in different parts of the empty building. Making an old hospital, especially a veteran's hospital, into condominiums seems much more unbelievable. Layers of what went on there still exist, from the land itself to the various souls who passed through its doors over the years. Then there are the little children who left a lot of various energies behind them, as well as a spirit or two, from the psychiatric unit. One can remember all those little, silent abuses from their own family members or maybe an employee or two, as well as the juveniles who visited. The little multi-handicapped ones who were taught there weekly cannot be forgotten. All this residue still hangs on, along with the experimental laboratories where animals were tortured in the days before animal activists were bringing such things to light and before an awareness of these experiments changed things. The military is historically notorious for occasionally experimenting on its own men with drugs which have been newly discovered and certainly not analyzed enough, actually causing illnesses under the guise of protecting troops. Don't forget that animals can haunt a place too.

If such things seem too far-fetched, visit our VA Hospital today. You will be taken on a prearranged tour through the parts that they want you to see, and told how wonderful their facilities are, which they are. You will never see the places where the permanent residents are locked up or hidden away. Guys who would rather that their parents don't know about them and men who don't remember their former lives at all. Older or younger, they are the patients who must reside in their own memories in a time or place where the most tragic or most startling events of their entire lives happened to them. They are the forgotten ones, with few visitors, but a lot of stories to tell. Living in their memories and stilled in time by whatever war which maimed them; every year when I deliver Ann Lander's idea of taking Valentines To Veterans from my students, I sit down and listen to a few on my own.

Most importantly, I understand that some neglected places might be angry, and that this old Veteran's building is one of them. It will not stop being angry until the misrepresentations stop. It does have a history of its own to tell and a prevailing sadness that should not be forgotten. It would be best to stop a few minutes there and pay your respects to those who passed through or even lived there and who might have left their memories and even a part of who they were behind them. They are the men and women who in one way or another stood in our place on the battle lines. They fought for whatever they were told to fight for, from our very freedom to some obscure and obtuse reason that perhaps made no sense to them or anyone else for that matter. No matter the reason, they stood where we might have had to stand, and that is the real issue.

Someone once said that we are all responsible for war, even those of us who protest against such conflicts. We should never blame the warriors for the war in which they fought, but instead, treat them as our own brothers and sisters. All of us, every single one of us, must take responsibility for what happens everywhere in the world. For we all contribute whether we wish to or not, simply by being here. Perhaps by staying a few minutes in this little plot of grass, or really anywhere that monuments have been built to honor the fallen, this will help to quiet their spirits for a while. Even the hand of God drew its line around this place, when an unexpected city tornado wound its way up into the Avenues and then was gone. The storm focused our attention not only on an old Veteran's Hospital, but a beloved veteran's park as well, because no trees were left standing to obscure our vision.

BUSHNELL VA HOSPITAL

INTERMOUNTAIN INDIAN SCHOOL

THE EAGLE VILLAGE - TORN DOWN

Bushnell Hospital was the first and largest war installation in Utah's history. It was built on the south end of Brigham City right below the road which one must travel to go through the mountains to Logan. Several locations were considered in 1941 but Brigham City was selected for the 1,500 bed U. S. Army Hospital. The United States War Department acquired 235 acres of land east of Main Street and south of 7,000 South. The hospital was named after Colonel George E. Bushnell who had been commissioned to the U. S. Army Medical Corps in 1881 and served until 1919. He was known for his specialist work with tuberculosis patients and was a special consultant to the U. S. Surgeon General in World War I. On March 1, 1942, the hospital opened and the first patients were admitted October 10th of that year. There were 60 buildings on the grounds and the facility could handle 3,000 patients if need be for both neurosurgical and neuropsychiatric needs. Each war era hospital became specialized for something and Bushnell became the hospital for plastic and maxillofacial surgery, neurosurgery, an amputation center, penicillin therapy, a neuropsychiatric center, and tropical diseases and malaria therapy and investigation. It also served the basic medical needs for soldiers from Utah, Arizona, Idaho, Montana and Nevada.

There was a full time staff to operate a brace or artificial limb shop and Harry S. Truman visited Bushnell in April of 1945 just before the death of Franklin D. Roosevelt. The hospital offered vocational and recreational therapy with such classes as photography, needle work, a metal work shop, and mechanics shop. It also offered dances, movies, baseball games played by both patients and staff, a swimming pool and field trips to points of interest locally. Many film stars and other celebrities visited the patients there and amputees were taught to ski at nearby Snow Basin. Brigham City was the first city to provide accommodations for the handicapped on city streets and in buildings and both the Peace City Apartments and the Bushnell Motel were built to house visiting relatives and family. People opened their homes to visitors and restaurants offered free steak dinners to amputees. Townspeople also provided private transportation and overnight stays in their own homes to visitors coming and going as housing and transportation were limited. Brigham City's economy was affected in many ways by the new hospital, providing hundreds of new jobs for cooks, construction workers and hospital personnel.

German and Italian prisoners of war were both treated in the hospital and also worked as hospital aides as well under the close supervision of American soldiers. German prisoners also worked for farmers around the county on work details and some prisoners of war and Americans became friends. The hospital served over 13,000 patients during its 4 years of operation which ended after the war was over.

In 1943, Bishop Duane G. Hunt of the Catholic diocese established St. Henry's Mission at Brigham City where Bushnell Army Hospital had been constructed during early W.W.11. There were 60 Catholics in 6,000 people in Brigham City at the time. The hospital officially closed in 1946 and by the 1950s the huge facility had reopened as the Intermountain Indian school. In 1950 Bishop Hunt raised St.Henry's to the status of a parish and transferred Box Elder County to the jurisdiction of the new parish, though services were still available to the students who attended the residential facility from all over the region. The LDS church also provided services and had been instrumental in getting the Indian school opened because of beliefs at the time, of providing better homes and families to these children away from their own families on the various reservations. The LDS church has a belief that the Indian peoples are the descendants the Lost Tribes of Israel and therefore of great importance to church doctrine and spirituality. Stories told in Indian lore and passed down through the generations seem to many to match the same stories told in Mormon church history and doctrines. The LDS church had a program in which families would adopt an Indian child just for the winter months while the child attended school and then the child would return home to his or her family each summer.

Brigham City had been assured that the hospital would run for many years after the war but this did not happen and the campus of the Bushnell facility became a huge albatross for which nobody had any plans for use. In 1949, a proposal was made to turn the campus into a boarding school for Navajo boys and girls; at that time, LDS

President George Albert Smith took a personal interest in "improving the lot of the Indians." A meeting was held at the Box Elder LDS Tabernacle, but the president was very ill and would not be attending. Halfway through the meeting he appeared anyway and spoke eloquently and powerfully about the plight of the Indian people. He then made a promise to the people of Brigham City that they would be especially protected by the Lord and greatly blessed and prosper upon completing this Indian project. The boarding school opened in 1950.

A seminary and chapel were built across the street from the school and by the 1970s the school had become an intertribal high school only. This caused many tensions among the various tribes who lived and attended school there. The Native American Nationalist Movement had begun across the whole United States with tragic incidents at both Wounded Knee and Alcatraz only a few years before. The Native American leaders demanded that the United States government abolish Indian boarding schools and that the government had no right to take Native American children away from their homes seeking to purge them of their rightful cultural knowledge and ancestors. The mounting publicity and violence managed to close down all of these schools around the country and the Intermountain Tribal School shut down in 1984. The buildings stood idle for some time until the Bureau of Indian Affairs sold the property to the Brigham City Corporation, who then made various agreements with private developers.

Some buildings are now single family dwellings, others are condominiums and townhouses, and still others are being converted into office buildings, while some have been demolished. According to an article in The Salt Lake Tribune published February 2, 1999, this massive urban-redevelopment project was moving ahead with a seven year plan. Eighteen of the buildings were to be demolished and 19 of them would have been be totally remodeled to make nearly 1,000 townhouses, apartments and detached homes. There will still be stores, flats, a senior citizens center and affordable homes and the whole complex will probably still be called Eagle Village, though all the buildings will now be built from scratch. Right now there are several families living in the village since the time when, abandoned and deserted, the Indian school had fallen prey to vandals and those who cavorted in the halls breaking windows and the like. These families say that they love it and thus far no such nonsense as ghosts from the past have bothered them. But with converted barracks and hospital wings, it is difficult to believe that all will be quiet there even when the buildings themselves are gone. The developers of these new structures want no part of this ghostly talk because they want the city to catch the vision of what is being done. At one time they talked of citizens who kept thinking of the place as an albatross and how they would be the model for other places to turn old buildings into new ones. Then they just found it too expensive to remodel the buildings and changed their tune. It was easier to just tear them all down and build brand new low cost housing, especially financially.

I have always been fascinated by this particular place. When we lived in Logan the first time, we would drive by and see the high school kids all over the grounds of this huge place; and when I lived there the second time as an adult, I would drive by and was very intrigued by the skeletal remains of the place sifting there so silent and empty, with echoes of which I then had no understanding. I never knew it had originally been a hospital and I read many an article about World War II at the State

Historical Society of the men who had stayed in its wards during the war. There was very little about the boarding school, although I am sure that somewhere more can be found. But I don't feel that I need to investigate further, having had many Indian friends at Utah State from the area. White fellow employees who had grown up in Brigham City also had many stories to tell. My husband is part Northern Cheyenne and so we attended many pow-wows in our younger days and saw a few basketball games on the Fort Hall Indian Reservation.

For me and my husband, the idea of taking Indian children from their own families is neither a comforting nor insightful solution to anything. I suppose that in those days my intuition was feeling two layers on that land, both the suffering soldiers and then the young Indian men and women either filled with a contained anger or a hidden embarrassment for their own past and cultural heritage. I have seen both in my years of teaching resource and certainly heard all the Mormon stories about seeing Laminite spirits on the land as echoes of their own and another people's past. Now Indian children do not live with LDS families for the program has been discontinued. The Mormon church is now culturally diverse and needs to be so because many new members from other countries or cultures are joining the church. This is a positive step, for diversity breeds understanding and cultural knowledge breeds informed solutions to very old misunderstandings.

As for me, the buildings stood silent, screaming out at me in so many ways that I was haunted by the sounds and images every time I simply passed the place. It was like the skeletal remains of an ancient city where events and people had left their imprints on its walls and within its heart. I could catch only pieces of these things as I passed by, not wanting to do more because the sea of emotions was just too overpowering. Now, I stand by and within these old buildings filled with new people and new stories, I can still hear the echoes of what went on before. The stronger of the two is the boarding school where horrors happened that no one talks about, or perhaps are even known by the immediate community. These stories can be told only in bits and pieces which make very little sense. This phenomenon is why most psychics are not very successful in helping detectives solve specific crimes because nothing is ever whole or accurate enough to really help. Sometimes the information can be enough so that policemen and detectives can take off on new leads and find real evidence. I can only tell what I felt, what I saw, and especially in this case, what I heard at the old hospital and school years ago, and what I can still hear to this day as I stand in the place and listen.

From the time Eagle Village began to emerge and while the place stood abandoned for several years from the end of the war until 1952, people I have talked to who grew up in the area say that they came to call it "The Homeless Capitol of the World." As many as 16 residents were found at any one time whenever the police swept through the area making these homeless vagrants vacate the various buildings. Local people also talk about the prejudice that existed in the town between their own kids and the Indian children. Apparently in many situations things were quite good, but there were always those situations where relations between students at the school and students at the local high school turned sour. There were also incidents with adults in town who owned shops and businesses that the Indian kids frequented.

Recently there was a newspaper article on Navajo Mountain, a sacred place to the Navajo. The mountain lies about 20 miles from Lake Powell and is even less distant from Rainbow Bridge National Monument, where a little community exists very near the mountain. Navajo hogans are scattered and isolated from each other, along with a government housing project in the area. The nearest grocery store is 27 miles away. There is a 40-student Navajo Mountain High School and a 140-student elementary school called the Naa Tsi Aan school, both run by the Navajos themselves. Although the schools are both modest structures they are talked about with pride and the fact that Indian boarding schools are now a thing of the past. There are many who remember the boarding schools where children were taken away from their parents for nine months out of the year and where military discipline was the rule, with required short haircuts, drills and rigid ceremonies and English as the only language allowed. If the students used their native tongue their mouths were washed out with soap. Adults watched their children change with the introduction of television and computer games and all the rest that replaced respected traditions. Their children brought new unwanted things home with them including gang membership, drugs and drinking.

Tribal leaders still fight for things in education on the reservation to this day. They work hard getting schools repaired quickly enough so that a broken window doesn't remain open for two weeks in sub zero weather with students inside, or finding a way to get more high school students home at night instead of having to stay in the dorms during the week because of long travel distances. A four day school week has been discussed and the students are taught the Navajo language, stories and traditions, as well as the regular curriculum requirements. Recent grants to Indian schools from the BIA, across the nation, have offered continued funds while letting a community-elected board run their own schools. Two years ago these two little schools became part of this grant. A successful lawsuit against the San Juan County School District allowed the building of a high school on the reservation, so that many of the students could return home at night during the week. Things are as they should be according to Indian families, and not as they were when children were taken from them and forced to live clear across the state for the better part of each year during the school year. The albatross that is the Intermountain Boarding School's skeletal remains is slowly being swallowed up by the White man's progress and will some day be completely forgotten, at least by those who live on or near it.

My husband and I were both overwhelmed by an oppressive dark sea of emotions and an all encompassing and pervasive sadness when we first saw the school. Perhaps my husband's intuitiveness comes from his Northern Cheyenne great-grandmother or his experiences on the Vietnam battlefield or in hospitals with men wounded in war, for this was one place where he felt just as much as I did and wandered through the abandoned buildings hearing and feeling things from both layers of history. I had told him nothing of the place's history and the only thing he knew was about the old Indian school and nothing about the hospital that came before it. He stepped into one building and heard in the far distance, and yet louder than the pigeons who roost there, men moaning from pain. When I told him about it being an amputee hospital among other things, he talked of how during Vietnam it was called debredment of the wound, while he and the other hospital corpsmen nicknamed it the "stumping" of the wound. They would clean and dress a wound, give the man some morphine which would wear off in about an hour and a half and then the man would moan and cry until the pain stopped. He was once in a room full of such cases. It surprised him because I had not told him what kind of hospital the Bushnell hospital was, and he was expecting to get flashes of things about the Indian children who stayed there. He said later, that he could not figure out why little children or even older ones would all be moaning in pain in a dormitory. I said the word amputee and then he understood. Both of us felt that there were still very powerful and strong spirits on the land at Bushnell and that they will not leave no matter what becomes of the buildings.

Intuitive flashes included the following: some of the students who were schooled there experienced apparitions of amputees from World War II. A whole layer of pain and suffering both mental anguish and physical continues to remain from that time period. Students saw and felt such experiences in various buildings. Walking through some of the dorms was extremely negative and sad and even the buildings themselves looked like giant skeletal remains. Although it was bright and sunny and positive when the soldiers entered the hospital, many of them left residuals from their emotional traumas behind them. One man haunted a particular dorm from World War II and I was told that I needed a map of the area to entirely understand what I was seeing. The entire place made my husband angry, recalling his own PTSD from Vietnam and feeling sensations both from the patients and the Indian youth was just too much for him. He said, "You were right. I was expecting to feel things about the Indian children, but instead, I felt things about the men who were brought here from all over the nation." He told me a story soon afterwards about his father, who drove a tank during World War II, and how his superior officer had ordered him to go up to the top floor of a building which he had been ordered to fire upon, and showed him a room full of 8 to 14 year olds being trained for the SS, all dead. My husband said, "Now why did that man have to do that? Wasn't it enough that my father had to help liberate Dachau? Did he have to see what his guns had done?"

As I walked though I felt little hands touching me on the legs and back. I heard voices, snatches of phrases from little children, the younger elementary ones I guess, the ones to whom I would naturally be drawn. We thought of it as a beautified concentration camp with people operating it who had no idea that separating children from their families and heritages might not be the right thing to do. There was a barrenness to the place. I did not respond to individual stories or faces, but rather felt the entire weight on my shoulders and chest. I felt that I would have dreams later, that they would come to me when ready, and that I would remember these dreams vividly. My visions would not be of the hospital, but of the many years after when Indian children and teens populated the place leaving sights and sounds and impressions of imprintings behind them. I also felt the weirdness of the covered-over apartment complexes. Although I knew that the buildings had been completely renovated from the inside out, it still felt as though the developers had simply dropped a shell over the top of the dorm to hide its previous history. My perceptions reminded me of an old Disney film where a giant paintbrush swept its way across the old and made it bright, colorful and beautiful, where once darkness prevailed.

Usually the old is just gone and only the ground speaks of what came before. But here, unlike the old Veteran's Hospital in Salt Lake City where the renovation into condos has never happened, this place was actually in the process of moving from the old to the new. One actually got the opportunity to see the changes as they occurred, and could walk right between the new and the old. It was eerie and creepy and amazing, all at the same time. There is a center for the Spanish speaking, a preschool for little children at the north end, and various merchants' shops which are located at the south end. In addition there is the Eagle Village real estate office and construction company workers renovating the next dormitory. Tenants enjoy their beautiful new apartments of every hue and color; some residents perhaps having even gone there years ago as students. Pigeons being pushed further south or north into the center of the complex, and are still roosting there, waiting until the time when they will have to leave altogether. The Bushnell hotel, remains as a single monument to the four years that the hospital stood on those grounds. It was all very strange and bizarre and haunting.

The whole scene reminded me of being in Kanab at my great grandmother's boarding house and literally arguing with the new owners who have been working on the place for 11 years now, that yes indeed there was a second giant house right next door to their house at one time. I thought, am I going crazy? We remembered the long talk we had had with the old man next door who lived in this big house and hearing him tell us how he had placed a board across from his second floor window to the old man's house next door. Only both had been little boys then and best friends and had crawled across both ways to visit each other. The new owners were absolutely sure that no house had ever been next door, and it was then that I remembered that it had been about 30 years since this experience. Another 14 years had passed since my husband and I had visited the place, and he confirmed that he remembered the ruins of the house next door still lying on the ground. I thought of all those baskets of old photos I had once come across in a store in Cripple Creek, Colorado. When I asked the woman where they had come from, she said that there had been an entire warehouse of photos which different stores had bought for sale as part of their merchandise. Thousands and thousands of pictures of people that nobody knew anything about, were now for sale for a dime or a quarter apiece. The story of the pictures is somewhat like the old man and his house, or like the old dorms and buildings at Brigham City that will soon be gone or replaced by something to wipe out their memory.

But there was a major difference. The old house in Kanab was not a blight on the land like the buildings in Brigham City, a place where men lost a part of their physical and spiritual selves after a war which had purpose, but was still a war. The old hospital and Indian school had provided places where townspeople worked and did their part and were proud of it. Also it was a place where the government of our nation made a decision that the previous owners of this land needed to be taught our ways. BIA officials determined that Indian children would be taken away from their families for the winter months each year and taught the white man's ways. Government officials called such proceedings an education, and for some it probably was. But the school also saw both good and bad things happen to the student children, and this decision, good or bad, took place anyway. Then a time came when philosophies changed and many people knew that what had been done was wrong, while others never did understand what was happening. Then came a brief time when the homeless and downtrodden lived within its walls, seeing their own apparitions and sights or hearing their own sounds. Finally, the covering over of the past to make way for the present produces a future, where those who will live there will argue that nothing ever happened worth remembering. The conveniences of a selective history or a selective memory tend to hide what was very probably a poor decision on the part of many.

After trying to renovate a couple of the dormitories at the old Indian school in Brigham City, it has now been announced that most of the buildings will be demolished and brand new low-cost housing will be built on the property. The 90-acre area has become a real problem to its new owner who is going to start from scratch according to the latest reports. The Cape Advisors, a New York based company who bought the campus in the early 1990s want to transform Eagle Village into a mix of single family homes, townhouses, apartments and shops. All that will remain of the old original campus will be two buildings which have already been converted into townhouses. The project will stand out as a symbol of "new urbanism" says the owner because of its use of high densities and wise land use to provide homes for average wage earners. The decision was made because developers lost money on the first two dorms that were converted. While developers say they hate to see the old buildings go, the mayor of Brigham City says he is glad the eyesore will disappear. He reported that he had only one resident call him concerning the demolition.

In March, when the demolition began, some people did indeed come out of the woodwork in some rather strange ways. "With Memories Painful and Sweet, Indian School, Heads for Demolition." - the first thing that appeared was this article by Kristen Moulton in the *Salt Lake Tribune*, for which several people who had taught there or gone to school there were interviewed and this brought the whole issue to the attention of the public. It was amazing just how much was to be made of this "old eyesore" the city wanted to eliminate. Rose Curley, a Cherokee from North Carolina had taught there, along with her Navajo husband, for over 20 years and was very sad that the history-rich buildings were to be torn down. She talked of the first bus load of students to arrive at the school in the predawn hours of a January day in 1953. Thirteen hundred students arrived that day having been plucked from their hogans and towns in Arizona and New Mexico; some would continue to live there in the winter months for as long as eight years. They ranged in age from 12-18 and brought what they had in cardboard boxes. They spoke no English and yet by the time they graduated, Navajos, Utes, Seminoles and Sioux children spoke English, had a trade and an education.

The peak enrollment reached 2,300 and like any sudden mixing of so many different cultures, the relationships between the townspeople and the students was a mixed bag of both good and bad. One store owner would not allow Indian students in his store and there was another incident in which the superintendent of the school sent his son to see if the ushers at a local theater were indeed making his students sit at the back of the theater. On the other hand there were many shoplifting incidences and shop owners took to hiding their glue and paint behind the counters because students would come into the stores and try to sniff them to get high from the fumes. I suspect that just as many white students were doing this too. They dealt with runaways all the time, students who wanted to return home to the reservations or their homes in other towns. Many town citizens did however heed their LDS Church President and did the best they could in hiring students from the school for part time jobs. Former students interviewed had fond memories as well as bad ones, such as having the luxury of an indoor pool and seeing more water in one place than they had ever seen in their lives. Former students talk of what they did learn and all the sports in which they could participate, and the trades that they learned that helped them later in life.

State preservationists and a local group of citizens petitioned the city to save at least one little corner of the campus -as a museum or memorial to what had taken place there, good or bad. The biggest fight was for the saving of the gymnasium for a museum- Johnny Begay heads an alumnus group who have a reunion in different places each year, though the next year's was planned for Brigham City. He is the one who recognized the value of saving the gymnasium for one very important reason. The gym has a mural painted in 1954 by a renowned Indian artist, Allen Houser, who taught at the school several years in the art department. It is painted directly on the foyer wall. The developer says that he will not save anything and that the gymnasium building would be one of the most expensive to save. He is questioning where these people were when he was trying to redo the dorms, "I've been here for a number of years and never have these people come forward with the brilliant ideas that they now have." ("Developer Says Renovation Too Expensive," by Kristen Moulton, *Salt Lake Tribune*, Monday, March 19, 2001, A7.)

There are others who never wanted the schools shut down in the first place because they believe that the school leaders were developing an Indian pride that has somehow been lost in today's modern world. The community leaders say that the local school, instead of being shut down for the reasons given, should be returned because the children need to be returned to their native cultures to attend schools built locally. These people argue that it was simply a money decision on the part of Congress who did not want to spend the money. More was accomplished at the Brigham City school than on the reservations because students were encouraged to speak their native tongues and to learn about their own cultures while gaining other skills to survive in society. Just as the children were reaching their peak in Indian pride and development, Congress chose to shut down the facility. Other observers say that the whole idea was a clash of existing cultures and really hurt tribal pride and development and invaded personal rights and freedoms. While some boarding schools might have been worthwhile, there were plenty that were not where bigotry, abuse and other unfortunate things took place. Now that Indian children can have their own schools close to home, matters are really moving forward in a positive manner.

An article in the local newspaper said that a New Mexico foundation, called the Allen Houser Foundation, based in Santa Fe has entered the fight. Their leaders have written letters to Senators and Representatives and others asking for support to save the building or at least the mural. One of the artist's sons says that the mural is important to American history, Utah history and Native American history and that it should be saved. The developer has now agreed to give the foundation more time to find a benefactor to save the gym or at least the mural which would cost around

$40,000. About 20 paintings on doors and windows have been saved so far and the woman spearheading the hope of saving the entire gym is extremely pleased with this additional help. She wants to turn the gym into a community center for sports clinics and the city's youth. She contacted the historic preservationist organizations in town and the Houser Foundation in hopes of enlisting help. She has petitions and the help of the foundation which hopes to find someone that will give that mural to the National Museum of the American Indian. They only had three weeks and that was very little time. The city has now decided to raze all the buildings except the two which have been renovated. The graveyard of buildings will no longer remain to be a reminder of what took place

"Houser was a Chiricahua Apache whose ancestors lived in Arizona, New Mexico and Mexico. Born in 1913, he became a world famous painter and sculptor. He was the first Indian to receive the National Medal for the Arts, from President Bush in 1992. He died in 1994. He was selected as a featured American Indian artist for the 2002 Winter Olympics. Twenty of Houser's works will be on display next winter in Salt Lake City .... This international recognition of one of the most important 20th-century American artists is seemingly incompatible and in direct contrast to the desecration of Allan Houser's mural as a part of Utah's history." ("N.M. Foundation Wants Indian School Mural Saved," by Kristen Moulton, *The Salt Lake Tribune*, Wednesday, March 28, 2001, D2.)

Note: In spring 2002, the entire Indian School will be gone - demolished and gone. A few buildings will remain - the two that have already been made into low-income apartments and a few others where businesses have already been established. As to the fate of the gymnasium where Allen Hauser's mural is housed, we will have to wait and see. It is such a big mural that they will have to take the whole wall out if that is what they decide to do. Perhaps the better route would be to preserve the little gym as a museum for and about the old school and the old Bushnell Hospital before it. The school covered such a vast area of land that it will be interesting to see what, if anything, happens next.

Surely the spirits will not rest there, but then perhaps they are happy to see the place gone and forgotten too. This will be a true test of a haunting. Did the land soak up the images and emotions of these places or did the buildings take all the spirits with them? And what will trigger a replay? Will those who haunt the place still insist on interacting with the living even though life and time itself has moved on? The old stories about the place still persist however, with the entire area being dubbed "the old Indian School." Windows seem to break out all by themselves when no one is around either outside them or inside. People who visit there have had things thrown at them from inside the empty buildings. Ghost hunters who tried to take their equipment there have not only had things thrown at them, had their equipment shut off or break down on them, but have had doors shut or open in their faces all by themselves. On the other hand, they have come away with some great EVP recordings of all sorts of voices and banging sounds, etc.

Most interesting is the fact that there is a solid rumor that has been floating around for some time that there is blood all over the bathroom walls in one of the bathrooms in one of the buildings. And that when people go there who know which buildings came from the original hospital, some find these buildings all boarded up, while others find all the doors and windows open wide as if to invite them in. Perhaps these stories and rumors will disappear with the demise of the huge complex of old buildings, perhaps not. The Bushnell Hospital carries a layer of residual energy from one mighty strong generation and probably a few lost soldiers as well. The "Indian" school carries another layer of even more powerful energies stemming from the subtle injustices of not only boarding children away from their families, but from their cultural heritages as well. Even with the buildings are gone and some in this town are ignoring the past, the spirits and apparitions of these times will not allow themselves to be ignored. They will wander still, through whatever else is left there or built there in the future

THE OLD LEHI HOSPITAL

"IT'S JUST AN OLD EYE SORE; IT OUGHT TO BE TORN DOWN."

Lehi was settled in 1850 when the first group sent there by Brigham Young voted to camp by a place called Sulphur Springs. By November, 13 log cabins had been built in anticipation of building a fort. Fifty-two men, women and children first wintered there and a few others settled by themselves nearby. The first baby was born in that same month, but Lehi's first citizen only survived three months and then became the town's first death with burial in a makeshift cemetery up Dry Creek a few miles. This place remained the town cemetery until 1871. By February of 1854, the city council voted to erect an 8 foot adobe wall around the cabins, thus creating Fort Lehi. In a visit by Brigham Young and two of his council members, the settlers were urged to build a larger fort than they had planned and the fort eventually held 128 acre lots. Every man in the community had to build 4 rods of the wall or pay an equivalent in money or bushels of wheat. When it was done, portions of it were 12 feet high with a bottom thickness of 6 feet and a top thickness of 3 feet. There were watch towers on each corner. These towers were located at 2nd West and 1st North, 1st South and 4th West, 3rd South and 2nd West, and Center and 2nd South. The fort had three entrances.

Like any building that has survived this long, the old Lehi hospital has layers of history behind it. The old fort was the first layer where the hospital eventually stood. The next layer, the People's Co-operative Institution, was built on this same ground as competition for the Lehi Union Exchange in 1871. Three men, upon learning that the Utah Southern Railroad intended to build its line through northern Lehi, began to build a small store across the street from the probable location of the railroad depot. The railroad stayed only one year, in which time the Co-op flourished and actually took over all other business by the time the railroad left; the other stores did not survive the railroad leaving the area. A second Co-op store, and a bigger one because it had two stories, was built in 1878 and still stands at 193 East State today. In 1890, an attempted robbery of the store resulted in an attack on a night watchman. He was clubbed over the head and shot. Another young man just arriving home from the train was almost shot by the sheriff, who mistook him for the thief. The thief was captured the next day and both men who had almost died lived to tell their grandchildren the story.

On July 16, 1891, Thomas Cutler, the president of the Lehi Commercial & Savings Bank, temporarily established a bank in the newer People's Co-op Store while waiting for the permanent bank to be built on the site of the original Co-operative store at 206 East State. The old Lehi Hospital, the third and final hospital in town, would eventually serve the community for many years. The new permanent bank was a red brick two story building with a sort of central tower in the front. In the meantime in 1900, bank president, Thomas Cutler built a seven room home nearby at 150 East State Street. It became the finest residence south of Salt Lake City and included an interior of hand carved oak wood throughout. Fireplaces and mantles were in almost every room. Cutler moved to Salt Lake City a mere 3 years later to be closer to his businesses there, but various Cutler children and their families continued to live in the Lehi home periodically. One of these children, Marion Cutler, remodeled the home to take advantage of the traffic in town. He named it the Reltuc Inn, Cutler spelled backwards. Unfortunately, while the Inn was a luxurious place to stay, it only lasted about 6 months, was considered a financial failure and was sold. Dr. Fred Worlton bought the mansion, moved his family into the lower floor and converted the upstairs into the second Lehi Hospital.

In the meantime, the Lehi Commercial & Savings Bank continued to do a thriving business, especially with the Co-operative Mercantile. In 1905, the bank reached a peak with 60 percent gains over the previous 12 months and had over 700 depositors. By 1907 things began to change, as an as yet unfounded fear of bank failures was influencing people across the nation. There were bank closures and this added to the paranoia. The bank, however, continued to operate successfully until the stock market crash of 1929, when it was forced to shut its doors. The bank was sold in 1929 to N. O. Malan. Malan was one of Lehi's real characters. His small gas station was called the "Keep Off The Grass" station because of the funny sign which he had hung over a gas pump. He was also the town undertaker and apparently was a flirt with the girls. He owned several very different but successful businesses in town including a confectionery. He moved both his mortuary and his automotive business into the bank building in November of 1923. As author Richard S. Van Wagoner who wrote *Lehi: Portrait of a Town* in 1990, p.209, puts it: "Apparently mixing two types of body work did not catch on." Dr. Fred Worlton bought the place in 1925 and began converting it into a hospital.

Before the old bank was made into a hospital, it had also been used as a place for town dances, balls, Virginia reels, horn pipes, quadrilles, cotillions and other such town gatherings because of its ample floor space. Until new schools were built, the upper floor was also used at times as a temporary school room for the overflow from buildings that could not house all of the students. In 1910, so many fifth graders showed up for school that they had to be sent home. There were 765 students and despite the new additional 16 classrooms that had been built, temporary classrooms had to be housed in the southeast end of the second story of the Utah bank building. In 1895, the Ancient Order of the United Workmen, with all of their secret names, passwords, ceremonies, initiation rites and fraternal orders was also established in the upper floor of the Lehi Bank. In 1891, Mosiah Evans, head of the local Deseret Telegraph Company, established an office in the bank.

While there had been several doctors in town, it was a native born young man, Dr. Fred Daniel Worlton, who did the most for medicine in Lehi. He studied at the University of Utah in 1908 and received his M.D. in 1912 from Rush Medical College in Chicago. He returned to Lehi in 1914 and leased the John Y. Smith mansion at 518 North First East to establish the first hospital in Lehi. John Y. Smith who was married to Emerett Cutler, was director of the Lehi Silver Band, cashier at the Lehi Commercial & Savings Bank and eventually a Utah State Senator. He lived a block south of his father-in-law, Thomas Cutler, president of the bank. Dr. Worlton leased Smith's home and located his hospital on the second floor while housing his family on the first floor. Many years later in 1984, parts of the movie "Footloose" were filmed in the home. By the mid-twenties, Dr. Worlton's hospital had outgrown its surroundings and the good doctor had enough capital to buy a place for his second hospital. He bought the Cutler home in 1925 and moved from Smith's home into the Cutler's roomier surroundings, establishing the second Lehi hospital. He established ten patient rooms and an operating room in the upstairs of the mansion. In October 1921, he took the first x-rays ever taken in town under the supervision of a representative of the Victor X-Ray Corporation. He again outgrew his facilities and purchased the old bank building from N. O. Malan in 1925.

This new and very spacious hospital had 14 beds, an operating room, bathroom, reception area, and kitchen, all on the ground floor. By 1928, the Lehi hospital had treated over 150 patients and Dr. Worlton was very pleased with his new facility. Unfortunately, the beloved town doctor died suddenly that year of a heart attack while out duck hunting near Ogden, Utah. It was soon after this that Dr. Elmo Eddington received a phone call from his brother in Lehi. Dr. Eddington had been born in Morgan, Utah and had served in the medical corps in the U.S. Navy in World War I. He received his M.D. from the University of Pennsylvania in 1924 and had opened a medical practice in Chicago. "While driving along State Street Eddington's brother had hit a small boy riding a bicycle. He rushed the slightly injured lad to the hospital, where he learned that Dr. Fred Worlton had recently died. Eddington phoned his brother in Chicago, told him the circumstances, and within a month Dr. Eddington and his family had relocated to Lehi, purchased the hospital from Dr. Worlton's widow, and established his living quarters and office in the facility." (ibid, p.318.)

Business was very slow at first for Dr. Eddington. He waited and waited for days and days for a first patient to come into his hospital; his first patient turned out to be a cow. A man came in asking about his cow which had milk fever and wasn't growing very well. The doctor demonstrated his abilities by working with the udders and the cow began to grow. Word spread and human patients soon followed. There were still many patients who did not like to come to the hospital, so Dr. Eddington began making house calls. Once, in a terrible blizzard, Dr. Eddington was paid three dollars in all for making eight house calls. The hospital struggled financially at first and the doctor's wife canned fruits for sale and cooked for the inpatients at the hospital to help pay expenses.

I am struck by the comparison to modern medicine, reading about these things, because in our modern day what we have gained technologically in medicine and pharmacology, we have lost somehow in compassion, humility and individual human caring. Especially when one thinks about a real live doctor making house calls for little or even bartered payment and providing this care in the comfort and security of the patient's own home. Perhaps someday this will happen again because doctors will have minute and hand held equipment that can remedy most less serious problems without the patient having to go to a hospital. Doctors of today are being taught classes now in human compassion and caring along with their other technical curriculums and more and more in the medical field are giving credence to the role that belief can play in the healing process.

In the 1930s, Dr. Eddington obtained a substantial grant of money - pretty difficult to obtain during those depression years - to remodel his hospital. The east part of the ground floor was rearranged into a reception area, a rest room, a nursery, a delivery room, an emergency operating room, x-ray facility, kitchen and dining room. The west part of the ground floor housed a business office, the doctor's office and reception area, and three examination rooms. Upstairs there were private and semi-private rooms, an operating room, labor room, shower, bathrooms, nurses' offices and bedrooms, showers and closets. A central heating and air conditioning system was added, as well as a water-powered elevator on the south side. People remember that even in those days the elevator rose slowly going up but then descended rather quickly. If the water pressure in the system was low, and patients had to be moved quickly from the labor room upstairs to the delivery room downstairs, it became a very close race because of the elevator. In 1956 the system was converted to an hydraulic one which solved the problem.

Dr. Eddington was also the town quarantine physician and he placed many a public forum notice in the local newspaper when an epidemic was anticipated or even after one had arrived. Scarlet fever and the polio epidemic were among the most serious diseases. Children were kept home from school for a whole extra month in 1943 as a result of the polio scare, and there were still 178 cases in the county that year. Dr. Eddington warned townspeople about the spread of polio, and asked that children under 18 not frequent any public facilities at all. He even asked that church gatherings not be permitted during the polio season, a real affront to an essentially all Mormon town. He and Dr. Boyd Larsen spearheaded the massive vaccination field tests in 1954 when the Salk Vaccine became available. In 1940, the hospital came under the control of a newly established hospital board instead of Dr. Eddington. Five or so other doctors had offices in the building, though Dr. Eddington still maintained an office there for himself. He and Dr. Larsen became the prominent activists for medicine in town.

Dr. Boyd Larsen, who had also been born and raised in Lehi, had chosen medicine over physics as a career. He later married a nurse who was part of Dr. Eddington's staff. He had attended Washington University and had done his internship at St. Louis City Hospital, working mostly in the maternity ward. He had served as a medical officer in the U.S. Navy in World War II, and then returned to Lehi in 1946. His office and home was at 700 North Center, but he worked closely with the hospital where all of his patients were admitted.

In 1950, there was a widespread push to build a new hospital in Lehi and Dr. Eddington was quite involved in this venture even though he seemed to be nearing the end of his practice. Dr. Larsen and Dr. Eddington explained to the people not sure about financing a new hospital, that the Lehi Hospital was losing patients at an alarming rate because the facility was old and needed many new additions. The two doctors spearheaded a drive for this hospital in 1952, and a plot of land was even located for the new structure. The city decided that it couldn't afford to build a new hospital, especially since there was already a new one in the neighboring city of American Fork. By October of 1954, patient attendance at the old Lehi Hospital and operations performed there had dropped by 50 percent. By 1961, the state department of health told the hospital board that the outdated facilities would cause them to lose their state license, and it happened in 1965. The hospital continued operating until March 1, 1967, when the last patient, Mrs. James King had to be transported to University Hospital by ambulance.

Dr. Larsen began sending his patients to the American Fork hospital. Dr. Eddington, who had left town for a while, returned to Lehi in 1967 and reestablished his old office in the hospital but only for about a year. Because the old building was sold a year later, he established his practice in a home office at 101 5 East Ninth North and ran his practice there until his death in 1975. He and his wife had had a beautiful New England-style home built for them a year after they had first come to Lehi; it can still be seen at 617 North First East in Lehi. The house was restored and is now a private residence. Dr. Eddington was obviously a doctor of the old school, and dedicated and caring, he must have been well-loved by the townspeople.

Wally Olsen became the new owner of the old Lehi Hospital building. He rented it to a health elixir manufacturing company, and then to a furniture upholstery business. Then Max Chapman bought the building intending to convert it into an apartment building but he was denied a multiple-housing permit. In 1985, Russell Daly operated his music studio in the building, now called Studio Five. One apartment was built on the ground floor of the building, which has been occupied on and off ever since. The rest of the old hospital remains relatively the same, especially the upper floor, though it has stood unoccupied for years and years now. My first question of course was, why? How could this building, that so many people consider an eyesore, have survived? In a city where both the wonderful Lehi Opera House and even the Lehi Tabernacle came tumbling down, though not without some protestation, one can guess that preservation seems to be a brand new consideration. Again, in the many fascinating pages of Van Wagoner's book about Lehi, I found my answer. A couple named Wallace and Arlene Olsen, who obviously are preservationists, have purchased almost every historic building that they can get their hands on. They run The Outpost Antiques in the old second Co-op building, and also own the old Lehi Hospital among many other structures. Their ownership may be why the building is probably still standing, though unoccupied at present.

Neither Dr. Eddington nor his wife are still living but I was able to talk to a daughter-in-law and to a former nurse at the hospital, as well as to someone who was a former patient . I had started on this piece because of the rumors I heard, from people who had grown up in the Lehi area, about the place being haunted. At present much of the hospital still stands as it was, though rumors are that more than one apartment was slated to be constructed in the building, before the owner was not allowed to proceed. There was a long period of time when only a small portion of the hospital had been renovated and various renters in this one single apartment came and went. Anyone who lived in that apartment could walk straight into the old hospital from where they lived. Some of the tenants said that it was indeed eerie to do this when part of the hospital still existed, and many of them had strange experiences when they went into that part of the building. One renter reported seeing a man sitting on the stairs with a t-shirt tied around his waist, wearing nothing else and grinning at her with that sort of odd grin that the mentally ill have. He then promptly disappeared before her eyes.

According to rumors it was once a psychiatric hospital which is totally untrue. Another rumor is that the various renters that have tried to live in the apartment have chosen not to stay very long because of the "ghosts". Others who have lived in the place accepted these " ghosts" as part of their lives and are not frightened by them. Doors slam without people around; things move around in apartments when no one is there to move them, and then show up in odd and unusual places. People report seeing shadowy figures run across doorways or at the end of halls. Most interesting is the rumor that the old elevator which might not even be there anymore, runs up and down by itself. It runs up very slowly and then back down very quickly, like the original elevator did. And sometimes it is only the distinctive sounds of it running that can be heard.

The former patient that I talked to summed it all up by saying that he had lived in a house near there all of his growing up years as an only child, sometimes alone in his house. Many years later a reporter wrote a story about the former patient's old family home being haunted and the patient thought this was a real hoot. Surprisingly, soon after the article was published in the newspaper, a man did commit suicide in the the patient's old family home. But the former patient said there were never any ghosts and he wondered just where on earth this reporter had gotten the material for her story. He ended by telling me that there weren't any ghosts in the old hospital either and that it was an eyesore and ought to be torn down

I thought about all those many people who had passed through this building's doors, both living and dead - customers, bankers and cashiers, a secret order of men, telegraph operators, teachers and historians, doctors and nurses, patients and entrepreneurs, morticians and car salesmen, renters and vandals, just the plain curious, but especially those who came to dance. I thought about the dedicated doctors who had worried and struggled and given their all, so that the town of Lehi could have a hospital. And how now, just like their beloved tabernacle and their beautiful opera house, this old "eyesore" might come tumbling down at any moment because it was never as beautiful as either of the other buildings. I thought mostly about how this same former patient that I had talked to, had once, as a small boy, had his arm set in this hospital while smelling the strong odor of ether. He had told me about Dr. Eddington shushing him when he began to cry out, saying if you cry you'll wake the babies. Babies that some say can still be heard today from time to time if one is in the building alone at just the right time of evening.

In the closing years of his own life, this once young patient at the Lehi hospital had his own memories, but somehow couldn't see the value in preserving the place where these experiences had occurred. He still insisted that the old hospital building was an eyesore and ought to be torn down. And while I can concede that it really is nothing to look at and probably will go at some point, when one thinks of the spirits which once inhabited the place and of the many layers of uses that this old building had, it would be sad to see it go. It might be wise of the community to remember these two doctors with a plaque at least, though the spirits inside this place still actively remember them to this day.

STATE MENTAL HOSPITAL
ST. MARY'S OF THE WASATCH
BONNEVILLE COUNTRY CLUB

In 1870 the first state mental hospital was erected on a beautiful 160 acre tract of land on the foothills of the Wasatch Mountains at 24th East and 9th South. The Salt Lake City Insane Asylum, established by the Salt Lake City Corporation, was run by the City Physician. Doctor Seymour B. Young was appointed City Physician in 1876 and ran the institution for many years. He was from New York City and not only studied under some very famous physicians at the College of Physicians and Surgeons, but graduated as the third ranked student there receiving a bronze medal for his efforts. Stories told about him attest not only to his great skill as a doctor, but also his great devotion to his work and his ability to lift the spirits of all who knew him. He was the first to graduate as a physician and practice in the Utah Territory. In 1878, Dr. Young purchased the hospital and the place became known as Dr. Young's Insane Asylum, though its nickname was "The White House On The Hill."

People came not only from the Utah area but from all the surrounding states, both the sick and what were called the "feeble-minded" or the "insane" in those days, and lived or stayed a short term there. The grounds in those days were absolutely beautiful so the stories go, full of lovely shrub-lined stone walkways and bridges, as well as flower gardens and special rose gardens. The hospital staff cultivated wheat and other crops. There were vegetable gardens, as well as various fruit trees around the place. The building itself was made of plaster and cement with many gables and porches, and kept immaculately white. Locust trees surrounded the main building. The hospital maintained a herd of cows for the various dairy products needed and had hogs and chickens to supply the patients with food. While the individual apartments had bars on the windows, many of the patients were allowed to work in the gardens or the fields, as well as to roam the grounds. Some of the patients spent time at the Young's home when convalescence required hourly treatments, which was considered a privilege, as according to stories, the Young family was very hospitable.

Mrs. Elizabeth Riter Young did all of the purchasing for the institution and made most of the clothing for the women patients. She helped feed the hundred patients or so on a daily basis, as well as the many visitors to the the hospital. She also bore 12 children, many of whom went on to college. A local superintendent and matron lived at the Institution all of the time. One of these couples caught my eye, as they were named Mr. and Mrs. Richard McAllister. McAllister is my mother's maiden name so I at once became interested when I first visited the site. I knew about St. Mary's of the Wasatch but absolutely nothing about the state mental hospital that was there before it. I just knew that something else had been there besides the girls' school, because I kept seeing three women older than high school students; I thought at the time that perhaps they were teachers. Yet, whenever I saw them walking about, they were dressed in white uniforms of some kind, laughing and whispering together as though in a huddle. But their attire just didn't fit with a school. They also seemed to be on the wooden bridge, though I felt there had been an older bridge at the place and they were standing on its long-gone foundation instead. Perhaps I have an ancestor who managed the place and will have to research this further.

Dr. Young thought that the mind should be kept busy to insure the best in health and happiness, so besides the various garden, yard and farming jobs, many crafts were taught. The women did various kinds of sewing, including producing some very beautiful quilts. The more violent inmates remained locked up all the time. At one time, part of the building had been set on fire or accidentally 'fired" as it was called then; three women had burned to death. The caretakers got everyone else out as quickly as they could, or many others would have died as well. There is no date given for this event. This incident was my after-the-fact explanation for the eerie feeling I had on the grounds as we walked about, because for me there were people all over the place. Since there is no linear time when one goes walking in the other world, these individuals could have been girls from the school and hospital inmates as well, all intermingling together.

To run this institution in the late 1800s must have been quite a feat indeed. The institution had its own water rights but the springs were a half mile away from the buildings. There were no heating or lighting systems. Many large heating stoves were used in winter and oil lamps and candles were available for lighting. It is probably quite a feat that only one major fire occurred during these years. Coal was eight miles away and ice was five miles away. No railroads were close by and of course there were no automobiles. Literally everything had to be hauled by heavy wagons. The whole place had to be totally self-sufficient.

When we went there and saw the gate it did puzzle me about how old the entrance looked and how there seemed to be a sort of little guard tower. I thought it was an unusual place for people just to sit in for fun, and why would a girls' school need a guard booth? Now I understand that I might have been looking at a guard station; the stone gate possibly built much earlier than 1921, though this too could be wrong. I could find no information about how long the place stood empty until it was purchased for the girls' school, nor exactly when it was torn down. I would dearly love to see a picture of it, because I do have my own private "visuals" which I "stored away" and would like to see if they match.

The Congregation of the Sisters of the Holy Cross arrived in the Salt Lake Valley from Indiana on June 6th, 1875. Two sisters had responded to Bishop Lawrence Scanian's request for a school. They purchased property on the present day Second West and First and Second South Streets for a convent. Sisters M. Augusta Anderson and M. Raymond Sullivan opened their school in the convent building. It was the first site of St. Mary's and was called St. Mary's Academy. The first year they had 100 day pupils and 25 boarding pupils. In 1877 a violent storm damaged the building and major repairs had to be made. In 1878, the sisters purchased more land and added a steam house and new kitchen and music hall. In 1913, Bishop Scanlan blessed a statue of the Sacred Heart which was moved to the foyer of St. Mary's of the Wasatch in 1926.

In 1921, the Holy Cross Sisters purchased 400 acres, almost 3 times the size of the grounds for the asylum and slightly further north and west than where the asylum itself must have stood. Located at the foot of the Wasatch Mountains the new institution had its own reservoir and piped water at 13th East and 13th South. The ground was broken in 1925 by the Bishop Joseph M. Glass. The Knights of Columbus and the student body of St. Mary's Academy planted trees on Arbor Day of that year on the new property. On September 11, 1926, the old St. Mary's Academy was shut down and everything was moved to the new facility. On October 7th, 1926 the school was dedicated with a full liberal arts college program for women. The laying of the cornerstone took place at this time and Bishops from San Francisco, New York and the new Bishop of Salt Lake City were present. In the next years the Shrine of the Little Flower and the Grotto of Our Lady of Lourdes were completed and blessed and a statue of Our Lady was placed above the front entrance. At about the same time, a 700-pound Angelus bell was installed. The Our Lady Grotto had a 5-foot high statue of St. Mary of Lourdes within it.

In 1930, the basement of the school was damaged by a violent rain storm and the rushing water from the mountains behind caved in an upper tunnel and several water pipes. A collection was taken to pay for repairs, but the lower tunnel was not restored until 1939. The college was placed on the "A" list of four year colleges by the Northwestern Association of Secondary and Higher Schools in 1930 and placed on the list of junior colleges by the same organization in 1933. The University of Utah also accredited the college in 1930 as well. In 1935, the college's pre-nursing program was recognized by the American Hospital Association. The college continued to operate until 1959 when the Holy Cross Order made a case study of the facility and decided that the Sisters could best serve somewhere else. For a while after, it served as a high school academy and infirmary for Sisters of the Western Province of the Holy Cross Order. Then from 1964 to 1970 while Judge Memorial served as the Catholic boys' high school, St. Mary's continued to serve as the Catholic girls' high school. To know more about the history of Catholics in Utah, consult the following book, from which most of the previous text was taken: Bernice Maher Mooney's book: *Salt of the Earth: The History of the Catholic Church in Utah*, 1776-1987, published by the Catholic Diocese of Salt Lake City in 1987, pp. 1 71-174.

In 1970, the school was closed permanently and was used temporarily for the next two years as the Provincial House of the Holy Cross Sisters. In 1972 the building was sold and demolished and all of its beautiful grounds were maintained as a golf course, which is what it is today. If you would like to see where it was and the last remaining brick wall entrance and small stone retaining wall as you drive into the golf course, turn as if going to Hogle Zoo in Emigration Canyon and then take the very first right turn. Go down this street and

enter the golf course where to the right is the old brick tower wall and to the left will be the low stone fence as you wind around the hills to the parking lot of the golf course. Before you enter the gate there is a privately owned and completely remodeled home which was part of St. Mary's at one time, a private residence for faculty. There is an old walking bridge still there over a rather deep tiny canyon and the high hill where the gazebo held the Grotto of Our Lady of Lourdes. Though the property is silent now, there is still a very beautiful feeling of what once was, a myriad of ghosts and spirits of a time when this held all the hopes, fears and dreams of many young women and of the Sisters of the Catholic church who resided there for so many years. The buildings were huge and covered quite a bit of the grounds there, although the beautiful gardens seem to be gone now.

There are many women still living in Utah today who attended this school. I would never presume to know what they do today, nor try to get into their hearts and understand what they felt as they were going to school there. I am only writing about the place because of the stories of the 5-foot high statue in the grotto of Our Lady of Lourdes. For those who know neither the story of the Little Flower nor that of the miracle of Lourdes, a brief background might add to your understanding. The story of the Little Flower was made even more meaningful recently because an exhibit of the relics of "the little flower of Jesus" made a worldwide tour and passed through Salt Lake City in January of 2001 to honor the centenary of her death, a ceremony which began in 1997. Relics in the Catholic church actually have various classifications: first-class relics are parts of the bodies of the saints; second-class relics are items of clothing and objects that belonged to the saint or even instruments of torture used on a martyr; and third-class relics are objects or pieces of cloth actually touched by a saint. Originally relic worship was a way of stopping idol worship in the church, but eventually it became a way to celebrate and educate the public on the lives and teachings of the saints, as well as to inspire spiritual renewal.

Therese Martin of Lisieux, France passed away in 1897 at the early age of 24 due to tuberculosis. She was made a saint because of her amazing devotion to her church and to her God. She was born in 1873 into a family of nine children; both her mother and father had themselves wanted to be in the cloistered life of the Catholic church but had chosen otherwise. Early on, St. Therese showed signs of her mystical, clairvoyant and healing powers. When she was ten she healed herself from a deathly illness by praying to the Mother Mary fervently. From the beginning she wished to be a nun but everyone opposed her until at the young age of 15 she went to Rome herself to see the Pope. She joined two of her older sisters at a Carmelite Convent in Lisieux and devoted herself to prayer, meditations and to the writing of an autobiography called *Story of a Soul*. This autobiography gained her a huge following among the Catholics. After her death many miracles were attributed to her intercession and 28 years later she was canonized by Papal Exception In 1925. In the nineteen sixties, one of St. Therese's ideas was adopted by some people to put flowers in the end of gun barrels, although few know this now. Many a war protester took this idea to heart.

Her remains, really only three bones, are traveling about in an ornate, plexiglass covered case of Brazilian jacaranda wood decorated with very ornate silver embellishments. The coffin is 3 feet wide and 5 feet long and weighs 300 pounds. Many Catholics have waited all of their lives to see this, some never being able to go to Rome where she was interred. Although I am not Catholic, I visited the exhibit, for it is said that the healing powers of ones so holy continue on even after their mortal remains have passed on. Those who have come to respect her words and those wishing to find some sort of healing also came. St. Therese is the patron saint for AIDS sufferers, florists, France, missionaries, and the restoration of religious freedom in Russia. ("The Relics of 'the Little Flower of Jesus' to Make Stops in SLC" by Bob Mims, *The Salt Lake Tribune*, January 1, 2000, Section C and "Relics of St. Therese of Lisieux to Visit Oakland This Week," by Carrie McLish, *The Catholic Voice*, January 10, 2000, p-3.)

The miracle at Lourdes happened when three young children began to have visitations from Mother Mary which continued over the rest of their lifetimes. Thousands of people have since traveled to Lourdes to be cured. Today, people still travel there and many miracles and cures have come about because of energies released when one bathes in the waters of the grotto or just simply sits there. St. Bernadette became the most famous of the three children. The most famous miracle was when Mother Mary caused the sun to fall out of the sky towards the hundreds of people at Lourdes watching it. Then the crowd saw the sun return to its place in the sky. Many prophetic visions of the future took place and many of them have since come true, including both world wars of this century and various other disasters. Some of these prophecies have not as yet been revealed by the Catholic church. It is said that when Sister Bernadette died, her legs had become almost wooden from wading in the muddy waters of the grotto for so long. Although few people claim to have seen the Virgin Mary there, her miracles continue to this day at Lourdes.

Over the years at the College of St. Mary of the Wasatch, girls who attended said that of an evening they would walk to the Grotto to contemplate or pray as the sun went down. Gazing at this statue, as the lights of the evening played upon it at dusk, the robes of the statue would begin to move and sway as they watched. It was as if the hard stone became like soft clay and the robe would ripple in front of them. Many of the girls tried their best to discover a natural cause for this. Most of them dismissed it as a way in which the lights of a particular type of sundown created the illusion, however people saw it at all times of the day or evening and so this couldn't explain it. There were others who felt that they were witnessing a miracle and truly believed that the robes moved and swayed in the canyon winds. Still others, though fewer in number, saw tears run from Mary's eyes as her gown swayed around her. The tears being more typical of a Catholic miracle and consistent with those who knew why she wept. Rumor has it that the statue went to either the foyer of Judge Memorial High School when St. Mary's closed down or it stood in the rose garden by Holy Cross Hospital where I used to sit to rest on my walk back from town to my apartment on South Temple in my college days. I remember the statue but do not remember anything unusual about it There are so many such statues but I am not sure which one it might be, and even if I were sure, I don't think I would tell anyone, only to keep her safe from harm. Perhaps the statue is in storage or at another Catholic facility somewhere in the valley, maybe at the new church and school that just opened recently in the south end of Salt Lake Valley. Though the robes of the statue moved and her face sometimes had tears on it, I would imagine that these were not the central issues, but rather that some came away from their meditations healed in one way or another, sometimes without even knowing that they had been made well.

The feeling of the grounds, golf course now, are very real. Blessings of sacred ground cannot be taken back once they are given. This ground is most definitely eerie and yet blessed at the same time. One feels it as one walks about and various spots seem more sacred or more frightening than others. I am not Catholic but am sensitive to what I feel wherever I am. On these lawns I walked about to the spots most holy to me or most strange, and saw about me many images of what once was. I saw three young women on the old walking bridge talking and laughing together as they stood tossing small pebbles down below, trading the secrets that young women do, though they seemed slightly older than students, perhaps teachers or caregivers from an earlier time. They seemed to be dressed how they might have dressed in the twenties and thirties but they were in what appeared to be all white outfits which I did not understand since they had the old bobbed hairstyles of the times. The high hill where something must have been located, perhaps the grotto or shrine, or even an event which took place before with a meaning not so holy, gave me the shivers. The parking lot where some building must have stood once resonated with me because I could feel its heaviness and height above and felt as though I could put my hand out onto the warm brick which wasn't there anymore. As I walked I felt as though various people passed through me on walks of their own from different places and times far removed from my own. I was conscious of people walking about the grounds in pairs or threesomes or in small groups as well.

I am now on a search for the statue, because I would like to touch it and be satisfied within my own feelings of what others saw there. I should like as well to ease my unsettled feelings about the sparkling reputation of the old mental hospital, which just does not feel right to me. For this is not what I heard and felt as I walked about, instead there were secrets and misbehaviors which I guess are of no consequence now. Standing in the exact location of the old hospital, wherever that was at the south end of the golf course, would tell me what I need to know. And the statue would help me to know more about the girl's school as well.

THE OLD LDS HOSPITAL
- THE EAST WING HAUNTINGS

This story began because some people mentioned that the original hospital building, now so surrounded by other buildings that it has disappeared entirely, is haunted. Only those employed there and possibly patients, know where this original portion of the hospital is located. Still, their stories of hospital beds going up-and-down on their own or having been moved into a new position from the night before when no one was in the room, are interesting. Windows opening and closing on their own and lights flickering or going on and off have also been observed from time to time. People have heard voices coming from the empty patient rooms late at night and have discovered beds or whole rooms of furniture rearranged whenever no one was even there. But such things are going on to this day and sometimes right before their eyes and this has everyone baffled. Originally an LDS hospital, people would talk about this within the hospital walls but never publicly. It wasn't until later on when the IHC corporation took over that some of the employees began talking about all these strange happenings and discussing openly the occasional strange incidents that took place in the old original hospital section and the first wing built onto it some time later.

It was in January of 1905 that Dr. W. H. Groves dedicated the Latter Day Saints Hospital in a simple but impressive ceremony. The building was five stories with 80 beds. One thousand patients were admitted and the cost of building the new hospital was $175,000. This first grand hospital had been the culmination of a dream to bring modern medical practices into the Salt Lake Valley. After years of individual doctors and midwives and the early formation of the "Council of Health" in 1849, which was formed to identify and collect plants to be used in healing or in botanical medicine, it was decided that the Mormon people needed a modern hospital facility. St. Mark's hospital had already been in existence for several years, but in those days it was considered the Gentile hospital and Mormons were leery of doctors and their patients using St. Mark's, so that the hospital was only used in the most dire of circumstances.

Brigham Young had fostered a common sense approach to medicine. He told his followers to ask the Lord to help heal them but also told them to apply any remedy that they had knowledge of on their own. He was not fond of doctors but understood that sometimes a good surgeon was the only thing that could save a patient. In the 1850s and '60s doctors in Utah practiced only part-time, soon left the area if they were Gentiles, or if they intended to stay in the territory left the profession after awhile, because the LDS people did not go to them as a general rule. At the same time in the outside world the medical profession was making enormous strides. At the time of statehood in 1896, the medical field had become much more acceptable to the people of Utah. In 1872, even Brigham Young's attitude had changed because he agreed to send a nephew to medical College. In 1874, Seymour B. Young graduated from Columbia University and came home to practice medicine in at Salt Lake City. Soon other relatives of Brigham Young followed suit, and Brigham paid their expenses. When Brigham Young passed away, not only Seymour Young, but three other Mormon physicians were in attendance.

Brigham also began to encourage women to become midwives, nurses and even doctors and several Mormon women did become doctors and practiced in Utah long before other areas of the nation could boast of so many women doctors. It was these women who established the first Mormon hospital in the valley in 1882, called the Salt Lake Valley Deseret Hospital. This hospital, though short-lived, had a woman doctor as president, a woman doctor as vice president and several women resident doctors. It was first housed in the old LDS Ward Chapel on Fifth East and First South and South Temple, but soon moved to First North and Second West. The hospital managed to run only until 1890 due to a lack of financial support.

Dr. William H. Groves from Nottingham, England had joined the LDS Church in 1862 and moved to Salt Lake City to practice dentistry. "He had accumulated a fortune of $85,000 when his lifestyle changed abruptly and mysteriously. He shunned his friends, retired from practice and became a recluse living in a poorly furnished room above an undertaking parlor south of the present Temple Square Hotel." ("About LDS Hospital," author unknown, *LDS Hospital*, Chapter 2, page 2, 1980-http://www.ihc.com/xp/ihc/lds/about/history/chapters1-11.xml.) Groves suffered a heart attack in April of 1895 and mentioned to the doctor in attendance at St. Mark's Hospital that he intended to endow a library with his money. The doctor, Dr. Joseph S. Richards, asked him if he had liked the services he'd gotten from the doctors and nurses at St. Mark's hospital and once Groves said that he had, Doctor Richards proposed to him that he endow a hospital instead, one for his own LDS people.

The Deseret News offered great praise when the hospital opened, saying that it was perfect in arrangement, equipment and accessories "not surpassed in all the world." The hospital would stand in perpetual sunshine above the city with a warm canyon breeze, cooled in summer and warmed in winter by the strong sunlight. The hospital was a "magnificent structure with its cream-colored brick with white stone and red sandstone base. Located on a 2 1/2 city block 175 by 40 feet, the high wall that surrounded it afforded patients and staff much privacy. English inlaid linoleum covered even the basement floors and the enameled tile and marble walls reached to the ceiling on all sides. One large main hall ran through the middle of each floor. These hallways were 13 feet wide and 11 feet high. There were 80 patient rooms and the main floor housed doctors offices, surgeons rooms, and chief nurses quarters. The men's ward was opposite the women's ward on each floor. The third-floor also had nurses quarters, the fourth floor included a few private rooms and the fifth floor had a series of three towers which had operating rooms located within the main room in the middle section. Each operating room had a glass roof and all three were completely tiled. Preparation and sterilizing rooms were also completely tiled and even the doors to the operating rooms had glass knobs with a unique device at the washbasins, allowing one to turn off the water with a knee.

There was also a rooftop promenade so that patients and visitors could view the Wasatch and Oquirrh Ranges unobstructed by any high-rise buildings in the city. Two 60 horsepower boilers and stokers were situated nearby to power the hospital. One of the first in the valley, the automatic elevator was a major attraction at the new hospital. There were 30 tiled bathrooms in the building, chutes for soiled linen that went all the way to the basement and other designated dust chutes to carry sweepings and refuse to the basement as well. An X-Ray machine, invented only 12 years earlier, was another popular new attraction at the hospital. The hospital was modernly fireproofed, had an up-to-date telephone system throughout, red lights installed that attracted the nurse's attention rather than patient bells that could disturb others. Temperatures in the building were regulated on an automatic system.

The first year, 987 patients were treated and there were 707 surgical operations. The hospital averaged 43 patients per day and the daily cost per room or bed was $2.24. Forty-five people were on staff and 87,000 meals were served that first year. There were also many small complications the first year, but hospital director, John Wells and his staff weathered them all. Wells had absolutely no experience as a hospital administrator and had worked his way up in the LDS Church wrapping packages at the Z.C.M.I. Department Store. He had gone from clerking finally to streamlining the LDS Church's out-of-state business and membership record systems. But then he had to add to these responsibilities by in running a hospital and working 7 to 10 a.m. at the hospital each day and 8 to10 p.m. at night. Being appointed to this job, Wells simply learned the new business day by day. At the time the death rate at the hospital was really high, so Wells hired more nurses including one experienced nurse who came from a former job at the Insane Asylum in Wyoming. He also added much-needed services such as a nurse's training school, a laundry and nurse's home. He obtained more suitable furniture, more proper equipment, and a better light system for patients to use to call their nurses, repaired the walls and painted them a more pleasant color than stark white, installed doors to partition off the huge elevator on each floor, updated the heating plant and built additional storage spaces for supplies. In so doing he probably saved the lives of many a patient simply by reducing the chances of infection from the surroundings themselves.

Mr. Wells served the hospital until 1914, making sure that improvements were made in the following areas: employee training, better handling of supplies, food handling and regulation, hiring more well-trained nurses, developing a method to pay for charity cases, reducing sound pollution from outside the hospital such as coal wagons and other vehicles, and establishing one of the first nurse's training schools in Utah. Illness forced him to resign his "second" position at the hospital, although he maintained a great affection and fondness for the place until his death in 1941.

Miss Leila Hard came from the Wyoming State Mental Hospital in Rock Springs to supervise the first six nurses at the hospital. Several other supervising nurses followed, directing the three-year nurse's training program. Nurses rose at 5:40 a.m., completed their morning devotional, ate breakfast at 6:20 a.m. and then went on duty from 7 a.m. to 6 p.m. at night. They got an hour off for dinner and two hours for classes and rest. If a nurse did not attend devotional, she lost one afternoon of off duty time each week. Nurses had to retire at 9:30 p.m. and were allowed to stay out until 10 p.m. one night and on special permit until 11:30 p.m. once a week. Nurses were paid $7.50 a month for room and board, textbooks and uniforms. And of course all nurses in those days had to be female and single.

Patients were treated for as much as 40 days in the hospital for common ailments: pneumonia, abscesses, hemorrhage and numerous other conditions. Blood transfusions were used only as the last resort for dying patients. The donor was directly linked to the patient through a gauze sieve and when the donor paled and the patient gained a healthy looking color this indicated enough blood had been transfused. Recovery from any kind of surgery took a minimum of 10 days in bed for fear of rupture or hemorrhage, although this long bed rest often caused other postoperative complications, which caused a higher death rate in the early days from pneumonia, phlebitis and pulmonary embolism. Patients and their families paid 3 dollars a day for a room when the average wage earner brought home 2 dollars a day. Operating costs were from $5 to $10 per operation. Even in those days the cost of medical care was very high. No smoking, tobacco chewing or spitting or any other disagreeable habits were permitted, loitering in hallways, loud talking, or gossiping while visiting patients or walking into restricted areas.

In 1913, the East Wing was added to the building at a cost of $382,000. This wing housed a modern kitchen, dining room for employees, 66 private rooms, five more operating rooms and a laboratory. In 1915, David A. Smith was the new hospital director for the next two years. Alfred W. Peterson took over for one year and then in 1918, B. F. Grant took over and stayed with the job until 1929. In the 1920s, the hospital began to become very overcrowded going from 987 patients in 1905 to 5,420 patients in 1925. The drug room and X-Ray room were directly across from the morgue, not a trademark for good hygiene by any means. Patients in the wards had little privacy except for temporary wooden dividers sometimes brought in from the hall. Everything was painted white once more, nurses wore white uniforms and even the metal beds were painted all white. Winters were warm but in the summers, patients roasted in the heat. Nurses learned how to outsmart curfew regulations by climbing ladders into the engine room and then crawling upstairs into the windows of the nurse's home. The atmosphere was however, full of laughter and community at the same time.

In the 1930s, a West Wing was added to accommodate the more than 5,800 patients, boosting the patient accommodations to 240 rooms. There were 295 employees and 62 medical staff members. Average patient stays were around 13 days at the cost of $4.75 per day. The 1929 stock market crash almost closed the hospital but the hospital weathered this crisis. Finances were in the red in the 1930s and although several more administrators kept the hospital afloat through second World War and with more renovations. The LDS Church eventually wanted to sell hospital. The decision was made at this time whether to spend more money or sell. The original sandstone steps of the hospital's entrance had deteriorated and were not safe, the laundry complex was long outdated, the coal power plant was polluting the neighborhood, and people were complaining loudly about this pollution as well as the noise that the trucks which rumbled up and down the street all day long to dump coal into the bunkers underneath 9th Avenue made. Every part of the hospital was overcrowded, but eventually a consensus was reached to spend money on new construction and renovations on the existing structures.

Homes were purchased around the hospital to allow for expansion and for the next 14 years remodeling and expansion went on, although some beautiful old mansions were lost along the way. By 1953, two deep water wells had been drilled, a new central supply section was completed, the new Radiology Department doubled in size; a chest surgery unit was opened; a greenhouse was added; and the old heating plant was replaced with electric power for a hospital city of some 30,000 people. The old laundry building was razed and the seventh and eighth floor additions to the East Wing were dedicated. The nurse's residence on 9th Avenue and "C" Street was reconstructed and rededicated. At the end of this time by 1959, a seven story Center Wing was added and all parts of the hospital's exterior went through a three-part paint and ceiling process to make the whole hospital look like one building again. Many other new units were added including air-conditioning and modern intercom and televisions.

In 1968, a $3.5 million North East Wing was added with seven stories, 88 additional beds, 9 new X-Ray rooms, surgical suites, an intensive care unit and computer equipment on the top floor. In 1970, a parking plaza, purchasing department, printing office and storeroom were built. Finally in 1974, the LDS church greatly studied whether the running of hospitals was still a religious concern or if church monies should be more appropriately spent in other ways. It was decided that the management of a set of regional hospitals was no longer central to the mission of the LDS Church. One April 1, 1975, Intermountain Health Care, Inc. assumed operation of the LDS Hospital as well as 14 other regional hospitals that the LDS church owned in Utah, Idaho and Wyoming, including Primary Children's Hospital then located on 12th Avenue. IHC currently runs over 21 hospitals in the intermountain area. In the late '80s, the hospital went through another expansion program to keep up to code. Today LDS Hospital covers quite a few blocks and buildings, has received awards for patient care and continues to serve the community well.

The little five floor original hospital still exists inside this huge conglomerate of buildings at precisely Eighth Avenue between "C" and "D" Streets, including the first wing addition in 1913 to the east. These are the two areas purported to be haunted, the original hospital and the first wing addition. The irony is that now the entire hospital will be moving to a new location out on State Street and 56th South by the year 2005. The place where the controversial Murray Smokestacks came tumbling down, once being readied for a huge shopping center, has been bought instead by Intermountain Health Care which has plans to build a three hospital complex over the entire area where once many smelters covered this ground. It is also ironic that hospitals for the health of people will be sitting over the tailings of several smelters and refineries that were once located in the area. These new facilities will provide for plenty of parking and expansion in an area not so enclosed by the beautiful old historic homes in the Avenues. These hospitals will be centrally located for the whole city and will be much more accessible.

Plans for the old hospital at present are to tear down much of it but to leave a specialized 50 bed hospital in operation in the area. Thus providing the opportunity for not only more new Avenue homes to be built, but for the return to a quieter neighborhood minus a huge hospital complex in such a crowded area. However, there is something else very ironic about all of this and that is that in returning the hospital to its original 80-bed facility, it will become once again serene, small and private. Primary Children's Hospital has moved three times. Once located in the Avenues, it has been torn down and disappeared along with the hauntings that were purported to be there after it stood vacant for a while. It moved to a brand-new facility next to the University of Utah hospital. And now it will be moved again to this new location on State Street as one of the three new hospitals being built there. One wonders what the old primary Children's Hospital will be used for, since it is such an unusual and quite uniquely designed building.

The specter of a brand-new hospital being built over toxic tailings and quite a few ghostly happenings, should produce a lot of more interesting stories in the future. Back in the Avenues, the old LDS Hospital will probably continue to be haunted by former patients and employees, although at the new hospital an occasional minor smelter worker will walk through its walls, mistaken for an hospital employee from time to time, or maybe just a shadow on the wall. Things will move in both places when no one is around. Lights will flicker, and the old world will meet the new, as what came before meets what is yet to come. Both places are likely haunts, especially the huge smelter area, as neighboring West Jordan has also had plenty of reports of hauntings over the years. When the beds move about or place themselves in upright positions without any human help and things in the room rearrange themselves all by themselves, those working there will know that some of these spirits have decided to remain. In the Avenues, what remains of the old hospital with its history of patients who either got better or slowly expired, such hauntings may continue. Life goes on and so do the cycles of buildings, from birth to death and back to life again, in a slightly or even greatly altered form.

THE OLD GRANITE WARD HOUSE

"THE WHITE CHAPEL" OF "RAGTOWN"

One cannot talk about the old Granite church without mentioning a bit about the now deceased town of Granite, or "Ragtown", which sprang into existence in the 1870s along with the town of Alta due to the mining in the area. Teamsters from Alta needed a halfway station to rest and feed their teams, and Granite town extended from the Murray Power Plant along the creek to the Glacier Park Stadium which no longer exists. For about 5 years it was a very busy place and Bishop Solomon J. Despain was Justice of the Peace at the time. There is one tale of the Bishop having to perform a wedding in his nightshirt from his second story window because the couple just couldn't wait until morning. The Despains were very prominent in the founding of the town. A teacher I worked with for many years still lives in the area on some of the land that her husband's family retained for many years; she is the real historian of this area and has lots of information about her family and the area in general. A book, The History of Granite Ward, by Rosemary Fairbourn was published by the local LDS ward. There is also information which can be garnered from two volumes written by intermediate boys and girls from the 1945 - 46 school year in Jordan District called Communities of Jordan School District Volumes I and II. There are valuable and interesting tales of the founding of all the little towns in this area, many of which no longer exist as separate little communities. Volumes were being discarded one year and when I found out about them, I ran down to get a set.

J. B. Woodman and his partner were the first to prospect in Little Cottonwood Canyon three years after pioneers first came to the valley. Within 30 days they had opened the famous "Emma" mine after digging in a ninety foot tunnel. Soon after, the wife of an army surgeon from Camp Douglas in Salt Lake City, found ore on a hill north of Little Cottonwood Canyon and General Patrick E. Connor, Commander of the Camp, allowed his men time off to prospect for silver. Some of them found nothing, but a few others were able to locate rich ore veins in the area. Overnight, people came from all over the country to Alta to strike it rich. Ore was hauled down the Mountainside in ox hides on horseback at first and then later by sleighs and teams of horses. In the summer stone boats or flat drags were used and then eventually tramways were built to take the ore to the canyon floor where the town of Granite was located. In 1873 the Wasatch and Jordan Valley Railroad was completed to Granite and this was basically the end of the town because it was no longer needed as a halfway station.

The first school for children in the area was built in Alta but it burned down along with much of the town two years later. The school was then moved to the mouth of the canyon and this school ran for four years. A school was then built east of the "White Chapel" or old Granite church. The boys came in the west door and the girls in the east one. The boys and girls were separated by a partitioned wall and the school was known as the Forty-Second District School. A Mrs. Hatfield and a Mr. Vawdrey were the teachers. It was heated by a coal stove in the middle of the room and the students sat on hard wooden benches, two to a bench. This school was abandoned in 1905 and a new school was built a little distance away. That school ran until the new Granite building was completed. All of the previous schools were torn down, and the new school is to the west of the church. The old Granite church is now surrounded by beautiful homes in what is considered a very nice part of the valley with gorgeous views of the mountains. I often wonder if the people in this very nice suburb east of the old church, hear old school bells or even church bells from time to time, or it anyone around there hears children laughing, though the laughter is coming from the old church or where the old school used to be. As described in the 1940s, Granite was still its own little separate community though there were no stores and one had to drive into the "city" for anything that one needed. Even a bear or two might be spotted near town when both the old original school and the old church were still in use.

The first chapel in the area was on present Wasatch Boulevard and was really too far away from Granite. LDS Granite Ward had met in individual homes and in 1892 in the little adobe school house. The Granite/Butler building on Wasatch Boulevard was built in 1892 and then abandoned in 1901. Land was purchased in 1903 to build the White Chapel at 9800 South and 3100 East. William J. Despain, the oldest citizen in Granite, held the plow while Oscar N. Despain drove the team to plow up the field where the chapel was to be built. The cornerstone was laid on May 12th, 1905. It required over two years to complete the building and everyone in the community contributed to the construction. It was heated by wood stoves with one chimney on each side with three pot-bellied stoves attached to them. Wooden steps were used at the front entry at first and then stone steps were built later. Young men of the congregation had the responsiblity to build the fires early every Sunday, but the building was still cold when worshippers arrived because of the high ceilings. There were no indoor bathroom facilities until the 1930s and at this same time a furnace and thermostat were installed. The church was red brick at first but later was painted white. Someone at some time walled up many of its beautiful windows, probably to retain heat and to have more privacy.

When I first drove by many years ago, people appeared to be living in it like a home and it was really run down. Avard Tennyson Fairbanks, the famous Utah sculptor, later purchased the building and used it as a studio. His father began an artists' dynasty in Utah. John B. Fairbanks was born the son of John Boylston Fairbanks in Payson, Utah in 1855. The LDS Church saw his promise as an artist and financed his trip to Paris in 1890 to go to art school as a painter. His work was never quite as gorgeous as was that of his son, Avard. Art books say that he had a "certain archaic quality to his work." John B. moved about the country most of his life before returning to Utah in his final years to become a great advocate for art in Utah before his death on June 16th, 1949. Avard became his most famous son though several other children became artists as well. Avard was the tenth son and youngest child of Lilly Huish Fairbanks and John B. Fairbanks.

Avard was a child prodigy born in Provo, who traveled to New York with his father at the age of 13 to study at the Art Students League. He even had an exhibition of his work that same year at the National Academy of Design, and then in 1913 he was off to Paris too. He eventually taught at the University of Michigan for several years, but then was called home in December of 1946 to become Dean of the University Of Utah's College of Fine Arts. He retired in 1965, but still continued to be the "best known traditional realist sculptor working in Utah." It is said that he was the one who "legitimized the nude figure in Utah art ".

One of Avard's brothers, Jonathan Leo, reached some acclaim as an artist as well; probably others of his brothers simply did not pursue their family tradition or just were not talented enough to gain fame. Jonathan Leo was born in 1878 in Payson, Utah. He attended the LDS University in 1901 and then went to Paris to study. He returned home in 1904 and had a "style more polished and naturalistic than his father," John B. Fairbanks. He was the Salt Lake Public School's Arts Supervisor until 1923 and then went to Oregon State College to chair its art department. He only outlived his father by 6 years, thus cutting short what might have been a long and productive artistic career.

Ortho Rollin was Avard T. Fairbanks nephew. He was born in Salt Lake City in 1925 and got his Master of Fine Arts at the University of Utah in 1953. Ortho taught at the LDS Church College in Salt Lake and then at the LDS Church College of Hawaii. He lives in Salt Lake City today and some of his sculptures are exhibited alongside his uncle's in the Utah State Capitol Building. Avard's sons have continued the dynasty. Grant S. Fairbanks was born in Salt Lake City in 1935 and became a medical doctor. He has been involved in collecting, organizing, presenting and in the preservation of his father's works all of his life, as well as being an amateur artist in his spare time. Jonathan Leo is another son born in 1933 in Ann Arbor, Michigan. He studied at Brigham Young University and the University of Utah and eventually became Curator of the American Decorative Arts and Sculpture at the Museum of Fine Arts in Boston, Massachusetts. He served as a professor at the University of Boston and continues to do his own work as a sculptor and landscape painter. Justin Fox was born in Eugene, Oregon in 1926 and worked with his father until the late 1960s at the University of Utah. He then moved to Thatcher, Arizona to continue his work. He is the father of Daniel Justin Fairbanks born in 1956, a grandson in the dynasty, who lives in both Provo and Salt Lake City, continuing to produce wonderful artistic works.

A couple of other Fairbanks are mentioned only briefly in *Artists of Utah* by Robert Olpin, Gibbs-Smith: Salt Lake City, Utah, 1999. One is William Fairbanks who exhibited some of his work in the Springville April Salon in 1922, a possible relation to the dynasty, He has since disappeared from public notice. The other is a woman who married into the family, Velma Parker Fairbanks, wife of Merwin Fairbanks, another son of John B. Fairbanks. She was born in 1923 in Orem and did beautiful landscape paintings until her death in 1983. Right here are a handful of mysteries. Who were these people and what did they do with their lives? Were there many more such talented artists in this family that we have never heard about? Will we ever see their work? Or are these pieces lost in some attic somewhere, or worse, destroyed over time by lack of interest or even ignorance of their location or value? I know when I visited the 104 year old Maeser school in Provo, they even had two of Avard Fairbanks sculptures purchased many years ago for $29.00 dollars for the pair.

Former art students or even current ones probably have the same question that I do, if you are a woman that is. Didn't John Boylston and Avard Tennyson produce a few girls as well? Were they devoid of artistic talent because they were women? Were they just too busy having babies and raising them to have time to sculpt or paint? Perhaps it is because no one expected that they could also work as artists, and so they didn't? Or worse, did they become artists but no one ever gave them the recognition that they deserved? It certainly can't be that the women in the family didn't have any talent, though I do understand what the times were like and how difficult it would have been to try and have an art career while being a wife and mother.

Consider all of the other women who sacrificed for what they thought they were supposed to do, many of whom were forced to try to love what they were told they should, while others, more silent and tragic, gave up all of their dreams, sometimes to very ungrateful children. It is not the quantity of time spent with loved ones that counts, but the quality of it. A woman living only half a life or even less, cannot show her children how to live a full life of their own. In fulfilling her own talents and dreams, she then by example shows her children how to live with and fulfill their own visions. While our mother felt trapped by what she both loved and disliked for herself, this message gave all of us the strength and abilities to go out and seek more than the closed world from which we came. Fortunately in our day and age, it is now acceptable for women to pursue their dreams.

Avard Tennyson Fairbanks left behind sons, grandsons and nephews who now own the old Granite Church property. They have been trying slowly over the years to renovate the place for a museum dedicated to their father's work. Just a couple of years ago they put in a wonderful stone fence around the place with black wrought-iron-fenced openings. They also put up two plaques dedicated to their father. One was on the building itself and the other was on the outside wrought iron fence with information about their father and uncle's lives. Unfortunately, vandals took it upon themselves to steal both of the plaques and they are no longer there. I do believe that this work will go on however long it takes. In talking to neighbors around the area, I found that because the sons and grandsons have been working on the place for such a long time most think it will never be finished at all, a sort of "white elephant" in the neighborhood. The place has been rumored to be haunted for years and years and even people who live clear across the valley, know about this haunted church, hidden away in a suburb. Even such distant observers mention the resident ghosts at this old white church from time to time in my own travels about the city

Some neighbors near the church, including the elementary school across the way say that they have never heard of such things. The LDS ward in the area is very proud of the history of not only Granite City but the old church as well. Church goers seem happy that the old church is still standing and there are a few who live around there talk about the ghost lights that come on in the place, while teens seem to want to vandalize it from time to time. Now that the place stands empty awaiting its museum and art gallery doors to open, I can't wait to have a chance to go inside and sit for a while and see what my intuition brings, as it says that the place does have a lot of residual energy, though probably not an active ghost on the premises. However if anyone would haunt the place it would be the artist who used it as a studio along with perhaps an earlier bishop who also loved the place. And with so many ghost reports, though none of them substantiated, I had to investigate the place anyway.

I hope that Avard's sons do not give up on the idea of renovation, because it is a wonderful way to preserve this old building and keep it from being demolished. I want to go there as soon as the doors are opened to the public, since often I can only sense things from a distance, without a more detailed close-up visit. I am still looking for neighbors who will talk of strange happenings there, though I hear plenty of stories from others who have never lived by this "White Chapel of Ragtown." The only thing I worry about is that the owners will prove its neighbors right and never get the place done, thus jeopardizing its very existence. And I will never get the chance to enter its doors as a museum and receive more of my impressions of times long past.

OLD ROCK CHURCH

PROVIDENCE INN BED & BREAKFAST, CACHE VALLEY

Construction of the Providence Rock Meeting House was initiated in l869, about 10 years after Cache Valley settlement began. It was completed in 1871, thirteen years before the Logan Temple and 22 years before the Temple in Salt Lake City. It was used for church meetings, community meetings and for theatre entertainments by the Providence Players which attracted well known actors from Salt Lake City along with local artists. In 1869, rocks were quarried from the nearby mountains; the timber milling was local, as was the forging of nails and braces. Over the years, it has been variously called "The Hall", "The Rock Hall", "The Rock Meeting House" and The Old Rock Church", and it predates most historic buildings in the state. In 1926 another wing was added. The meeting house is now on the National Register of Historic Places.

It had the finest dance floor in the valley and many an all-night dance took place on its smooth floor. A wonderful stage, proscenium, paintings and curtain provided the setting for an excellent pioneer theater group which performed in the hall. Many of the player's names are on a plaque on the outside wall of the meeting house. The house has three foot thick walls and a south wing was added in the nineteen twenties. This wing held the bishop's office, a kitchen, relief society meeting room and Sunday School classes for the LDS church. In 1968, the LDS church sold the building to Dennis and Edith Carlsen who own a Bernina sewing store in town. They converted it to a wedding and reception center called Rosella Manor with a chapel and cascading staircase, while other parts of it were used as a storage facility and warehouse for their fabrics. They also took out the old wood burning stoves and put in gas heating.

Cliff and Elaine Mayfield bought the place in 1979 and lived in a portion of the meeting house until 1993. They continued the reception business while remodeling and converting another portion of the building into a residential facility for the elderly. They put in an elevator, two fireplaces, a large kitchen and really put their souls into the building's care and maintenance. They imported poured glass windows from Germany for the chapel to replace the non-original windows. Cliff Mayfield contracted cancer and was forced to sell the building. A buyer who planned to gut the building and make it into apartments came forward, but the community rallied. A petition was presented to the Providence City Council to save the building. As the area was zoned for residential use, the citizens were able to discredit the apartment idea and in 1993, a new owner promised not only to renovate the building slowly over time, but also to find a way to use the building in a more appropriate manner. Thus the idea for a bed & breakfast inn was born.

A long term process of renovation is in progress in conjunction with an architect from Design West and Elizabeth Rogers of the College of Family Life at Utah State University, who has been working on the Inn as an interior designer. She specializes in historic preservation and the various rooms in the Inn are a product of her care and guidance. The first thing the proprietors did upon buying the place was to scaffold the chapel and try various paints and colors at various times of the day and evening to achieve the right combination to enhance its atmosphere. The old chapel is now a grand assembly hall once more with Palladian windows, a cascading staircase, mirrored backdrops and exquisite furnishings. The design in the chapel was coordinated throughout the building to make it into the bed & breakfast Inn that it is today. There are fifteen guest rooms, each one designed in a specific style such as Georgian, Pioneer, Victorian, Neoclassic, English, French Provincial, Nautical, Rustic, Attic, and New England style. There is a parlor and library, and the whole Inn sits on 1.35 acres of land out in a country-like setting in the middle of the small town of Providence. All the modern conveniences have been added such as air conditioning, TVs and VCRs, hot tubs, and telephones. An extensive remodeling in 1999 upgraded the reception center, bed & breakfast, food service and storage. In the year 2000, a home to the east of the Inn was purchased to provide for a twentieth-century arts & crafts bungalow and to help maintain an exclusive residential atmosphere. There were other exciting developments along the way, and one shouldn't miss visiting the old time gas station across the street with its marvelous collection of memorabilia.

On visiting the Inn and the old church, I found the owner and manager to be one of those few people who really understands the heart of his property and enjoys showing people around. Anyone who would keep some of the hundred-plus year old nails from the roof repair work and bring them out for display as you hear all the interesting tales about the place, is someone who truly loves what he does. I told him outright that I was writing ghost tales and he invited me to visit the place anyway because there might be a few angels about the place according to various guests who have stayed in its rooms. As I talked with the staff, they said nothing of ghostly consequence ever happened, but that if I wanted to visit the basement I would find it quite eerie. Indeed it was, as most basements seem to be. No spirits though! However, the stories were really fun. The chances of spirits in the old rock church were quite a bit higher as the atmosphere within this social hall was heavy with energy, for all the gorgeous remodeling and wedding chapel quaintness. I would suspect that any spirits inside are quite happy with their church being turned into a wedding reception center, because after all, who doesn't love a wedding?

Visiting Providence brought back a few memories too, of visiting my mother's relations, especially one of her cowboy uncles who really entertained us kids with his stories of cowboying on the Kaibab Plateau near Kanab. Back in Providence, we were shown various beautiful rooms like the Rose Room, English Cottage, Mountain Stream,

New Orleans, and the quite ornate Honeymoon Room. A wonderful breakfast room on the first floor and a hallway of articles from all around the country highlight the Providence Inn as one of the premiere bed & breakfast inns in the west. The manager took us up to the attic to see how the old church was constructed. He spoke with reverence and awe while telling us that in his 29 years of managing the place, he still hadn't learned all of its historic secrets. He also explained how at one time after its church, theater and social hall years, the building became a reception center, then a nursing home and finally a bed & breakfast inn.

An elevator has been installed for those who can't climb the steep three flights of stairs. I wondered if it was in place when the structure was a nursing home, realizing that people could have died or been near death in such a place. Yet, the atmosphere was never dreary, nor seemed to have ever been that way. This is hard for me to imagine, though, since having visited a few such retirement places while shopping for a nursing home for my mother. The entire place was full of a warm, homey and loving atmosphere perhaps infused into it by the wonderful down-home staff, or perhaps by attracting people who love such buildings. Either way, a "Hammond boy" was messing around one night and shot the beehive over the front door of the old church. He later became a "pillar of the community". Below this beehive is a small "lamb of the lord" symbol and the cement arches around the windows and entrance lend themselves to something I would never have noticed if the owner hadn't told us about it. All around the archway on either side were deep scratch marks, apparently made by men putting out their cigars before going inside, or striking a match on them when they came out to light up.

In those days these smokers were probably attending a theatrical production put on by the Providence Players, the biggest theatrical troupe north of Salt Lake City and second only to those in that city. The names of the actors and actresses on the plaque read: Chas. and Joan M. Johnson, Harry Brown, Jesse Hammer, John Wilson, Alizina Hammond, Jas. Nye, Thos. Priday, Jos. A. Smith, Mary Naef, Lucinda Monroe, Wm. Reading, Jas. Fife, Ammon Harmon, Geo. and Mary Marier, Wm. W. Low, Henry Bullock, Lorin Bassett and Rudolph Hugg. In those days the Chautauqua's often included traveling troupes and it was not as often that a hometown troupe did all the performing. There was a plank dance floor as well and when the pews were taken out, it was found that quite a few names and initials had been carved on the backs of them. Between the dances and theatrical performances and church meetings, the old rock church would have been quite a lively place. A few old pioneer homes nearby attest to it prominence.

If anyone is around it would be Old Tibbetts, though the staff hasn't noticed anything in particular except a few guardian "angels" watching over the place and keeping the atmosphere friendly. Tibbetts was the caretaker of the old church long before the 1926 addition was added. He retired in 1909, which means that he took care of the place from its inception. Some say the place might have worn him down a bit as he looked quite tired in the photo taken on his retirement day. He really loved the place and probably still does drop in from time to time to check out how his building is being treated. And finding it treated so well, he probably doesn't need to stay that often. As far as my own impressions, I could sense others wandering around in its rooms: a woman who must have died while it was a nursing home because she seemed to have rented a room in the place when the building was not available to renters, a woman who either worked or managed something in the building who lost two children while she was working there and left some of her grieving energy. The possibility exists of another caretaker from a much more recent time hanging around the grounds and not necessarily inside the building. Also I felt that a man died while attending church or a performance in the hall. He seemed to have choked to death from lack of oxygen or fluid in the lungs. However, this was a mere imprinting, like an old painting of an event and not something currently disrupting the beautiful room.

Regardless of these little impressions which only add to the charm of the place, this Inn has to be one of the most entrancing and quaint places that I have ever visited. The Inn has an owner who obviously loves and honors the past of this place, while at the same time looking to the future to expand. People who love old quaint places would really love to stay here. What a wonderful place for a wedding with all the guests staying in the Inn enjoying the food, quiet and the lovely landscapes outside. Look for it on the internet, which is where I initially found the information about it, not knowing before of its existence. While the ghosts there are nebulous, the angels are not!

HANSEN PLANETARIUM

SALT LAKE CITY PUBLIC LIBRARY

Built of Sanpete limestone which is very soft, this library building has weathered the years quite miraculously. In 1898, the Utah State Legislature permitted a special tax for libraries and was able to purchase a huge library of books from the Grand Masonic Lodge of Utah, but without a place to house the collection. The books were stored in the new City and County building. It was the Ladies Literary Club of Salt Lake City whose valiant efforts finally brought about the building of a city library. The members lobbied the Territorial Legislature for a mill levy to support the first free public library in the city. They also found a mining millionaire, John Q. Packard, to donate the land and help finance the building. The library was finished in 1905. It is pretty much today just as it was then. A few minor changes have taken place such as a center door and staircase which were replaced by a large glass window and later, the hidden planetarium, where large scale changes were made on the second floor.

In 1964 a new city library was built and the old building sat idle but only for less than a year when Beatrice M. Hansen donated $400,000 in memory of her husband George to save the historic building and do the renovations and modifications necessary to reopen a year later as the Hansen Planetarium. The interior of the building had to undergo a few drastic modifications such as punching out the middle of the second floor to make room for the planetarium dome. This planetarium is one of only a few in the world in which the dome cannot be seen from outside the building. The dome is perforated with millions of tiny holes to give it better acoustics and avoid echoing sounds. Also the star projector- the original one was affectionately called "Jake" - once rose and still can be used, out of the ground from the floor below for performances and thus can remain hidden when other kinds of performances take place.

Until 1978 the Salt Lake Library System still owned the building, but then it was sold to Salt Lake County. Other interior changes to this four-story building were a remodeling of the lobby, third floor mezzanine and basement offices. The beautiful wood carved staircases and wood walls have remained the same since the library opened in 1905. Now the planetarium has become a huge science center offering all sorts of outreach programs for the schools and wonderful programs of both informational and artistic and musical varieties. Hands-on experiences for children have always been a part of this building's history, whether a library or planetarium. The building itself is absolutely beautiful and worth seeing for that reason alone, although there are many wonderful exhibits, including a huge pendulum hanging in the center of the building on the second and third floors.

One of my college roommates worked there and we spent many a night inside this building or attending shows while waiting for her to get off her shift. I have always been fascinated by the night sky and anything that had to do with the stars and planets, though I was never very good at either math or science. So I read about them and write about them in any way I can, as an outsider. We went to star parties up Emigration Canyon and got to wander about the building when no one else was there. I didn't know then what I do now, that there was a second reason for my fascination with this building and what my intuition was picking up there. Feelings from the past and images and emotions of the various decades passed through my thoughts and emotions. Whatever happened in the second floor " Education Room" has fascinated me to this day.

The basement is also full of activity but my questions about that got answered when we talked with various employees. There were eight library directors, five of them women and two of them named Elizabeth. My own impressions say that one of these was a very difficult personality who fiercely loved her library to the point where she still inhabits the building today. She seems to have been offensive even to the patrons of the library and just hates the thought of all these people coming and going in a situation that she cannot control. The second is a male patron who comes there practically every day to read and just doesn't have anywhere else to go. A fourth fellow might have had a heart attack in the building, though I don't know how often he decides to appear. Of course there is the famous suicide in the basement where a librarian hung himself, possibly in the stairwell. All of them like the place quiet and don't like things moved or changed around. They certainly don't like attention being brought to them at all.

Employees related the following stories to us. A male librarian hung himself in the stairwell that leads to the basement. During performances on more than one occasion a black shadowy shape has been seen walking through the audience, often towards the projectionist and right through the people seated in the theater. Figures have been seen running across the front archways on the first floor and when they go to look no one is there. One employee saw the face of a man floating in the air where, it is suspected, the suicide took place, and it scared her so much that she went home immediately. She was sure that it was the "suicide man".

Another employee left a vacuum cleaner outside the main theater doors and went upstairs to check on something. He was alone in the building at the time, when he heard the vacuum turn on and begin running. He ran back down the stairs, checked all around and switched it off. Then he went upstairs again to finish what he was doing and when he came back down the vacuum had been moved clear across the floor. All of the employees we talked to said that the activity around the building seems to be more prevalent in the early morning when they first come in or on Sundays when they are open a partial day with fewer employees. Many things happen when someone is alone, with no witnesses to corroborate the story.

Perhaps the library was never open on Sunday and some of the spirits think it a sacrilege. Or perhaps they want one day of absolute rest with a building totally at peace and quiet. I only know what comes to me when I am allowed to walk through such a building, or sit quietly in the corner and listen to its sounds and feel its feelings. My great love is the science that it holds now. As a lay person, I hope that I have learned enough to inspire some of my students to be the ones to explore space even more than it has been thus far. To them, I say, go there and dream your dreams. Search the Heavens for whatever they might hold, and understand that the greatest scientists and the most earth-shattering discoveries came from both night and day dreams often ridiculed in their own time.

Note: "Planetarium Stars In Local Debate," by Phil Miller in *The Salt Lake Tribune* Section C, July 7, 1999.

"Space is its focus, and space has become its biggest limitation. The Hansen Planetarium's many educational exhibits have outgrown the 94 year old... building.... There is little room for special attractions, virtually no parking, and office space so limited that it has to be subdivided among several staffers. Nearly everyone... agrees that more room must be found. But two competing proposals are galaxies apart.

The University of Utah's Museum of Natural History, which has operated the county owned planetarium for two years, wants to keep using the current ... site for entertainment and tourist-driven temporary exhibits ... while moving its educational and permanent exhibits to a new building near the Hogle Zoo....

The Boyer Co., developer of the $300 million Gateway project on Salt Lake City's west side, wants the planetarium to join the Utah Children's Museum in the company's ambitious retail and residential blueprint. ...the Salt Lake County Commission will determine the Planetarium's future .... The University (of Utah) which... set aside 14 acres of Research Park for the new facility, must know whether to design the building to host only the Museum of Natural History or the Hansen Planetarium as well. Meanwhile the opportunity to move or relocate into The Gateway will last only about six more months .... Only one problem, said the planetarium director Sarah George:

the commissioners never told Hansen officials that the county was considering Boyer's development." The planetarium learned of this through a third party. though many agree that splitting the Planetarium into two separate locations would be silly.

At the time this book was written, a new building for the planetarium was being constructed in the Gateway Mall. I think the old library building is never going to be in jeopardy not only because of its historic registry protection and ornately built building, but because of its location near Temple Square which will probably help it to become absorbed into the Mormon dynasty. The old Wasatch Springs Plunge might be in question if the Children's Museum moves because it certainly has no value as a beautiful building. It is protected by the National Historic Registry and this should see it safely into the future, but its location might leave it standing in disrepair until local politicians can bring it down on those grounds. It will not be by any means an easy renovation. Both the planetarium and the children's museum will eventually be moving to the new Gateway center downtown the news said recently, making the future of both old buildings in jeopardy.

Writing this book has turned me into a preservationist, not only of histories but of the buildings which house them. As one European visitor to our fair city said in 1928, upon hearing about the old Salt Lake Theater being razed because it wasn't producing money for the LDS church and the telephone company was offering a mighty sum in exchange for the land, "We in Europe do not understand American thinking when it comes to this. We would discuss preserving the old building first and then discuss alternatives." Writing this has also given me new-found respect for both the Utah State Historical Society and the Utah Heritage Foundation. Most of all, I respect the group which existed long before any of these, the Daughters of the Utah Pioneers. They were radical preservationists in their day, and still quite a force as the preservers of history today.

Even the Daughters of the Utah Pioneers will leave their own ghosts behind them and the planetarium ghosts will continue to thrive as long as the old library is left standing. Just recently, they have begun moving many of the special artifacts from the old planetarium into storage while the new Clark Planetarium at The Gateway is being completed. It will take several years for everything to get moved to the new planetarium, so such things as a special moon rock are being housed in a bank vault downtown. One wonders just what will happen to the old Hansen Planetarium and we can only hope that various rescuers will find a new use for this magnificent old building. This first city library and its many first librarians, will probably continue to haunt the place for as long as the building is in use.

SALT LAKE CITY LIBRARY GHOSTS & APPARITIONS

Having already mentioned the ghosts of the old original Salt Lake City Public Library, which is now the Hansen Planetarium, it is interesting to note that some of the employees have over the years claimed that one of these ghosts decided to follow them to the new library. An even newer library is in the midst of being built on an entire city block downtown with an unusual architecture that is sure to be one of the showpieces of the city. So one wonders if this ghost or ghosts will decide to move over to the newest library when it is completed. The apparition is described as having long hair to her waist, which is worn in a bun and a long dress to her ankles. Employees and patrons have heard someone saying "hi!" to them when no one is around. One year they were having a book sale in the courtyard and some employees stayed overnight to guard the books. They had an encounter with a ghost but will not talk about it, except to say that they had one particular encounter that scared them quite enough.

This ghost seems to enjoy the Special Collections area of the library because librarians there will be looking for a particular book and that book will fall on the floor across the stacks from them or even at their feet. Having been brought to their attention by invisible hands, the librarians may have been looking for this book for quite some time when suddenly it miraculously appears on their desk or at their feet. When they go look for a book, it will be pulled halfway out from the shelf as though someone came just before them and found it and pulled it out just to get their attention. Employees also report, "knocking ghosts" who like to knock on the library walls, especially in the Special Collections section to get people's attention. Many people who work at the library now wonder if one or more of these ghosts will follow them over to the new library. Or they speculate that the ghosts may choose to stay put on the land next to the new library where the old library is being torn down. The question being do ghosts follow objects, books or artifacts to wherever they are placed, or do they stay with the building? Do these ghosts stay with the land itself or do they simply leave when their original haunt is torn down? The new library will be completed soon, so we will just have to wait and see.

In my research on libraries, it was interesting to find out that very often ghosts of libraries hang out in the Special Collections departments. Either this is because information on their decade attracts these apparitions, or people who work in Special Collections are more sympathetic to understanding the ghosts. Perhaps these employees are even a little more intuitive with a stronger curiosity than most concerning history, or the ghosts are simply seeking anything that might be a little more familiar. For example, at the University of Utah Library rumor has it that a Fort Douglas soldier has been seen for years roaming the Special Collections department in full dress uniform. The famous "Clem" of the Fort Douglas Museum is but a few blocks up the hill and some people have wondered if it is the same soldier, or if there are several soldiers roaming the area clear from the fort down to were the University library is located. The whole University of Utah campus was once Fort Douglas property and soldiers would have been all over the place over a hundred years ago. Even the old theatre on campus, Kingsbury Hall, has been known to have a few sightings of a soldier from the fort now and then. (More on this in my next book on the early history ghosts of Utah, *Shadows in Mormon Country*.)

Besides the main Salt Lake City Library ghosts, there are two other libraries in the city system that have rumors of apparitions although they like to keep a low profile. One of these is the Sprague Library has been on the main street of Sugar House since it was built in 1923. The other is the Chapman Library, which was one of the Carnegie Libraries and was built in 1918. Both of these old buildings are still being used as libraries in the city system. While the Sprague Library has only rumors, the Chapman Library has a legendary ghost woman, along with a very interesting history.

SPRAGUE LIBRARY - SUGAR HOUSE

The Sprague Library was officially opened November 1st, 1914. This library was named after Miss. Joanna Sprague who was in charge of the Salt Lake library system at the time as well as the head librarian at the Packard Public Library. Guest speakers at the dedication of the brand-new library included Governor Spry, Senator Smoot, and Mayor Samuel C. Park. The original building was replaced in 1928 with the English Tudor style building that stands there today. This building was dedicated on December 5th of that year. In 1940, the old Post Office was built next door and 1971 major renovations were made to the building. In 1978, the library celebrated its 50th anniversary and from 1989 to 1990 many new upgrades were done to the building, as well as a lot of new landscaping around it. In 1999, this library was voted the "Most Beautiful Branch Library in America" by the American Library Association.

Jack Goodman wrote about these renovations in December 1989 and the *Salt Lake Tribune*, where he mentioned a few other interesting facts about the old library. There is an old canyon stream meandering down right near the library and into the park below it. It is called Parley's Creek and has over the years, caused the foundations of the building a few problems. The Denver and Rio Grande Western Railroad used to run right by the library, through the old park behind the library and clear up through Parley's Canyon to the mines in the mountains. The old two acre park directly behind this library is now completely gone and in its place are several shopping centers. But when it was the park it was well known in the area as a bird refuge, before the word "refuge" came into popular use. Birdwatchers and many others would go to this park to enjoy the various songbirds, many of which have been depleted in numbers over the year since. During this time 300 schoolchildren gathered in the park at the dedication of something called the Bird Inn. It was a two-story bird hotel hanging in the trees with the words "Bird Inn" painted on the top and on the roof was painted the words "Proprietors: Children of Sprague Library, Sugar House." Children would visit the birdhouse before going to the Story Hour Room through its own entrance on the side of the library building.

The Sprague Library has an enticing architecture and is fun to visit, reminding one of those old-fashioned small town English Tudor Libraries that one might have visited as a child. People hear footsteps when no one is there and many patrons and employees have reported this phenomenon over the years. The copy machine will turn on or off by itself when no one has been near it. Some of the ghostly rumors revolve around a transient who broke into the library several years ago by shattering a window. It was a very cold winter and he was trying to keep warm, but instead he gave himself a deep cut, fell asleep and while he was sleeping, apparently bled to death on the library floor. They found him in the morning, and the story goes that he was either already stone cold, or he was rushed to a hospital where he died shortly after this. Some believe that besides the decades long footsteps and a visit from Miss Sprague upon occasion, the library is now haunted by this transient who died in the building.

CHAPMAN LIBRARY - WEST SIDE

The Chapman Library was built in 1918 and was designed by one of Brigham Young's grandsons, Don Carlos Young who also designed the original University of Utah campus layout. This library has two wings that intersect at a corner entrance with several columns, stark against the dark brick. There is a Gothic element to the building with the main floor and basement providing ramped passageways and an elevator for the handicapped. It cost $23,000 and was partly paid for by Andrew Carnegie Funds, which funded some twenty-three such libraries in Utah. There is only one other such library on the west side of town and that library is located in Rose Park. The library was named in honor of Annie E. Chapman who was the first librarian in the Salt Lake City Public Library System. ("Chapman Library Restored To Former Glory," by Jack Goodman, *The Salt Lake City Tribune*, October 31st, 1993.)

The well-known legend is that Annie Chaplain, who had a leg ailment, can be heard "thumping" around the library late at night because of the permanent limp she had. She never married and dedicated herself to her work in building up the library system. It ended up that the library was only partially funded by Carnegie Funds because of some disagreement between this organization and the architect. Don Carlos Young stuck to his agreement to build the library and took less pay so that it could be completed. Schoolchildren at the old Riverside Elementary across the street raised the rest of the money for the building. There was always a very close relationship between the children of this elementary school and the Chapman Library. However, the old Riverside Elementary was torn down many years ago and only the old library remains. The library has fanned-light windows which are the original lead glass and the whole building has remained pretty much intact since 1918. Not only is it a magnificent building, but is also the pride of the neighborhood.

In January of 1993, the roof fell in on the east wing mainly due to heavy snows. The east wing roof rested on the book stacks so that only the books on the top row were ruined. The snow was dusted off of the rest of the books and they remained in good shape. 50,000 books were rescued and no one was in the library when the accident occurred. By December of the following year, the library reopened with a ribbon cutting ceremony and quite a crowd to welcome it back. The old ceiling was completely duplicated in a labor of love by local construction crews and local businesses donated a lot to the restoration of the building and to the employees of the library, both in funds, goods, and volunteer hours. Even "the long curved desk where patrons returned books & the new ones was completely rebuilt." (Ibid, p.2.)

However, the real ghost of the Chapman Library probably has nothing to do with the Annie Chapman legend. Librarians as far back as the beginning of the library have been aware of and reported, at least privately, the sounds of a woman's long skirts swishing through the library stacks as well as a hand going along the stacks and straightening the books invisibly. Books will straighten themselves for the librarians and they say that closing time is when most of the activity starts. However the swishing skirts have been heard anytime day or night.

The most interesting full-fledged apparition is that of a sobbing woman whom at least one person from the past claims to have seen in back of the library. Apparently she will cry and sob very hard right before any major event happens in or to the library. For example, just before a beloved and longtime librarian in the building was transferred, three separate employees heard the sobbing woman at three separate times. She was heard over a period of two weeks before the transfer took place. Also, several employees heard a week or two before the roof fell in, the sobbing woman again. The woman cries so loud and so long that it is really frightening to those few privileged to hear her, thus they are shy of talking about the apparition's presence.

The Chapman Library is not only a piece of the true history of our city and state, but has also become a representative of the cultural diversity of our city. Bosnians, Hispanics, Vietnamese, Islanders, Germans and others come to this library to studying or checkout books, and even the staff is multicultural, the head librarian says. Giant pine trees that were planted as seedlings in 1918 still surround the library to this day. Several movies have been filmed there such as Disney's "Don't Look Under The Bed" as well as episodes of both the old series "Promised Land" and the still ongoing series "Touched By And Angel" on television. It is still surrounded by a community neighborhood that very proudly and sometimes even fiercely protects her. There are librarians who have worked there for many, many years, who are very proud of this library and have a deep love for the Chapman.

Along with each library's individual and interesting history are the ongoing evolutions of each building and the ghosts that inhabit these various libraries. Besides the libraries containing stories about Annie Chapman's thump, invisible librarians who arrange the books and swish their skirts, footsteps and dimming lights, and occasional sightings of full fledged apparitions, there are reports in some of the older libraries of objects and equipment being moved about or rearranged overnight by invisible hands. Most enthralling however, is the woman who sobs and cries when anything affects her library for the worst or even for any kind of change at all. She must have loved the place so dearly, that she could not leave it behind. One can speculate that perhaps she was never a librarian at all, although this would be the most likely scenario. Perhaps she was never even an employee of the library, but a patron of it instead. It might even be that when the old Riverside Elementary School was torn down, this ghost lost her immediate home and relocated to the library across the street. This is something quite common in ghost lore when two buildings are so closely connected to each other. This could be one explanation for the apparition's fierce defending of the old library. It may be the only home she has left.

FREEMASONRY IN UTAH

THE SALT LAKE MASONIC PUBLIC LIBRARY & TEMPLE

The Masons have been around since Solomon because much of the Masonic rituals deal with the builders of King Solomon's Temple. Much of the phrasing in these various rituals has to do with significant building terms, methods, tools and practices used then. The real start for the Masonic Order was in the Middle Ages with the rise of alchemy and all sorts of secret organizations. Chapters were located all over Europe, and England especially had an interest in such fraternal organizations. Benjamin

Franklin could be considered the father of Masonry in the United States, although George Washington was also a Mason. Signs and symbols of the Order can be seen everywhere in the founding of our nation, right down to the dollar bill with its all-seeing eye. Joseph Smith became a Mason when he was young and studied their secret rituals and degrees. The Masons politely asked him to leave when he started to found his own Masonic groups without their permission. At the same time, he was about to found his own religion. It is said by the Masons that he never really forgot their Order because his last words before his death were supposed to have been a very secret Masonic phrase known only to some. It is well known that many of the rituals and symbols in the early Mormon church are based on Masonic rites and symbols, which was a part of Joseph Smith's base of knowledge at the time. This partially explains the later animosity between the Saints and the Masons. Masons were angry about their stolen and misinterpreted symbols, and Mormons wanted to disown any such symbolism within their newly-founded church. A lot of people are aware that many of the LDS temple rites have direct links, even to this day, to some of the Masonic rituals.

The Free Masons in Utah began with 23 officers in Johnston's Army who used a dirt floor building at the military post as their first Masonic Meeting Hall. Sixty-two more candidates became Masons and spent a lot of their charity money on poor migrants passing through Utah going west. With the advent of the Civil War, all such activities ceased in Utah. In 1865, the Mormons and the Masons squared off because, while many prominent Mormons were also Masons at the time, a petition was sent to the Grand Lodge of Nevada for a temporary authorization to start another lodge in Salt Lake City with the added stipulation that no Mormons could hold any high degrees or even be admitted as visitors. The Masons finally found a state that would allow them to exclude Mormons from their lodge. The Kansas Grand Lodge took a lot of criticism for this reverse prejudice at the time. Other lodges soon followed and the growth of Masonry became slow but steady. While anyone of any religious persuasion could join the Masons, who do not consider themselves in any way a religious organization, the Mormons could not.

As the years went by, and the Masons slowly grew in numbers in Utah, various buildings were used as a Masonic Hall. The Camp Floyd building was occupied from 1859 to 1860 by Rocky Mountain Lodge No. 205, registered in Missouri. This indicates how the hostilities might have begun, because Missouri at the time was a hotbed of anti-Mormon sentiment. In Utah, the Saints readied themselves to fight the same type of people who had so viciously run them out of the Midwest. The first official Masonic

Hall was located at 128 South Main in the Commerce building where the Mt. Moriah and Wasatch Lodges met on the second floor above a Stoves and Tinware shop from 1867 to 1872. The third lodge was located in the Trowbridge building from 1872 to 1876. The fourth lodge was located in the Wells Fargo building at 161 South Main until 1896. Then from 1896 to 1907, Masonic Hall was in the MacIntosh building at West Temple and Second South. An actual Masonic Temple was built at Second East and First South and this building was used from October of 1907 to November of 1927. In a supplement to *The Salt Lake City Tribune*, an entire section entitled "Masonic Temple Dedication Edition," came out on November 20, 1927, and has been reprinted by the Masons for all to enjoy reading today. This edition describes the plans for building a magnificent structure and has pictures of all the other Masonic Halls used in Salt Lake City before this.

The Masons were soon complaining about how scattered their members were, and that they needed a central location to increase attendance and to focus more on their finances and programs. The land for the new temple was purchased on South Temple and the ground was broken on July 28, 1926. The cornerstone was laid November 5, 1926 and the building was dedicated with over 1,400 Masons from all over Utah and the surrounding states in attendance. The Masonic band played in the new auditorium and the Grand Master of the Grand Lodge spoke. The new Egyptian-motif structure had been built at a cost of $750,000. Before construction started, the two architects spent months studying and investigating scores of other Masonic Temples across the nation and overseas. They decided on an exterior with an Egyptian temple motif which was quite popular at the time, but with adaptations for modern needs. The building covers an 186 by 132 feet area and was constructed of Utah granite with a tapestry brick building on top.

Eight columns three stories high provide for seven openings at the front with the ascension of three, then five, then seven and finally nine stairway steps. Two sphinxes guard the entrance to the Temple and between their paws are figures which represent the Celestial and Terrestrial spheres. The sphinxes contemplate these spheres symbolizing the inspection of earth and the heavens. The Sphinxes were carved locally; the spheres are onyx. The three stories of the building signify the three degrees of Masonry. The ground floor is for public meetings, while the upper floor houses all of the lodge rooms for ritualistic functions. These Lodge rooms each hold a special meaning or aspect of Masonry and are designed in a certain style which the candidate is to contemplate for its historical and symbolic significance. There are two of them on the main floor and these are designed in a Colonial and Egyptian style. On the upper floor is a Moorish Lodge and the largest of the four Lodges is decorated in a Gothic style. All four Lodges have a flight of three, five, seven and nine stairs with an outer and inner door leading to a middle chamber: "To have the middle chamber open on the Lodge rooms so that the members can hear the work is original to our Lodge rooms." ("Masonic Temple," pamphlet given out by the Masons at their temple with no acknowledged authors or dates.)

The auditorium is decorated with gold leaf and is very much in the style of art deco Egyptian meeting rooms. The scenery or backdrops to the stage are considered to be priceless because they were painted by a famous scenic artist of the time for the very first temple on First South and Second East. There are 97 backdrops used in the Scottish Rite degree ceremonies. They were created to give a three-dimensional effect with two or three backdrops for each scene. In the new temple the drops were too small for the stage, although members were reluctant not to use them. It was then discovered that the artist was still alive, although 70 years of age. He was asked to come to Salt Lake City to enlarge and finish each of the drops. He agreed to do so and added ten to fifteen feet to the width and five to ten feet to the length of each drop. It was necessary to cut and splice a new piece for the center as well as the sides and bottom of each piece. The older parts were retouched and all of this work became the last artistic contribution of this famous artist, Thomas G. Moses, who died in 1934. The curtains can be drawn over four arches to create smaller and smaller rooms.

The dome ceiling in the auditorium has magnesium glow lights which symbolize the canopy of Heaven. There is a control panel for these lights and different colored lights can be used for different effects in the room. Costume storage areas and dressing rooms allow for those being inducted to change into replicas of costumes that represent the various degrees such as the Revolutionary period and Egyptian periods. These two rites include a priceless collection of historic costumes and accessories which no other Masonic Lodge in the United States can claim. The Banquet room is decorated in an Aztec style and in the nineteen thirties and forties the area would be cleared for dances on the original inlaid wood floor. There is a complete kitchen off this area and the column caps in this room were designed and built by the architect himself. He found that when he tried to explain what Masonic beliefs required in the space, the skilled molder could not understand or produce what was desired. While crude by comparison to other areas in the building, these molds hold almost every important part of the three degrees of Masonry in their designs.

The animosity between the Mormons and the Masons continued until sixty years later, when Mormons could once again join the Masons if they so desired. This seems not to be the case now; most Masons are not Mormon. The Salt Lake Public Library system owes its beginnings to the Masons. It was Christopher Diehl, the Grand Secretary of the Masons in Utah, who worked unceasingly to bring this about. He along with the Ladies Literary Society composed mostly of Masonic member's wives, gathered funding and books until there were over 900 volumes in storage. The Masonic Public Library, which never really came into being, ended up donating over 9,000 books to the city, which became the original volumes in its first public library.

Carl W.Scott and George W. Welch were the architects for the temple. In 1944, Scott wrote an article about the temple entitled, "Symbolism In The Masonic Temple At Salt Lake City, Utah" and presented it as a speech at a meeting of the Wasatch Lodge No. 1, F. & A.M. on March l0th of that year. In this article he spoke about the various symbols he had incorporated into the structure of the building. He said that the main goal was not to disclose Masonic secrets to those not entitled to know them, and yet on the other hand, to provide public access to parts of the structure so that people would feel comfortable visiting the building. He also wanted to show good taste in all that he did, and decorate in a Masonic style, while at the same time maintaining the secrecy of the Masonic rites. "Legend tells us that rulers in the past often blinded or put to death their builders upon completion of their work, that they might not disclose the secret wine vault or do a better job for another client." (ibid, p.2) While of course this is no longer a practice, it falls to the architect to decide what is sacred and what can be viewed by non-members.

Scott said that while it had now been a few years since the building of the temple, he could still recall interesting facts which had not been mentioned at the time. Several committees helped to build the temple, he said, and not just a handful of men. Also when local Masons visited the various Masonic Temples, they found that their Salt Lake City design was the first to include Masonic symbols on the exterior of the building and in addition, had a great deal more symbolism on the walls and ceilings of the interior. He also mentioned that since the building of King Solomon's Temple had a lot to do with the Masonic rituals, he tried to use related phrases and images within the building he designed. He also mentioned that non-Masonic artisans and draftsmen had a hard time understanding what he wanted done, and that he had the additional problem of not disclosing Masonic secrets, while illustrating the basics of Masonic beliefs throughout the building. Logistics of how the entire building and certain rooms within it were located had to be considered in the context of Masonic beliefs. For example: "Prior to being initiated, passed and raised, the candidate wandered in darkness as to Masonic secrets, which is symbolized by the North, and it is fitting that convenient doors should be provided inviting him to pass into the Temple to be enlightened in the Masonic ritual." (Ibid, p.4.) Doors open the wrong way and light switches are behind them which forces the person to "wander in darkness" until they can grope for the light switch!

Ancient measures were used, such as the cubit, to follow what might have been done in King Solomon's time in laying out the entire building. The numbers three, five and seven in Masonry have significant meaning and so the architect tried to use this symbolism throughout the structure. The spacing of the front columns and all other columns in the building used this theme. Three stories were provided on purpose, as well as a seven-finished course of ashiar of Utah granite in the base of the temple. The cornerstone contains a sealed copper receptacle of mementos from past Masons. Many people, especially Masons, asked the architect why he used the Egyptian exterior. One reason he gave was that with the ornate style, it was very easy to conceal Masonic symbolism and yet to include more of it than in other Masonic buildings. He also said that, "Several Egyptian structures and those best preserved today were built in honor of the Egyptian God Horus, described as the 'God of Light or Life,' and from them could directly be taken symbols of light so appropriate for our structure. The God Horus is variously depicted, perhaps more often as a falcon or a falcon-headed human. But in some cases the symbol used was a double-headed, feathered serpent and solar disc, and this suited our purpose better and was used. This device in large scale was used in ornamenting the cornice, signifying that this is a Temple dedicated to Masonic light." (Ibid, p.7.)

This same symbol was used on the funeral gates west of the Temple to symbolize life as well. A funeral procession escorting the dead Mason's body would leave by the west exit symbolizing the last time he would leave his temple. These gates were only opened for the Mason's funeral cortege, symbolizing a break in the life span of a Master Mason. Above the main gateway on the lintel is carved an Egyptian scarab signifying resurrection and immortality and along the ramp of this west exit were seven urns containing Acacia plants for the Masonic Funeral Rites of the day.

The sphinxes had a man's head and a lion's body which signify strength, intelligence and mystery. It is interesting to note here that the Mormon stonemason and LDS bishop Thomas B. Childs and his friend Maurice Brooks, the sculptor, spent a lifetime creating an unusual garden called Gilgal. Gilgal means "circle of sacred stones" in the Old Testament and I will have a section on the gardens in volume two, though I did want to mention the likenesses to Masonic ritual in this garden even down to a large sphinx with Joseph Smith's face carved into it. While sphinxes are Egyptian in origin and most of the world was fascinated with Egyptian art in the twenties and thirties, thus both the Masonic Temple and Gilgal, the similarities between Mormon symbols in this garden and Masonic symbols in the temple in Salt Lake City are striking. There is even a quote carved in stone from Ralph Waldo Emerson about the feminine nature of the sphinx. "The Sphinx is drowsy, her wings are furled./Her ear is heavy, she broods on the world." ("Going Gaga Over Gilgal Gardens: Salt Lake City attraction has a new lease on life," by John Keahey, *The Salt Lake Tribune*, Monday, May 13, 2002, Sec-B2.)

"The lighting or reflections on these two guardians of the Temple took considerable time to get just right. Various colors were used until it was noted that red seemed to be the only color which muted the white floodlights to make them appear mystical rather than grotesque. Sometimes in the granite a black blotch would appear in the stone which made it necessary to start over again to carve the piece into something smaller. The blocks for the sphinxes were therefore chosen carefully. However, upon completion of one of them, a large dark blotch appeared on the throat of one of the statue and no amount of polishing and cutting could get rid of it. Rather than start over, the artist was allowed to cut the piece out and insert a new piece of granite into the throat. It would be of interest to examine them and figure out which one had the piece inserted, as the architect claims it would be very difficult to do so, or at least was in 1944. The clay for the brick on the building was from a new deposit and only samples had been made of it at the time. After the Masonic Temple was built, this brick was always referred to as Masonic Temple brick.

While the lodges are available at times for the public to view, the architect said that he did a good job of hiding Masonic symbolism because only practitioners of Masonry can discern them. Concealed spotlights are directed onto the Master or the candidate in these rooms to highlight the event. Every detail in the various period designs for each Lodge room was taken from original pieces that were studied and copied as accurately as possible. All carpets and all pieces of furniture were specially selected for the various rooms. When the furniture for the blue room and for the red room arrived with the opposite leather color than intended, it was considered a minor disaster, as the furniture fit the period and the color did not fit the room. All of it had to be sent back and the leather changed to the appropriate color for each room. Everything intended and attempted did not turn out as well as it might, the architect concluded, but all in all, the Temple design fell into place as it should have.

Today, the Masonic Temple on South Temple, is gated off in the front and all members go through the back entrance to the various functions. The oldest order of Masons dates back to about 1390 and the oldest lodge in the United States is in

Virginia. Masons contend that they are not and never have been a religion, but that many famous Americans have been members over time, including Will Rogers and Charles Lindbergh, as well as presidents, congressmen, governors and other great leaders in their fields. Members do not consider themselves a secret society as they share much of what they do with others. The masons basically teach their followers the principles of the brotherhood of man, the fatherhood of God and the basic golden rules of mankind. Only men can join and reach the various degrees therein, though there are organizations for both the women and children of Masons. Unfortunately there are many who view Masons as people who are obsessed with control and money. But then aren't we all in one way or another? Our own leaders in whatever group or religion do much of the same. How fascinating are the rituals of man!

Friends who are Masons or their wives and children have told me ghost stories about the Masonic Temple. The very atmosphere of the place is conducive to the esoteric. I sometimes wonder if the architect, knowingly or unknowingly, incorporated ancient Egyptian constructions which trapped and used energies that we still do not understand to this day, thereby bringing about the ability to record even more of the past than another such building might. There has always been a theory in esoteric circles that the great cathedrals of Europe were all essentially planned by the same two architects who purposely had them built along "ley" lines around the earth. These natural energy spots are said to be conductors and amplifiers, and the structures the architects designed create immense energy fields within them that can pick up and record feelings and emotions in the stones themselves. Everything left over the years as people have visited these cathedrals can sometimes be re-released as sounds, sights or even smells. Perhaps right here in Salt Lake City, we have a temple designed to magnify and capture the esoteric and obviously in more than one such temple.

Upon interviewing the various people at the temple, I found they all knew about the resident ghost named Charlie Valentine and that he was once a "real" person. Finding out about his real life story was a bit more difficult. The custodians of the building did have ghostly stories to tell however. One man said that after his initial experiences in the temple, he thereafter locked up the building early and stayed downstairs by the door. There are four levels with the Gothic room on and Moorish room on top and the Colonial and Egyptian rooms on the main level. These huge very ornate rooms are like small auditoriums and are decorated in distinctive styles with the Egyptian room being the lightest and the Colonial second in lightness. The Gothic has a bit darker atmosphere while the Moorish room is the darkest and most active. Over time I have learned that when a light flickers dramatically on and off or a door slams or swings slightly open or back and forth of its own accord, I am in the presence of spirits. It is their way of getting my attention as both of these things happened as we toured the building more than once. Whoever hangs out there, the Moorish room is not the place to be, especially with a crypt that somehow rises from the floor. The upper two floors are the most eerie, probably because they are used less often.

One evening as one of the custodian was locking up, he was on the third floor, he looked down the hall and saw three people engaged in conversation. No one was supposed to be in the building and he had just finished securing all of the areas within it. He walked towards the three people, and they flicked the lights on in a room down the hall and walked into it. When he got there, the room was dark and locked and the people had disappeared. It spooked him and he left. He called and asked what to do and his supervisor advised him to check the whole building and make sure that everything was secure. It was and apparently had been all along. Another night he heard a man calling "Hello" from the fourth floor, but could find nothing when he investigated. After a few more experiences like this, he was quick to check everything and then return downstairs. He said that he didn't mind when these spirits talked to him, but he was not the least bit interested in seeing any of them again.

As we were allowed to see the rooms, the main floor where the Colonial, Egyptian and large auditorium are located, was really very cheery and inviting. Many films and television shows have used the building for filming, such as "Touched By An Angel" and the TV movie, "Avenging Angel," among others. The top floor was a bit more interesting and the Gothic room did have a feel to it of some activity, but it was the Moorish room on the third floor which intrigued and at the same time repelled me. There is a narrow passageway or room between the door to it and a second door which opens up into the chamber and with all of them, it's like walking onto an old movie set for some "when knighthood was in flower" movie. Also, the light switch is behind the door on the opposite side so that one has to enter into pitch blackness, walk around the door and grope for the light switch, which certainly adds to the effect. As we went into the little room in front of it with a very low roof, the light would not come on at first and then when it did, it flickered quite dramatically. I asked our tour guide if this happened often and he said just once in a great while. I thought to myself, yes, whenever someone intuitive enters the room! In this room I was actually touched by something and had a very strong feeling that women were not supposed to be in there and they, whoever 'They" are, definitely wanted us out.

I was also warned by a friend not to visit the temple again or to dwell on Masonry too much, as it was indeed a dark force to be reckoned with. My husband who has studied the Masons and Rosicrucians quite extensively, says that in the very beginnings of these organizations hundreds of years ago, the occult and black arts were incorporated into some of their rites. While in the modern day no such things exist, there could be some residue from certain individuals who continued to investigate such things in the past. I found the modern day Masons to be some of the finest people I know and quite friendly and open. They were very well informed and interesting people who really enjoyed themselves as a community, for all of their secret ceremonies for men only. The resident ghost, Charlie Valentine, was a worker at the Murray Smelter all his life. He came to Salt Lake from New York and was a member of the Mt. Moriah Temple or bethel somewhere in Salt Lake City. When he died he was cremated and his ashes were placed in an urn which was supposedly shipped back to New York state to be buried near his family. For about thirty years or so, stories and sightings of the ghost eventually nicknamed "Charlie," were told by members who came to the Masonic Temple.

Five years ago, while a big cleaning of the storage areas in the massive building took place, someone discovered an urn with a man's ashes in it in the back of a closet. A little research revealed that these were the ashes of Charlie Valentine and that the urn had been around even before the temple was built in 1926. It had been moved with all the other stuff from the old original temple downtown. People had been calling this ghost "Charlie" all these years and now, here was the real Charlie with a real story about him. Perhaps it was coincidence, or merely that someone a very long time ago had known the story and had started the whole account with the right name after all! Or maybe someone really did use intuition to find his name along the way. Charlie may have acquired the name by calling out in the middle of the night when somebody was there to hear him. Charlie has been blamed for all sorts of unexplained incidents at the Masonic Temple over the years, which could probably be blamed on many other spirits active in the building.

A decent burial supposedly gave the building peace, or did it? As far as anyone knows, they had no place to send Charlie's ashes to by the time that they were discovered. There was no family left and so it is a mystery still as to just where his ashes were sent when they did send them. It seems that even though sightings of Charlie are gone now, others have taken his place as spirits in the building. Sightings of groups of people who walk into a room and disappear, continue, as well as all the other usual phenomena of more than one haunting. With warnings of a fine line between the black arts and Masonic arts back in the old days, one wonders what portals might have been opened that would be of an unsavory nature to those not prepared by all of the Masonic ritual to handle them. And more than this is what the architect created unknowingly or perhaps even intuitively in this particular Masonic Temple, that would make it a place where souls can slip in and out of its many rooms unannounced and whenever they wish too.

TROLLEY SQUARE

- UTAH TRANSIT AUTHORITY BUS BARN
- TROLLEY BARNS
- TERRITORIAL FAIR GROUNDS
- LDS TENTH WARD SQUARE

The LDS Tenth Ward Square was located in Salt Lake City until 1865 and was used as a public space to be farmed jointly by local farmers as part of the Tenth Ward industries which surrounded the area. Then entire Tenth Ward boundaries, one of the original 19 wards created by Brigham Young, ran from 300 South to 600 South and 600 East to the foothills of the mountains. Some of the industries which existed closer to town inside these boundaries were such things as the Troy laundry and the Salt Lake Brewing Company as well as the Tenth Ward church building, a co-op store and a lumber company. The square which had been used as a communal farming area was purchased and used as the territorial fairgrounds from 1865 to 1902 for the annual state fairs before the electric company purchased it. This means that for 37 years hundreds of people attended the state fairs on this property and stories of both tragedy and triumph have surely been lost from this era. The Utah Exposition building was located in the southwest corner of the Tenth Ward Square but was torn down when the land was deeded to the electric trolley car company in 1907.

From 1908 to 1910, the Utah Light and Railway Company, under the direction of E.

H. Harriman, built car barns and repair shops for an electric streetcar system, one of the first in the nation. The first line was electrified in 1889, but when Harriman bought the company he intended to build a state of the art, trolley car system as a model for the whole world. He and other investors sank $3.5 million into the project constructing mission-style car barns, which were unusual for the time. Lots of people who go to Trolley Square as tourists wonder about the very ornate Queen Anne Revival mansion to the south of Trolley Square along 7th East. I did to, until finding out that it has always been a private home and had no connection to either the fairgrounds or the trolley and bus barns after that. It was built of red brick around 1890 and has an unusual box-like tower with gables and spindled woodwork all around it. Built for Abial B. Sawyer when he and his family moved to Salt Lake from Illinois, Sawyer was a lawyer who formed a partnership with a man named Putnam and his son and his family remained in the home until 1935. After this it had a series of owners who could look across to the trolley barns every day.

The largest or southern building housed berths for the trolley cars. The middle building was used as a machine or "rip" shop, as well as housing a blacksmith's shop. The north building was for the painters and carpenters who worked on repairs and making new trolleys. The small east building, where the trolley and water tower now stand, was a sand house. The water tower held 50,000 gallons of water and was designed to be used in case of fire. The trolley cars operated until August 19th,1945, though gas buses and automobiles had begun to replace them sooner than this. The Salt Lake City Bus System took over the barns for their buses and used them until 1960. I can remember going on an elementary school field trip to the bus depot and riding inside our school bus through the giant washing and drying machines as we watched. It was one of the highlights of my elementary school years. I was just fascinated by the giant rollers and brushes and rinsers and to be riding snug and secure inside our bus while all this was going on around us, was a real thrill!

When the buses moved out around 1960, the buildings stood vacant and dilapidated but by 1970 the city had plans to turn the place into a giant shopping mall. It was the first large-scale renovation that the city of Salt Lake had ever undertaken. The remodelers converted the whole place into what they called a 'festival marketplace." They also collected relics of all kinds from around the whole west and installed them around the place to add atmosphere. I can remember being sad at the lost of the bus barns and wishing that things did not have to change. In June of 1972, Trolley Square opened and it really was a smash hit. It is full of all kinds of little shops and eateries and restaurants and is a showpiece for the city, though the prices now discourage a lot of us commoners from spending too much time there. The place is wonderful to visit at Christmas time, or any time for that matter, even if you plan only to browse.

Everyone has his or her own hauntings and stories about Trolley Square. My stories come often to haunt me, not unlike those of the Old Spaghetti Factory where stories of ghostly encounters have been told throughout the years. In the north building there apparently is a painter or carpenter who still plies his trade to this day. Years ago, when the bus barn was being converted to the shopping mall that it is today, we used to watch them working on it from across the street at Bill and Nada's. Their sign is still on the old building which is now abandoned but once was a locally famous restaurant that reached a sort of cult status among its customers and especially college students around the area. Nada died many years ago and Bill ran it for a long time until he died just a few years ago. One was always guaranteed very interesting fellow diners including a ghost or two as well. I can remember a hitchhiker coming in at three o'clock in the morning, who was so exhausted from walking that he ordered a hamburger, smothered it in ketchup and then fell face first into the ketchup as he passed out onto his hamburger. Ketchup was all over the place and he slid down onto the floor, a bronze god spread-eagled before us. It was therefore very sad when a year after Bill's death it was announced that Bill and the employees had made a pact to close the place forever at Christmas time, 1999. Bills and Nada's is now gone forever.

My own haunting happened when I first returned to Salt Lake City after an 8 year absence and ran into an old college friend at Trolley Square. He was actually an old boyfriend whom my girlfriend and I had both dated. She had gotten serious with him after I had moved away to Colorado and they dated for a couple of years. The guy came to Colorado to see if he and I could go any where. He said he was drawn to both of us and could not help himself- what a line some might say- though the three of us being young had a very awkward time of it. With the cultural background and heritage that we all three shared and then turned away from, perhaps in an earlier time, during the polygamy times that is, it would have all worked out. But a lot of years had gone by, and he had a gorgeous blonde on his arm, which was typical of how he managed things in his life, "a girl in every port" so to speak. He ran up to talk to me and even looked like he might have dropped the blonde for me, but I was married by then and so was he as far as I knew. I thought that perhaps it was not the appropriate thing to do. At this later time, we were in the south building of the barn on which employees were doing some maintenance work. I remember that he had a scarf tied around his head under his leather hat, like a pirate. I was a little intrigued that the attraction between us was still strong. We chatted away as though the blonde was not there at all, but I walked away from his offer to get together later and never saw him again. This became one of the great regrets of my life, because he was dying of leukemia and I did not know it. The scarf, the hat, the way that he looked at me all got past me and I walked away oblivious. I was too afraid, I think, to pay attention to the very intuition that had drawn all three of us together, and apparently still did.

The other girl, who had married, had children and divorced, now lived across the country from me. One day she just showed up at my school and found me and said,

"Jay has died. Do you want to go to the grave side service with me?" It was the only time in my teaching career when I simply ran out of the school, regardless of the consequences. My old friend was home visiting her mother and had read about the death in the newspaper. We went to the service and stood as strangers among a crowd that had once long ago been familiar. Later, when we went back to the grave to have our own private funeral, we found two red roses placed diagonally over the grave. One had a long stem and the other a short one, as I stood a foot taller than she. We picked them up and pressed them in our own separate books, not knowing whether Jay had left them for us after his death or someone else in the funeral party had purposely placed them there for some entirely different reason. Over the years the two of us who remain have called each other and reminisced about our memories of Jay. We recalled the premonition dream that my friend had had several years before he died, about the three of us in a classroom somewhere where we were being instructed in important things about our lives. We all stood up and got into some clear plastic bubbles in threesomes and began floating across a huge ocean towards a beautiful tropical island. Halfway there, Jay fell out into the water and the other two of us continued floating on to the island.

Jay had contracted leukemia perhaps a year before I saw him and he was divorced at the time. He fought the disease for 5 years and eventually had to quit teaching and move in with his parents. In the obituary, like many in the heart of Mormon country, were the comforting little white lies about his lifestyle, which only dug my regret even deeper into me. I had stood in the south building where the trolleys once were berthed and where construction was now going on, watching the wind blow through the huge plastic rolls that hung there, talking to one of my best friends for the very last time. All the time I was oblivious to his suffering, or his desire to speak with me when perhaps he had needed it most. A youthful pride in having once been deeply hurt by his actions and those of my girlfriend, had blinded me to my own intuition about this supposedly chance encounter. Years later, when I woke up to the real me - the person who must live within the heart of the intuitive life whether she chooses to or not - I would never forget the importance of this chance encounter and the need never to ignore such things again, regardless of the consequences. I had thrown away my chance and one never gets a second one when the veil shuts down or so I believed at the time.

I do hear from Jay upon occasion, though it has been years now and life, as always, flows on. A favorite song of his comes on the radio with words that I am supposed to attend to carefully. His old letters and poems will fall out of a stack I am going through and I will read a certain one and recall that there is something I need to do for someone: I do it as soon as I can. I remind myself that his sons need to have all this stuff as soon as they are old enough to appreciate it, which is not now, because they are still too young and might just pass it all by. He visits in a dream now and then, or when my old friend and I discuss our old memories. I remember his kindnesses, intimacies and lack of loyalties. I wonder if he forgives me for having been so stupid or blind at the time to what I should have known. I will hear him say something to me as I drive along on, always on a strange cloud-formation day. I then notice, and recall our youthful times together.

It is Trolley Square, which I don't visit very often, which brings back this memory every time I am there. I walk through the south concourse, recall the plastic blowing about us, the blonde's invisible face, and Jay standing there with a scarf under his hat, speaking to me through the wind about what is really important in life. Later on I found out that the blonde was a sister-in-law and felt even sillier about my behavior then. I have to admit that death comes to me much more often now in the intuitive work that I do for others and I am more comfortable with it now as well. In helping others cope with the loss of loved ones, I still fail to recognize moments when it would be important to pass on information that I get, and when it would be inappropriate to do so. The dead spot on my own soul gone forever now, I accept the responsibility of not fearing and walking into my inner self to assist others with their journeys, farewells, and visits. Though sometimes I do not recognize my own bravery when it comes to this, nor that I just have to do it, no matter the consequences which do indeed come along with it. I journey now in a country without signposts or directions, stumbling forward supposedly guiding others, while I am pressing forward in the darkness myself. I cannot go back to who I was before. I can only go forward.

More years pass, and another friend and I sit in the middle building of Trolley Square where she has gone to spend her extra Christmas money. I had placed it in her hand at her husband's funeral, remembering her kindnesses from before and how much this Christmas needs to be a good one for her. Her last son is out spending the extra money, purchasing little gifts for his sisters, not knowing our secret as this is one that she has been told to keep. She and I sit on one of the benches reminiscing about her years with her second husband. Near us is a window display of a huge, very pink and shiny chrome Harley-Davidson, parked among white fluffy clouds and a bright blue sky. Her son comes up and brings our attention to it. The three of us walk over to look at it. By this time I am able to offer comfort in some intuitive readings with her and her son. Her son, who is fourteen, says, "That's what dad is on in Heaven, mom. He always wanted a Harley and those are the kind they would have there." I think of Jay again and thank him for recognizing in me, something that all three of us had - the very connection which had brought us together. I am now very aware of this connection at every step in my life, and one which Jay knew we had. Unlike we two women, he failed or perhaps was not allowed enough time to pick up the mantel himself.

The ghosts of Trolley Square have been talked about for years. I guess that I just added a few of my own to those which I am sure many others have in their memories and reminisces about the place. It is a gathering place of souls, those who worked together on the church farms, those who came to enjoy the entertainments of the annual state fairs, those who traveled through on trolleys or buses, and those who brought friends and either lost or found them at the premier shopping mall. The Old Spaghetti Factory ghost is the most famous one and has been talked about ever since the Square opened as a town showpiece and mall. Everyone knows about the ghost, but so far no one seems to know any specifics. Even the employees know an apparition is supposed to be in residence, but can't recall any stories or experiences of their own. I did manage to find a few people who could tell me about the rumors of ghosts and this will have to suffice. It is an urban ghost, whose legend has no basis in fact as far as I know.

The other ghost of Trolley Square is supposed to be a workman who died there in the twenties and likes to hang out at the north doors of the north building. I found at least two versions of how he died. One is that there was a fire and he died in the fire, right in the building. The other is that he was injured in an accident inside the shop, lingered for days or weeks and then died. He loved his work so much that he then returned later to haunt the place. He supposedly will materialize out of one of the two large grates in a road which runs between the bus barns and the old carpentry shop around 3 or 4 o'clock in the morning. This story has been told for years. He has coveralls on which makes sense, as this particular building was the carpenter and paint shop when it was a trolley or bus barn. The story goes that he really loved or took great pride in his work and that is why he cannot leave his job, not even for what eternity might offer him. He apparently hangs around this area and has been seen as a wisp of light smoke or a dark shape walking near the grate or by the north doors, both outside or within that area inside the north building. There have been several sightings of the apparition over the years and even more sounds of whistling as well as odd experiences. On a recent Halloween, a new story about this ghost surfaced thanks to Paul Fleming who writes a column for *The Salt Lake Tribune* called "Law Enforcement." (Monday, October 19, 1999, p. B2.)

Fleming starts his article by talking about being a newly hired security guard whom the other guards are trying to scare by talking about the north building ghost. They swear that it is true that he comes out of the north grate and walks through the north doors into the car barn building dressed in a pair of bib overalls. They are just warning the new guard because they don't want the ghost to sneak up on the guy and then just disappear right in front of him. After all, it is his first night on the graveyard shift. The other guard leaves to go home and then remembers as he gets to his car that he must remind the new security man that the ghost only appears in the wee hours of the morning. The night maintenance crew is preparing to strip wax off the first floor and replace it as the new security guard makes his rounds, locks and secures every door and window and goes upstairs to the security cage to read.

At 3:05 one of the custodians comes up and asks him to unlock a door so they can go and get some food. He walks them to a door and lets them out and bolts and locks the door. Then he walks around all the equipment they dropped in place and noticed that they still have a lot of the floor to do. The men return within the hour and bang on the door. He goes down and lets them in and then they all hear this eerie sound drifting through the car barn. One of them thinks that it is someone whistling "Danny Boy" and they take off en mass sprinting through the building to where the sound is coming from. They all round the bend on the north concourse at the same time. The whistling suddenly stops and they all come to a quick halt. They stare at the scene in front of them and all of them gasp together. For there before them is the entire corridor, waxed and buffed perfectly and all of their gear is stacked neatly against the wall. The foreman asks, "Who did this?" The young and very new security guard says, "Let me put it this way guys, come Halloween, we'll have one heck of a ghost story to tell."

Ghosts can be seen by many people over time or they can be the kind that are personal only to us as we sleepwalk through our lives as ghosts ourselves. In the hallways of a sleepwalker's time, most of us remain oblivious to what we should be hearing or seeing or sensing. It has often been said that we are the ghosts and what people report as ghosts are the real thing instead. We are the ones who are not real or merely brief flashes of light on the long walk through eternity. While others, who are much further along than we, and who know a great deal more about matters of the universe than we do, are trying to guide us in our blindness. This is religion or spiritual faith or superstition or wishful thinking on our parts. Some believe; while others trust in the blind faith of their walk and do or do not come into their own understanding of things once the walk is over. When my friend's husband died of liver cancer, he had lived a very hard and precarious life, but then had found "religion" in his last years. When Jay died, religion had been a contention in his family and I will never know what he came to believe in the end. For me, the little severely handicapped children, many of whom died, taught me that death is not only a process but also a door to a new beginning. I had known this, but had not experienced it, until I awakened and found that I could know things that others did not. I had assumed everyone knew about these matters, and had spent many of my adult years being frustrated or angry because people seemed to be blind on purpose to these things. These feelings and intuitions have become routine to me now and not the least bit odd or foreign to my nature.

Now I know that when Jay looked into my eyes or those of my friend's, it was not romance that we saw there but a connection of another sort. It was instead, a recognition. It was the recognition by an intuitive person that somehow many others choose to remain oblivious to, fear greatly, or really, truly do not know such things exist. Spirits do indeed walk among us, some merely recordings of past events, others attempting over and over again to appear before us, and still others accomplishing this feat and communicating either randomly or self-centeredly. It is when actual contact is made to help or assist someone dear to us or perhaps just part of our work in the world which we can see, that one feels the warm golden rain of love failing on our skins and into our persons. This is an energy beyond description, one in which I must now live when I am lucky enough to have it come to me, with its companion pain that also comes along with it.

Misunderstanding, ignorance, fear, perhaps even unrecognized denial, and strong intellectual and scientific disbeliefs - all these factors contribute to dividing and compartmentalizing what is to me a normal, natural part of who we all are. It is something that is a part of a whole integrated universe and not something that one can divide up into little categories and label in a lab. I remember being at such a place one time in my life, so that on some level I understand this way of thinking but can never return to it now. Too much has happened, too much unexplained and real phenomena that cannot be studied with our present methods for proving just about anything. Someday, way beyond my time here on earth, this grand illusion thought of as our reality now, will be thought of in the future as the darkest age of mankind. We will not only be using all of our brain power, but all of our hearts as well.

The trolleys have long been silent now, though ghosts still run some of the machinery it seems. Every night like clockwork, a single worker climbs up out of the ground and goes about his business in the barns. We day people, who have memories there, recall them when we can. Our own individual hauntings are enough it seems.

When I get a chance to walk around the hallways of Trolley Square, certain sights and sounds trigger these memories. A single face flashes in front of me and I am reminded of regrets and broken promises. I assume that many others have their own stories to tell of meetings and partings, regrets and fond memories at Trolley Square. I have lots of company, being among the haunted.

Note: Shortly before this book went off to the publisher, my experiences with Trolley Square had a sudden continuance. My husband and I had just arrived and I had walked perhaps four yards away from our car to take a picture of the tower when two girls probably in their late twenties yelled out to me if I this place was for tourists. "Oh, yes!" I said. And then they asked me if I knew any history about the place. "You certainly asked the right person," I said and began telling them some of it. When they found out about my series of books on places around the state they asked me if I wanted a miracle. They then explained that they were from southern California and here for a few days for a "Quest" seminar. They had never been to Utah before and apparently part of their experience with what I assumed was a sort of Christian-New Age encounter group, was to create one miracle every day. "Go for it," I said, while my husband readied himself to retrieve my camera just in case.

One of the girls grabbed both of my hands and began a rather long prayer in which she blessed my books and me and even the ripple effect that they might have for others, as well as giving me a protective shield for any bad stuff that might come my way and even including the people of Utah and how much they would enjoy reading them. Finally she finished, pulled her hands away and the two of them, forgetting all about visiting Trolley Square returned to their car, with the one who had held my hands lifting her arm in that pose of the "Yes!" posture and saying to the other one, "Alright! We have created our miracle for today!"

From Tenth Ward farmer fields to state fair visitors, to trolley cars and gas buses and finally to the shopping mall that it is today, Trolley Square has always been a meeting place for both the living and the dead. With so much energy still hanging around, and so many, many people visiting the place over the years, perhaps you too will meet someone there from your past, present or even future, without really realizing it at the time. And just perhaps, the land on which Trolley Square stands, provides for a few dozen more miracles just waiting for those who pass by to find them.

UTAH'S HAUNTED SCHOOLS, COLLEGES & UNIVERSITIES

OLD MAIN SPIRITS

SOUTHERN UTAH UNIVERSITY

Cedar City is located at the mouth of Coal Creek in southern Utah. On November 11, 1851, thirty-five men from Parowan established an ironworks on the north bank of Coal Creek. These settlers and miners were of English, Scottish, and Welch descent and they opened the way for a hundred families to arrive a year later for the iron mission. They built small cottonwood log houses and named the place Fort Cedar. They used their wagon boxes as a temporary fort wall and then moved the fort near their blast furnace for the ironworks. When Indian hostilities arose and the fort became too small to house the new settlers, the fort was moved once more to the south bank of the creek. The Walker Indian War in July of 1853 forced the settlers to evacuate. In June of 1855, Brigham Young had another site surveyed where flooding would not be problem and this is where Cedar City is no located. The ironworks closed in 1858 due to several difficulties including flooding, hard winters, crop devastations, finding skilled workers, fluxing the ore, and Johnston's Army bringing in their own iron. The town changed its focus to agricultural endeavors and by the 1920s there were many cattle ranches in the area. In 1923 the railroad came to Cedar City making the town a gateway to the many nearby National Parks and providing an outlet for the iron mines.

There are some historical buildings left standing from Cedar City's early days. Among these are the Union Pacific Railroad Depot, the Old Rock Church or Mormon 1st Ward Chapel, the historic Hunter Home and the Old Main Administration building on the Southern Utah University campus. In 1896, Cedar City was in the midst of planning a new school for the area's youth. The State Branch Normal School opened in 1898 under the control and management of the Board of Regents of the University of Utah. However, the University had no money for books, furniture, and teacher's salaries.

University officials appealed to the citizens of the town to raise enough money so that the school could open in September of 1898. Over the years the Branch Normal School became a two-year college under the University of Utah, Utah State University and then in 1965, it became an independent four-year college. Southern Utah University sits on one hundred acres of tree-shaded land in the middle of the city. The college owns a thousand-acre farm to the west of town and to the east of town it owns a 3,700-acre ranch in the mountains. Interesting places on campus include, William R. Palmer Indian Museum, Braithwaite Fine Arts Gallery, Adams Memorial Theater and one of very few American full-sized authentic replicas of an Elizabethan Playhouse. The Utah Shakespearean Festival is an internationally renowned theater company. It began in 1962 and the Festival has been held every summer for five weeks or more in July and August with a company of one hundred and fifty actors, musicians, dancers and stage personnel. In 1981, the Royal Shakespeare Company from England felt that this theater was the most authentic of its kind in the world and as a result staged segments for their Masterpiece Theater series for the British Broadcasting Corporation.

In order to understand the evolution of the Bell Tower Ghost in Old Main there are a few interesting events in the history of the college that explain the colorful student stories told today. There was a special committee appointed when the school was originally being planned that included one member named Rebecca Little. This is possibly where the name Little came from in the later story of the Bell Tower Ghost, or Rebecca Little might have had an ancestor involved in this story. Another interesting possibility is that Lillian Higbee MacFarlane was well known in the early days of the school as renowned pianist. She gave a remarkable recital that included music by Beethoven, Chopin and Mozart that was considered legendary for many years by the music department as well as the college and the whole town. It could be Lillian who has become confused with the later girl who plays the piano at night in Old Main. The library and the music department were located on the third floor of Old Main for many years after the school was first built.

Above the third floor of Old Main is a small bell tower that for many years did not have a bell. The Home Economics Club was begun in the 1920's by prominent local women to give financial assistance to special contributions for the high school. One of these contributions was a large cast iron bell that the high school's flat roof could not accommodate. So the women offered the bell to the Branch Agricultural College to be placed in the cupola on top of the main building, which was at the time called the Library Building. However, there was one major problem, the bell weighed 1,800 pounds and the small tower would have difficulty housing it. Using the department hoist and some steel cable, an inventive teacher and some of his students managed to fit the bell into the small tower. They fashioned a way for it to be rung by extending the bell rope from the operating crank to a loop below the ceiling. Every morning at 8:00 the bell rang to remind students and townspeople of the hour and it also rang for special events both in town and at the college. Some of the mystery of the tower surrounds the ringing of this bell even after the bell was no longer in the tower. Even though today the college has replaced this bell with a mechanized system, there are some in town and at the school who believe the old bell is still in the old bell tower. The great fire in December of 1948 signaled the demise of the bell when the roof of

Old Main was destroyed and the bell crashed through all the floors and landed in the basement

The lore of the fire on December 12, 1948 has also contributed to the many rumors and stories about the bell tower and Old Main's various apparitions and ghosts. On a wintry Sunday morning a newspaper boy spotted smoke coming out of a ventilator on top of Old Main. The first to arrive were the manager of the college farm and the school custodian. The custodian cut the power to the building but flames were already visible on the roof. Students rushed to the scene and formed a human chain up the fire escape and passed precious books and artifacts back down the stairs in an orderly fashion. As the third floor began to be consumed by fire students grabbed armfuls of books and threw them out to the ground. Only moments before the roof collapsed the students left the building and no one was hurt in the fire. The bell could be heard clanging from floor to floor almost as if crying as it fell to the ground below. When the fire was finally put out only the roof and third floor were damaged. One professor, Mary Bastow lost her entire massive collection of materials, books, and paintings. Twenty per-cent of the library's collection survived, and while space was found for classes it was difficult to find space for the books anywhere on campus, so books and artifacts were stuffed in closets, and stairwells all over the campus until a new place for the library could be located. According to student tour guides there are still two little rooms near the bell tower, although no one knows what they were used for on the third floor.

In 1984 a book was published on *Popular Beliefs and Superstitions from Utah* collected by Anthon S. Cannon and published by the University of Utah Press, page 335. "People going past the old Branch Agriculture College Auditorium at mid-night have heard weird strains of 'Deep Purple' coming from a piano somewhere in the darkness. The performer is said to be a young woman, and accomplished pianist, who had suddenly died of a heart attack after completing a rendition of 'Deep Purple' at a recital in the auditorium." One librarian at the school said that an elderly Cedar City native, gave this account of the haunting of the Old Main building. The woman claimed that this incident had taken place some seventy years ago. "A young lady by the name of Little was practicing playing the piano in the Old Main Building for the Junior Prom. Apparently there was a piano in the upper room. The piece she was going to play for the dance was something like 'Deep Purple'. The day before the Junior Prom Miss Little died of a broken appendix and did not play at the Junior Prom. Since then people have heard her playing this tune on the piano in the bell tower of Old Main. When people pass by late at night they can hear this music coming from the building." Most people agree on the song being entitled "Deep Purple" and that for many years after this, the song was never chosen for the Junior Prom because it was considered bad luck and this was the song that people heard echoing from the bell tower around midnight.

Over the years students at the college have added amazing stories to this original haunt. Their creative additions can be traced to various parts of the school's history and Old Main itself. One of the stories began with the laying of the foundation for Old Main's construction in 1897. According to the student stories over the years, ". . .a laborer was guiding a large slab of sandstone into place when letters began to appear as if written by the finger of a supernatural being. As the finger traced the letters the workmen read them aloud, "Virginia." As the workmen said this, the stone began to bleed human blood where the inscription had been. It is claimed in this article that the inscription can be seen in the special collections section of the college library, though the librarians' in the special collections department say they have never seen any such thing in their library. However, the stories of bloodstains on the brick in front of Old Main have persisted. An example of this is the story the student tour guides used to tell to visitors on campus. The guides had been asked to stop telling the story by the administration because they believe that this story is not true. A little old couple lived up in the rooms by the bell tower. The man was a custodian for the school. The couple had a fight and the man got very angry with his wife. He ended up murdering her near the bell tower and dragged her down the stairs to the front of Old Main. Her blood dyed the bricks red there. ("The Haunting of Old Main," by Tom Braun, *The Thunderbird*, SUU, Thursday, October 31, 1991, p.5 and "Dr. Spear exposes haunted Old Main," by Chris Taylor, The University Journal, SUU, Monday, October 31,1994, pp.3-4.)

Until the fire of 1948, the haunting of Old Main consisted of hearing piano or flute music coming from the bell tower around mid-night as young couples strolled by. They were treated to the mystical strains of a beautiful waltz. Also over the years, unearthly lights glowing from the third story windows were reported as well as shadows moving around in the belfry. There was also the fact that only black crows and no other birds, would perch atop Old Main. In the old days people believed that crows knew where spirit had passed and that black birds always visited farmhouses of people who had died on the anniversary of their hour of death. For example as a child my husband stood with his grandmother on a small farm in Indiana while she told him of his great-grandmother's passing on that very day a year before. "It was just around this time," she said, and then asked everyone to have a seat on the front steps. From the timber about a mile or so from the house a clutch of crows rose out of the trees and flew straight towards his grandmother's yard. They landed in all the trees of the yard and barnyard around the whole place and cawed and cackled for five or six minutes and then just flew off to the west. His aunt Cora piped out, "Same thing they did last year!"

The college fire on December 12, 1948 happened at 7:30 on a Sunday morning and most of the bell tower, third floor and the bell itself were destroyed. This fire started a whole new set of rumors about Old Main. The prominent rumor was that a Dr. Jerode Spear, supposedly a famous parapsychologist from the University of Utah in 1948, was hired to investigate the hauntings at Old Main. His dairies about this investigation were returned to Southern Utah University by his grandson who was a student at S.U.U. in the late eighties. Although it is very hard to believe that there were any parapsychologists at the U. of U. in 1948, it is possible to believe that a psychic might have passed through town at the time and made a comment or two about spirits in Old Main. Regardless the fire inspired two stories, one being that when the bell crashed to the basement it took an employee of the college with it, smashing him into the basement floor, although no skeleton was found. The second story is that a malevolent force inhabited the bell tower as the result of some violent incident that had taken place. After this fire, many stories were told down through the years of murders being committed on the third floor in Old Main. People were supposedly axed, strangled, gutted, chopped up into pieces, and then disappeared into the old coal furnace sitting in the center room of the third floor. Others said that the remains were carried down to the basement and thrown into the furnace. However, this mysterious Dr. Spear started the rumor that old Main's bell tower was dimension door to other worlds or at least the netherworld. To this day there are people who believe that spirits from other dimensions come through this door to visit or do evil. Dr. Spear claimed that such an event caused the fire. Although probably none of this is true, Dr. Spear also recommended that Old Main be torn down, to rid the town of an entrance to the nether world.

The premiere murder story about Old Main was probably fabricated, although there is the possibility of some historian investigating any part of it as truth. The story concerns a young sixteen-year-old girl murdered near the site of Old Main in 1886. Perhaps the murder has some truth to it, although the rest of the story is rather hard to believe. Two years before Old Main was built a young woman named " Virginia Loomis, was murdered east of Cedar City in the red hills. Her throat had been slashed and her blood soaked body was left lying over a large red sandstone boulder. The stones used in the construction of Old Main in 1898 were out of the same red sandstone boulder quarry in which Virginia was killed." Supposedly the only suspect was her boyfriend but he was released due to lack of evidence and left town. Years later the boyfriend returned to Cedar City just two weeks before the fire in 1948 when he took a job tending the furnace in Old Main, at the unbelievable age of 78, if he was 16 at the time of the murder. Either this boyfriend was the man crushed under the bell in the basement during the fire or even more bizarre, in Dr. Spear's version the murdered girl's apparition appeared in the flames laughing as her murderer received his retribution. It is rumored that one can hear the voice of Virginia in the dead of night echoing through the bell tower along with other voices from the spirit world.

"Virginia" is probably a made up name, for the real young lady was a senior in high school at the time when she contracted appendicitis in the late 1930s. This local high school student was making a name for herself as an accomplished pianist by the year 1939. She was especially known at her high school and at the college for her rendition of " Deep Purple." Among the people of the town, "Deep Purple" came to be known as her personal song. A local doctor performed the surgery and soon after this she developed peritonitis and died of septicemia. Not long after this people began to report lights flashing on and off, crows on the roof, and the strains of piano music coming from Old Main. One young woman who attended the school at this time and had her own experience with the phantom piano player, had to have the exact same operation performed by the same doctor soon after her classmate. While she thought nothing of it, her parents had been afraid to let the same doctor perform the operation.

Winona Cowen relates her experience in the following quote: "There were three students in the Old "A" building one night for some reason and all of a sudden they heard music coming from somewhere upstairs. They went upstairs to find out where it was coming from. When they got to the auditorium they could tell the music was coming from the piano at the front of the hall. Even though it was dark at the time they could see that no one was sitting at the piano. That's when they realized something was strange. They got a little closer to make sure nobody was really at the piano. When they discovered there wasn't, they practically fell over each other trying to get out of there." After a few more experiences like this one, she and her classmates also decided to quit sliding down the very large tin rain gutters outside the old administration building on pieces of waxed paper. Probably because they suspected that someone was playing the music to scare them away from the building.

While many other students who went to school during the thirties and forties didn't believe the ghost story, variations on this story became well known around campus. Many people wondered why any spirit would choose to play the same song over and over again. However, the lyrics in the song suggest that nothing is really final and that just because the physical body isn't there doesn't mean that a spirit or two can't linger about. "... When the Deep Purple falls over sleepy garden walls, and the stars begin to flicker in the sky, Thru the mist of a memory you wander back to me, breathing my name with a sigh." Those who did not believe the ghost stories at the time explained the whole thing away stating that there used to be a lot of instruments stored in the music room on the third floor. The building was very drafty and the wind would blow down through the various instruments causing many different noises to reverberate through the huge old auditorium. The sounds would get louder and louder and begin to echo. However this does not explain the playing of a tune. ("The Ghost Song of SUSC, "by Dean O'Driscoll, *The Thunderbird*, Thursday, May 26,1983, p.14.)

Even in those days students came up with wild stories based on this tale. Bessie Dover remembered the story that she heard from friends who went to the old agricultural college in the 1940's. "I had always heard that it was a ghost of a former ballet dancer and she had died from an infection she got in a blister from dancing a lot," she says. "I heard that the ghost was dancing up in the auditorium to that old poplar song "Deep Purple." While the stories of today far surpass the ones of old in their colorfulness and blood and gore, the one thing that has been constant for decades has been the reluctance of students to pass by Old Main late at night or especially to enter the building and stay on the third floor alone. I am sure school officials discourage this practice as well. The transformation of this ghost from a forlorn and mournful yet gifted artist whose life was cut short, to a malevolent force out to spill blood on the stones from which this building was built, is quite interesting. It is a reflection of our changing times and decades, and the many students whose generations signal those changes. One can assume that we step over quite a few stones where history has been laid down and then transport these same stones to somewhere else to build an even newer story in an increasingly unsteady world.

BRIGHAM YOUNG UNIVERSITY

- BYU ACADEMY - ACADEMY SQUARE

Founded in 1875, the BYU Academy was to provide a religious and academic education for young Mormons in Utah. The Academy was first held in the basement of a downtown mercantile store and was called Lewis Hall. A fire destroyed this building in 1884. Several temporary facilities were used while the new building was being built

on University Avenue. It was completed in 1892. Several other buildings were added on the block, until finally the Maeser Building was added on Temple Hill in 191 1. Karl E. Maeser was a German convert who believed strongly in education and he was the principal contributor as well as director from 1876 to 1892. There were then 700 students at the school, though only 30 of them were college-age. My grandmother was always very proud of having attended the BYU Academy in Beaver for one year around 1908. Though even then for young ladies, it was considered more of a finishing school, my mother used to say with a bit of amusement in her voice. My mother, coming from a poorer family, had really had to struggle through college on a scholarship, which was difficult to get in those days, especially for women

The college was under a deed of trust from Brigham Young and when he died, those funds were gone. The Academy had to look for other funding then and found it in several local wealthy constituents like Abraham O. Smoot and Jesse Knight. This kept the place alive until World War II when the LDS church began once again to fund it. The Academy was renamed Brigham Young University in 1903 and the first real college degrees awarded there were in 1897 for Bachelor of Pedagogy, in 1902 for Bachelor of Science and in 1906 for Bachelor of Arts. Master's Degrees were first awarded in 1916. The rest of the story is well known, with Brigham Young University now having an annual enrollment of around 28,000 fulltime students and around 4,000 part-time students. It covers quite a few blocks and buildings now, has an honor code and dress code, religious course requirements and a system of LDS wards and stakes with a huge foreign missionary program.

In the 1960's the main BYU Academy building housed a demonstration training school and a Brigham Young High School, but the high school was moved to a new building and the other classes were moved to the main campus just before 1975. It was in that year that the magnificent BYU Academy building was sold. From 1975 to the nineties it sat idle, the victim of a silent war between those who wanted to tear it down and those who would not let it die. Yet at the same time no plan had been developed to save it. During this time vandals and vagrants used the building, as the area of town it is now in is somewhat run-down. A satanic group moved in and used it for various ceremonies which then gave the building an even more unsavory reputation. The only other building left standing, except for possibly an older home near the old campus, is the Women's Gymnasium across the street from the Academy building, built in 1912. The gymnasium's Greek-columned exterior is the only thing left of a once magnificent building. It is now used for a thrift shop and an absolutely marvelous used book store which winds around through what must have been the old locker rooms in an eerie sort of way. Once the library is opened, with a better sign to tell people about it, this bookstore will most definitely be discovered and business just may boom there.

An internet site was established by those groups wishing to save the Academy building from demolition and a proposal was made to make major renovations on the building to convert it into a city library and city auditorium tentatively titled Academy Square. There were many in city government who opposed this idea, including the former mayor, who now applauds the efforts of so many private citizens to obtain a 16.4 million dollar bond and 6 million dollars in private donations. An article in the Salt Lake Tribune on Saturday, October 9th, 1999 entitled "Library Writes New Chapter for Academy Square" by Brooke Adams, tells more about how these renovations came to be. Ms. Adams called it "Provo's most notable wreck" and then went on to tell of how the 108-year-old building was being transformed into the new home of the Provo City Library. The building renovation was completed by the year of 2001 after once being ranked by the National Trust for Historic Preservation "as the No. 1 endangered building west of the Mississippi."

Doug Smoot was chairman of the BYU Academy Foundation and a BYU professor. He explained that the original building was designed by Don Carlos Young in 1891 and the building was dedicated in 1892. It was his great, great grandfather, Abraham O. Smoot who was charged by Brigham Young to look after the academy. So Dr. Smoot felt obligated to continue this trust by finding a use for the magnificent old building before it came tumbling down. The grand opening threw its spotlight on Dr. Smoot's ancestor, Abraham as well as two welcomed additions to the building, a small square monument with a beehive in it and the seven and a half foot bronze statue of a bearded Brigham Young with cape and cane created by D. J. Bawden.

Provo City purchased the square in 1994 and it is located on a major thoroughfare now between 500 and 600 North and University Avenue, surrounded by fast food places, chain stores and all the typical accoutrements of a thriving college town. Eleven different projects were proposed for the square before the city was persuaded to make it into the city library. No one on the library board approved of the idea when the foundation was organized, and neither did the mayor. But when the Provo residents voted on a bond, it was overwhelming approved. Four major contributors kept the plans afloat: George S. and Dolores Dore Eccles Foundation contributed a million dollars, the LDS church contributed, and the Carnation Company and the State Legislature gave 950,000 dollars. Just a week before the deadline given by the city of June 30th, 1997, the foundation pulled in the last million dollars. Though it was the people who saved the building from destruction, many in power positions still had misgivings, considering the building a sort of white elephant. If construction costs went beyond the budget, the foundation had to make up the difference. So they continued to raise money for the 95,000 square-foot facility which is four times the size of the present city library. A new 2-story building that complements the older one, houses an adult library and support services with a glass conservatory linking the two buildings. The old building has become a children's library on the first floor, administrative offices on the second floor with meeting rooms available on the third floor. The third floor has a 4,000 square-foot ballroom available for concerts, lectures, receptions and dances. An underground parking lot has been added. But the fourth floor is empty for now because there is no more money to finish it, though the city is thinking of eventually leasing it for a small museum or educational program.

The renovations had not been without their own troubles. The parking structure had to be redesigned because of a high water table on the block. Shoring up the existing building turned out to be much more expensive and extensive than anticipated, but this only put them a few days behind schedule. During the renovations and construction, two workmen were injured on the job. A father and son were working outside the building when an old wall suddenly collapsed on them. They were both 40 feet in the air in an elevated bucket. Brick and mortar from the chimney landed in their bucket pinning the father down and disabling the operating mechanism of the platform. It took 15 firefighters to rescue them by using an aerial platform. The firemen then positioned themselves above the victims and rappelled down into the bucket to treat the two men. The father suffered chest and back pains and the son an injured knee. Other mishaps were possible, simply because it is such a high, ornate and very old building, having not weathered the course of time as well as other such structures. And maybe, but only a speculation on my part, there are some unquiet spirits there just waiting to speak their piece or show themselves once the building is completed.

When I drove past during the construction and stopped where I could on such a busy street, it was covered in scaffolding and plastic and not much of it was visible. Yet my overall feeling of this structure was one of an ancient and overwhelming sadness. It was a strange impression to be having on such a modern and populated street with many lanes of cars passing by. I tried to imagine it as it once was, out in the country in a quiet and bucolic scene. What brought on the sadness I wondered? Was it just me, seeing it surrounded with so much of our modern world, or was it more? Perhaps something yet will be discovered beyond opening day. When I wandered through its halls and gathered my own private impressions, I was struck by the odd combination of new and old in the building and wished that I had been able to wander there before all of the renovations. It is a magnificent structure, saved by the people to be used once more for a place of learning.

People now are calling it the cultural heart of Provo, preserving the roots of the nation's largest private university. The inside of the building has been completely redone except for 5 cast iron pillars and one small stained glass window. The builders took great pains to capture the flavor of the original interior, modeling things in the building after the early 1900s and replicating them with new materials. Tiles in the bathrooms were copied from those that might have been used in those days; oak paneling and rosettes can be found throughout the building. The re-created Academy Grand Ballroom looks as much like the old one as the builders could make it and it is available for receptions, public meetings and maybe even a dance or two. At the same time, the modern touches make it a good blend of the old and the new with underground parking, a children's reading circle and stations for over 100 computers. The people of Provo should be very proud of their efforts to save this building, especially since the atmosphere of its occupation will bring many good apparitions back to life.

As for ghosts, time will tell. It would be no surprise to me to hear stories about voices and laughter and music from the grand ballroom or windows and doors opening or closing by themselves after lock up at night. Or it wouldn't surprise me to hear of lights going on or off of their own accord. While the building is new inside, it is the original building and the original ground where once young men and women walked through the halls of higher learning with their lives and tragedies and hopes playing out. I got a taste of this wandering about in the gymnasium across the street where those spooky winding hallways hidden from view unless one enters the labyrinth of books in the store, transported me to other places and times. I would expect that the new library will have a few stories to tell as well, though in Provo they would have to be guardian angels rather than ghosts. Someone may think of dedicating the building privately to make sure that nothing unsavory lurks there.

Begun on a vision, the largest private university in the country at the time, Brigham Young Academy has endured fire and the weathering of the ages to become the showpiece of a town in love with its religious history. Any building of such majesty and ornate design will surely house a few apparitions and secrets, though in a town like Provo, they will do so quietly. On the other hand, many in town worried that the energy in the building would be hard to get rid of from all those cult rituals and satanic symbols spray painted on the walls. Since the only occupied area of the old Academy building is the wonderful children's library, this would be the true test of anything unsavory. But so far no one has experienced anything according to the lady librarians there, except fabulous storytellers and great memory boxes along the entranceway of people and their favorite books as a child.

On my first visit to the newly opened building, I was sad to learn that only the basement floor was occupied with a really wonderful children's library. Much of the gorgeously renovated and restored old academy still sits empty awaiting evening receptions, meetings and other functions. There is a small art gallery with traveling exhibits, but most of the rooms were locked up, though one could see into many of them because of the extensive glass windows. An incredible stained glass window crowns the archway from the library to the covered crosswalk, which connects the older building to the new one. A delightful children's sculpture greets visitors at the door to the children's library. It is made of bronze and is a little boy in a rocker reading a book. This library is wonderfully decorated with big glass shelves on both sides where individuals can place items from their childhood and favorite books; it really is a magical place.

I spoke with the librarians and asked about the new home for the McCurdy Doll Museum, which houses over 4,000 dolls at present. They said that the BYU Academy board had considered this, but had wanted to put the dolls on the fourth floor up many steep stairs, although they had installed small elevators in the building. The owners of the doll museum also felt that the atmospheric conditions of the building would cause the dolls to deteriorate at a much faster rate. Recent news is that a place called Thanksgiving Point might house the doll museum, with a guarantee of the right atmospheric conditions for the dolls. Thanksgiving Point is halfway between Salt Lake

City and Provo, and is a place devoted to children and gardens, with a big dinosaur museum as well. Still it was sad to think of those dolls being somewhere else, as the BYU Academy building would have been a perfect location for them, right above the children's library with librarians who would have felt honored to have them and care for them. The old carriage house where they had once been housed in downtown Provo was indeed a haunted place of which I write elsewhere. It is sad to think that the Provo carriage house, with every nook and cranny turned into a display case, will no longer house these dolls. College students now rent the place and are probably being disturbed by a ghost or two without realizing it.

As for the ghosts and apparitions at the BYU Academy, time will tell, just as it does in other such magnificent buildings. Other authors who have written about the Provo area have mentioned the Academy ghosts in their books. Authors have also noted the Utah Lake stories and early Indian tales of ghosts and spirits that roam the hills at night, just as the early settlers mentioned what they saw near the lake and along the foothills where subdivisions have replaced orchards. Many of these spirits might be someone's grandmother or grandfather who attended the Academy so many years ago, enjoying every minute of their time there and I am sure there are many stories about this school that I have not heard as yet. If one multiplies just one of these stories many times over, these ancestral tales and anecdotes often become ghost stories over time. And the real ghost stories, those which have many people telling them with very little variation for decades, will present themselves as the years roll along as well.

The work has been done in renovating the building to keep the spirits alive, and although the people in Provo might not talk about these spirits publicly, in private I am sure that they are there just waiting to be discovered. In the women's gymnasium across the street things are different. Nothing has been renovated or changed except that now it is a thrift shop similar to a Goodwill store. In the women's old locker room there is one of the best used bookstore collections that I have ever seen with twisting and turning passageways and lots of built-in bookshelves. One would never know that it was there because the rest of the stuff is pretty junky. The energies in the whole building are quite high and especially where the bookstore is located. I would imagine that things are really hoping there at night time, what with all of the spirited phenomena that I felt there.

There is one other building from the old original campus built in 1904 now part of the Brigham Young University, the Maeser Building. It is a little known fact that this building, now the Science Department, is built over and near an old pioneer graveyard. When the building was built, relatives of these departed ones were given the option of moving their relations to the Provo Cemetery. Quite a few were moved but the rest remain buried under this building and on the grounds near it, another possibly haunted location, though no one so far has reported any activity in the building.

WESTMINSTER COLLEGE

SALT LAKE COLLEGIATE INSTITUTE
- GRADE & HIGH SCHOOL, 1875 TO 1895
SHELDON JACKSON COLLEGE - HIGH SCHOOL & JUNIOR COLLEGE, 1897
WESTMINSTER COLLEGE - CONVERSE, FERRY HALL & FOSTER HALL

(All of the historical information in this story is taken from R. Douglas Brackenridge's excellent historical account of the history of *Westminster College of Salt Lake City* by Utah State University Press: Logan, Utah,1998.)

Westminster College has an interesting and varied history with two original halls and one newer building which stands in place of a third older one on campus, all of which are supposedly haunted. One can ask the faculty, students and custodians from over the years and definitely get quite a few stories about the two buildings. The two original buildings are the oldest on campus, though the main building, Converse, is the most striking because of its gothic design, and Converse and Ferry stood empty for many years before being used and coped with such things as massive fires. The Salt Lake Collegiate Institute opened its doors on April 12, 1875 in the basement of the First Presbyterian Church to 27 students who ranged in age from 5 to 21. Mary, Lemma and John Coyer were the three teachers. Graded by departments with individual instruction, within a few weeks there were 36 students and by the end of the year, 150 students with more wanting to come. Without enough room for any more students, a search was soon started for more space after the first year. Sheldon Jackson was one of many who helped to finance and bring a scholarship program to the school, motivated by a Mormon woman separated from her husband. She had attempted to enroll her two children but had neither goods nor money for their tuition.

An adjacent lot was purchased by fund raising and a four room schoolhouse was erected there. It was dedicated on August 22, 1877 and the Territorial Governor spoke at this dedication. To reach the last portion of their financial goal, Coyer went door-to-door in his buggy for contributions in order to open the school on time for the new year. He even made his own contribution in the name of his deceased daughter, Lemma. In 1880, construction on a second building began because of the overflow. When it was dedicated in August 1880, Coyer -raised the last $2,000 on its steps in less than ten minutes by making an emotional appeal to the attendees. In 1883 a third building was opened, called the Octagon House - a female boarding house which the Presbyterian church had just purchased nearby. Fifteen females boarded there and soon other buildings were needed as the primary, intermediate, grammar, high school and music department grew to 225 students. A second story was added to the original school in 1881 and a parsonage was built. Another building nearby was purchased and became the Liberal Institute gymnasium and temporary dormitory facility. The school was quiet and orderly and soon gained a reputation for being one of the best in the entire west.

However, the growth of the college seemed to threaten the Mormon community and the rift between the two groups began to widen and deepen further, due to the polygamy-caused anti-Mormon sentiment of the times. Coyer did not help any by making public statements that Mormonism was 8 parts diabolism, 3 parts animalism, 1 part bigotry, 4 parts cunning and treachery, 2 parts Thugism (from India), 2 parts Arnoldism and shaken all together, or "...shaken over the fires of animal passion... you had the outer appearance... of the forms and ceremonies of the Christian religion..." (*Westminster College of Sakt Lake City* by R. Douglas Brackenridge, Utah State University Press: Logan, Utah, 1998, p.53.) He also attacked his neighbors politically, and the Mormon press responded in like form by calling Coyer a Presbyterian bigot and a hypocritical pedagogue. The LDS Church leaders also warned Mormon families against placing their children in his school as the influence there might turn their own children against them. However, enrollment at the school continued to increase with both Mormon and non-Mormon families enrolling their children.

Meanwhile, protestant women started a campaign to enroll more Mormon children in hopes of converting them, though they knew that the financial heart of the school were those students who boarded from the east from wealthy Presbyterian families. The first visions of establishing an institute for higher learning began around 1883, the same year that a branch school was opened on Fourth West between First and Second South to accommodate the overflow of students. Enrollment stood at 245 students in 1885 when Coyer announced his retirement from the school because of his wife Mary's debilitating physical illness; she also had a deep fear that he would be assassinated for his public anti-Mormon statements, either by an individual or members of that secret Mormon organization, the Danites. She was so depressed over this, that the Coyers felt they should retire from public view; they moved to Pasadena, California where also Mary's rheumatism would fair better in the warmer climate. Mary Coyer died a few years later and John Coyer became a successful rancher, returning to Salt Lake City only once in 1890 when there was a movement to name one of the buildings on campus after him. The suggestion was rejected because the board wanted buildings named only as memorials, an ironic statement to his life's work as a financial donor.

The next administrator, Dr. Jesse Fonda Milispaugh, continued to support equality for women in education at his school, as well as to raise the academic excellence and tighten the discipline. He liked order but he also liked innovation and one of his more famous pupils was Maude Adams who attended the school for four years while living with her grandmother. However, she left after this to pursue her stage career, not liking the rigorous academic life and yearning for the stage lights. Free public schools opened in Utah in 1890, and Millspaugh had been working diligently to mend the fences that Coyer had built against the Mormon community. He left in this year and a series of other leaders ran the school, continuing to build bridges with the community and at the same time being threatened by the public school system. The diversity on campus in the 1890s with 325 students in attendance was quite amazing considering its unique role in the city. The campus was made up of Mormons, apostate Mormons, Evangelical Protestants, Roman Catholics, Jews and even some Spiritualists. This was also a time of financial crises at the school, but most of these crises were weathered. One major event would effect the future of the school, however, and that was when members of the board appealed to Sheldon Jackson to use his influence in the community to gain funds for a new academy building and better salaries for the teachers who were working for half-pay at the time. The new building was dedicated on June 5, 1895 and Sheldon Jackson was by this time deeply involved in creating a college of higher learning. The Collegiate Institute continued to prosper even though it often had to accept goods or promissory notes from students, such as, for example, several bushels of potatoes for one student's tuition.

By 1910, the trustees of the school were college trustees, having obtained ownership and preparing to make the Institute into Westminster College. It became a high school preparatory and junior college. The original incorporation of the school was in 1895, however, as Sheldon Jackson College. So from 1895 to 1910, Westminster was known as the Sheldon Jackson College, with the motto (in Latin) of "For Christ and Liberty." Jackson recommended the first president of the college and unfortunately reinstated the issue of anti-Mormonism, calling his college an antidote to Mormon evangelism. The college portion of the school officially began on September 7, 1897 in some of the rooms of the Institute, with seven men and women. But several wealthy easterners were being courted to build a new college facility - John Wannamaker, Nettie McCormick and John Converse. At the same time, anti-Mormon sentiment grew there because of the anti-polygamy campaign nationwide. Another problem was that as long as the Collegiate Institute and Sheldon Jackson College operated independently, the college had no chance of growing on its own.

Plans for a new campus for the college were envisioned but failed to materialize, so the college continued in a struggle with the Institute for control of the board and its finances. Various money-making schemes failed to work and the college was in jeopardy, as the Institute continued to control the school. Once again, Jackson's anti-Mormon stance did little to generate funds locally. In 1902, the college officially became Westminster College, though still operating in rooms on the Collegiate Institute's campus. With some of the funds raised, the college looked around for a suitable piece of land, finally settling on 21 acres at a place called Perkins Grand View where Westminster College is located today. The Ferrys owned the land but while her husband did not want to sell, Junta Hollister Ferry did. The land was soon theirs and plans for several buildings were underway. In 1905, Nunemaker Memorial Chapel was the first building dedicated. Next was Converse Hall as the result of John Converse's generous contribution to the college. Converse Hall was dedicated on August 23, 1906 and completed by July 1907 as a modern Gothic administration building. However, it stood empty for several years and was vandalized several times with smashed windows, and stolen museum artifacts that had belonged to Sheldon Jackson.

Following the death of her husband, Junta Ferry almost single-handedly kept the college alive through donations and widespread traveling to gain more funding, though the buildings stood empty at the time.

The next structure to be built was a woman's dormitory called Ferry Hall, which was located 200 feet south of Converse Hall. It had a colonial style architecture and was to house at least 40 female students and 6 teachers, but work on this building was halted for two years before finances became available to finish it in 1909. In this same year, the original Collegiate Institute was condemned by the city building inspector and shut down. With only three students and 2 instructors, the college had no where to go. The new campus wasn't ready and the Collegiate Institute now had no space to offer them. Sheldon Jackson died in 1909 and the push to get the new campus funding was on, as the college had had to agree to suspend classes at the high school with no space being offered them. In 1910, there was enough support that the Collegiate Institute became Westminster College and officials were working quickly to get their students housed on the new campus. By 1913, there were still only about 42 high school students and absolutely no college students in attendance. The fear of losing all that had been gained was imminent.

Herbert Ware Roared became president of a virtually nonexistent college in 1913 that had not had a president in over a year. With him came his secretary Elmira Dodge, who spent a lifetime living in Ferry Hall and contributing to the founding of Westminster College. Roared was determined to have college students on his campus by the following year and traveled to the eastern states to obtain funding. He worked once again to mend fences between his college and the community and had plans for a boy's dormitory as well. In the fall of 1914, the college re-commenced with 10 college students and 62 preparatory students. The students were finally on the new campus. By 1918 there was a Student Association on campus and quite a few more college students.

This same year was the year of the terrible flu epidemic and due to the ban put on attendance at public places, local students received their assignments by phone and on campus students were eventually quarantined. All classes were suspended and the second floor of Ferry Hall became a hospital. All faculty and students who were treated there eventually recovered and a faculty member, Dean McKirahan, set up a carpentry shop in Converse Hall to keep the on-campus students entertained while they waited for the resumption of classes. The impending World War I armistice brought the students out of their confinement when they rallied to have a mock burial of the Kaiser against orders of the school. When the real armistice came they dug up their effigy and dragged him around campus on a chain behind a farm wagon. They also sang songs and built a huge bonfire on the athletic field.

By 1920, the college had 123 preparatory students and 16 college students and a big deficit. Once again supporters plunged into a huge fund raising campaign nationwide and Westminster College obtained the most publicity that it had ever received. In the meantime other buildings were being constructed on campus, such as Foster Hall in 1926, with its fourth floor left unfinished for expansion.

That same year, Converse Hall had a devastating fire. Early on the morning of March 12, 1926, the fire began. It collapsed the two top floors of the building which destroyed a library of over fourteen thousand books, most of them classics donated by hundreds of individuals and organizations. The University of Utah and the Salt Lake Public School System offered temporary facilities and school officials reconfigured how to house their students in the remaining buildings: Foster and Ferry Halls, as well as the Nunemaker Chapel. Sponsors launched a campaign to rebuild Converse Hall immediately and it opened for classes the falling year. Apparently no one was in the building at the time or students were evacuated successfully, because no one was injured in the fire. As an intuitive however, I found the fire smell still there, the mention of books, and the suggestion that there was at least one severely injured person during the attempt to put out the fire. A few others had minor injuries while combating the blaze.

Thirteen more acres east of the college were purchased in the same year that the gym was dedicated as the Payne Gymnasium in January of 1929. Though the college continued to have low enrollments, the doors were kept open. During President Rewords administration, the college grew slowly, developed traditions and customs and established various rules about campus behavior. In 1915, two students at the college wrote the song that would be performed over and over again, eventually becoming the school's alma mater "Westminster Evening Song." There were various silly events like the time when the faculty served the students on George Washington's birthday while dressed in white wigs and powder, wearing colonial costumes. The athletic program really got off the ground in those years. After the twenties, Westminster College began to become financially stable. However, the Great Depression once again threatened closure of the school and unemployment and poverty continued to plague both the college and the wider community until the beginning of World War II. It was in 1935, though, that Westminster College officially became a four year college and the phrase "Old Collegiate" was rapidly relegated to something only mentioned on Founder's Day or occasionally at official functions from time to time. World War II was a boost to the economy everywhere and Westminster began to settle into a very stable existence from that time on.

Additional buildings have been added over the years and two quite famous teachers at the school attained legendary status: Viola Evans Chapman, professor of English from 1948 to 1972 and Professor of Speech and Drama, Dr. Jay W. Lees, from 1946 to 1983. Westminster weathered the sixties without many protesting, unlike the University of Utah which had a lot going on at the time. I remember that Westminster was indeed affected by those years. I remember going to a huge rock concert there on one occasion when a “streaker”, who of course didn't streak, ran up on stage and dropped the only thing he had on, his coverall pants. Facing the huge crowd with his arms outspread to the sky, he bared all for the crowd until campus police pursued him and he had to take off on a run. Modern day Westminster, while quite expensive to attend, has a nationwide reputation for excellence and is really interested in recruiting the older students returning to or just starting college, as well as students who come having to learn English as a second language.

When I asked people who had gone to the college at Westminster, or friends who teach there, they all said there was a ghost in Ferry Hall that they had heard about from older teachers or students. Ferry Hall was built in 1908 as a women's dormitory and the ghost apparently scared the women students on more than one occasion over all the decades that the dormitory was in existence. However, Ferry Hall has long since been demolished to make way for the present day Gore Business School which apparently continues to be haunted anyway. Converse Hall was built in 1906 and it is said officially that it has never really had rumors of ghosts, though there are those who claim something walks the corridors of the artist's studio on the top floor. Foster Hall, whose first floor was originally built in 1917 as the men's dormitory, is now the next oldest building on campus. Happenings in the old dormitory seem to center around objects being moved about or re-arranged or even just carefully placed in different positions over and over again. Many professors have their private offices on the top floor of Foster Hall and many of these teachers have related their own stories privately about the ghosts there. While both Converse and Foster have been completely renovated and modernized in the interior, the exteriors remain the same.

The old Ferry Hall ghost was rather famous, with several sightings of a full three dimensional image, as well as various sounds and odd movements in the building. No one seems to remember however, whether the spirit was a woman or a man, or even a child, as apparently Ferry Hall was demolished some time in the 1970s. Foster Hall, on the other hand, was completely renovated in the mid 1990s. It had originally been intended to be a three and a half story building. The first story was built in 1917 and the other stories were not added until 1926 when more money was donated to the college from The Women's Board of Missions and a private donation from a T.D. Foster. Even after the exterior of the building was completed, the interior took a while before it eventually was ready to house some 102 male students. During the renovations in the nineties, it was found that the four gabled dormers had very leaky roofs and had to be completely redone. The unused attic space became faculty offices and the lower floors became classrooms and conference rooms. With 47 offices needed, a dozen of them went into that attic which was once used simply for storage. After the remodeling, the architects thought that no one would want those offices because of the many stairs to climb. The opposite proved true, for faculty members have fought for those dormer rooms under those new leak-proof gables.

The Foster Hall happenings are quite interesting and are simply based on various professors over the years telling their students about the movement of objects in the building and especially in those attic offices. One can speculate that these various events are students playing tricks on the teachers or night-time custodians re-arranging things, though on the other hand there are so many odd stories, students don't have access to this area and the custodians usually clean these offices earlier in the day or even rarely clean them because of all those stairs. The consistency of these incidents make one wonder just why anyone in their right mind would do these various rituals over and over again for decades without variation in an attic. Or one has to question why two different professors who inhabited the same office in entirely different decades would report the exact same incidents when they both occupied the office. It is also interesting to speculate on why so many different people would tell so many different stories about these offices over the years and yet some of them were exactly the same. All the signs of an interactive presence are there as well.

Every morning or at least quite regularly, the professors would come into their offices and find something done repetitiously to the furniture. For example, one professor used to tell the students about a ship in her office. Apparently there were several model ships in her office with heavy glass covers over them. No one knows where they came from or how long they had been there, probably made or collected by a student, professor, or a former tenant of the office at one time or another. Anyway, on a very regular basis, she would come in the morning to find the ship on end, a Viking boat with its heavy cover removed and placed just so next to the boat. There would be a pair of tweezers placed nearby as if someone had been examining or looking at the ship at close range. This would not be that unusual if not for the fact that the cover was always placed exactly the same way, the tweezers were always in the same spot and nothing else was out of place. Either this was a very boring person, someone intent on playing a practical joke that was always precisely the same, or a ghostly professor who loved Viking ships and tweezers. Apparently such incidents happened to others in the building - finding things moved around. Most people just attributed the strange goings-on to a practical joke or two, though others could see a pattern to these events.

The funniest one is about a professor who liked a little nip of whiskey between classes. The professor would go into his office pour a half glass and leave it on his desk to drink. Then he would remember that he had to get something from another room, lock his office door and go get it. He would come back, unlock his door and find the whiskey glass empty on his desk with nothing spilled anywhere. He began to test this out on his own and always locked his door to eliminate that possibility. Sure enough every time the glass would be empty when he returned. He placed the glass in different places in the room and still the glass would be empty when he returned. He poured various amounts into the glass and sure enough the glass would be empty when he returned. He changed the type of drink and this did not matter either. Then one day he rearranged his office and moved his desk to a different area in the room and the phenomena stopped. Missing this game, he moved the desk back to where it had been and the phenomena started up again. Of course skeptics would say that perhaps the professor was taking a little too much of a nip in the middle of the day!

Another thing that happens, students say, is that things will move around right before their eyes and because they are alone when it happens, most people just usually talk themselves out of having seen what they just did, by letting the incidents dwindle over time into something that they must have imagined. That's why it is important to have witnesses so that one can keep checking with others to make sure one saw what one did. We were in one of these buildings when a large bottle flew off a top shelf, propelled itself through the air almost hitting an older woman student and then slid across the floor as though drawn to a magnetic place on the other side of the room. There were seven people who saw it and four of them said immediately afterwards that nothing had happened or that a large truck going by had knocked the bottle off of the shelf. I and another woman saw this event from opposite sides of the room and the person who was almost hit by the bottle and had to duck to avoid it, stuck to our story and corroborated it with each other. To this day the three of us stick to the story of what we witnessed while the other four make fun of us for not only imagining what we saw but adding on to this story as well.

The residuals of so many events do hang around, and do make their presences known usually in the quiet of evening or late into the night or when you are the only one there as a witness in the dead of winter. So it was my mission to visit in as quiet a time as possible where dramatic events had taken place, such as the fire in Converse or in the once temporary hospital on the second floor in Ferry Hall. The latter is now a new building but built on the very property where the hall stood. To spend time there waiting and watching and sensing can be very interesting. Looking at the old photographs of the two places over the years, one does get an eerie feeling about them, especially the "cracker box" boy's dormitory and the old campus barn and haystack next to the wide open spaces where Ferry Hall with its huge columns and beautiful brick designs once stood in an open field. Similar feelings come from visits to Converse Hall across an alfalfa field with Coyner Gate to the right and the old barn to the left, towering above everything else around it. Its gothic twin towers and turrets rise up to be seen in the distance, with gorgeous brick designs of their own. Having stood there since 1906, first alone and empty and then filling with the sounds and emotions of so many for so many years, Converse is an enthralling place.

The story on campus about the Gore Business School is that there is an auditorium with a stage and at the back of the stage is an old elevator which goes from the first to the second floor. Apparently it has a habit of traveling up and down by itself, or opens its doors on the stage unexpectedly when no one has pushed its buttons and no one is riding inside it. People say that talking about the ghost in old Ferry Hall that once stood in the building's place, only serves to heighten the surprise opening of these elevator doors. When the new business building was being dedicated by the college president at the time, he was giving his address when suddenly behind him the elevator light came on and the doors swung open with no one inside the elevator. The president made mention of this in his speech, saying something to the effect that he hoped the ghosts approved of the new building too.

A common occurrence for intuitives, is that when a ghost is discussed openly, it will make its presence known by slamming doors or opening them invitingly, or even dimming lights or turning them on or off altogether. Elevator doors also like to do this sort of thing, opening and shutting on their own when no one has pushed the buttons. Either the Gore building has a ghost all its own, with something having occurred on the land before the building was built or it is the same spirit which haunted Ferry Hall for so many years. One would think that most likely pranksters are involved, although performers and speakers and those who work there would beg to differ, having seen this phenomena first hand. Since Ferry Hall might have had more than one ghost with all those women benefactors as well as the young man who might have died there, one wonders if perhaps they just decided to stay on even though the original building is long gone. There are the Ferrys, two possible Hancocks, the young man and then the housemother, all of whom might have decided to stay for a while or at least have their images imprinted into the walls of both the old building and the new one.

There is an old church in England where people have seen the apparitions of a group of monks for centuries. They appear over the crest of a small hill, walk towards the old church and down the center aisle to the altar, where they promptly disappear. However, they are walking on the old foundation of the original church so that they appear to be walking inside the earth, as they can only be seen from the waist up as they walk forward. The replaying of such events can also be "modernized" in the sense that though the ghost is no longer actually seen, it can still affect electrical things within a building. In finally locating the original story of the ghost of Ferry Hall I also found that it had been told over and over again throughout several decades by students and faculty alike, perhaps into the forties and early fifties. After this the story died out and students and faculty today don't know the story at all, but many of them have heard that there once was a ghost in residence in the hall. Whether the story is true or not, it does fit all the criteria for an active haunting and I am sure was added onto through the years. Best of all, it is a good one!

A group of male students often did panty raids on the girls' dorm in the middle of the night; certainly this is nothing new, though I was surprised to learn that this practice had been going on from way back when. However at Westminster, the old dorms had narrow and very high fire escapes on the outside of the old buildings. They were pretty dangerous to begin with. Anyway, one night, in a very early decade, a group of students from the boys' dorm slipped out and began, climbing the fire escape on the outside of the building to the top floor where a certain girl's panties were especially desired. When they got close to the top, one of the students slipped, lost his grip and fell all the way to the ground. He apparently died from the mishap and the fire escapes were off limits after that. Various students over the years claimed to have seen the dark shape or outline of this student moving up the fire escape of the girls' dorm and in his hand he held a glowing light, which upon closer scrutiny appeared to be a pair of girl's panties. People saw the shape or light, or even the panties floating by themselves on the side of the building; this was the ghost of Ferry Hall. He was also supposed to have been seen inside the building at the end of a hallway as a shadow or even as a full manifestation which then turned and walked around the corner and disappeared. Over the years many a coed was frightened by this apparition walking down a hall or even leaning over her bed in the middle of the night obviously searching for her panties, though she usually didn't know this!

This was supposed to be the famous ghost of Ferry Hall, though others say that a second apparition has been sensed or smelled or even sighted - a never married, former female teacher, secretary or dorm mother who loved the place so much that she just didn't want to leave. Her identity seems to have been lost to time and rumor. Students living in the new dorms report various ghostly activities all the time, if one is to believe all of these tales. However, given the age of the campus and the various buildings that were once there and are now gone forever, I guess it is possible that spirits would haunt the newer facilities where once an older ghost resided. Former students say that they saw objects move back and forth by themselves or that trash cans would swing back and forth in the rooms. It is said that a young male student is often seen in Hogle Hall at the end of the halls, and then he simply vanishes. Most interesting are the students who have been standing talking in the evening, when all of a sudden a mist will form to the side of them and then walk right through their group as though a human form were inside it. This has scared them enough that they at once leave the building or at least vacate the area.

All in all, Westminster is quite a haunted place, though non-believers scoff at the notion, while others swear by their experiences in the place. Professors who have had their personal items moved about in their offices, or have observed items belonging to the school from a more ancient time being transported, do shake their heads and wonder. Former students from years long past say that, whether true or not, the ghostly stories have been around for decades. Present day students have their more popular stories to tell, now that scary stuff is all the rage among the young. Still, hidden within all of this is enough to know that Westminster College does house its own share of those who have gone but refuse to be forgotten. And perhaps one or two who have never gone, and just keep right on doing whatever they please, to the living.

MAESER ELEMENTARY
- UTAH'S OLDEST SCHOOL IN USE UNTIL SPRING 2002

At Hollywood Cemetery in Los Angeles a young entrepreneur has revitalized an old but very famous cemetery by offering among other things fifteen-minute biographies of the people buried there. There will eventually be two theaters located on the beautifully groomed grounds where one can go and watch the life story of a loved one, famous or not and even several generations removed from the person's passing. Historians, preservationists, archivists and many others have been doing the same thing for old buildings for decades. The death of a building with this amount of people involved with its life over the years, makes those who have any connection with such a place, mourn through memories and events, silently and most usually alone. Sometimes there is a celebration or "wake" if you will, and in a very few instances the people who inhabited the building will even have a funeral of sorts. There are dedications or birth announcements, re-dedications or graduations, holiday celebrations which would be like weddings or even divorces in some cases, and finally there are wakes and funerals for buildings about to be torn down.

Built in 1898, Maeser elementary school has had thousands of students and hundreds of parents, teachers and some administrators pass through its doors. Its history follows the timeline of its building, from the first section which saw the turn of the new century, the industrial age, a world war, a worldwide flu epidemic, the roaring twenties and Prohibition. The second section of the building behind the original school was added in 1914 according to a teacher who ought to know her facts having taught there for 24 years and acting as the resident historian for the school. However other articles were quoted as saying that it was added in 1939. But no matter because beyond the seam which she showed me of where the two buildings meet would have been The New Deal, a second World War, the Cold War and Korea, and the final edition to the main building in 1956. After this came a kindergarten building all its own, portables and various other additional buildings, which would have seen the Kennedy-Johnson era, discos and finally the age of computers, cell phones and laptops. Maeser School has been wired with a state of the art computer system, although one had to climb several flights of stairs to get to it.

I visited the school just after the chaos of moving everything to the brand new school. There will be a huge warehouse sale, the very complex and convoluted basement rooms and tunnels were in the process of being emptied of all sorts of things stored there for 104 years, and one last hurrah of a short summer school will be followed by the school's demolishment on the tentative date of July 16, 2002. The school's various staff members over the years kept up the art of scrap booking and they had already packed up those kept from the turn of the century through the twenties and those kept more recently since the sixties. But scrapbooks for the thirties through fifties had been missing for quite some time and some wondered if those years had been skipped somehow. One day, a teacher acting as the principal stepped into the teacher workroom and found a whole stack of scrapbooks that no one had ever seen before, stacked neatly by the door to the main office on the floor. No one in the building laid claim to having found them and how they suddenly appeared there is a mystery to everyone. Either someone outside the school had them and brought them back, which is highly unlikely, or the person who found them inside the building won't admit finding them, or as one teacher says, the building itself just decided to cough them up knowing of its impending doom.

Most important however, is that everyone who has memories with the building and everyone who is currently leaving its premises, feels helpless before the powers that be. Maeser School will fall. It will fall because school districts desperate for money these days will do anything to make a buck because their priority is housing students and educating them and with so little funds to go around, old buildings are a huge deficit to them all. It will fall because it is too expensive to save even the old original four-classroom building. It will fall because there are not enough people who care to save it, although it has great potential for a museum which larger towns; especially University towns have no need of. It will fall, pass away and become a piece of grass added to the little block park that is already there. Someone will take an interest in putting up a little plaque or memorial to the school in its place and eventually even that will be forgotten. The park will become either homes or businesses and no one will remember this school except the few who record its existence and recall that it was the oldest still operating school in the state. Those who attended there however, will remember their experiences and shake their heads sadly as they pass by, until the last set of students and faculty pass on to dust as well.

Although there are stories of ghostly happenings at the school in the form of the portrait of "Pinkie," "Blue Boy," and other interesting traditions at the school, apparently the spirits that inhabited the place remained hidden from most who attended there. Therefore it was with great surprise that after my tour and looking through some of the newly discovered old scrapbooks, I came home thoroughly exhausted and did something that I never do, took a nap in the middle of the afternoon. I fell asleep and dreamed and was awakened by my husband which made me remember what I had dreamed and I got up and wrote down what I could remember of my visitors who spoke with me about their time at the Maeser school. In the dream I sat in that old easy chair with a scrapbook in my lap when four teachers came up to me and casually surrounded me, leaning against walls or sitting down beside me. They were from different eras and all four spoke to me about their school, although this part I could not remember. I do however remember their sex, approximate age, era of dress, basic description of how they looked and some about each of their individual stories. After I tell the history of the school I will return to this dream and tell the rest of what I remember of this rather odd and very unusual circumstance.

Maeser School is named after Karl Gottfried Maeser who was the first Principal of Brigham Young Academy in Provo, Utah. He was born in Saxony, Germany in 1828 and worked as a teacher in Dresden, a private tutor in Bohemia and then a school Vice Principal in Dresden where he met and married the Principal's daughter. He heard of the Mormon Church through an anti-Mormon pamphlet, wrote for information, and then worked hard to get the missionaries to come to him and was baptized in the Elbe River in Dresden. Before coming west to Utah he worked in Scotland, London, Philadelphia and Virginia in various capacities for his church.

In 1860, he arrived in Salt Lake City and immediately began organizing church schools, tutoring some of Brigham Young's children, did accounting work and played the tabernacle organ on the side. He served LDS missions in Switzerland and Germany, took a second plural wife and taught at the University of Deseret, which eventually became the Brigham Young Academy. Brigham Young asked him to go to Provo and head up the academy where he did every duty, from chorister to janitor, to help build up the school. He headed this institution for the next sixteen years and then was appointed head of the Mormon Church Board of Education in 1888. In 1889 he received an Honorary Degree and continued to build up the education system throughout the state until his death in 1901. Throughout his life he was known as an "electrifying speaker" who could move others to action. There is an amazingly life-like portrait of him which hangs in the Maeser school library, which will no doubt be purchased, moved to the Brigham Young University archives or perhaps end up hanging in the newly revitalized BYU Academy and city library building. As I looked at it, it had the effect of following one with its eyes and if the artist did indeed capture the soul of its model, he must have been a stern man who could speak of hellfire and brimstone in the same breath as he could in expressing caring and compassion for the young whose education he cared deeply about. (*Utah History Encyclopedia* edited by Allan Kent Powell, "Karl Gottfried Maeser" by Jesse L. Embry, pp. 341-342.)

Maeser Elementary School was one of Karl Maeser's projects to build a bigger and better school for the children of Provo. The old Webster School had become entirely inadequate and so plans for this new school were begun in 1898. The eight-room school building wasn't even completed when the students moved into the first floor classrooms in November of that year. They gathered at the old school and gave three rousing cheers for it and then marched en mass to the new school where they again gave three rousing cheers and then entered with their four teachers and some two hundred students. J.M. Jensen was the first Principal and taught the sixth and seventh grades as well. The first teachers were Ethel Pratt who taught fourth and fifth, Mary C. Nuttal who taught second and third and Ella Kirkwood who taught beginners and first grade.

Twelve hundred school children gathered with their teachers two days later for the opening ceremonies of the new school. Dr. Karl G. Maeser was the opening speaker and the cost of the new school was $8.661.45. At the evening festivities, Dr. Maeser was the only speaker, as he inspired some in his audience to pursue their own higher education. The Maeser Trio, Mandolin Guitar Club and the Pyne and Boshard Brothers performed the musical numbers for this event. A huge cake decorated with miniature American flags was presented to the new school by the students at Timpanogos School and the new playground was dedicated the next morning. Homes alongside the school were purchased so that the school grounds could be enlarged and more playground equipment provided.

On Arbor Day of 1899, trees were planted around the grounds of the new school playground. The outside row of trees were given names of the presidents of the United States and the inside row were named after teachers, famous statesmen, authors and educators. On Maeser Day in 1900, before Dr. Maeser passed on, he had written a quote on each of the blackboards of the lower four rooms. For years it was a matter of honor that no one erase these four sayings, but after a mysterious but unwitting substitute erased one of them, they were framed and covered in glass and can be seen in the original rooms of the school to this day, one tiny section of the old blackboard visible under several layers of walls added over these. It is an amusing story in the sense that everything can be blamed on a mysterious Substitute. Substitutes have been blamed for lots of things in schools; it is practically a time-honored tradition to do so. So if anyone else was to blame, there is a poor but anonymous Substitute probably dead in her grave somewhere who cannot defend herself against such a terrible accusation!

Maeser Day was celebrated every November 7th and the entire school would meet together for holiday celebrations in the assembly rooms upstairs during the first twenty years of the school's existence. The students also met every Monday morning in these two rooms for devotional exercises and general instruction. On Thanksgiving the children were taught lessons of giving by bringing food, flowers and money to school, which they then distributed to the poor of their various LDS wards, as nearly everyone at the school and in the town of Provo at that time was Mormon. The school also celebrated "Tag Day" when money was raised for various community projects. In the beginning the children were divided by what was called beginners, first, second, third, fourth, fifth, and sixth and the seventh graders, who were taught by the Principal.

In 1908 the school and town experienced a measles epidemic in December and many students were absent for a month or more including four teachers who had measles in their families. The school also had its first fire drill that year and was visited by the fire marshal, a man who traveled around the town specifically to time each school's exit from the building. Fires back in those days were a much more real threat because once it got started enough to engulf even one section the chances of saving the building were very limited with few resources except simple manpower, bucket brigades and a few fire hose carts available then. Maeser beat the time of any other school in the state by having their students exit the building in 40 seconds after the alarm sounded with the 4,000 pound hose cart arriving in just 3 minutes and water being thrown onto the roof. Over the years the school did have at least two fires, which caused very little damage in the building.

In the next decade from 1910 to 1917, the United States became involved in the Mexican Civil War because of various economic investments in Mexico. There were various fights between dictators and the people and finally the wars dissipated and the last of the American troops were withdrawn in February of 1917. By 1911, it was a tradition at the school that the first and second grade students lined up along the hallway to perform a little ceremony before school started each morning with the boys holding flags and the girls holding flowers. Using this daily tradition the school held a special ceremony for the Grand Army of the Republic veterans of the Civil War and the men entered the building having flowers strewn along their pathway, after which a patriotic program was presented in the assembly hall. The G.A.R. veterans presented the school with a huge American flag. In 1917, the students at Maeser welcomed F Troop home from the Mexican border where they had been stationed. A huge celebration involving a parade and hundreds of students waving American flags in a special flag ceremony was held in the assembly hall. A school flag was hung from the top of the tower at the front of the school. A sixth grader would climb the stairs to the attic, cross a narrow plank to the front and then climb a ladder to perform this task each day. It became another tradition to write one's name and date on the wood beams around where the flag was displayed.

A heavy wooden wall about one foot thick hangs from the ceiling in the attic having waited at least sixty years or more to be lowered to the floor below as it often was when the school first opened. Heavy metal counterweight blocks about one foot in diameter hang down from the top of this wall waiting to be released so that the wall can make the assembly room on the second floor into two classrooms again. Long since, other walls and ceilings have taken its place and the wall just sits up there covered in the earliest of names written by those who hung the flag out the window near it. Over the years dozens of wood beams around this area became covered with the names of students who performed this task, so that as I toured the school it was fascinating to see all of these signatures starting with the oldest near where the flag was once displayed and going back to the most modern signatures near the stairwell where teachers had merely allowed their students to peer into the place while writing on the beams closest to the attic door as a lesson in history.

During this decade historians say that the second addition to the school was added and while the new addition is the same size as the original school it also looks flawlessly like the original with the seams between them being barely visible at the sides of the school. On the outside the same colors of brick, mortar and designs made it close to impossible for the layman to distinguish the difference. This addition was made between 1912 and 1914 and the school soon had thirteen teachers and 565 students. Students at the school during this decade also held a field day at the BYU Academy each spring and celebrated their 15th year with a ceremony where they decorated the assembly hall in the school colors of gold and white and began the tradition of voting for a May queen who received her coronation on May Day along with her twelve girl assistants whose main duty was to braid the Maypole. This was often followed by a parade with the May Queen riding on her float. Maeser students won the local track meets for nine years in a row during this decade as well.

When America joined in the fight, which had become World War I, that Thanksgiving the student brought in thirteen bushels of apples to send to the soldiers at Camp Kearney. They also began what were called "war gardens" on the school grounds to raise food for the war effort. They held fundraisers for thrift stamps and organized a Junior Red Cross auxiliary with 275 members who then collected 290 pounds of old underwear to make into baby shirts "for the suffering Beligumns." The students made 250 wash cloths, seven quilts and fifty baby booties to be sent along as well. The first school nurse was hired in 1918, which might have been a lucky thing as the influenza epidemic then struck and the school was closed for three months from October to December of that year. Teachers were required to visit homes to make an accurate count of those stricken with the illness and when school opened on December 30th, both teachers and students had to wear masks and every student's temperature was taken each morning until the situation cleared up. Schools were closed again during the month of February but the students at the school still managed to adopt a French orphan named Gaetan Lahorgne Poulot and the sixth grade adopted a second orphan from France whose name has been lost to history. This program was entitled "The Fatherless Children of France."

The years between the end of World War I and the second World War are basically chronicled in the scrapbooks in a series of student writings, attendance books stored in the basement along with old books, the oldest of which have already been boxed up for the University archives, along with old textbooks, desks and other items which will be sold at the warehouse sale in the Maeser auditorium at the beginning of July just before the demolition date which is tentatively July 16, 2002. During these years Maeser had only one principal, Oscar Bjerregaard was the longest serving Principal in the state of Utah with a record that began in 1921 and lasted until his death on April 11, 1946. Also the Page library was the first public school library in the state and was named after Mrs. Gertrude Page who taught at the school for 36 years. The scrapbooks during these years also consist of photos of the May Day celebrations, parades, and various fund raising projects both for the school and for charity along with student writings and teacher meeting minutes with an occasional school newsletter here and there. I am sure that there are many former students that could tell us more about this period of the school's history, and though my favorite story was told to me by a long time teacher there who sometimes acted as the assistant Principal when the Principal was away.

It seems that an old man, who looked quite poor himself, came walking up the sidewalk to the school. The Assistant Principal could not remember the exact date, but figuring her twenty-four years at the school and the age of the school almost a 104 and the man who was in his eighties, one would have to assume that the man probably went to the school somewhere between 1920 and 1940. He asked to speak to the Principal and since the Principal was not there this teacher said she could talk with him. He insisted on going into the Principal's office wherein he related his tale. He and another boy had been fighting and during the course of the fight his head had struck a window, which then broke the windowpane. Neither boy ever told anyone what had happened and there had been no witnesses. This incident had apparently bothered the man all of his life and he had come to the school to pay for the broken window. He handed the teacher five dollars and left, looking as though, she said, he probably couldn't even afford the five dollars.

According to records it was not the second addition to the school, which was already in existence at the time, but a huge remodeling project that took place in 1939 while the children were in attendance at the school. "As soon as school reconvened, the Board of Education decided to immediately remodel our building with the help of a P.W.A. grant. So walls were torn down and rebuilt, plaster was slung, and when I say slung I mean nothing but a flip of the trowel would toss it from one side of the room to the other and many decorative effects were bestowed on the pictures, moldings and furniture. An insulating machine made a bombardment over our heads; a concrete mixing-machine banged and squeaked its noisy way under the windows and door cracks, bricks cavorted around in the air, narrowly missing our heads, plumber's hammers banged on the pipes and the water was shut off frequently and at the most inopportune moments; painters bestowed polka-dots on male and female apparel alike, and electric wire men left nooses hanging where the unwary might hang themselves. Doorways were blocked, and to see five hundred children try to get in one door all at the same time was an inspiration and education for teachers." (Author unknown, taken from excerpts from the scrapbooks and written up by a teacher at Maeser, also unknown.)

The biggest enrollment the school ever had was during World War II when 950 pupils were enrolled. Starting in 1956 the school became surrounded or integrated into a larger facility when an auditorium, modern kitchen, offices and workroom were added as well as doors to close off long hallways and storage cabinets within the individual classrooms. Since this time it appears that additional classrooms have also been added though the school only houses around 500 students at present. A separate but permanent kindergarten building was added to the south of the old building with its own fenced in area and playground. Like all school districts today, strapped for cash and continuously battling funding cuts, old historic schools are always in danger of being torn down without much hope of being saved. The 104 year-old School is on the National Registry of Historic Places and has been studied by the Utah State Historical Society with recommendations that it find a renter or buyer. However, the school board voted four to one to raze the school in the summer of 2002, unless those interested in saving it can come up with the needed $300,000 it would take to upgrade the building, plus an additional annual rent of $100,000 to be paid by the tenant.

The students will vacate the building for the last time in June of 2002 and attend a new school nearby called Spring Creek Elementary. While the school board has considered lots of options none of them have panned out. After considering the place as their district office and proposing office space or rentals, the local residents voted down the decision. The board is left with only two options. Either they raze the building to cut their costs or the local residents raise the money to save it. The campaign to save the school has already begun although they have a long ways to go just hoping to raise the $50,000 it will take to stave off the razing in July and to give them time to find a renter. The committee to save the building hopes to make it into a museum at a later date, but right now they just need a renter so that they can work on raising money for renovations. Maybe this is an Eccles Foundation project, although at present, saving this particular building has nothing to do with the arts!

Locals and especially some of the students talk about the ghosts in their school and say that they will not miss them, although a few residents probably will. Students call it "spooky wiring" when the lights dim or go out unexpectedly. The "talking plumbing" is sometimes entertaining and sometimes scary they say, while the occasional failure of the old furnace is no fun in the wintertime. Some say that Dr. Maeser must certainly hang around once in a while, especially with his favorite sayings encased in glass, which will probably be saved and transported to the archives when the building is left to the wrecking ball. Maeser is also said to be hanging around his portrait in the library which one could really see, as the painting itself seems to be one of those live ones which follows one around in the room with its eyes and might upon occasion even appear to be breathing. Then there are the usual things that all old buildings can attest to although most don't agree on any of this happening; doors swinging open and shut, windows locking or unlocking on their own and any of the other sounds in the middle of the night that no one can probably tell us about except for those students over the years that might have tried to get in and a late night custodial visit or two.

Art works seem to be the most haunted objects at Maeser Elementary School. Besides the painting of Maeser, this includes two small art prints, a couple of Avard Fairbank's reliefs, and murals painted on the walls which will disappear with the building. Fairbanks was one of the most famous of Utah's sculptors who reached international fame and the school bought both of the two-dimensional relief's for $29 dollars. Probably worth thousands now, these two casts have only been lost once or twice over the years while the two cheap little art prints of Gainsborough's "Pinkie" and "Blue Boy" which are in those gold ornately scrolled frames and were hung in various places throughout the school's lifetime, have been lost time and time again with no human hands involved, say staff members.

The pictures and especially "Pinkie" have been found everywhere imaginable in the school and not once could any culprits be found to own up to their disappearances. Hung on a wall in the main office where it could be watched, the picture still was found in a locked basement room and even once in the attic, which is also locked. Placed in a locked closet, the picture would turn up hanging on a wall somewhere, or vice versa. Each time, custodial staff swore that they had not only, not taken the pictures, but didn't even know about the history of the pictures. Also, "Pinkie" has been known to hide one of her feet under her gown upon occasion, first one foot and then the other. One never knows which foot will disappear for a while. Her eyes follow you around the room and this really spooks some of the children. Some teachers at the school have also been known to take their upper grade classes down to the basement to tell ghost stories or write ghost stories there. One day such a class found the "Pinkie" portrait down in a basement room when she had been lost for quite some time and nobody knew where she was.

No one knows how long the pictures have been around although they look like a perhaps nineteen fifties addition and the "haunted portrait of Pinkie" as the children and staff call her, continues to disappear. When I visited "Blue Boy" was missing but "Pinkie" was in the Principal's locked closet next to her desk. The two pictures were supposed to be there with all of the other old pictures to be auctioned off. Just last week though, they told me that "Pinkie" had disappeared from the closet and was found in a basement room and returned to the locked closet once more. They are hoping that the building doesn't decide to not let them have the two prints at the last moment because then they will not be able to find them anywhere and the two pictures will go down with the building. With the maze of tunnels, shafts, rooms and closets in the place this could very well be possible. On the other hand, perhaps the building will want them to be saved and will return them before it goes down. This game of cat and mouse had gone on for more years than anyone can remember and certainly before any present staff member's time in the building because others have talked about the same thing happening before this.

The other haunted artwork involves some murals painted on the walls by more than one custodian. Joel Rodriguez, a custodian at the school some fifteen years ago, painted most of the murals. An article about him appeared in the *Provo Herald* in May of 1989 where he was invited by the administration to paint two murals on the walls after someone saw his drawings and suggested this. He never became an art teacher and never went on to more school after high school but continued to draw and paint and was an excellent artist. One mural is of "Pete's Dragon," a scene from the Disney movie with the added attraction of the boy who is playing tic-tac-toe on the dragon's stomach. The other is a scene of students of different races going to school in a rural setting and playing together near farm fields where horses are raised. He painted before and after his work time and students would watch and make suggestions such as one student who suggested that there should be a few flies around the horses, which Rodriquez then painted in. According to another teacher I talked to there were some other murals around from a previous custodian but I only saw one of these. The feeling is that while these murals were in the building, things moved in them, though I would guess that if the building had survived the artists, these two would have experienced a few hauntings.

Then there are the spook alleys which were held in the basement of the place for many years on Halloween with its many finished rooms, dirt and stone tunnels and caves all over the place, including shafts which a child could get into but then would fall all the way to the basement from the attic. Two old and very small but ornate oakwood desks with iron lattice work on the sides sit down there as a testament to the many Spook Alley years because they are covered in red paint to represent blood and covered over with clear Elmer's glue so that the paint is permanently sealed to the desk tops. Around the corner along the walls are a few handprints and signatures in the same red paint. Some of these little basement rooms were used by the band and orchestra and even at one time were special education rooms, which frankly gave me the willies having been a special education teacher for many years as well. There are absolutely no windows and doors and passageways open up in all directions with only one entrance or exit from the whole basement. In fact the special education room was an active area for me and I wouldn't have wanted to remain in it for very long at all.

One teacher at the school even started a program with a local junior high school teacher based on shows like "Scariest Places On Earth" or "Fear" which was a short-lived program on MTV. She explained to me that the idea for their Fear Experience program was to introduce the students to this experience in hopes of some of them gaining confidence in themselves as well as in their newly discovered survivor abilities and skills. Some of the students did have some scary experiences as they carried out the various tasks in the spooky basement rooms and tunnels of Maeser Elementary School. The two teachers did this experience three separate times and students could sign up for the nighttime experience with permission slips from their parents. The students drew a colored disk, which then led them to a particular ghost story which they had to read in the room they were assigned to in the school, after of course, getting to the room with a flashlight in the dark in groups of two or three.

All the groups had walkie talkies and the command post was in the faculty room of the school. The students and teachers began their experience at 8 p.m. and ended it at 11 p.m. Once they reached their assigned area and read the story, they then had to maintain radio silence for 15 minutes. Here are some of the unexplained things that the students reported. One group was assigned to the room where the attic door was located and things kept falling off shelves and papers were being shuffled with no one in the room but them, so those students came down early. Another group reported dramatic changes in temperature in a room in the basement where they were stationed. Another student group heard sounds that couldn't have been there and were convinced that they were not the pigeons, which live in the rafters of the school. In fact they were very positive that they had overheard people talking to each other. One group reported that a voice had come on the walkie talkie telling them that their experience was over and it was time for them to come down. When they got back down to the command center in the faculty room, no one was there. When the rest of the groups returned they asked who had called them and everyone insisted that they had maintained the radio silence as planned. This group also felt that they could not recognize the voice on the walkie talkie. It had not been the right time for them to leave and no one else had left their post.

One group of students reported that in the area they were pictures kept falling off the walls. They would hang them one back up and then another would fall. They would hang that one up and another would fall. It just kept happening and so finally they got scared and came down early as well. Another group found that the lights in the room kept going on and off and they were nowhere near the switch at the time and in fact didn't know where it was. The kindergarten building is separate from the main building and on one of the fear experience nights, a kindergarten teacher was in that building working late, saw the lights coming from the basement and called the police. When the police arrived they were startled to find all these kids and teachers, even though the whole experience had been cleared with the officers in the first place. Nearly all of the groups reported hearing footsteps and doors opening or shutting when no one else was there.

As for my own encounters during the final days of this grand old school, I had not expected any as I was assured that no actual hauntings had ever been reported beyond the footsteps, doors, windows and lights. While I was there, this was true, although certain areas seemed active to me and there were so many of them that this energy made me tired. One could not distinguish between the energy and chaos of the final days of the last days in this school, and any energies that had existed from long ago. I went home and felt very drained for some reason and found myself falling asleep in my chair, which never ever happens to me in the middle of the day. Then I was awakened by my husband, which was also unusual, so that I remembered part of the dream I was having while sleeping. I was also struck by how easily I had transitioned from a sleep state to a waking one inside the dream. In the dream I was sitting in the same chair in the little workroom at Maeser with a scrapbook on my lap and looked up to see four individuals appearing around me. They had not walked into the room but had just appeared and some seemed to be leaning against walls out in the hall though I could see them plainly as though the wall between where I sat and the hallway had melted away.

They talked quite casually to me about things that concerned them although I will probably never remember any of this part. I do however remember what they each looked like and what they wore. The main person who talked to me was of what appeared to be of Mexican-American descent. He was of medium build though he had powerful looking shoulders and arms and slicked back black hair and small mustache. He may have had glasses though I can't be sure about this. He was from the World War II era and probably died in the war. He may have been a teacher or more likely some other part of the staff at that time. The second man was thinner and slighter and appeared to be quite the intellectual type from the World War I era where he might have served but I don't think died in it. He was more interested in telling me about the school and the grounds and might have taken care of the gardens although he could also have been a teacher. The other two were women, one being slight and thin and short in stature with a longer skirt from the very early days of the school while the other seemed to be from the thirties and forties and was tall and portly with dark hair drawn back from her face in a fancy sort of braid or bun.

The earliest woman seemed to have never married while the later woman seemed to have devoted herself to the school even though she did marry and have children. What I do remember was that all of them were concerned about getting information to me about their school and they were also there to let me know that they did exist and were around from time to time at the school. They pointed out to me that a boy that attended Maeser had drowned in 1918 and that someone important to the school had lost this boy who was their son. They said that this boy came back to the school from time to time and was sometimes responsible for things disappearing from one place and reappearing somewhere else. They also pointed out a dark presence that had no face with the shape of a very tall man, although it was more like a dark sort of cloud moving through the halls Somehow I knew that this was a tall man who liked to wear one of those high top hats for some reason and was very stern. I felt he owned the place and might have been a Principal or teacher there in the very early days. Mostly the four of them had been waiting apparently for someone to tell their stories to and I felt bad that I did not remember any of what they told me. I was convinced that they were really there.

One wonders if the school will resist this tearing down like other such magnificent old schools have done in the past or just die quietly. Hopefully this story will have a happy ending with ghosts and apparitions intact, when in the future it becomes a city museum in the park much more magnificent than the little building that stands in another park in town and is run by probably very old members of the local chapter of the Daughters of the Pioneers. Other towns have done this, turned magnificent old schools into town museums, libraries and centerpieces or at least office buildings or little private schools. However Provo residents might think that they have already done this sort of city renovation with their showcase restoration of the BYU Academy building. The new city library was Karl G. Maeser's greatest love as well. The most likely scenario though, is that the old buildings, built in different decades will all come down to dust with no funeral held and the cremation being hauled away or left to filter its way down into the ground from which it came. I may never know more about the stories of these four people unless somehow they are in these various scrapbooks and are salvaged for the BYU archives. Perhaps I will go there sometime in the future and see their faces in a scrapbook.

Update: "Historic Provo School Wins Reprieve," by Martha Murvosh, *The Salt Lake Tribune*, Thursday, June 20, 2002. "Foundation has six months to raise refurbishing funds and find a buyer or tenant." Provo City School District voted unanimously to extend the date for the wrecking ball from July 15 to December 3, 2002. The board had voted 4 to 1 in March to raze the building and build a new school there. The "Friends of Maeser" nonprofit foundation needs to raise $50,000 dollars toward the $300,000 needed to renovate the building. Kena Matthews is the vice-chairwoman of the foundation and she says that they are hoping to find either a tenant or buyer so that some day the building can house a private charter school or museum. If a buyer is found they will have to agree to upgrade the building but also leave the older portion intact as the old school, in other words no offices or apartments. The cash-strapped school district can't afford the school's annual upkeep. "What needs to happen is somebody with vision has to come forward and show us what they can do with it...." Says Darryl H. Alder, a school board member. Neighbors and the Friends of Maser are also hopeful that someone out there with the funds will match what they raise so that the old school, at least the old original portion of it can become something that the community will be proud of.

"Housing Proposol Offers Preservation Solution for Maeser," by Kirk Huffaker, UHF

Assistant Director, *Heritage*, The Utah Heritage Foundation Newsletter, Winter 2003, p. 16. "The Provo City School District Board of Education set December 3rd, 2002, as the date it would decide the fate of the historic Maeser School...In December, Overland Development and Cooper Roberts Simonsen Architects presented a well- received plan to the Board of Education, the neighborhood, and the Maeser School Advisory Committee. The Overland is proposing to convert Maeser into unique condominium type housing units and preserve all the historic portions of the school. The rest of the school site would be developed with additional housing units designed to be compatible with the style and massing of Maeser school, as well as with the single-family nature of the historic neighborhood that surrounds the school property. We believe this project brings together expertise that can redevelop the school site with sensitivity to the neighborhood and historic school building, while revitalizing the historic Maeser neighborhood after the loss of its public school." Making it still possible for the original part of the school to become a neighborhood or city museum perhaps dedicated to the history of Maeser school as well as the city's history and also making it possible, for the ghosts of Maeser to continue their occasional haunts.

WASATCH ACADEMY - MOUNT PLEASANT

Sanpete County

"Let it endure like the Wasatch Mountains ... call it Wasatch Academy."
-Founder Duncan McMillan

Wasatch Academy, then known as Mount Pleasant Academy, was founded in 1875 by a Presbyterian minister, Duncan McMillan. Sheldon Jackson was an apostate Mormon well-known in the area as a slightly more radical thinker than most. He was the one who encouraged McMillan, along with other apostates in the area, to establish an alternative Christian school. Duncan McMillan was a missionary in this region who had come to Utah looking for a drier climate. The first person to approach him about a school was the postmaster, Jeremiah Page, representing approximately 30 Mormon apostate families. McMillan was given the title to a building which he called Liberal Hall, although it had been originally the Liberal Dance Hall. He assumed its debts himself. Liberal Hall was located on Mt. Pleasant's Main Street. He then made the adjustments necessary to turn it into a school with a ready-made curriculum. The school opened April 19th, 1875 with 18 students in the lower grades. This soon became 44 students and then grew to 109 students by the end of the first term. By 1887 the school was offering classes up through 12th grade and that spring the first two students were graduated from the Academy.

When McMillan had troubles paying his debts, he asked the Presbyterian Church in Salt Lake City to help him out. He then deeded Liberal Hall over to the trustees of the Presbyterian Church in Salt Lake City and its patrons sent him $500 to buy the real estate. McMillan always hired female teachers because he thought they were better teachers. His very first teacher was named Miss Delia R. Snow. Other teachers followed and in the early years it was a school only for the elementary grades. In 1880, the Board of Home Missions took it over and ran it until 1891. That year, a new two-story structure was erected with $10,000 donated by the Ladies Missionary Society of the Synod of New York, plus $2,000 from the Sanpete County Co-op. Named Hungerford Hall, the administration building and a few other older buildings were scattered in the southwest part of town. By 1896, 24 students enrolled as the first boarders. Boys who boarded stayed in Hungerford and the girls stayed in a home nearby.

By then, the school served through the high school years and offered such subjects as Latin, physics, bookkeeping, government, rhetoric and all the other usual subjects. By 1894, the typical enrollment was about 120 students and several different Principals took charge over the years. The Principal then was George Marshall and he added the boarding school so that students from other areas could attend the school. He served until 1904 and in 1908, the school's administration building was erected. In 1911, Charles L. Johns became Principal and it was under his direction that several other buildings were added including a boy's dormitory and a hospital. He acquired two nearby Victorian homes which became Lincoln Hall and Indiana Hall. He also added the nearby brick schoolhouse and its grounds. Finks Memorial Hall was built in 1913 for the girls' dormitory with money raised nationwide for this endeavor. Three years later Darlington Hall was built for the boys' dormitory with donations from Charles Darlington of New York City.

In 1912, public schools were draining away the student body and so Wasatch Academy took a new direction and became a college preparatory school. At the same time however, the Academy received a lot of equipment, supplies and good teachers when two other Presbyterian schools shut their doors: Hungerford Academy in Springville and a Boarding school in Logan. In 1917, the property for the gymnasium and the Johansen Cottage were purchased. In 1921, the Frances Thompson Memorial Infirmary was built and a year later "John's Gymnasium" was erected. In 1923, Olivia Sage Memorial Hall was raised and in 1924, the Duncan McMillan Memorial Hall was completed. In April of 1933, a fire destroyed Hungerford Hall and almost shut the whole school down. It was still the Great Depression and school officials out of funds discussed closing down the school. But in 1934, a Miss Alice Craighead whose father had been a close friend of Duncan McMillan's, left the school a gift in her will. She had listened and been impressed by her father's stories of his friend's dream for a school. Instead of closing, the school was able to expand even more and built both Craighead Industrial Hall and the Craighead Administration Building in 1934-35. The new administration building was built on the foundation of the old one.

By 1938, a few more historic houses had been purchased and the Seeley Mansion was purchased to serve as the Principal's residence. By then there were 24 staff members, 160 boarding students enrolled, and 80 day time pupils as well. In 1958, Wasatch Academy dropped its lower grades and became a high school only, with high academic standards. To this very day, Wasatch Academy is still this type of school. The school maintains a low teacher to pupil ratio of one teacher to every 8 students and enrollment is kept at a constant 125 students. All the students are required to perform community-oriented tasks such as domestic chores and religious responsibilities. Faculty members and students maintain a close relationship through such things as eating meals together and teachers helping students to study in their dorms. In 1972, Wasatch Academy became an independent, interfaith school. The grounds now cover some 14 acres of land which include classrooms, dormitories, a gymnasium, playing field, faculty homes, and a museum. Extracurricular activities include such things as soccer, baseball, skiing, swimming, music and the arts. A hospital is located only a short distance away in Mount Pleasant.

Today the school is no longer an alternative school for non-Mormons. Students who choose to attend school there do it for various reasons from liking a rural area, to individualized attention and a reputation for academic excellence. There are 160 students at the school from such countries as Japan, Bulgaria, Kenya, Rwanda, Latvia, Lithuania, Sudan, Pakistan, Korea, Bulgaria and 15 different states with 11 percent of the student body commuters living within a thirty-mile radius of the school. The school is accredited by the Northwest Association of Schools and Colleges and is a member of the National Association of Independent Schools and the College Board. It is one of only 11 such schools in the United States under the administration of the Presbyterian church. From 75 to 90 percent of their graduates go on to colleges and universities. Other Presbyterian schools that were established in the area did not survive but did have some success. The Manti Presbyterian School and one in Gunnison as well were active in the late 1800's. These schools offered better trained teachers, more money for supplies and sturdier buildings. When the public school system came into being many of these schools died out.

The "Tigers" have won numerous awards for academic excellence as well as athletic awards. Many graduates have gone on to become community leaders or have distinguished themselves in various professional capacities. Students now come from various religious, racial and cultural backgrounds, small mining towns, Native American reservations, and from overseas military or diplomatic corps families. They come from at least 12 states and 5 or more foreign countries. The school now exceeds two blocks in size and while non-denominational, still maintains a close relationship with the Presbyterian church. In the 1990s, a $2 million math and science building fund raiser was completed and plans to build a new dining hall are underway. Updating with major renovations and restorative work on the now historic buildings are in these plans as well. Mount Pleasant, which houses this now historic school, will always be known as the "Liberal Town" to people in the area.

As I walked about the grounds of this absolute marvel of a place, school was out either for the summer or it was between quarters or semesters. I was there because graduates of the place had reported to me the various hauntings on campus that they had experienced. I was simply enthralled by the magnificent old buildings and Victorian mansion houses in the middle of this small town on an historic drive through Fairview, Mount Pleasant, Ephraim, Manti, and Spring City. It is an enchanting place, especially when I was lucky enough to arrive when no one was about. The feelings there are overpowering and the magnificent architecture is something to behold. I was aware of various entities and while all of them were puzzling, they all very much belonged. Each one of them had either loved the place deeply or had departed the place in some sort of tragedy which held them there still.

Only a few years ago, a residence hall which housed some 30 students from all over the world, caught on fire. It was a four alarm affair which started at 2 p.m. in the attic of the Alice Dormitory which is a 62 year old building on the 125 year old campus. By 4 p.m., firemen had the blaze on the roof under control. The 11th grade boys who lived there were allowed to return to their rooms the next day to sift through their belongings and see if anything remained. Unfortunately, it was the water damage more than anything that wreaked havoc on the building. The local media reported that the historic building had burned to the ground. However, what really happened, was that a student's cigarette butt probably started the blaze which gutted only the attic of the building. Students from foreign countries had to look for important papers like their visas, so that they would be assured of getting home when the time came. The attic room was locked when firefighters arrived after being summoned by the Mount Pleasant Mayor who saw the smoke from City Hall.

It took over 30 fire trucks from three surrounding towns to put the blaze out. The building was empty at the time so there were no injuries. On the second floor, the main damage was to personal computers which were entirely ruined by the water damage. A new roof for the building was immediately begun and the students who were living there were housed in other dormitories until it was done. The Alice residence was named after Alice Craighead, a wealthy benefactor who bequeathed her fortune to the school. On the ground floor of the dorm buildings are rooms for dorm parents and a common room with a grand piano. Upstairs are the tiny student rooms. Class sizes are around 12 students and ninety-eight percent of the students go on to college. Locals say that they like having the variety in their small town and really are proud of having this historic school. As for ghosts, well a fire is an interesting start!

There have been a few fires at the school over the years and there are the usual former student claims of the paranormal, such as lights flickering, doors locking and people being locked in. There are also stories of objects moving by themselves in dormitory rooms and footsteps following young women down hallways. Students find that windows locked the night before are wide open in the morning. There are strange mists floating past one in the dark and perhaps even a few of those floating orbs people talk about. This is the usual stuff that kids on campuses often claim happened to them or that they saw. A teacher or two also haunt the place, spirits who seem to have decided to hang around for a few decades just to see the progress of the school. While these stories are told, not one of them so far can be pinned down to a particular era, event or person. This makes them somewhat suspect. I wonder if a reader who went to school there can tell me something more substantial?

A former resident of one of the homes for faculty, a Victorian-style home which was given to the school in 1954 by Frederick Jensen Stedman and called the Jensen residence, Donna Glidewell is quoted as saying: "Several people asked me if I felt I was living with ghosts. My reply was that they were friendly ghosts. Their only concern was that the house be cherished and restored as a memorial to its unique past." ("Wasatch Academy: A Lesson in History, Longevity, and Quality," by Laurel Brown, *Preservation Magazine*, Volume 6, pp. 32-35.) Other homes on campus include the two-story Victorian-style President's house built in 1895 and the Indiana House which is another Victorian house built in 1900, now named the Pierce Historical Hall. The First

Presbyterian Gothic Revival Style Church on campus was built in 1922 and the rest of the buildings were built of brick between 1915 and 1920 in a bungalow style. Last there is the Johns Gymnasium built in 1921 in a time when brick was costly and so discarded glass was used to make the dark bricks which therefore gives the surface of the building a shiny look not seen anywhere else. There is an old folklore story that states that dark brick attracts ghosts more easily and they can pass through it more easily as well. So one wonders what dark brick with glass in it would do to apparitions since they are also prone to not liking their own reflection and like to turn mirrors around whenever they can!

Alice Craighead made her donations in the 1930s and literally saved the school from ruin. A dormitory, administration building, and industrial hall were built in the next decade all named after Alice. Alice never came to Utah but instead remembered stories that Duncan McMillan had told about Wasatch Academy when he visited her family in Washington, D.C. when she was a little girl. There are 12 buildings altogether on the Wasatch Academy campus in a beautiful tree-lined area in the middle of a very historic district of which Wasatch Academy became a part in 1978. The middle of the block is a quad just like most colleges and a Nancy Jones is quoted as saying that "Thinking about the buildings on the Wasatch campus always fills me with a strong sense of history. Each building has a story to tell and within these walls are the memories of the people who have been there over the years...I feel blessed and fortunate to have been a part of this great story." (Ibid, p.34.)

While the campus appreciates its rich heritage and all the gorgeous wood paneling and oak staircases are still there, problems with heating and upkeep do exist. On the other hand, Wasatch Academy just matched a grant from the E.E. Ford Foundation to complete a project that makes it one of the few wireless campuses in the western United States. This means that their entire computer network works without cables and wires, thus eliminating all problems connected with being a state of the art school where technology is concerned while being housed in historic and very old buildings. The ghosts of Wasatch Academy will appreciate this when traveling about during a campus evening in the small rural town of Mt. Pleasant.

SANPETE ACADEMY & SNOW COLLEGE

Sanpete Academy was housed in Ephraim's co-op building from 1883 to 1903. It was then decided that the academy needed its own place and the administration building was dedicated on November 5th in 1909 in its new location. Newton E. Noyes went begging to the LDS church when the school hit financial woes in the beginning and when then President Lorenzo Snow helped them out, the college was renamed Snow Academy in his honor. Noyes was principal until 1921 and built and lived in a beautiful mansion with his family not far from the academy. In 1923 the school changed its name to Snow College and managed to survive that difficult time when the public schools were taking over or forcing the private schools to go under. In 1932, Snow College became a state college with state funding and James A. Nuttal presided over the school for a long term, from 1936 to 1953. A celebration of the first fifty years in

1938 showed just how many community, state and distinguished patrons the school had and the term "Spirit of Snow" came into being.

In 1951, Snow College became a branch of Utah State University until 1969, when the college was separated from its Logan connection and became its own state institution again. Floyd S. Holm ran the place from 1958 to 1974 and really took the college out of its financial woes and into the mainstream. Snow College has a great reputation around the state as a junior college. The school has won awards for its theater productions, music contributions, awards in several sports fields, ESL and forensics programs, and even an award winning yearbook. Many high school students from the state of Utah choose Snow College for their first two years, not only because of finances and its reputation as a good second choice to Brigham Young University, but because of its reputation as a friendly and attentive small town college. In its 112 years of operation, it still has at least two places on campus which can boast of a ghost or two. The administration or Noyes building and the gymnasium were built in 1912, as was the old Noyes mansion, complete with carriage and guest house in back. The Noyes building has its famous story of the "eggs."

"In 1897, 200 students and faculty gathered at the chosen site for a new building, drove a center stake, and then learned of a halt called by the LDS First Presidency, which had to pay off indebtedness caused by federal seizure of church property during government efforts to put a halt to polygamy. Two years passed before academy principal Newton E. Noyes got the okay for construction to begin .... Ephraim families had pledged $7,500 toward an estimated cost of $25,000. Soon teamsters were bringing wagon loads of oolitic stone to the site - but there was no construction money in sight until the 'Sunday eggs' program became a reality. This was matched with money from donations of 'quilts, cloth, carpets, socks, soap and sugar' plus donations garnered via 'nickel Sundays,' parties, banquets and bazaars." ("Snow Building Owes It All to Eggs" by Jack Goodman, *The Salt Lake Tribune*, Sunday, December 5, 1999, Arts section.) Any eggs collected on Sunday and their profits went to the school. To this day, in the Noyes building are display cases with various types of decorative eggs which have been donated to the school, as well as things found about the place when major interior renovations were made.

Faculty and students moved into the uncompleted building in the fall of 1904. The huge building housed 33 classrooms, a 600 seat assembly hall and was built from 750,000 red bricks with an oolite stone foundation. In the twenties the administration building got its official name of the Noyes Building in honor of its first principal. The huge reconstruction project that was begun in 1996 with 6.6 million dollars from the State Legislature, has just recently been completed and now the building has three stories instead of two, even though the outside remains the same. Handcrafted wooden beams and nails were found as the building was given steel supports, fireproofing and wired for computer use. It is strange to walk inside and see half windows between two floors. The student taking us around talked about the sorts of things found in the renovation and informed us that the only thing original to the building was the safe on the second floor. Before she told me this and I had walked about looking for someone to help me, I felt really drawn to that particular space and when our pictures came back, there were lights around and within it of a peculiar nature. But then who would believe me? I asked her about ghosts and of course got the same answer that I often get, that there were none. I had decided at one point not even to write about the place, until we took a drive around town and I saw the old Noyes mansion. This mansion was very active to me, though it is privately owned, and of course I could not enter it.

We did, however, run into some students who said that they felt the gymnasium built in 1912 was indeed haunted and everyone on campus knew it. They told us a timeless and ageless story of someone having drowned there or of a young girl having committed suicide there. No one knew any details and it was not a friendly place for ghost hunters. However, I do feel that if I could spend time in that gym - which was locked at the time, by that safe in the main building alone, or within the Noyes mansion, there would be a great deal more to tell. These are the oldest places on the campus and, while the Noyes Building is the most striking, it is the gymnasium which enthralls. Perhaps someone out there has more to tell, and someday I'll be able to visit in a different way and write down the impressions of these energies that I think are really still there.

HARRINGTON SCHOOL

AMERICAN FORK

A one room log schoolhouse was erected in 1852 when the settlers first came to the valley called American Fork. It was located on First East and Second South along the creek bed where the settlers homes were located and served both as a church and for other public gatherings for three years. In 1853, the people had to move into a fort and the loghouse was relocated to LDS Bishop Leonard E. Harrington's property across the street and a little to the east of the LDS Stake Tabernacle, another interesting building which still stands today. Sometimes in winter the schoolhouse had to be shut down for periods as long as two weeks because it was so cold that wood in the little fireplace was not sufficient to keep the students from freezing. In 1861, a new adobe church meeting house was built on the property with a granite foundation and a basement and served as the new schoolhouse as well. In 1877, a thirty by fifty foot addition to the side of this church was built and christened "Science Hall."

Science Hall contained prison cells in the basement, and with no ventilation and complete darkness, this city jail must have been as the author, George F. Shelley, of the book *Early History of American Fork*, says: " - a rather interesting coincidence to have Heaven above and Hell below." (p. 75.) In 1867, a law was passed in the Territory establishing free public schools, largely due to Harrington's and Lorin Farr's (of Ogden) efforts. East and West schoolhouses were built in the city, but eventually one big central school was needed to accommodate the growing school population. In 1892 - 1893, a new brick school house was built at the cost of $13,000. It was named the Forbes School after Joseph B. Forbes. In 1903, the school district bought Science Hall from the LDS church and an addition was made to it that very same year, this being the original Harrington School right next to City Hall. Leonard E. Harrington was both the first mayor and an LDS Bishop in American Fork. A second unit was added to the building in 1924 and a third in 1935. This schoolhouse had 16 classrooms of elementary school children and housed the seventh and eight graders for a while, although they were eventually transferred to the high school building which finally became the junior high school building. The Forbes school next door was torn down and became a playground for Harrington School. The high school was completed in 1912.

When we arrived in American Fork, looking for the Star Flour Mill, we went to City Hall to ask for directions to it. Right next door was this magnificent and yet abandoned school. You might say that it called to me, those of you who believe in such things, and I just couldn't get away from it. There were voices and images all about the place and yet being in the city center the school was very much ignored, like an eyesore that people wished might be torn down. When I asked about it, the only thing people could tell me was that it had still functioned as a school in the 1950s and possibly into the 60s, that a Dr. Carl Bell owned the building, and that no it was not haunted, although the good doctor claimed that a house that he lived in for just two years was subject to apparitions. According to the gals at City Hall he had held Halloween parties in it just to talk about the haunting. Not knowing whether they were pulling my leg, I figured that Halloween meant that it was all in jest. We walked around the building several times and so much information was flooding my mind that I decided to take notes just in case I would be able to find out more about it. All I did find out was that Dr. Bell was in some legal battle with the city over this property and was stubbornly and amazingly refusing to sell.

Walking around the building, I was fascinated to see all of the old school equipment still inside, including what looked like a science lab in one room. All the doors were chained and padlocked, probably due to vandalism in the building and some sort of construction was going on which was encouraging, since the structure seemed in jeopardy of being demolished. Perhaps it was the dream of another man who did not have the finances to turn it into whatever he planned. Anyway, these are the "spirit" people who spoke to me from the windows and doorways as I stood taking my notes. I saw photos of an old stage in my mind and was told that someone's grandfather helped to build the platform. A girl student had fallen out of the south second story window in the 1930s and there had been at least two fires in the building, although no one was seriously hurt. However, a carpenter was seriously injured in a fall and three students who had attended the school died, probably in a car accident. They were all together it seems, though it could have been an earlier era, as time Is hard to judge in such places. One of the Principals had been a very unsavory individual whom students and faculty disliked immensely. He was a dictator, had a nasty temper and was very abusive as well. I could see the students running down the hallways in terror for some reason, and a little girl stumbled and fell and was trampled over by the others before they all got out of the building. There were between 5 and 7 "character" teachers over the years who the students either really loved or at least found quite interesting.

Harrington School was the showpiece of the town when it was built. I saw a young man from the 1910 to 1920 era walking through the halls alone; at least his attire indicated this time period. He is the single haunt in the building, while the rest were merely impressions left behind. Apparently there was an accident in the science or chemistry lab and this young man, either student or custodian, was injured in the accident and somehow disfigured. Two of the custodians over the years of the school's operation did some mighty weird things in the basement, as the vibes from that area were heavy. Over the years the school lost 5 students due to natural occurrences such as illnesses and diseases. I felt that for a short period of time the school had served elementary through high school students. I also felt strongly that there were people in town who know that it is haunted but they don't talk about their experiences. The brand new chimney on the place made me wonder if, after the school officially closed, the building was used for some other purpose for a while. In summary, the whole downtown area is of interest with the old City Hall, Harrington School, the old church through the block, the old Veteran's Hall across the street and of course the old Tabernacle just a few blocks away. After visiting these places one can drive on up the hill and visit the old Star Flour Mill which is a general store now and quite a place to explore.

The Harrington School has also been the site for various short scenes in some movies over the years, though few would know about that because old schools aren't given credits in the movies. My favorite one was in the made-for-television bio of the Osmond children's parents with Marie Osmond playing her own mother. Sam Bottoms played the father and there is a scene shortly after it is discovered that the two oldest sons are deaf, one with a 45% hearing loss and the other with a profound one. The two boys were taken to the Utah School for the Deaf in Ogden, but the scene is actually filmed at the Harrington School in American Fork. A big sign was placed over the front door in an arch and the actors walk through those doors into the interior of the old school as though it was the institution for the deaf and blind. Having worked for the Utah School for the Blind and having visited the other campus developed for deaf students when they separated from each other, I was quite amused to see how all these places were pieced together. In the movie, the Osmonds decide to teach the two boys themselves, which they really did, accomplishing more than "experts" could have done back then. The sons once came to speak to us at the school for the blind and brought one of the old communication boards that their parents had constructed and used with them. This impressed me very much. Here was a family of singers and musicians who had dealt with sons who could not hear much of what their family produced. Harrington School got to be in the movies!

ROWLAND HALL - ST. MARK'S SCHOOL
MEMORIES AND NEW MOVES

Rowland Hall was vacated this spring, as the Episcopal school will be moving to its new location by the University of Utah. The old school, which has been functioning for over a hundred years only a block behind the Cathedral of the Madeleine in downtown Salt Lake City, will be used in some other capacity by the Catholic Church which bought the property. Many people I know attended the school at one time or another, and they had stories tell. I am sure that upon reading this, others will come forward with stories of their own. It is a beautiful little campus and has been kept up very nicely over all these years. It has some interesting history to it, although someone else will have to research the truth or accuracy of most of these tales, as I can only tell what I see, hear or feel intuitively in scattered pieces as they fall around me. There are no official ghost stories about the place, I am told by quite a few who attended the school, although others who went there beg to differ on this point sighting the vacant third floor of the main building as the haunted part of the school. My impressions, as always, are simply laid down for those who can later confirm or deny them.

An Episcopal reverend and deacon established the first non-Mormon day school in Utah in 1867 in an old adobe bowling alley on Main Street between 2nd and 3rd South in Salt Lake City where the old Walker house later stood. It was a two-room schoolhouse with 16 students and enrollment doubled within a week. Episcopals and some apostate Mormons ran the school and it soon outgrew its quarters. The second year the promoters occupied Independence Hall and the third year they rented an old store on Main Street. The Catholics and the Episcopals soon joined together and the school overflowed into two old stores next door. A new schoolhouse was built opposite City Hall in 1873 and 118 students attended this one. The school soon gained support from gentiles, apostate Mormons and orthodox Mormons alike, as the first good schools were started by various other churches in Utah. By 1871 there were 310 students at the St. Mark's school.

In this same year it was decided that the school needed to be divided to provide all of the types of education demanded. St. Mark's Grammar School became the boy's school and a second school, St. Mark's School for Girls was started in the basement of the new St. Mark's church. However, both boys and girls under the age of 10 attended this school while the older children went to St. Mark's Grammar School. Students coming from out of town and surrounding areas were first boarded with Episcopalian families in the area, and then later, they boarded at the new school. This school was built at 141 East First South and cost $20,000. It had a large chapel, a large library and several classrooms. By 1876 the school had 463 students. School began August 20th and ended on June 14th each year. The St. Mark's School for Girls had three departments: Primary, Intermediate and Grammar or high school. Some students still continued to take classes in the basement of St. Mark's as well.

Rowland Hall's beginnings are a bit fuzzy historically, but most agree that the school began around 1880, though some printed material indicates that the second year was 1882. The school on the hill came from a 13 room adobe farmhouse built between 1855 and 1860 by Brigham Young's private secretary, George Darling Watt, with several apple and mulberry orchards nearby. The land was eventually deeded to a parishioner of St. Marks and the home on the land had probably already become a boardinghouse for girls at the school. The property was probably bought either to continue the expansion or to provide a bigger facility for the basement school in the church. Reverend Reynold Marvin Kirby came to Utah in the Spring of 1871. His wife Virginia had died only a year and a half before. She had come from a wealthy industrialist father whose family name was Rowland. Kirby married again and the youngest of his four daughters was named after his first wife. His first wife's mother visited Salt Lake City, became interested in the school where Kirby was on the board and taught mathematics, she donated the rest of the money needed to purchase the property and the Watts-Haskins house. The school then had its name, Rowland Hall.

Some of the teachers who first taught at the new school, included as Principal Miss Lucia Mason Marsh and as teachers Miss Semons, Miss Emma Chandler, and Miss Abby Marsh. The first official boarder was Farnetta Alexander and the first official graduate of the school was Daisy S. Senter in 1882. Theresa Godbe, who was the daughter of the leader of the famous Godbeite movement, graduated from Rowland Hall early on and became a school teacher. Only 13 girls and one boarder attended the school that first year. Other teachers soon followed: Professor Radcliffe taught piano, Miss Fedelia Hamilton taught voice, and Madame Fitzgerald, who was from Paris, taught French. The old original house had two classrooms, a dining room, kitchen, sleeping rooms upstairs, with swings and a ball field outside. One of the favorite pastimes of the girls was to chase away the neighbor's cows who liked to graze on the alfalfa field on their grounds. Books were donated and in one year a library was organized to serve the 17 boarders and 30 day students. Like so many schools for girls in those days, it was more of a finishing school than a serious academically oriented campus.

By the time Utah became a state, St. Mark's School had closed because there were so many other ways for local boys to gain an education. But Rowland Hall remained open. By 1894, however, the new Principal Clara Claiburne had begun to establish a high standard of academic excellence at Rowland Hall. Enrollment at that time had been limited but a spirit of excellence was being fostered and soon enrollment increased, a new school and chapel were built and even a tennis court was added. A huge donation at the turn of the century enabled the school to expand and the new school building was completed in 1906 and a chapel around 1910. By this time too,

Rowland Hall was becoming like any other girls' prep school where late night talk-fests and other rule-breaking adventures were conceived and sometimes carried out in what one teacher called "their Adamless Eden." ("Rowland Hall - St. Mark's School: Alternative Education for More than a Century," by Mary R. Clark, *Utah Historical Quarterly* Volume 48,1980, p. 286.)

Girls were not allowed off the campus without a chaperone though they could go to a movie once a week with a group or visit day students alone on the weekends. Rowland Hall was now a prep school for college like so many others. By the 1920s girls were being required to take such courses as Latin, three years of Math, four years in English and History courses, as well as have involvement with the athletic programs at the school. While many students over the years found a lot of classes demanding or dull, they had great praise for the college preparation that they received. Katherine Browne Stehle is the oldest living graduate of the school and she graduated in 1920.

She also talks about how hard the curriculum was: "Rowland Hall was a wonderful school. I wasn't a boarder, but there were many of them sent from ranches in Wyoming or Montana. Contrary to what children may think now, we didn't just take the piano or lessons in etiquette. We had a very heavy academic load. We had three years Latin, beginning in the seventh grade, followed by other languages. We took Geometry, Algebra, Biology and Physics....in our gym class we wore midi blouses and bloomers....We learned rudimentary ballet steps. We played tennis on the tennis courts and we performed our Grecian dances." (RHSM, Alumni News, Review, Spring, 1997, p.12.)

"Maypole dancing was a wonderful tradition and a huge celebration at the school. Each class wore something different to signify their class. Maybe an extra ribbon in their hair or something. Only the older girls were trusted to go in and out around the Maypole....We received all our news by telegraph. It was difficult, but somehow the most important news got through....Tour buses would come by the school and we could hear the comments of the drivers. They would say: 'This is Rowland Hall, a girl's finishing school. The only male allowed on this campus is the U.S. Mail.'" (Ibid, p. 12 &13.)

During the depression, Rowland Hall suffered financially like most private schools and almost closed. But a few people found an ingenious way to keep it open by incorporating it as a non-profit institution and the school survived World War II as well. Nancy Streater who graduated in 1947 remembers graduation in St. Mark's Cathedral and the Candle and Carol tradition done at Christmas time. Both events were very colorful and by then they wore two uniforms, an every day attire and white dress attire for special days at the school. For graduation they wore white caps and gowns and carried bouquets of pink roses and blue delphiniums. Candle and Carol was held in St. Margaret's chapel on campus and the choir practise the songs in their original language months in advance. The chapel was decorated in live greens and the girls came in each carrying a lite candle which she says the fire marshall would surely not permit today.

Rowland Hall's academic excellence was so good that by the 1950s, parents and the Episcopal community were asking for a college preparatory school for boys as well. St. Mark's School was reestablished in 1956. The boys school was flourishing so well by the 60s that a new location and school were needed. But the probable expense brought an even better idea; why not make Rowland Hall co-educational? In 1961, the two schools were merged and Rowland Hall became a school for both Adams and Eves. However, merging the school symbols, practices and traditions proved to be more difficult than anticipated. The cross and motto and the winged lion all had to be integrated into one symbol. For many years boys and girls maintained their own separate traditions and practices, including sitting across the room from each other even though they didn't have to.

By the early 1970s, the schools had successfully merged. Economics however, forced the school to close the boarding facilities and a new upper school building was built. Students from other countries and states now live with families in the surrounding areas paying room and board. Through the 70s, 80s and 90s, Rowland Hall continued academic excellence with a large enrollment of both boys and girls. It was only recently that a new school was proposed and was built further out from the city. It is now the year 2002, the new school is complete and Rowland Hall plans to move this summer to its new location, leaving the old Rowland Hall abandoned for the first time in over 120 years.

The original school is now a National Historic Site, which should help its chances to survive and I had speculated that perhaps the Episcopal church would find another use for it rather than selling it. If they sold, I said, then it should be protected from business development, but one never knows in these cases just what will happen. One sure thing was however, that all those graduates and teachers and contributors would probably put up a pretty good fight if anything like demolition came up in any negotiations at all. Today, Rowland Hall has a campus full of beautiful gray colored buildings with black and white trim and lovely flower gardens and trees and walkways. The older buildings have been blended in with the new beautifully, and on a Sunday afternoon, joggers and passersby stop to admire its tiny campus and read its little historic sign.

Rowland Hall's fate, just recently decided, has turned out to be a good one. Performing an elaborate medieval ceremony the elementary school turned over its Avenues buildings to the Madeleine Choir School of the Roman Catholic Diocese of Salt Lake City. Students posing as town criers opened the "Transfer and Seizen of Land" ceremony which was attended by judges, sheriffs, the Catholic Monsigner and the local Episcopal Bishop. The two school's headmasters presented each other with trees to be planted on the grounds. Students exchanged handmade memory books and the choir school fashioned a journal with blank pages for the Rowland Hall students to begin recording new experiences at their new school. The choir school consists of fourth through eighth grade students and raised the money to buy the school through various donations. They plan to build a gymnasium and performing arts center on the grounds.

As for ghosts at Rowland Hall, there definitely are some, though just strolling the beautiful grounds might be enough for some. There are also secret passages which the students discuss but will not reveal their locations to anyone, as well as favorite hiding places within the old buildings. The main ghosts however, are said to inhabit the third floor of the main building, a floor which has been vacant for many years and is probably filled with spider webs and all sorts of creepy things to fuel the student's imaginations, the staff says. However, there are those who found a way up there and claim that the ghosts are quite active and alive. If you are one of these students, let us know what you found or experienced there!

ST. ANN'S ORPHANAGE AND SCHOOL

CATHOLIC DIOCESE, SALT LAKE CITY

In 1888, Bishop Lawrence J. Scanlan, who is pretty much the father of the Catholic Diocese in Utah, wanted to build a cathedral. He purchased a house for his rectory on First South and Third East and then a large plot of land on South Temple. He wrote to an architect in Chicago asking if this particular site could house a cathedral of magnificent proportions and height. In 1890 a new cathedral rectory was completed on the east side of where he wished the cathedral to be built. The old rectory where he had lived before was converted into an orphanage. Bishop Scanlan had for a long time been considering starting a place where orphans and children of neglected parents could receive attention. His old rectory was used temporarily for such a place. Bishop Scanlan preached to his congregation in St. Mary's church all that summer, asking for help in building a more permanent building. In 1899, after a committee had been formed and some fund raising had been accomplished, Mrs. Thomas F. Kearns stepped forward with a $50,000 donation towards the orphanage building fund.

The corner stone was laid on August 27, 1899 and Carl M. Neuhausen was chosen as architect. The Kearns-St. Ann's Orphanage opened in 1900. Not only did Jennie Kearns give a donation, but in 1901 Thomas and Jennie Kearns, who had leased the property to the church for the orphanage, then gave the land to the church. The Kearns said that "...the said premise shall forever be used for and conducted as an asylum for the shelter, training and education of the orphan or destitute children of the State of Utah Irrespective of Religious Belief and for such religious or educational purposes as the grantee herein or his successors as Roman Catholic Bishop of Salt Lake deem proper." (*Salt of the Earth* by Bernice Maher Mooney Catholic Diocese of Salt Lake City Copyright 1987, 1992, p. 110.)

In the winter of 1900, the Scofield Mine Disaster occurred. The widows of the men killed in the disaster asked for help from their state legislature. A special session was convened but nothing happened. The women had to sue the company and even then their compensation was minimal. Bishop Scanlan opened the doors to his orphanage and school to these women and children while they got themselves back on their feet. The church provided transportation, free room and board and schooling to these families and also took in any children orphaned by the blast. By the time the later Castle Gate Mine disaster occurred there were compensations in place for the widows, although any orphans without relatives were again taken in at St. Ann's. In 1902, Patrick Phelan, a miner, left his estate of $76,000 to St Ann's Orphanage and one can't help wondering if what Bishop Scanlan did in 1900 contributed to this windfall.

In 1917 a first rectory was built at 430 East and 2100 South. A second rectory was built around 1920, after the first one burned to the ground, killing the Father William T. Hart's dog. Then something must have happened to this one or the number of residents just outgrew it because in 1935 a third rectory was built at 2003 South and 500 East. What we thought might be the remains of this rectory could still be seen sitting at an angle on its property across the street from the new church. It is covered in trees and is now privately owned. However in talking to a former resident of the school in the thirties, this house was a residence for elderly men, many of whom attended mass at St. Ann's. Although it still seems odd that the house is facing the school at a parallel angle and is the only big old mansion house which matches the architecture of the times and sits in the southeast corner of the property facing the northwest corner. The house is the correct vintage, and looks very much like a rectory. If it were in a small town, it would be considered the haunted house of the town. Best that it remain hidden!

In 1925, Bishop Joseph S. Glass made extensive improvements to the building, grounds and interiors. By 1926, there were 36 boys and 30 girls in residence, and 50 day students from the area who attended grammar school. Jennie Kearns continued her generosity to the orphanage by, among many other things, providing Christmas presents and Christmas dinner every year. A Catholic Men's Club sponsored twoweek summer camp trips and the Community Chest group gave the orphanage $9,000 annually. St. Ann's Orphanage Sewing Society and the University of Utah Mothers' Club also supported the orphanage for many years. The Knights of Columbus sponsored trips to Lagoon and Saitair starting in 1908.

In 1929, Bishop Kames E. Kearney arrived in Utah to take over, among many other duties, the running of St. Ann's Parish and school. He was from Omagh, Ireland and his mother, Rosie O' Doherty, had been a gifted singer and poet. Bishop Kearney had inherited these gifts and had sung with the Priest's Choir of New York and had also had some of his poetry published. He loved to write poems for the children of St. Ann's Orphanage and School and always entertained them with his beautiful Irish tenor voice at all the holiday dinner parties. He was a legendary and generous man who was always giving to those in need and especially to the orphans.

Agnus Palmgren attended the school in the thirties. Her father had been a miner at the Bingham Mine and her family lived in Highland Boy. Her father died young of a heart condition brought on by being gassed in World War I. With her mother the sole support of the family after this, the priest talked her into putting her nine children into the boarding school at St. Ann's School so that her mother could earn a living and support her children. Apparently many children went to St. Ann's during this time because they were from a single parent family. There were no more orphans by this time at the school but most of the children boarding at the school had only one parent. One of Agnus's sister became a nun at seventeen years of age and eventually worked at the St. Mary's of the Wasatch School.

Life at St. Ann's at this time consisted of a lot of work she says. They got up at 5:30 a.m., went to mass, ate breakfast and then completed whatever duty was assigned to them before school started. Each boy and girl had what they called a "charge" who was a younger boy or girl which was assigned to them. You washed and ironed their clothes too, made sure they got up and got dressed, went to mass, had breakfast and completed their "duty" as well. You had to watch out for them all of the time. Monday morning was wash day and every girl took turns helping cook in the kitchen. There was a big field in the back that was like a huge garden which they all took turns helping in. They harvested at the different seasons and then had canning and bottling days where they were assigned a duty again. She said that the nuns were very nice and helped them a lot, not like they are sometimes depicted by school children of today.

She remembered the big Christmas party that they had every year in the rec room downstairs and how the very elderly Mrs. Kearns would come with her son and grandson. Though she stopped coming after a couple of years and only her son and grandson came to deliver the presents. And they did have parties on all the holidays in the downstairs rec room or dining hall, although most of the time they were not allowed to talk when working. Boys and girls dorms were on the second floor separated by some of the nun's quarters and they ate on separate sides of the dining hall downstairs. On the main floor was a parlor and offices and on the third floor was the infirmary and other nun's living quarters. All of the children from her family that were smaller went to St. Ann's until they graduated from the eighth grade and none of them had any complaints except for the dishes they had to eat out of, her sister didn't like them.

By the 1950s, the orphan population was gone as well as single parents needing to use the facility like they had in the 1930s and 1940s. It was decided to make St. Ann's a complete day school. The school started in 1955, after the Holy Cross Sisters found it necessary to withdraw from their work and the Sisters of the Charity of the Incarnate Word were asked to come to Salt Lake to start the school. Father Thomas F. Butler, Pastor of St. Ann's Parish, went to the Mother House in Houston, Texas and made his request for the sisters to the Bishop there. A two year transition period ensued between 1953 and 1955 while this all took place. In 1954, a fire in the orphanage destroyed the sacristy, damaged the altar and the sister's community room and the adjoining stairs. All of these were in the basement where a temporary church had existed from September to December of 1954. I have always wondered if this maybe started the rumors of a couple of hauntings.

Bishop Duane G. Hunt was working to turn the first floor of the orphanage into a school and a convent for the sisters. The renovations were completed and the new convent was opened that year as well. There were 260 pupils enrolled that first year. At first only kindergarten through fourth grade classes were enrolled, but each year another grade was added, so that now kindergarten through eighth grade classes are held. The unusual St. Ann's Church right next to the school was constructed in 1968. It cost close to $500,000 and was designed by Scott, Louie and Browning. The Thomas F. Kearns Sports Complex was built behind the church in 1981. The entire debt for the school and church was paid off in 1982 and a recreation center was built between the church and the school in 1986.

By 1982, the school was badly in need of repairs and once the council parish learned that the school could be renovated for less than the cost of building a brand new building, they jumped right in. The current Principal was a student at the school as well and she was a big advocate for saving the building. The renovations began with the third floor which had been originally used as a chapel and living space for the nuns running the school but had become storage space for many years. This floor was turned into classrooms for the seventh and eighth grade students as well as creating a science lab and math lab. On the first floor the parlor was kept as it was originally because of its historical significance. Staircases and walls were returned to their original oak finish on this floor as well. Repairing the leaking roof became more difficult than they had anticipated because they discovered several charred beams from the previous fire years before. The building was made as seismic proof as it could be by adding brick stair towers on each end of the building. All of the renovations took over ten years to complete and faculty and students had to work cooperatively with construction crews by moving to different classrooms, etc.

"As a private school, Kearns-St. Ann has more flexibility in regard to saving its old building than the public school system, where old schools are routinely torn down and discarded. 'The parishioners did not want to see the building torn down....They were committed to its preservation and to saving a part of history.' The students also feel a sense of history with the building...." ("Neighborhood Schools: Kearns-St. Ann & Columbus" by Susan Petheram, *Utah Preservation*, Volume 6, Spring 2002, p.77.)

Rumors of hauntings there have been discussed over the years, and with two fires and such an intriguing building built way back in 1900, one can easily speculate why. It is a spectacular building similar to the Salt Lake City and County Building or the old BYU Academy building in Provo. Wild stories have been circulating around for years about St. Ann's. There is one about a one-armed nun who died there and roams the halls at night, or a kind of psychotic janitor who did weird things, then committed suicide, and does some roaming of his own through the halls. None of these are substantiated, but there are plenty of former students and maybe even a few orphans left to tell these tales. The Catholic church would of course discount such silly ideas, but I will probably have my own impressions when I get a chance to walk through the school's halls.

Recently, Bishop Scanlan's main life dream, the Cathedral of the Madeleine. celebrated its 100th birthday as well. The Cathedral of the Madeleine, after eight grueling years of work, was completed in 1906, the ground breaking ceremony had been held on July 4th, 1899. Bishop Scanlan wrecked his health campaigning for his cathedral and had only 6 years to enjoy it. He died May 10th, 1915 and he was buried in the crypt in the basement. The 1991-1993 renovations required his body to be moved; it was placed into a new casket which was buried beneath the cathedral's original altar. It was he I am sure, who in his quest not only to find refuge for children but also to build a grand edifice to God, oversaw the planting of a pear tree, Sunday July 4th, 1999. It was planted as a symbol of the growth of the Catholic Church in Utah and as an example of the parable of the mustard seed that blooms into a beautiful tree to celebrate life and its creations. The Cathedral of the Madeleine was built for the celebration of God say the Catholics of Utah. To me personally, the once St. Ann's Orphanage and School, now Kearns - St. Ann's School, was a greater gift of life to many and their September 1999, 100th year celebration was well deserved.

JORDAN HIGH SCHOOL
- THE BEETDIGGERS: GONE BUT NOT FORGOTTEN

PART I

There have actually been four Jordan High Schools. The first high school in Midvale was in the basement of the Midvale church. It was 1907 and seven students attended the school. Very quickly there were more high school students than the church could accommodate and the first Jordan High School was built at 8800 South and 250 East. This served the students from 1911 to 1914. Growth again demanded a larger facility so the Old Jordan High School was built at 9351 South State for $165,000.00. Wagons were still being used to transport students and the new high school offered only six classes: Math, English, Domestic Arts, Music, Oral Expression and Book Keeping. There were 750 students and 20 faculty members. The school was sometimes known as "the college" because there was no age limit to attend. Lunches cost 2 or 3 cents and tuition for a full year was $2.50. Some students rode their horses to school and stabled in the barn that was behind the school. The individual students were responsible for feeding and taking care of their own horses.

Sixty-three freshmen entered their first year at the first Jordan High School basement church in September of 1908 and 11 seniors were the first to graduate in 1911. The horse drawn wagons that picked most of the students up were called "kid-wagons" and the first showers for the football team consisted of 50 gallon wooden barrels filled with water for the team to cool off in. In 1912 the LDS. church offered two rooms in the Sandy Bishop's storehouse and land was purchased in 1913 for the new school, or the third Jordan High. In 1915 a third floor was added to the building. In 1917 school was recessed for two weeks because so many students were not attending. They were either enlisting in the military or harvesting beets and potatoes. Some say that they could just as easily have been called the "potato diggers" instead of the "beet diggers." The school also bought 3 large auto vans, 4 model-T Fords and 4 stages to help transport the students.

Cottages for the Superintendent and Principal were also built south of the high school. In 1919 auto mechanics was added to the courses offered as well as a shop department. The boys repaired 134 automobiles in just three months that year for the cost of $5.47 each. School directors also added an Agricultural Department and Domestic Arts became Home Economics. By the 1920s, Jordan was the first in the nation to have a fleet of buses to transport its students. The athletic field was added in 1928 and a vocational building in 1937. Since 1925, Jordan has participated in drama competitions and had won first place on 10 separate occasions by 1977. The gymnastic team took the state championship six times by 1977 as well. The football and basketball teams shared at least 18 championships over the years up until 1977.

The superintendent and principal cottages were razed in the late sixties. Construction began on the fourth or New Jordan High School in the early nineteen-nineties. Once the new high school was completed the Old Jordan High sat empty for quite some time while its fate was decided. I used to drive by it upon many an occasion and wonder what would happen to it. It was a great old building and deserved better than what happened to it. Larry Miller bought the property and a huge fight ensued while those who loved the old school tried to save it for a museum or whatever. In the end power and money won out and the supposed compromise was that the outside of the huge movie theater, hotel and shopping complex would have some of the outside facade of the Old Jordan High on the west side of it. Watching this monstrosity develop one can now see that the outside walls resemble a giant false front of the Old Jordan High School. It would be almost comical if it were not so sad. Because what looked okay in a normal-sized, not necessarily pretty building, looks down right ugly blown up.

In the end none of this will matter. People will go there any way to see this unusual building and the rest of the complex. They will be attracted to its newness and size and whatever awes them about it. All will be forgotten in the name of progress, though had it been my alma mater, I could never have forgotten it. I expected that the new construction would do nicely as it is there to entertain people which is a great American pastime. School districts desperate for added funds don't fight very much to keep old schools anyway. The ghosts at the Old Jordan High School may continue their pranks, even in new surroundings. This, only time can tell us.

I had heard of ghosts there but did not connect them to the 1938 Jordan school bus-train accident. Then when I heard some of the stories, of course it made perfect sense. The high school kids I talked to either never heard a thing or had heard plenty about the crossing incident. The stories are plentiful, many of them obviously made up entirely and others, more close to the time of the tragedy, sound a bit more poignant and plausible. One asks, how can a ghost be plausible? The normal answer being: "Judge for yourself." But there is not a school building left anymore, only the property on which it stood and the new place built on top. Ghosts sometimes go with their buildings, in which case they will be gone now. On the other hand, sometimes it is the place that means more to them, and they stay for good. We shall see.

Common reported occurrences were the night janitors bringing a dog with them that would then proceed to bark at the doors and walls continuously all night long when nothing was ever there. Footsteps could be heard behind the night workers, and then stop and when the janitors turned around, no one was there. Someone was always banging on the pipes, and doors opened and shut for no reason even when there were witnesses. Custodians said that they couldn't even begin to tell about the things that had happened to them because it was too scary.

Right after the accident, a PTA Commerative Plaque was placed in the front hall of the school and many people claim to have observed activity around this plaque, either an energy force, a mist, faces in the plaque or in the glass reflection from the display case and even full apparition sightings of a young girl. At the memorial service held at the school, the PTA was handing out a smaller version of this plaque to kids who had survived the accident and to relatives of those who had died. Some people apparently lost their miniature plaques and then found them later in some odd place, as though someone or some thing had taken them to get their attention. The custodian putting out chairs for this memorial service the day before, counted exactly how many chairs to set up. When he came back the next morning, there were exactly 23 chairs more than he had placed the night before . Twenty-four died in the accident and one was the bus driver.

A favorite male teacher at the school had had a student whom he liked quite a bit; this individual having died in the accident. It became quite plain to many of his students that something strange was going on because the teacher would leave things written on the board for the next day's lesson and the notices or assignments would either be erased or the wording changed when the teacher came in the next morning. Everyone with whom he checked about these happenings claimed not to have done anything. Things that he had left the day before would be rearranged. Sometimes he would leave his classroom for just a few minutes, there would be no one there, and when he came back little changes would have been made that only he and this student could have known about. The students began to joke about these events along with the teacher - that so and so had come to visit again. And since many of them were private jokes, people began to believe that the teacher's student was indeed making visits to his classroom.

The more modern stories are more horrible and probably less believable. For example in one of them, the custodian is working on the top floor and sees something out of the corner of his eye. Then he sees a girl floating towards him. As she gets closer he can see that she has no arms and legs. Then she floats down the stairs and disappears. He runs to follow her, and sees that she disappears on the main floor in the front hall. When he gets to the spot he looks up and sees the commemorative plaque about the bus-train accident. Next to it is a photographic display of the dead students' faces. He recognizes the girl who had floated towards him as one of those killed in the crash. She seemed still to be coming to the school.

Having read about the terrible accident and having had my own experiences at Schulsen's Crossing, I can only say that kids often don't have a feel for history like an older person can. They don't understand that real people with real children experienced this event. They don't know that ghosts more often than not come to communicate, comfort or warn, and much more rarely to frighten one out of one's wits. If the custodian's vision really happened, which I rather doubt, then the girl was seeking something that the poor custodian just couldn't understand. Other versions of this same story seem to be more believable and a bit more on the tame side. The more constant story is that the custodian saw a high school-aged girl standing by the gym in forties attire and said to her, "Can I help you?" At that point, she promptly vanished right in front of him.

Faces have been seen over the years reflected in the glass case in the front hall where some of the memorabilia about the accident has been housed with school trophies. Custodians have reported hearing a basketball game going on in the gym. They could hear the crowds, see the lights coming from the gym in the late evening and when they went to check it out, all was dark and locked up. Frightened custodians were known to have this happen to them twice or even three times in an evening, before all the commotion stopped. They also noticed that one year when they found some things about the accident in the basement, such as newspaper articles and other items, there was an upsurge of activity all over the building for a while after. One of my favorite stories is the one about the clock. A teacher was giving her lecture to a class when all of a sudden the clock literally floated off the wall, hung suspended in the air above her, and then all of a sudden crashed straight down to the floor in front of the whole class, narrowly missing the teacher.

Another good yarn is about the day that the huge auditorium screen was being lowered for an activity later on. A student was walking past the front of the screen and an indentation that looked exactly like a hand pressed against the screen from the backside, passed through the screen and followed him as he walked along the front of it from one side to the other. Other students also saw this phenomena and several of them jumped around the screen to catch the culprit, but there was no one there. As they stood behind the screen, the hand indentation continued to follow one student. When they all stepped away from the screen on both sides, the hand indentation was still seen! People were also constantly reporting the feeling of someone brushing past them in a hallway, but nearly always, this happened when the person was alone. Or someone would feel a slight push from behind and no one would be there. Then there were the usual things, such as doors being locked by themselves or unlocked after a careful checking of the area, and lights going out when no one was around to turn them off.

It was a tradition at the old Jordan High to tell ghost stories from this accident every year at Halloween, probably because students were so proud of the fact that they, among all the other high schools in the valley had the premier ghost story. The students made up all sorts of outlandish stories, though if one talks to former students, many say they never heard one. Others, probably the more imaginative and intuitive ones, had a dozen or so stories to tell you from those early days. Early fall and late summer seemed to be the most active times for ghosts. The gym and the case in the front hall were the most active areas in addition to the giant tree in the northwest corner of the front yard of the school. It was the biggest and oldest tree on the whole property. Over the years the folklore grew about how one could see on its trunk, the faces of the various children who had died. Especially around Halloween, many a student would claim to have seen more than one face on the trunk even in broad daylight. Steven Spielberg could do a lot with this one, especially if the faces actually moved.

When the school was to be demolished, the last graduating class invited Eva May Isrealsen, the 7th oldest person in the state, to speak at their graduation. She had been valedictorian of the first class to graduate from the then brand new high school in 1915. She was 104 years old, having been born in Butlerville at the mouth of Big Cottonwood Canyon in 1894. After graduation she went to Utah State University, met her husband and helped him operate a diary farm near Hyrum for much of her life. Eighty years later, she returned to her alma mater and received a standing ovation from the last senior class of "Beetdiggers" to graduate from the old Jordan High School. Two hours before she died, her grandson-in-law arrived from Switzerland with his wife to serenade her in response to her dying wish. He was Michael Ballam, founder of the Utah Festival Opera Company in Logan and a local celebrity singer in Utah.

The new Jordan Commons is now open. Larry Miller, the car dealer and owner of this extravaganza, promised at first to keep the front of the old high school as part of the new complex. When he found this an impossible task, he ordered a larger sized facade of the old high school be incorporated into the outside west wall of the huge structure as a rarely used entrance from State Street. Where it stands today, totally out of place with the huge movie complex, there are several restaurants including one with a Mayan motif with people diving into pools while you eat and a "South American" eating establishment with performers and lots and lots of atmosphere! The entrance is supposed to have been cast from the original building, which should make it the same size, though it seems to be much larger. This whole project started one day when Miller had a vision while watching children practicing a dance at the Delta Center, home to the Utah JAZZ basketball team which he owns. The word "commons" comes from the colonial era when towns had a park or town square where people would gather for all sorts of reasons. Along with 17 theaters, a 70-mm screen in one of them, a food court, restaurants and shops, he has over a thousand employees working to ensure the financial success of his enterprise. All those who scoffed at his idea can watch Mr. Miller laugh all the way to the bank, for the entire project has been highly successful thus far.

Miller sponsored a special alumni ceremony before the high school was razed in 1995, partially to placate all the angry citizens who considered this particular high school their own, even though it had stood idle and abandoned for several years. Even to this day, the mention of the razing of this old building brings up a lot of emotions from the people of West Jordan. Inside the State Street high school entrance is a plaque designating the area as an historic site. Next to this, way off in an isolated corner in a glass case are some memorabilia about the old high school. One has to wonder if such hauntings die with the building and the older walls which housed its memories, sounds and replaying of events, or if the ground itself holds on to such things. Maybe just a bit of memorabilia can keep such things alive.

In the future, perhaps memories will return if someone were to find some old articles and add them to the display in this hall. Would we see a resurgence of some ghostly activity in this specific area, late into the night, when all is quiet and all of the people are gone? Or maybe, even a bit of such happenings may occur where the big hundred-year-old tree once stood on the corner of State and 9400 South? Or perhaps even at the new Jordan High where they have memorabilia displayed from the old school, a bit of residual energy might produce a few strange phenomenon. On the other hand, does all of this die with the building, never to return? I suppose the true test would be to add such things about the original disaster to the glass case in that west hallway at the Jordan Commons or to watch such a display closely at the new Jordan High School and then stand before it in the middle of the night to see if faces other than your own would be reflected.

"EARTH'S ANGELS"
- JORDAN SCHOOL BUS DISASTER
SCHULSEN'S CROSSING, SALT LAKE CITY

"...NOW WE REST FROM EVERY CARE ...
TO GOD'S KINGDOM WE BELONG...."

PART II

On December 2nd, 1938, the nation's worst bus-train accident involving school children occurred at 10200 South and 300 West in Sandy, Utah. It occurred at what is known as Schulsen's, or Lampton's Crossing, which has a long history of accidents even since the 1938 tragedy. It seems to have poor visibility and a crossing gate is really needed at the spot. Though there have been worse Utah tragedies since, at that time it was so devastating that there was even coverage in *LIFE* magazine and *The New York Times*. Fog and snow were creating blizzard-like conditions that early morning and the crew of the Denver and Rio Grande Western Railroad's Flying Ute half-mile long train, was two hours late. They hit the Point of the Mountain and sped through Riverton at seventy miles per hour on the stretches; at the same time a Jordan District school bus carrying 38 of its usual 50 student load from Herriman, Draper, Riverton and West Jordan, headed north along side the tracks on 4th West towards the old Jordan High School.

The bus pulled up to the train tracks and stopped, and then as onlookers watched, it pulled onto the tracks with the Flying Ute only three train car lengths away. At a half-mile visibility, the train firemen were yelling at the bus and screeching on the brakes when the train hit the bus full force in its center and wrapped the entire school bus around its engine. The bus was carried two blocks before the crew could stop the train. The driver and 23 of the students died. But very few of them died instantly. Screams of the injured students echoed along the tracks, though many faded away slowly and then eventually stopped entirely. A hobo riding on the train was hurled forward and looked out thinking that the train had hit a herd of cattle with all the flesh and bone scattered about. Then he saw a young girl mangled and crying on the tracks. "...I got off. It was the most awfullest thing I ever saw. I saw a little girl sitting alongside the tracks. She was terribly mangled, but alive. She was screaming horribly, holding for dear life to a little pocketbook. I rushed over, but she died before I could reach her. None of them seemed to die right away. One by one they would stop screaming......" ("The 1938 Train-School Bus Disaster: Mormon Communal Response to Catastrophic Death," by Melvin L. Bashore, *Journal of Mormon Thought*, Volume 24, No. 1, Spring 1998, pp. 116-117 and *Riverton: The Story of a Utah Country Town* by

Melvin L. Bashmore and Scott Crump, Riverton Historical Society:Riverton , Utah, 1994, Chapter 7, ""It Was The Awfullest Thing I Ever Saw.")

Another girl was put with the presumed dead until she made some sounds and someone came and rescued her. "There was a lot of chaos that morning. I recall that they had piled bodies up. They was all trying to get anybody that was alive out. They had piled these bodies up and my sister-in-law .... was in a pile of (dead) bodies. A nurse walked along the track ... and heard a groan and took her out of that pile of bodies and rushed her to the hospital." (ibid, pp.1 18-119.) It was snowing and icy and the ambulances almost hit each other in their rush to take the injured, dead and dying to area hospitals. Band instruments, purses, briefcases, shoes and body parts lay strewn along the two block area. Parents, sheriffs, police officers, doctors, ambulance drivers and a milling crowd worked not only to try and save lives but also to find ways to identify the dead. One set of parents recalled that they passed several ambulances on the way there and that when they did reach the site, they could see that bodies were strewn for two blocks. Men were frantically loading them onto trucks, ambulances and anything else they could find and they, like many others, were forced to look inside each of the bags full of remains and body parts for their child.

One boy recalled that when the bus arrived, "It was snowing real heavy when I went out to catch the bus. They were big flakes and they were wet. There was no wind. They were coming straight down. I ran and got on the bus and when I got there I was wet from the storm." (ibid, p.1 15.) One of the firemen on the train said that when the crew saw the bus they were only an engine and two car lengths away from the bus when it suddenly pulled onto the tracks. He yelled, "Big hole 'er!" meaning a top priority emergency stop and the engineer quit pulling on his whistle to apply the brakes though on his side he could see nothing. Next thing they knew the hood of the bus was on the engine. One of the surviving students said that right after someone yelled, "Train!" she blacked out and then woke up in the snow with her back and side hurting. Another girl, not hurt in the crash, came over and helped her up and took her into the caboose of the train where it was warmer. Another boy who was also knocked unconscious, came to under something heavy at the bottom of the bus and then passed out again. When he woke up again he was outside and his buddy was asking him for some shoes because the force of the blow had knocked his shoes off. They found the shoes later and he was very thankful that his feet had not been in them. Lost shoes became a sort of symbol of this disaster.

One boy survived without injury but he carried the post traumatic stress of it throughout his whole life. He slept in his parent's bed for a year afterward. Others could not cross railroad tracks at all or at least without a great feeling of dread. One boy who survived had gotten up from his front seat to join a friend at the back of the bus. He had had a premonition dream that morning. He told his mother when he got up that he had had a nightmare about a bus wreck that night. The bus went down and hit the river bridge. He could see all the bodies floating down the river. It has been a life long conviction of his of the prophetic power of dreams because he had had this dream of disaster just before the accident happened later that morning.

A 16 year old girl who was waiting for the bus in front of her home saw the crash 300 yards away. The bus stopped, the train approached it, and then all of a sudden the bus pulled onto the tracks right in front of the oncoming train, she said. She heard the crash and all the screams. The train slowed just opposite her and the frame of the bus was on the engine. She and her father rushed out to the tracks but they were told to go back and call ambulances and doctors. All of the children were rushed to the Salt Lake County General Hospital and temporary morgue was housed in the psychiatric unit of the hospital. Teams of doctors and nurses worked around the clock in shifts setting bones, suturing and otherwise easing the pain of those who had survived. Some suturing jobs were done poorly and had to be re-done with very little available in the way of pain killers.

More than once a student would be listed as dead, the parents would go in to identify their child and discover that the body belonged to someone else that they knew. Then they would find their live child somewhere else later. There was one student who should have been riding the bus, who had skipped school that day and it took a while to learn of the accident and then to call home and tell his parents that he was okay. Seven others missed the bus and took a later one. It would have been interesting to see if any of these students had had premonitions that morning or even the night before. Parents sobbed in hallways of the hospital at the news of their loss and when Jordan High learned of the crash, school was dismissed immediately.

Two interesting side notes involve a man who went about in the area after the accident offering comfort to families and friends by relating his own near death experience to them in cottage meetings in their homes. The man claimed to have been met by a white-clad messenger when he had his own near-death experience and was taken on a five hour journey through Heaven. He offered great comfort to some of the families. Archie J. Graham was a Mormon bishop and farmer from Wyoming who had had a near-death experience when suffering from the flu epidemic in 1918. He moved to Salt Lake City in the 30's to be near his father who was ill. He had written a typescript called "A Visit Beyond The Veil" on his five hour tour of paradise, which is in the LDS archives. Many remembered that his visits had been the most comforting while he was visiting relatives in Riverton. He spoke of lush green foliage and a gorgeous place where no one suffered and everyone was happy. He told these parents that they would see their children again and told about his own near-death experience in detail to convince them that the after life was very real. He had left his body and floated over all these people he knew who were crying over him. Then the spirit guide told him that he could not die yet because he had things to do and he was pulled back into his body.

The other interesting event involved the Mormon view of being "called home" at an appointed time. Only the Prophet of the LDS church it seems, was willing to imply that God had called all of these children home to save them further trials and tribulations on Earth. There was no one else who could explain why God would "call them home" in such a large group, just as my husband, a combat veteran, could never explain seeing hundreds of bodies all at once being called "home." It made little sense and offered no comfort to the families to think that this was predestination at the hand of God. The Prophet's speech, in which he implied that the children might have been too good and too pure to remain any longer on earth, or that it had been a divinely appointed time for them to die, caused much debate and discussion for years afterwards. People then believed that being called home in a group had no explanation of its own, and that God couldn't possibly have had such a hand in so big a tragedy. Those families interviewed about this topic said that either no one ever asked about why it had happened, or that it was simply unforeseen circumstances that can befall any individual.

Jordan High School did not reconvene until a memorial service was held and all the burials had taken place. Mass funeral services were held in the Riverton Junior High School and the Governor, Apostles of the LDS church, State Superintendent of Schools, and many other dignitaries attended all of them. Nine hundred students attended the memorial service and several days later the president of the LDS church conducted a special service in the local Stake Center. All across the valley funds were raised to help with funeral expenses and rehabilitation programs. The Red Cross formed a special committee made up of civic leaders, school officials, business and church officials and the media to distribute the funds. The county and the LDS church made sizable contributions and even the area theaters offered benefit shows to raise funds.

A lot of different agencies investigated the crash but it was the Interstate Commerce Commission which had the final say. The members felt the bus driver was at fault by failing to see the train approaching from the side of the bus opposite his seat, although other investigators felt that poor visibility that morning had more to do with it. There was even a rumor that the bus driver had wanted to commit suicide which deeply hurt his family because of course they knew it was not true. After this all school bus drivers across the state and eventually the entire nation were required to open the front door and stop at railroad crossings. Parents of the victims brought a lawsuit against the railroad and received an out-of-court settlement of $80,000.

A common story now that seems to go along with many such school bus-train accidents and which started with one that occurred on the Villa Main railroad tracks just outside of San Antonio, Texas at a much later date, has rapidly become an urban legend. It involves the idea that if the tracks are in a rural area and run along a slight hill perpendicular to them, you can drive up to the spot, put your car in neutral and literally be pushed over the tracks by invisible hands. The idea involved is that the ghosts of those children killed will appear and push your car to safety if you stop on the tracks and wait while idling in neutral. On several occasions with the one in Texas, and then all across the country, people have put baby powder on their back bumpers, allowed their car to roll by itself over the tracks and down the slight hill while they were inside and then gotten out to discover the impressions of little hands and fingerprints left in the baby powder. There have even been several articles and local and national television shows which have documented this, though I was hard pressed (excuse my pun) to discern these marks as actual hand or finger prints. Many people who have actually done this claim to have had the prints form right before their eyes as they watched.

But none of this is so at Schulsen's Crossing. Nothing feels good there. Not even the physical features of the land would allow for this kind of movement, as it is a sharp "S" curve which seems to have caused a lot of the problems there over the years. There is not much of a hill and as I stood there watching for quite a while I noticed that cars still traveled this road tending to speed up as they rounded this curve and not often looking for trains as so few seem to pass by nowadays along these tracks. However, there are still trains and still a lot of people who take this short cut even though the way to the other side is blocked by a huge freeway. It is still a dangerous crossing, because of the way people drive it, even though huge signs pronounce it so.

A prevailing sadness at the crossing includes many other deaths as well as those children lost in 1938 in the winter snows. It seems that this corner is a very haunted one, with one disaster after another layered over the decades. Even to this day, people who live in the area and remember this accident and those which followed the initial one, talk about the corner's poor visibility and the sharp curve on it, and wonder why the old road is not closed down. It is hidden now by a huge freeway and a large shopping mail and one can only get to the road by searching to the west and studying the street signs. As one friend said who had a cousin, no longer living, who survived the crash and never would talk about it, most of the people who remember it will be dead in the next several years. Those affected by the car accidents which followed this initial tragedy are not willing to reminisce about the incidents, nor should they.

There have been a couple more single car and passenger collisions with a passing train at the spot. In 1953, five girls who were being chased by a carload of high school boys, rounded the corner and rolled and crashed at the crossing. Four of the girls were killed and the one that survived apparently was severely brain damaged and survived for only a short while afterwards. They were all on an LDS ward basketball team and another girl on the team has recently asked me to visit the spot again so that she can attempt to talk with her friends, before she herself leaves this earth. She herself is very ill and feels an urgency to talk with them, although she doesn't understand I think that she will get that opportunity when her own time comes. And I don't feel comfortable doing this as none of us really knows what awaits us on the other side or if it is really any of my business.

This is something I may or may not do, as the spot itself gives me the creeps and I already have too many horrific images rattling around in my head from my first visit there. If I can see a positive reason for this, rather than some sort of idle curiosity, then I might be willing to do it. However, as most who travel in that other world can attest too, layers of time can become intermixed and one never knows just exactly what will pop up nor which will be the strongest to come through. With so many tragedies in this one spot, it would be hard to differentiate, unless the sight of this other woman could trigger something. More recently, three teenage boys were killed there in another car accident. Watching the cars which do use this back road now, it is interesting to see just how people really do fly around that curve and come charging up over the tracks without looking because it is such a deserted place and no one thinks that anything will happen to them at the crossing. Freight trains still speed down these tracks to this day and despite the huge signs facing the western direction, there is not much of a warning system if one is coming from the east and headed west.

I suspect that there have been other accidents at this crossing, which I don't even know about. The air there is thick with something that I am pretty sure I would have felt without ever knowing anything about the place. It is almost as if it were, from the beginning, a bad energy spot on the earth, which then became a railroad crossing later and was unfortunately at one time a direct route to the old Jordan High from West Jordan. Now all of this is blocked off and the crossing is eternally condemned to local traffic only. I was still amazed however, that so many cars still found and used it as a sort of frontage road, although thankful that there was no longer a high school nearby so all those daredevil drivers of that age could navigate the road or play "chicken". I am glad that it takes some doing to find it these days, as I myself had to wander around a bit and kept getting confused as to just which crossing it was, although I would imagine that the locals know exactly where it is.

As I stood near the tracks that day and walked up and down both sides of them and the road as well, a song came into my head, a Mormon hymn actually. I recognized it from my childhood days but could not remember the words. The humming grew louder and louder as I walked about, and finally the title of it came to me: "Welcome, Welcome, Sabbath Morning." I could not shake it from my mind and it stayed in my head all the way home. Nor could I shake the strong feeling of it having to do with a specific mother who found comfort from this song upon losing her child. There seemed to be a young man lying on the tracks crawling forward with his arms, his legs being either crushed or broken, calling for his mother. He was still there calling for her and it was she who had listened to or sung this song over and over throughout her life as a comfort for her loss. I also felt strongly that this song had served a general purpose, either at some sort of ceremony for the children or within individual homes and families. I must have had great significance to many involved with this tragedy. I needed to know what the words were, as more information would come to me from knowing them.

Later, I called an LDS friend of mine and borrowed an old hymn book from her so that I could write down the words. At that moment I was engulfed in the cries and images of all that had happened at the crossing, as though remembering just the mere title of that song had opened the main floodgates and time had washed over me and around me, full of the sights and sounds of what was being released. Names were called out to me, family names, parental names, friends searching for friends and on and on. This was not a time that I was at ease or able calmly to write all of this down and remember it, for I had been taken by surprise and had not expected to be so overcome with the grief of others in this spot. I was told that I was supposed to give this song to someone's mother, and images formed in my mind's eye for which I had not asked.

Besides the young man, there was a young woman who screamed at me from the pieces that she had become. Then there were several others in various forms or odd angles and turns who seemed to be trying to get my attention, but yet with no sound, like a silent movie of past events long gone. Yet the ones that I could lock on to seemed to be alive at that moment and were vying for my attention, needing this or that. The images crescendoed like the crest of a huge wave in time, and then slowly dissipated as I stood transfixed, gradually realizing that tears were rolling down my cheeks and that I had not even been aware that I was crying. All the while that tune played in the background and I was eager to go home and find the words. That was all that I could take while at the crossing. It was like a battleground, and one expects such things when going to historic sites. This event had taken me completely by surprise and I was not prepared to handle any of it.

When I later learned of all the other accidents at the spot, I was not sure then just what had happened to me, nor just exactly where I was in the fabric of time. That song had been there, and when I did get the words, everything fit as my having at least been at the crossing at that moment in time while experiencing other events. Ten of the students who died were from Riverton. Much later, after writing this story blind to my own ancestral history, I was startled to be reminded by my father that he still to this day has many relatives from this town. My great grandfather was one of the founding fathers of nearby Herriman and lived there with his three wives. Two of his sons and their sister, Annie Crane, my great grandmother, lived in Riverton all their lives. Annie Crane married Carl Madsen and they lived in Riverton where my father spent a summer as a young boy working on their farm. I have often wondered since if perhaps relatives of mine, although none died in this accident, weren't friends with those who did die. This would partially explain my strong reaction to this incident of so long ago, although my intuitive sense would have strongly reacted to this event anyway.

"Welcome, welcome, Sabbath morning, now we rest from every care. Welcome, welcome, is they dawning, Holy Sabbath, day of prayer. Loving teachers kindly greet us as we meet in Sunday school, where they labor hard to teach us, by the Savior's golden rule. Hark! The Sabbath bells are ringing, hear the echoes all around. List! the merry children singing! What a pleasing, joyful sound! Every tender note entreats us, bids us come, no longer stay. On our way the music greets us; hasten, hasten come away. Here we bow in meek devotion; here we sing God's holy praise. Here our hearts, with fond emotion, seek to learn his holy ways. From the books of revelation we are taught while yet in youth. Words of Heavenly inspiration, guide us in the path of truth. Here we meet with friends and neighbors; parents too are in the throng. We are earnest in our labors. To God's kingdom we belong. Trials make our faith grow stronger, truth is nobler than a crown. We will brave the tempest longer, tho the world upon us frown. Welcome, welcome, Sabbath morning; now we rest from every care. Welcome, welcome, is thy dawning, Holy Sabbath, day of prayer." (Text by Robert B. Baird, 1855-1916 and music by Ebenezer Beesley, 1840-1906.)

My friend who knew many of the families and has memories of her own, thought perhaps that some of the students might have been singing this song on their way to school that morning. However, when I checked with the local historian who had interviewed many of those involved in this incident, he said that they all agreed that actually the students on the bus that morning had been very calm and quiet. My friend is also pushing me to hurry up and talk with a few of these people who remember this event before they are gone, for she sees the importance of this with her own desire to speak with her old high school friends who are in "spirit" that she hasn't seen for many years. However, I am still mired in doubts, doubts about what is really happening to me, and doubts about whether this is the right thing to do or not. I am already used to being considered foolish, but common sense tells me that this is a place best left alone, both with the living and the dead.

My friend, on the other hand, argues that I should use my ability to help those wishing to tie up all the loose ends here In this spot. She would like to talk to her "spirit" friends and wish them well or ask for forgiveness for whatever one does upon losing so many close friends so suddenly. She has things to say and they probably do too. She would like to at least try to talk to them, but she doesn't know how and I do. Most people would scoff at the whole notion and she herself doesn't really believe In such nonsense. Still, there is always that chance, and she has tested me enough with all her artifacts from digs she went on in her youth, to believe that I really could give her some sort of Information. Besides, she says, I want to tie up my own loose ends before I die. And she knows that her time is coming sooner than most as she suffers from an illness herself.

What I think about most is the one young girl they thought was dead and then discovered that she was still breathing and saved her. As her mother stood over her, speaking with family members the story goes, the mother said something to the effect that she was glad that her daughter was dead. The girl was apparently conscious enough to hear her mother say this and was never the same again. I think about how, my family, having left such a tightly woven faith and such a strong history, would to some degree feel as this girl felt, shut out from what was once familiar by a people who shun those who turn from their roots. And how just because a certain faith does not fit, one's ancestry is still very important in the scheme of things.

My mother used to say that upon leaving her small town in southern Utah, it was as if she had died and the only time she came to life again was when she visited there. People would say that they were glad she was back and not ask her how long she intended to stay nor how long she had been gone. This journey into other realms made our family very strong and able to withstand outward onslaughts from those who did not understand us. We were always assured that we had each other and told never to fight among ourselves as we needed to depend on each other in life. I have always known that had I been left behind for any reason, it was my family who would come back for me, lift me up and help me, our ancestral roots intact. That we would always be loved and supported, no matter our trials and tribulations in life, and no matter how distant or far away that drummer beat for us.

HAUNTED SCHOOLS
& THE FIFTIES BOMB SHELTER CRAZE

The elementary school where I currently work is haunted. Enough people have talked about this over the decades, so that one has to suppose some of it might be true. Having worked in several school buildings with absolutely no haunting tales, I was delighted to be working in one! It is also one of the schools built during the era of the bomb shelter craze, which is an interesting story by itself. The old bomb shelter was one of several built into the basements of schools all along the Wasatch Front between the 1950s and the 1960s, and something that I along with many others my age remember as being a part of our elementary school experience. We were the guinea pigs to our parent's paranoia, or at least our leader's paranoia, between Joseph McCarthy and his henchmen, the great Communist threat that culminated in the Bay of Pigs incident, and the old "B" monster movies where Communism was thinly veiled by monsters and aliens from outer space who came here to threaten our American way of life.

These shelters consisted of one large classroom sized room from which two long tunnels ran the length of the school at a slight incline upwards. In these tunnels, and all of them were designed exactly alike, at least in our state, were plain light bulbs evenly spaced along each side of the tunnel halfway up the walls. To get to these tunnels one has to walk through the spare room in the basement, which in most elementary schools now has become a storage area, although those over crowded ones have been used in the past for everything from an extra classroom to special art classes or other such specialists visiting the school, as well as a choir or music and band room. At our school a kiln was installed down there for teachers to fire their clay pots, and this was the only other time I went down there with another teacher on "school business." On either side of this room one walks around the big old octopus style heater to two metal doors which were set to automatically shut down over hundreds of school children crammed into these tunnels. There were no windows and very little ventilation. The storage of food, water and whatever else each school deemed necessary for temporary survival in the event of an "attack," was located on the other side of these doors. As school children we were told about the effects of nuclear attack in little talks with plastic overlays which explained the stages of such an attack, did our under the desk drills and then upon occasion went downstairs for the big drills down in the tunnels.

I was so fascinated by not only the absurdity of these tunnels, but also by my own memories of these drills, that I got permission to be taken down into the one in the basement of my own old elementary school. It was built when I was in fifth grade and I spent the second half of my sixth grade year there after being in a very old elementary school where such things as bomb shelters were a thing of the future. This was when I realized that the plan was exactly the same for all of them. As I talked to those my age or a little older, I found that in general, people remembered these drills as something fun to do rather than something scary. Children got out from under their desks and instead of going outside they lined up and filed down the basement stairs with their little bottles of water in hand, having learned to put a drop of vinegar in their drinking bottles to purify the water for long term occupation in the tunnels. Packed in like sardines they would sit on the floor and laugh and joke until their teachers told them that the all clear had been sounded. Then they waited while several classes in front of them filed single file back out of these tunnels, up the stairs and back into the sunlight that poured through the windows of the school.

When our custodian took us down into the school where I work now, it was interesting to view this from an adult's point of view, especially now that this whole idea of bomb shelters has become a really absurd one. At least home bomb shelters had reasonable lighting, ventilation and storage, while the school bomb shelters made one picture what might have taken place if a bomb of any kind had fallen on the school while hundreds of school children sat down there supposedly safe from nuclear attack. It makes one wonder just what was in the minds of those who designed them, even if these places were considered a temporary shelter. On our tour we were maneuvered through the storage area full of old desks and such, around the octopus heater which we had to duck through, to the metal door of one of these tunnels while the custodian found the light switch. The light switch on the other side didn't work and so that tunnel was more eerie. When he turned the light switch on with the metal door securely wired open above us, it was quite an awesome sight. This seemingly endless tunnel stretched before us with the wires running up the sides of the walls and the endless light bulbs running way off into the distance at a slowly increasing incline to the end where there was nothing, no exit at all. It made one think of the old *Twilight Zone* shows and certainly humming the theme music would have been appropriate.

One could definitely imagine floating orbs and the like down in this area of the building and looking down the other tunnel where the lights did not work, one could see a white image floating there, perhaps an after-image in our eyes if nothing else. My friend and I, both with intuitive abilities, did feel some things down in this area, none of it good, and I especially got some images best left to the past in this case. My own memories of these drills, which disappeared soon after my sixth grade year, were not fun and pleasant like those experienced by many others. I was unaware of my sensibilities then and wouldn't have known how to figure out just what it was that I was seeing while I was down there, except the feeling of it, which was of course suffocating. One has to understand the times that people were living in then, to understand what sort of minds could think up such a thing as closed-in tunnels with only one-end exits. Perhaps someone could enlighten me a little in this. I did wonder if perhaps the other end of these tunnels had been closed off over time, and that perhaps at one time they had an exit at the other end above ground? No one could tell me for sure.

Beyond the proverbial rumor of our school having been built over an ancient Indian Mound, this has made the very land on which it is built haunted by long ago spirits buried there. Such stories have been told over the years long before I began to work there. One of these is that when the school was first built the classrooms numbered from one on up and that when they got to twelve they simply skipped to fourteen, making the room south of my present one, the room which should have been numbered thirteen. This room has had a myriad of problems over the years in terms of lights blinking or dimming on and off, or going off altogether, as well as windows being left either opened or closed and found in the opposite manner the next morning. The huge old steam pipes will decide out of the blue, to bang loudly from the walls around it. The other classrooms in the hall have no such activity in their walls at the same time. In my room it sounds like the sixth graders are next door kicking the walls in unison for five to ten minutes before they stop as suddenly as they had begun. The custodian who has worked there for many years says that besides the heating breaking down more often in that room, he has been called over in the night by security to lock up windows that the teacher swears he had locked before leaving. Also, the present teacher talks about how he will leave the blinds either up or down and when he comes in, in the morning, they are either uniformly the opposite or some are up and some are down.

Most interesting in our hall is the smell of either sweet grass or some sort of sweet smelling pipe tobacco which nearly always permeates a room when one teacher sits alone in her room in the late afternoon and the building is quieter and still. Various teachers have reported the scent only in our hall. There are a certain two rooms where the pipe smoke can be smelled. Some say that it is as if someone smoking a pipe has entered their room and stands near them for a few minutes and then walks off, the smoky smell disappearing as suddenly as it appeared in the room. The former custodian, who was considered "strange that way," claimed to have had several sightings of at least one spirit in the building when he was alone there late at night. Since I live in both worlds, I of course would tend to believe that he had had some sort of experience in the building with this tall dark slicked back haired man who smoked a pipe and who was either Native American or just a former employee.

Even one of our Principals had a story to tell of her experience one evening when she and another person had to go over and patrol the outside of the building to make sure all the doors and windows were secure in the summer time when the teachers and students were long gone. When they got to the alcove behind the school outside where the two rooms are located and where pipe smoke has been reported, she said that the two of them had a strong feeling of being followed. A strong smell of tobacco like that from a pipe permeated the area and they felt as though someone had walked behind them until they got to the other side of the alcove. The principal was new to the building at the time and knew nothing of the other stories about the pipe smoke smell on the other side of these walls in those two rooms. One might think that perhaps this was a former custodian who made his own patrols of the building still to this day making sure that things are secure even though his time on earth has been over for quite a while.

An older story told around the place involves an old copy machine, which used to be stored in a closet next to where the secretary of the school greeted visitors. Sometimes she would be sitting alone in the office when most people had gone home and the copy machine would suddenly start up on its own and spew empty papers out onto the floor. Two teachers related a story that had happened to two former colleagues at the school when they tried to go down in the basement as part of a silly Halloween hunt that had been cooked up for the staff one year. They left the bottom door open and were hunting for their clue when suddenly the door slammed shut loudly and locked them in. They were stuck down there for quite a while before someone noticed the noise coming from the basement and unlocked both doors and let them out. They said that they had been down there screaming their lungs out and were surprised that no one had heard them.

For two years I would come back from summer vacation and ask the custodian if he had encountered any ghosts. A staunch non-believer in such things, he would joke with me about it and report that absolutely nothing had happened. The third year, I came back from summer vacation, asked him the same things I always did and he surprised me by replying that yes, he had encountered a ghost this time. At first I thought he was kidding, but then I realized that he was half serious. I asked him what had happened and he said that he had been in the stage area, which is spooky to almost anyone at the school. It is an area that he has always joked about being the only place where a haunting could be taking place, and that the usual phenomena was going on. This is a sort of game that he ends up playing with the building when if he is downstairs he will hear banging up on the stage and will go up to investigate. Then he hears banging downstairs and goes down to investigate and then the banging will start upstairs again, over and over. He has learned to ignore it most of the time now.

He says that most of the time, this "sound tag" doesn't bother him, although one time that summer the banging noises had been particularly loud and attracted his attention. He was working in the basement near the bomb shelter area and the banging started up above him. Suddenly the banging stopped and all was silent. He then saw a white light flash before him and then it began to float towards him, though it disappeared before it got to him. He said that it had really startled him because there was no natural outside light in the place and the overhead ceiling light had dimmed when this took place, he hurriedly finished what he was doing and left the basement. He had also had to repair a broken window in the dark one evening and had heard very loud banging, clanging and knocking noises coming from the stage area by the stairway to the basement. They were so extremely loud that he felt as though someone was trying to get his attention. The sounds were nothing like the usual "sound tag" that he had experienced before and as soon as he went into the school to investigate, all sounds ceased immediately.

The last interesting phenomena, which the people who live in the neighborhood can attest, are the flying objects. One story the sweepers tell is of being in one of the back rooms when a clock just simply flew straight off of the wall, propelled itself across the room and crash landed near the other side of the room from where it was hung. They say that this was around ten years ago. The other thing is that on the side of the building where the first and second grade classrooms are located, kids have looked through the windows during the summer months and have gone home and told their parents an incredible story. They will look in a room in this area the evening before and all will be well. The next morning they look in the same room and books are strewn all around the floor, from a few books to many books. The first time the children noticed this, they told their parents who did not believe them. Then the students experimented on purpose checking the rooms the night before and then once again in the morning. They found that this happened much more than once. Finally a few parents did the same thing, mainly out of curiosity or concerned that someone was getting into the building. They went after everyone was gone and looked through the windows of these rooms. Then early in the morning before anyone arrived they would go over and look through the windows again. Invariably at least one of these rooms had a few books on the floor. When I asked the custodian about this, he said that he had noticed the books but just figured that the sweepers might have done this accidentally. At which point he picked up the books and put them away again. It was rare he said, but it did indeed happen. One only has to wait to hear more about our "haunted" school, I would guess!

This spring I moved to a different grade just before school ended. I am on the other end of the building by where the first, second and fourth grades are located. It was the last day of school and the students had already gone. I was back in my workroom putting things away when all of a sudden I heard a creaking sound, turned around and watched as the top drawer of our poster storage area rolled out two and a half feet in front of me all of its own accord. I had not stomped the floor or whacked the cabinet or been anywhere near where this drawer was. I pushed it shut and out it came two and a half feet again. I shut it four times and on the fourth attempt it remained shut.

I had some other teachers come down to watch and the drawer rolled open but only for about three or four inches. One teacher got down and checked for anything rolled up behind the drawer that could have gotten there when we moved but there was nothing there. The teacher who had had the room had never, ever even had the drawer roll out a few inches on her, so we checked again, the rollers, the gears and looked for anything that might cause the drawer to roll out on its own. There was nothing that we could find. The funny part was that no one but me saw the drawer roll out two and a half feet, everyone else saw it roll out a few inches and thought I was making a big deal out of nothing!

OTHER HAUNTED SCHOOL STORIES
COLLECTED IN UTAH

MURRAY DISTRICT - GRANT ELEMENTARY - SLC, UTAH

The ghost of a former band teacher that died in a car accident on the way to school one morning seems to haunt the school. His favorite place for haunting is to play the piano in the school cafeteria, which is also the auditorium, when no one else is there.

UNION HIGH SCHOOL - NEOLA NEAR ROOSEVELT, UTAH

An ancient Indian Mound is supposed to be under this school too. The ghost in this school has a name he is called "Edwin." He has apparently been there for many years and likes to play tricks on those involved in school productions because his favorite place to hang out is in the school auditorium. His favorite trick is to turn off all the lights in the auditorium when only one person is there left to find a way out in the pitch darkness. He misplaces costumes and likes to hang them in unusual places such as on the curtain tracks. His most famous trick involved a time when the school was putting on a production of "Dracula" and the actor playing the count was in his coffin on stage. Unseen hands pushed the actor, coffin and all, off the stage right in front of the audience.

CRESCENT MIDDLE SCHOOL - JORDAN SCHOOL DISTRICT - SLC

The head custodian at this school for many years reported quite a few incidents that were difficult to explain. These were the usual lights going on and off as noticed by many witnesses over a long period of time, as well as doors being left locked and found open within the school in the morning. Doors also slam violently right in front of several witnesses and will unlock themselves later in the evening AS the custodian made her rounds a second time. Shadows or spectral figures have been seen moving across the end of hallways or in an open doorway. The custodial staff would change lights and then have them go out immediately, in this relatively new school. Strangest of all, the lock system for all of the student lockers was always going haywire. It is an automatic system for the whole school and yet the custodian would find combinations that had changed their number order or even had entirely new number combinations or be perfectly backwards or would contain half of each other's number order. According to the custodian such a feat was impossible with the system and no one could have figured out a way in which to change these numbers, especially in such a random fashion.

VALLEY ALTERNATIVE HIGH - OLD CRESCENT ELEMENTARY - JORDAN

This high school is located in an old elementary school on State Street and about 110 South. High School students talk about hauntings in the school connected to a young man and young woman who were once students at the high school and cared rather deeply for each other. The story goes that they somehow lost their lives and returned to the school as spirits to be together forever. The building was originally an old elementary school and has been there for many years. The original story is quite different from this because in this version it was two young elementary school aged children who were playing with something that exploded, possibly a blasting cap and they were killed either right on the playground or inside the school itself. Visitors to the school report hearing children playing in the gym but when they go to investigate, there is no one there. Staff members have actually spotted apparitions both in the school and out on the playground and also hear many voices and unusual sounds, which they only talk about among themselves.

Valley High is getting a new facility and the old elementary school will soon be deserted and put up for sale. Because it is right on a very busy commercial area, it is likely that unless a private school rents or buys it, it will be torn down for some gas and food shop or whatever else the new owners want to put there. My intuitive sense in this case however, seems to be that whatever is in and around this building will remain for the new owners to contend with.

DILWORTH ELEMENTARY SCHOOL

Jane Dilworth, for whom this school was named, supposedly walks its halls at night, haunting the place since she passed on.

CYPRUS HIGH SCHOOL - MAGNA

Here is yet another high school where the school auditorium is haunted. The school does have a history to fit the haunting in that it burned down at one time and was rebuilt two different times since it was constructed in 1910. The school has had problems with bats for years, they will mysteriously fly into the auditorium during an assembly and then disappear just as mysteriously. Over the years school officials and inspectors have tried to find the bat's nesting area or anyplace where they could be hiding, but they have been unsuccessful in finding them. The stage lights will on and off whenever they feel like it, and when no one is around to turn them on and off. The resident ghost has never officially been given a name but many have seen him walking about in the auditorium. The only description given is that he is a man dressed in clothes from the 1930s.

TAYLORSVILLE HIGH SCHOOL

This is a fairly new ghost story because of a senior who shot himself in a west hall school stairwell in the fall of 2001. I can remember that I happen to be driving by the school at the time that all the police and ambulances arrived, and wondered if a gang fight was going on because of all the official cars in the parking lot. Instead it was just once student who lost his life to some deep dark feeling that the rest of us will probably never understand. Somehow as a result of this suicide, the ghost rumor began. Taylorsville High School has a very large night class program and is affiliated with both Utah State University and the Granite School District. Several of us took a ghost hunter's class there. The course has become quite popular, and of course we started our investigations with the hall in which the student committed suicide. As for myself, not needing any ghost hunter equipment, there were just way too many people there to investigate anything. Besides this, every student locker in the place had a story to tell and this was quite enough of a hormonal barrage, to shut my intuitive flashes down entirely.

ROY HIGH SCHOOL & SAND RIDGE JUNIOR HIGH - ROY

Roy High School seems to have two ghosts haunting the place. One is supposed to be a little girl who laughs and talks in several areas of the building. The other ghost haunts the large auditorium. He has been blamed for moving the curtains and moving objects around on the stage, although no one has ever really seen any sort of apparitions. At the Sand Ridge Junior High, which is right next door to the high school, there's supposedly a boy who died while in high school and who walks back and forth between the two schools as an apparition. Supposedly there are 9 ghosts and one little girl who can be heard talking to people on tape recorders. Amateur high school ghost hunters have made their own EVP recordings and the 9 ghosts are supposed to be students who died either at the high school or the junior high over the years.

Stories about how all of these students died are quite interesting. One of the boys was riding his bike and got run over by train. Others were in car accidents. Teachers and students say that they can hear children playing in the gym when no one is there and that they have experienced soft breathing on the back of their necks when no one is present. There are cold spots and other strange activities that take place at both schools. The students there have even gone so far as to try to capture the ghosts on film using ghost photography techniques. They claim to have pictures of orbs and floating wisps that have been seen in the auditorium. These schools are fairly new and so one could consider this a modern-day ghost story.

Note: There are many other old and sometimes abandoned schools in the state of Utah, so that after this book comes out, maybe I will be able to include a much longer list of such stories in a future book in the series as others read these stories and tell me more such tales.

OLD SCHOOL HOUSES DIE HARD

TO MAKE WAY FOR NEW PLACES AND TIMES

The Utah Heritage Foundation, Utah State Historical Society and Jack Goodman, the definitive three when it comes to preservation, all say the same thing. Old school houses are the number one target for death these days. Whether it be small towns or big cities, nobody wants them except for the few who attended them and who put up a valiant effort to keep them for renters or as a museum or senior citizen center, and in some rare instances, a city library. Occasionally, preservationists win out and the school is saved, but more often than not, the school disappears into the past, never to be seen again. Knowing of a former school teacher couple who have made it their life's work to travel the country photographing such old places of learning before it is too late, gives me a bit of hope. Having been a school teacher of one kind or another for so many years, with the fantasy of having the opportunity just once to work in a one-room schoolhouse, I am fascinated by them. As an intuitive person, I love to listen to their walls and floors and ceilings, letting the old images of bygone eras flood through me, while those who loved the place tell me their stories. Children, even those of the spirit, seem to be attracted to me. So I let them visit me, as I wander through the halls and rooms of such places, hearing and seeing both the tragedies and the happy times that took place within them.

When I thought about writing their stories, all I had to do was collect tales from others, though the stories became more often than not the same sad repetitive one - that each school provides wonderful or sometimes terrible memories for a group or several generations, then sits idle, goes through a series of weird occupations like a car garage or nursing home, and then is torn down, disappearing into dust. Someone or some organization wants the land because it is more valuable than a bygone school and it is cheaper to build from scratch rather than to try and renovate such places. A few stragglers come out of the woodwork to fight developers and sometimes these saviors win, but too often they lose. Winning takes big bucks and backing with foundation monies or grants. Losing takes very little, for an old school has no value except to those who attended or taught there. The education system itself needs a giant overhaul, with no money of its own for the fight to save it, and with over-population becoming an additional burden for the system. In short, poverty stricken schools with bigger and bigger populations have to get money where they can and old schools are one of the easier things to get rid of.

Still, those of us who remember these little schools and see the value in trying to preserve at least a few of them, keep wailing in the dark just to hear our own voices and to remind ourselves that yes indeed we are still alive! Honoring what came before us and facing the future, we are taught by the past not to make the same kind of mistakes again.

My father was the Principal of a little four room schoolhouse in Pingree, Idaho. It was his first professional teaching job and he was hired because there had been some trouble with some oversized farm boys and my father was six feet four. After this he left public school and became a University professor. My mother taught school in Salt Lake City at Lincoln Elementary on Fifth East, at Momingside Elementary, and at a school in Logan. They both went on to other things, my father becoming a professor of history and my mother eventually became a linguist. And while Morningside Elementary is still running strong, Lincoln Elementary was becoming integrated into a new junior high for Granite District, or so I thought. Everyone else in the family but I chose something not related to teaching. My mother's sister taught all her life and I have one cousin who attempted it for a while and then went an entirely different direction, finding teaching old-fashioned and backward, though she herself still honors the profession. I taught severely multi-handicapped children, then special education in the regular public schools and eventually gifted and talented in a regular elementary school. And now the younger generation in the family has at least one teacher in it, the principal and sole teacher of an alternative high school in the inner city with his four Spanish speaking assistants to help him down in Southern California.

I was a child of the sixties when it seemed everyone was choosing a helping profession, or one to tear society down. It was a fantasy which soon crumbled, but I kept teaching, loving it for many, many years. In the last few years, however, I have come to realize that nothing can save the education system now, except an entire overhaul. It is like working for the post office - antiquated materials and books, not enough desks, too many children, two many opinions about how to fix the system from people not in the front lines and who oddly think that more testing is the answer, and way too many dissatisfied customers. My time will be over soon, like so many others who dedicated themselves to teaching and are leaving in the next ten years. We will be leaving a massive amount of empty positions where our younger counterparts will hopefully be.

Perhaps this next generation of teachers are either too smart, too self-absorbed or to aware of a not so positive future to take the punishments which we older teachers have been taking without question, though there are still many diehards around, idealistic and compassionate. They say that soon we will have an over abundance of doctors and lawyers who will not be able to earn a living for lack of patients and clients, while on the other hand the teacher and health care shortages continue due to a lack of funds. I for one am all for filling these positions with people leaving other professions where they are used to being treated better. For they have the energy and time to protest, and to ask for better treatment and standards and finances. Because they are used to better work-place conditions, they will perhaps protest and ask for better rather than leaving to find something better which one sees quite often in our profession with the younger teachers.

As for me, I honor where I have been, both in my many years in special education and then my many years in the classroom as well. But I too must go forward with the time I have left, to talk about the intuitive life and preserving things from the past. Across the state, or any state, one can find these old schools. Some of them have made the transition and have already found a way to survive like the ones in Fairview, Mount Carmel, Santaquin, or the Peteetneet Academy in Payson, which have become town museums. Others are in transition, becoming senior citizen centers and boys and girls recreation facilities although there are schools which may or may not make it in the long scheme of things, like the ones currently in the news from Brigham City, Logan, Provo or right here in Salt Lake. The Spanish-style Columbus school, became a real success story to many by being completely gutted, renovated and turned into a wonderful city library and South High still stands with the Grand Theatre within its walls as the south campus for the Salt Lake Community College. Still others sit idle, awaiting their fate, though a few of them have been taken on by private citizens like the one in Scofield and in Fairfield and some others that one can see simply by driving around the state. Schools whose names I don't even know, like the one west of Murray which is a nursing home now. Still others like the Whittier school in Logan and the South Jordan school here in Salt Lake, are in the midst of fighting for their survival, precariously sitting on the edge of some developer's abyss. Then there are the ones that become a part of some farmer's field, or sit next to gas stations or town halls, one step away from demolition either because a single citizen owns the property and can't or won't tear it down, or because the structures make good storage sheds, as in several towns on the old highway into Kanab.

The schoolhouse in Thistle is pretty much symbolic of all of these threatened buildings, as I personally came to see it slowly deteriorate from the magnificent and unusual building that it was, a monument to all those others whom no one cared about and let fall into dust over time. When I first saw the Thistle school we had rounded the bend on the old road to Fairview and there it stood in all its red sandstone glory very close to the highway but facing towards some company's closed gate. I imagine that the firm owned the property on which it stood. Thistle had been washed away some years before by a great mud slide, sat as a lake for a few years, and then was drained, with several ghost stories of her own to tell. I was visiting with a friend to a country that I had never seen before, into the heart of an area solidly Mormon and proud of it. I had a great time, visiting old graveyards and mountain hideaways, and even attending an old drive-in theater which still shows movies. A few years later, my husband and I observed that the Thistle school was still standing, though the deterioration was pretty obvious. A year or so after that, the roof had fallen in and only the walls stood up pointing to the sky. I can remember wondering if the elements had done this or if it was the work of vandals. A few more years went by and we drove through there again in search of more ghost stories and hauntings. We rounded the corner and there it was, half gone, the parts of a few walls still standing. An old traveler had made it his home. He had a blue canvas tarp stretched over his car from the school walls and was wandering about, busily getting done whatever tasks he needed to do.

The next time we passed by, most of the walls were gone, with a lot of newly added graffiti. I asked my friend if we had taken pictures that first year long ago, for time blends together as one gets older and I really couldn't remember how long ago it had been. She had none, the tone of her voice implying that it was an odd question in the first place. My heart fell, knowing that many, many people would think that it was just an old school, so why was I even wanting to have a photographic record of its former existence? I couldn't even remember the date over the door where the raised letters said "Thistle - 18--." I thought about those few whose homes which were taken away from them by the mud slide, and how among them must have been at least one or two old timers who had attended that school and had their own memories about it, good or bad. They themselves were probably spirits now, ghosts who haunted the area where once as a young boy or girl walked down to the sound of an old school bell and let themselves be "'taught."

I also thought about how this was true all over the country, as my husband and I traveled the back roads of the Midwest. He took me to all the old schools in the area, while I took rolls of film that would never be used for anything. I stopped at everyone and got out and touched and listened to them. I got my visions and stories from those who had left their echoes and shadows in the place, telling or showing them to me. I would remember some, while many others would be filed away in some dark recess of my memory, never to return.

Jack Goodman, before he retired, wrote about the Whittier Schools's fight in the Sunday Salt Lake Tribune's Arts section in October 22, of 2000. He also wrote about the Mt. Carmel school in the same section of the paper on Sunday May 14, 2000. The Fairfield Schoolhouse story was in the Sunday, October 31, 1999 column that used to appear every Sunday in the *Salt Lake Tribune*. He told Snow College's story in his Sunday, December 5, 1999 column and then had a couple more in his book *As You Pass By*, on the Uintah Elementary School and the Columbus School in Salt Lake City. He talked about the architecture of each building, former teachers and students, and of course the fact that the school has somehow survived. Since his book came out, however, the Uintah School has been torn down, as was the Lincoln Junior High whose demolition he does talk about in his book. The old Bingham High School out in Copperton also met its demise long after Goodman had written about this school.

Of course, there was all the controversy surrounding the demise of the old Jordan High School and Larry Miller's various ploys to placate people concerning its demolition. John Keahey wrote about South Jordan's fight in the *Tribune* with an article entitled, "Historic School Won't House S. Jordan Museum" in December of 2000. My own school district was instrumental in condemning the South Jordan building to death, and I can understand both sides of the issue. We need new schools to house our rapidly increasing population. School districts are pinched for money, and no one Is really helping that much. Community and preservation groups are struggling. too, and no one is really helping them much either. Government, big business and religion dominate our fair state; this is where the power and wealth reside.

Then there are the forgotten schools in out-of-the-way places, such as Jordan's Bingham Middle School which shut its doors after once housing the original Bingham High School. It stood ready for demolition because no one could come up with the $13 million that it would take to renovate it and it is now gone forever, a magnificent building that I rushed out to take pictures of before its demise. South High and Bingham High were both designed by a famous architect and again location was what kept one alive and brought the other one down. In Magna, in the same copper mining area, stands the Webster School at 2700 South and 9180 East. Designed by Cannon and Fetzer, it has six classrooms and a prairie style with a flat roof; It was built in 1912 at a cost of $13,512 and was christened the Magna School at first. Then it became the Hayes School and finally the Webster School in 1922 when six rooms were added to the original building, with six more being added in 1927. In the 1960s it housed 675 students with 20 teachers. In 1953, a gym and auditorium were built. By 1955 a new school had been constructed and the Webster school was closed down. At first, locals tried to turn the building into a mining museum and then into a county office space. This school is presently vacant and Kennecoft Copper owns it. The company may donate it for use as a community building.

With the city being emptied into the suburbs as are many other places across the United States, Salt Lake City is certainly not unique. Just recently the Salt Lake City District announced the closure of two more schools, one of which has been around for

109 years. The closing school is the Lowell Elementary School which many parents are still fighting to keep open. As an amateur preservationist now, I know that once the school closes, the strapped-for-money district looks for a buyer or tears it down and builds a new one in its place. Lack of students in the area means for Lowell School that it will be sold and either used as-is or torn down for office space. As Lowell was built in 1892, I am sure many former students or teachers have stories to tell about the school. Then there is the oldest still operating elementary school in the entire state in Provo, the Maeser school, which just shut its doors for the last time this spring and the fight is on to save it, though most say that it is too late and not enough people are behind saving it. The school board voted to raze it four to one, so I would very much like to meet this one person who stood up against the rest and would not change their vote! Eventually Maeser got a reprieve and a unanimous vote to sell it rather than raze it, possibly because of the publicity it received.

Like those who have spent a lifetime observing this destruction of the past, I can shed a tear too, at what it is that we value these days, compared to what must have been valued a hundred years ago. I am not saying that a hundred years ago there weren't mistakes made, nor that the schools were perfect. In fact, back in those days there was even less interest in preserving anything because people were too busy building up the world. We have now reached a delicate balance between the old and the new. Like many older countries, we Americans are trying to establish a way to preserve some of what came before us before it is too late. It has been said over and over again by many a famous orator that a world power which does not honor its own past is doomed to failure.

One theory about how we live involves the idea that when something happens far away from us we do not need to worry about it because it does not concern us. The theory is that this is far from the truth, because the closer something gets to us the more we become a larger and larger part of the warp and weave of the Universe. For example, there is a massive power outage in England and we don't know about it. The next day it is announced that there has been a huge power outage in the southwest area of Canada and we may or may not notice this. The next day it is announced that the power has gone out in several large areas in the western part of the United States and this we notice but remain unaffected by it. The next day the state of Utah has big time power problems all over the place and this we do notice because a lot of us have become affected by this. Next our city has a major power outage everywhere and soon its our neighborhood and then the house next door and then our house and finally the power goes out in our own body and we have to be hospitalized. We slowly get better and the news slowly recedes away from us as well, until finally England's electrical power is fixed and something else breaks down somewhere else in the world.

This is how old schools are for me. First it was what I saw in other parts of the country and then what I noticed in my own state and then my own community and finally schools were closing down all around me. After passing my mother's school for almost two years, thinking that Granite District was integrating the old Lincoln School into its new junior high, I was shocked to one day see the old elementary school in rubble and a few weeks later, hauled away into nothing. Yesterday they announced the closure of two schools in my district, Libbie Edwards and Holladay, the old school that I attended throughout all of my elementary school years except for the second half of sixth grade where the bomb shelter was located in my "new" school. They showed pictures of the empty library shelves and books scattered all over the floor and children saying their last goodbyes in the hallways or quietly crying for exactly what, they themselves probably do not know. Teachers as usual were in a rush to get out and off on their summer vacation, disregarding that fact that they would never return to this particular school again and only thinking about the next year's survival somewhere else.

I thought about Mrs. Parkinson, my sixth grade teacher who lived just up the street and had invested her whole life into teaching at my elementary school. She was of the old-fashioned variety, strict and stern and sometimes downright mean, but one always knew that she cared about you and would be fair to you even when standing in the corner with gum on your nose. I thought about Mrs. Anderton, my fourth grade teacher who the kids used to chant about on the playground: "Here comes Jennie and her ton." Both of them investing years and years into our school and certainly haunting it now or in the near future. I remembered my terrible fifth grade year when no one helped me and I and my slow witted girlfriend were surrounded each day on the playground and taunted and tripped and punched because she was different and therefore I was too. I can remember falling in a mud puddle while chasing a ball that the boys who taunted had thrown strategically, hoping that I would fall and I did. Those names they called us were what I carried with me for years and years before finally letting go of the hurt and forgiving those popular high school students who had done this to us each day of that school year until my only friend left in the spring to go to "special" school. Some of these same students became teachers too.

The seventy four year old Holladay School will meet a worse fate than that of the Libbie Edwards school because a private school wants to buy Libbie Edwards, while the Holladay School is in the heart of a business district. For now though, the school is being rented by a private Mormon school called Deseret Academy. Once again I will have to rush over and get pictures before the place is gone forever, only this time it is my own school and my own memories of a time and place that will never return. And again as I have learned in my travels, location is everything unless a person from out of town moves in and says I want to save this place or that. After location comes wanting to make money and tearing down is always the way to make it unless some foundation comes up with even more money than developers can make. Last is the consideration of how beautiful the site is or how historically significant, and even then this may not be enough to save something, like in the case of the magnificently ornate Orpheum Theatre in Salt Lake or the Maeser School in Provo which are both on the National Register of Historic places. Maeser has been temporarily saved with a new vote by the local school board and a foundation fighting to save it. The Orpheum has been demolished from the backside and the front wall has been saved to make it look like a part of the building was preserved. The old theater has been replaced by a terraced parking lot and offices and shops.

But my old elementary school has none of these things going for it, located where it would be lucrative to tear it down, being a not so attractive building of no historical significance in an area where nobody cares to save it for anything in particular even if they went to school there. Perhaps private schools will continue to try flourish in it, which would at least preserve the building for a while.

One parent at the Libbie Edwards School put it best when Connie Ward said that "We've had children whose parents and grandparents went here. It makes it more than the closing of a school. It's the closing of an era." ("Last Walks in the Hallways", by Heather May, *The Salt Lake Tribune*, Saturday, June 1, 2002. Sec-B.) This time I am being directly affected by the closing of a school right in my own neighborhood, which means if I don't do something to help change this, next it will be my own school where I teach and then me. The other part of the theory, the positive part, being that one or more people can effect change and completely alter the pattern of events from my little grade school to altering the course of future events such as preventing another twin tower catastrophe. It doesn't mean that I have to go down and chain myself to the doors of my old elementary school, it just means that I have to do something somewhere else that will then have a ripple effect on my old school or the land it stands or even some of the people effected by this school over the years or even those of a future generation.

It means that the ghosts which haunt my old school will still be there in the future just as they have been in the present or even the past, and I will and others will, still be haunted by them. It means that the kind of teacher I am now makes up for the kind of teachers that I had then, and that every time I and my students laugh together and have fun at school or I show compassion and caring for a child never forgetting the haunts of my own childhood, or I remember that test scores don't mean much except to the powers that be, I am erasing a part of what happened to me as a child and replacing it with an event that encourages someone of another generation to blossom. We do create our own ghosts and hauntings by the way in which we live our lives.

It would not be a surprise me at all to learn that most legislators who seem to be the enemies of education have at least one or more memories of a bad teacher which is effecting their decisions to this day. Behind what appears to be money motivations, are those people scarred by a bad experience in school, whether it was with other students, a teacher or an administrator. People carry their own personal experiences in the school system with them for a lifetime. Although there are others in political circles who remember a good teacher that they had or perhaps even two or three, and try to work towards a better education system but in a more positive way. I hope that every child I taught remembers a good experience, a lot of fun and encouragement, and nothing negative at all. And it was very difficult on my part to maintain these things, as it seems the system itself fights you on this at every hand.

- CHAPTER FIVE -

UTAH'S HAUNTED OLD MILLS & FACTORIES

WEST JORDAN & MIDVALE HISTORIC DISTRICT

GARDNER HISTORIC VILLAGE & OLD MILLS - HENDERSON HOUSE
RED ROCK MEETING HOUSE AND OLD PIONEER CEMETERY
SHERIDAN HILLS STEEL MINING OFFICE - THE BLACK GOOSE

Archibald Gardner married his first of eleven wives in Canada where he had joined the LDS church. At the time persecution and violence against the Mormons was so great in this area that he sent his wife and children to his father's house in the states for two weeks while he prepared for them to go westward. When he was ready to join them he found himself being followed by the Gentile sheriff and posse and the only way to go was across Lake Huron where the ice was breaking up and crowding into the St.Clair River. The crowd gathered there tried to warn him to turn back but with the posse right behind him he knew it was his only chance for freedom. So he said a prayer and began jumping from each block of ice to the next and somehow made it to the United States side safely. Archibald had owned two grist mills, a saw mill, and two hundred acres of land in Canada.

In October 1847, the Gardner family arrived in the Salt Lake Valley and with his brother, Archie built a grist mill in Millcreek Canyon. In 1848, Archibald suggested a plan for ridding the fields of the locust infestation by releasing 1,600 sheep across the fields early in the morning when the crickets were sluggish, claiming it would only take two hours to kill them. Archibald was the first person to settle in Riverton. "He situated his family in a house on a rise above a meadow on the bottom lands. In order to hold the land, he enlarged and extended an irrigation ditch which had previously been made by Hunsaker. Gardner subsequently sold parcels of his land to Pleasant Green Bradford, James Gordon, and Samuel Green. He also moved his family to West Jordan. But the Riverton region was locally referred to as 'Gardnersville' during those early years." (*Riverton: The Story of a Utah Country Town* by Melvin L. Bashmore and Scott Crump, Riverton Historical Society: Riverton, Utah, 1994, p.6.)

Gardner was then called to be an LDS bishop in the West Jordan ward. He began building many irrigation canals and bridges all over this area and after having built several mills - lumber, grist, steam saw, shingle, woolen etc., he began work on his biggest project, the Gardner Flour, Grist, Saw and Mercantile Mill completed in 1853. He also owned the Jordan Silver Mining Company. Gardner fathered 48 children and 270 grandchildren, many of whom lived in the West Jordan area. His first wife Margaret was a lady-in-waiting to a rich family in Quebec and Archie walked 10 miles through the snow just to court her. She drove a span of horses all the way to Salt Lake, but then left her husband for six months when he was called to plural marriage, until Brigham Young had a long talk with her and she accepted the doctrine.

The most interesting of Archie's wives was the beautiful and vibrant Elizabeth Lewis Raglan who, according to record, sang like a meadow lark, drank hard liquor and never bore Archie any children. Hers is the only house left standing on the Mill property, a little red adobe one right next to the museum at Gardner Historic Village. Elizabeth sang in Kansas City dance halls before going on tour and singing in a church in Salt Lake City where Archie first laid eyes on her. Archie got his other wives to accept Elizabeth and her wild ways by promising that she could cook for all of them even though Elizabeth couldn't cook at all. He built her a special house and allowed her to order all of her fashionable clothes from back east while the rest of his wives made their own. She was also the one who got new carpeting and furniture whenever dignitaries stayed at the mill and this was where Brigham Young stayed for the dedication of the Rock Meeting House directly south of the mill.

Elizabeth continued to sing in the local bars and never did become a member of the LDS church. Archibald often hid in her attic whenever the law was looking for him because of his polygamous ways. They were married 17 years and when Elizabeth left Archie, he was quoted as having said, "I lost her in this world, come hell or high water, I'll have her in the next." After having to leave Utah for Star Valley, Wyoming because of polygamy, Archibald lived there with his family for eleven years. At the age of 86, he returned to West Jordan to live with one of his sons. He died at the old St. Mark's Hospital and was heard to say on his deathbed, "Here I go to solve the great mystery."

In 1858, the tiny community of West Jordan wanted to build a meeting house. A log one-room school house was also built just west of where the Red Rock meeting house stands today next to the West Jordan Cemetery. The members hauled red sandstone six miles from the Jordan range and then trimmed the building with granite rock hauled from the mouth of Little Cottonwood Canyon clear across the valley. Those who worked on the meeting house were paid in produce from the resident's private gardens. There was very little money to be had and so when the building was ready for a roof they decided to have a military ball to raise the money, charging a dollar a head. Brigham Young and other officials of the church were invited along with all the officers from Camp Douglas. When the little church was ready for dedication, great preparations were made. All the great dignitaries were invited and new furniture and carpeting were installed, including building a stable just for Brigham Young's horses. The cornerstone was laid in 1861. Additions were made in 1875, including an interior balcony.

In December of 1913, the meeting house was abandoned and went to rack and ruin for a very long time. In 1937, the Utah Daughters of the Pioneers renovated the building and rented the hall out for various functions. With the renovation of the Gardner Historic Village about twenty years ago or so, the Red Rock Meeting House, which is directly across a very busy street now, garnered some interest and various groups now rent it out for private occasions. Just west of this is the West Jordan Cemetery, the first one for the city of West Jordan, though the old pioneer cemetery had served the area for many years between the Gardner mills and the mining headquarters northeast of this.

The old original pioneer cemetery was the first one in the entire valley and the legend of its beginnings has been passed down through the generations through oral tradition. At the "big field" where the Utah State Prison Farm is now located, women and men from the West Jordan community were working the field when a group of Utes came up to them. One of the men in this Native American party was very ill and some of the women went home and cooked foods and made home remedies for this man which they brought out and left with the group. Several days later this group of Indians came to West Jordan bringing the body of the man thrown over a horse. They formed a circle in the field to the east of the mill down on the other side of the Jordan River and began to dig a three feet long and not very deep hole. They then removed his body, folded his legs and arms to his body, bound it tight with rope and placed it in the grave. They placed the food and remedies that the ladies had brought around the body. When asked why they had not given the food or medicines to him, they said that they knew he was going to die and that he could take these things with him as gifts. A few days later they came back with more food for the ladies and spent time at the grave.

Soon several Indians were buried there and then the settlers began burying their dead in the same place as well. When all the mining and processing hit the area in 1862, all sorts of smelters and processing plants sprang up around the several mills that were already there. The people who worked in all of these places lived in little towns all around the area: Sandy City, Midvale, West Jordan, etc. And by 1870, the "Bingham District" got one more boost when the railroad started coming though the area. By 1873, two very large smelters were built by the Jordan River in the big gully past where the one mill stands today. The first two smelters were in Midvale and were called the Sheridan Hill Smelter and the Galena smelter or the Old Jordan Works. In 1902, the United States Steel Mining Company constructed another smelter east of the Jordan River at Bingham Junction. In all there were four smelters strung from Midvale to Murray by 1906 and the pollution problem became a huge factor in these communities. The other mill in the area having to do with mining was the U.S. Gravity Concentrate Mill built in 1914.

Even by 1906, the little pioneer graveyard with a run-down wooden fence around it sat in the center of all this on U.S. Steel property. The Pioneer Cemetery had been an Indian burial ground first. Tea plants and Matrimony vines marked off the corners of the cemetery and Iris bloomed on the southern edge. There were some monuments for family plots that marked the north end of the cemetery. Some of the descendants appealed to the U.S. Smelter to respect this plot of ground. Railroads were routed around it and the company put up steel fence posts and wire cable around it. Finally, in 1906 the Smelter offered to pay for removal of the bodies to other cemeteries in the area. Some families were able to do this, others did not take up the offer or had moved away. So quite a few still rest in this cemetery and at least in 1970, mounds of earth could still be seen there. Midvale created its city cemetery in 1923 and West Jordan fairly quickly began to bury its dead in the new cemetery right next to the old log school house.

Many men and boys came with their wagons and filled in the little swampy river that ran through the middle of the field. They leveled it and in later years lawn and shrubs and trees were planted. The log school house was about 300 yards west of the meeting house and school was held there from 1853 to 1864. Then the meeting house was completed and the school was held in the vestry. Students began to come from all the surrounding towns until the entire meeting house had to be used as a school.

In 1875, the vestry was torn down and the hall was lengthened and widened, and included a basement, kitchen, service area and small balcony which could be reached by some very narrow stairs. In 1885, a new school building was completed and the Red Rock Meeting House was again used only as a church and community meeting hall. In 1913, a new church was built and the meeting house was used as a recreation hall for a few years. Then it became over time, a barn, chicken coop, storage area and occasionally, a resting spot for homeless people. In 1927, the LDS church's basketball teams used it for a practice hall. Finally in 1937, the Archibald Gardner Camp of the Daughters of Utah Pioneers leased and restored the building and renamed it Pioneer Hall. It was then used as a dance hall, social center and church once again. People got quite dressed up and would go there to dance to the music of Moedi Steadman and his orchestra, dancing the Big Apple, the foxtrot and the Lambeth Walk.

In 1970 it was given to the city of West Jordan and can currently be rented out for various functions, though a recent article stated that the church was to be studied for restoration by West Jordan City Council voting in a $7,500 dollar restoration study project. The study will determine how much of the interior is original, how sound the structure is, plan more landscaping around the building and discuss building an annex with a kitchen and restrooms. Many older residents of West Jordan are excited about the prospect of restoring the old meeting house as they can remember reunions, basketball games, weddings, dances and church services that were held in the old building. Calling the place one of the roots of the community and that not many pioneer items were left to preserve in West Jordan, a former member of the historical commission there, said that the city needed to preserve the ones that they had.

A favorite story about the Red Rock Meeting House happened in 1909 when a dance was held there. The benches were moved to the vestry and mothers put their sleeping babies there while they danced. At this particular dance a mother picked up the wrong baby and drove all the way home before discovering this. She had to go to several homes until she found her own child. The two babies had on exactly the same shawl and she had never moved it from the baby's face for fear of waking her.

Both the West Jordan Cemetery and the Red Rock Meeting House have their own share of ghostly happenings, though getting people to talk about their experiences there is difficult. The Mill and Elizabeth Raglin's house, on the other hand, have a history of ghostly happenings. However, all of the other old farm houses at Gardner Historic Village were transported from other areas around the valley and so knowing their individual histories would be almost impossible to recover. One has to question whether any ghostly happenings are the result of the individual house and its individual history, or are the result of the land on which they stand. The land did house other mill and smelter buildings many, many years ago with certainly their share of tragedies.

Many people visit the place, being drawn to the mystical quality of the surroundings and the experiences they have there. Experiences have included voice phrases and words, objects flying across rooms from high shelves and then sliding across the floor to a specific spot as though drawn by a giant magnet, and the stories told visitors as they stand in various places. Clerks in the mill, which is now a furniture store, tell of phone lines lighting up when no one is in the building, first one and then all three. Most often, there is no one on the line or when individuals head towards the phone, all three lights will go off at once. Mirrors in the upstairs rooms will turn against the walls, and when the clerks turn them around, they may go back in twenty minutes and find the mirrors turned back around.

In the northeast side of the basement rooms there have been many times when beds that were made would be all messed up and the mirrors turned around. The clerks will fix them, turn the mirrors around, go back down to check and everything would be messed up again. Most of these happenings occurred when the store was closed and no one was there except the store workers who were all together in another part of the store. These various clerks have their own theories about the mirrors - that ghosts can't be seen at all or maybe can only be seen in mirrors and therefore want such spectral characters out of the store altogether. One bed had a canopy and drapes all around it. Something would draw the drapes back over and over again. An electrical engineer working on the building alone one evening had such an awful time that he now will only come during the daylight hours and will not go down to the basement at all . It seems that he cut off all the electrical power and that things either kept running anyway, or came back on of their own accord!

Most interesting is the story of the two girls who were putting things together for a big celebration at the village the next day. They worked late into the night hauling things over from the storage building to decorate for the next day's festivities and suddenly realized that it was actually 2 a.m. in the morning. They took the last of the things into the mill and then heard faint music and voices; it sounded like a party going on. But when they opened the doors, all of the music, laughter and voices immediately stopped. Apparently many parties did go on in the mill at one time or another in its history. Another time an employee was alone late at night and heard a child's footsteps on the second floor. She went upstairs and searched all over but could find nothing. She came down to the main floor and heard the footsteps again, running back and forth above her. She went up again and again but could find nothing. Finally, it scared her enough that she quickly locked up and went home.

One manager of the shop in the Henderson House, not purchased by the Hendersons until 1919, tells of many strange happenings there. She herself is fascinated by the independent and beautiful Elizabeth Raglin. No one really likes to be in the house alone. It was built in 1863 out of adobe brick and has two-foot thick walls. Over the years strange things have happened there, too. It is presently a dress shop and thus far has been one kind of clothing store or other. So it is a bit ironic that Elizabeth loved fashionable dresses and a dress shop would have suited her just fine. Some clothing items come off the rack, hang in mid air for a few seconds and then fall to the ground or whirl a few feet forward before falling. One day a whole row of necklaces just started to sway back and forth together on their rack. Another day employees heard knocking and went all over the house trying to find the source and couldn't. Sometimes when coming into the shop first thing in the morning, staff will find a pile of dresses on the floor, still on their hangers.

One night the owner came to the house late at night to do an inventory, and heard someone singing. She searched about and when she got to the steps to the second floor the singing stopped. The second floor and stairs are newer additions and so to hear footsteps on them, which they often do without a person attached to them, is very puzzling. Often those footsteps are right behind employees as they go up the stairs. Archibald did have some way of hiding in the attic upstairs though, whenever the authorities came looking for him because of his polygamous practices. People speculate that it might be him or maybe a later owner's grandparent or an invalid who had to stay in that upstairs room a lot, because every time the door to that room is closed, it is found open the next morning. There is a corner chair where, over the years, people must have read books or contemplated a lot because people have seen something there or felt it. People will hear someone call their name yet it seems to happen more often in the winter months than in the summer. Just as the footsteps and knocking noises are heard more in the winter, when it is colder and there are fewer customers around.

Archie never got official permission to marry Elizabeth and one can tell quite plainly that she was the favored wife. Four years before she left Archibald for good, she gave up her wild ways to care for one of the other very young wives who became ill and also her three children. It took that four years for the woman to get back on her feet. During this time Archibald gave each of his wives a parcel of land, making sure that Elizabeth got the most prime piece of property. While the other wives planned houses or gardens on their land, Elizabeth traded her piece of land away for a barrel of whiskey. She also continued to sing in the local bars and on many an occasion Archie would go and find her and drag her back to her house. Once the other sister wife was well, which was seventeen years into her marriage with Archibald, Elizabeth ran off for good and no one seems to know just where she ended up.

All in all, this whole little area has quite a history and lots of stories to tell from the old mill itself to Elizabeth's little adobe house, to the various transplanted houses now there. Three of the log cabin houses came from a little almost ghost town in Tooele county and all of the houses have interesting histories of their own with at least one of them bringing its haunting with it. In this shop the clerk was busy in the back of the shop when she heard the front doorknob rattling. She went out by the cash register and then heard it rattle again. This time she was only two feet away from the door when the doorknob began to turn completely around clockwise and then counterclockwise. She ran to the door and opened it and of course no one was there. She sold among other things antique replica doorknobs and had some samples hanging outside her shop, nailed to the wall. Somebody stole them one day and this was upsetting to her too.

In this same shop, although with different owners and different wares to sell, several of us witnessed a bottle of Lilies of the Field body wash float off the top shelf above our heads stay suspended there for a few seconds and then propel itself across the room almost hitting an elderly lady and landing on the floor where it slid as though guided by some magnetic force to the other end of the house's wood floor. Half the people who witnessed it said that it didn't happen that way and surmised that a train going by had simply knocked the bottle off its shelf where it fell directly down. Four of us stuck to what we saw, especially the elderly woman who had had to duck in order for the bottle not to hit her. We surmised that someone of the "spirit nature" in that shop didn't like elderly women with dark hair for it was definitely aimed at her head.

Recently, the owner of the Henderson House has decided to sell it. She began having sales on her inventory and talking about it around the store once in a while. At first there had been a long period of no activity at all in the store, so when things began to happen it was kind of a surprise. But now as she sells the store, she has had several incidents clearly indicating the spirits displeasure at her departure. At first things just flew off shelves, like a stack of papers or papers in a box moving around. Then the other clerk and a visitor or two had experiences on the stairs to the second floor, where they could both hear the footsteps and feel the presence of someone behind them as they went up and down the stairs. Then one of them was touched by it, and the other went up to turn the lights off and felt it so strongly that she had to just leave them on. Finally, the owner had put a little blue for sale sign on the door with a yellow backing paper behind it and it hung on the inside of the door. She locked the door and went to lunch. When she returned, she found that the for sale sign had been ripped into five shredded pieces and the paper behind it had not been touched. She found a second sign that she had prepared lying upstairs, and it too had been shredded into five strips. She asked me what I thought and I just said, "Well, I think that they are pretty much hitting you over the head with the message that you should not leave your shop!"

I did find several very old ghost stories about the mill itself, showing that such stories have been circulating for years and years. One around 1850 told of an aunt or sister wife who always seemed to have enough flour to make anything that was needed. Even when there was doubt that there would be enough, more flour always appeared in the bin. Every 'tramp" that came by headed for the gold mines was fed, still more flour appeared and it was always attributed to their faith in God. In another incident in 1893, an old man recalled this happening to him when he worked at the mill that year. One night the saw mill had been running extra heavily all day and it was shut down late. The two men both went to sleep in the next room as it was their duty to guard the mill at night. Suddenly the mill started up and was running full tilt in the middle of the night. They both jumped up and ran to the door and opened it looking for who had done this. When the door opened everything stopped. No lumber was gone and nothing had been sawed. So the men went back to bed and the sawmill started up again. They kept checking, and the mill always went silent when they opened the door to look in. This went on all night but the men stuck it out until morning.

Another store manager related a story about a man who had an experience on the property recently, but she was worried that the man, who is very reputable, might not want me to write it down. I feel safe enough, however, because similar experiences have been reported by other witnesses for over a hundred years These versions were also written down. There are several versions of the same phenomena from the late 1800s, the 1930s and 40s and again in the 1960s. The modern day version is no different from the rest. A man is alone on the property in the middle of the night for some reason and he hears noises in the distance. He begins walking towards where he hears the noise and suddenly he realizes that he is hearing the sounds of a mill running and that all the lights are on in the mill and that there is activity going on all around it. He then sees people working and the mill sounds become deafening. It is as though he was viewing a moving picture of the sights and sounds of the mill from a hundred or so years ago. Just as all of it registers in his mind, the mill suddenly stops and everything vanishes as quickly as it had appeared. The man is shaken and confused by what he has just seen, and so doesn't tell anyone for fear people will think he is crazy. Sooner or later, though, the story comes out and others get to hear about it, over and over again, decade after decade. Though no one ever thinks to link all these events together, the mill never changes. It is only we who are transformed, coming and going from one generation to the next.

Archibald built more than 35 mills in his lifetime, 13 of them in Utah. They were built very strong, without nails, with only mortises and pins, and yet hardly quivered when in operation. He located and recorded some of the biggest water rights in Utah and yet sold them all. When all the mining moved in, he would have been a very rich man if he had kept them. Today the Gardner Historic Village is a great place to visit with all sorts of shops and special events, even Moonlight Madness sales which seem appropriate for all that must have gone on around this whole area. There is even a lot of decorating a few weeks before Halloween when it is more appropriate to be telling ghost stories. There are both transplanted and continuous ghosts, making one think that this story should be placed among stories about haunted places rather than old mills.

Gardner Historic Village also owns The Black Goose across the Jordan River to the east and on a hill on the other side in Midvale. It is now an antique furniture store, but once was the former Sheridan Hills Mining Offices, which later became part of the U.S. Steel Mining Offices. As far as one can tell, its backyard is both an ancient Indian burial ground and the first pioneer cemetery in the valley. One can go upstairs, look out a west window and look right down on a single stone base. Recent news described how the city of Midvale is, after many years of neglect, not only renovating this graveyard but dismantling an old pioneer log cabin that might have otherwise been demolished to make way for a recreation center. The cabin is being moved to the pioneer graveyard as well. The 1860s cabin is being rebuilt and restored to sit beside the graveyard where the last actual gravestone disappeared in the 1930s. There is a legend that an Indian chief was buried at this place mounted on his horse, though there is little proof of such a thing. The Indians buried here were probably interred west of the pioneer cemetery on a plateau overlooking the Jordan River.

One hundred thirty-three graves were identified by a team of archaeologists who surveyed the cemetery three years ago, though many may be empty because some bodies were moved when the steel company made its offer to buy the property. The burials took place between the 1850s and 1897 when the new cemetery was established. When the team members surveyed the area they had to wear disposable coveralls, steel-toed boots, hard hats and respirators because the whole area is contaminated with the run off from the steel mills. One man fell into a grave pit as he was walking along and it took ten minutes for him to struggle out of the hole. When each grave site was located, the archeologists then probed for coffins with a long metal pole, though even this was not always accurate. The cemetery will have a new fence with a border of wild flowers and grasses and these same grasses will also be placed on the roof of the cabin of David and Sarah Drown, the parents of ten children back in the 1850s. The cabin will have new doors and shutters and a new stone foundation, which David and Sarah would have appreciated. The pioneer cemetery will at long last have the respect and consideration that should have been afforded it a long time ago. ('"Little House on the Park, Cemetery Getting New Life" by John Keahey, *The Salt Lake Tribune*, November 25, 1999, F-6.)

The mining offices above this graveyard kept rooms for visiting officials, for a doctor's office and for other purposes during all the years it has stood there. It is no surprise that such stories are told there! Winter time after dark seems to be the most active time for haunts and ghosts. There are two phone lines that ring and nobody is on the other end. Often there are sounds of furniture moving slightly or the knobs on the fronts of the drawers seem to be bumping against the wood in a sort of rhythm. When employees go to check no one is there. Once, some candlesticks flew off a table; they didn't fall, they flew. The clerk was alone and no one had touched them. The manager was working alone late one night and a whole stack of papers just flew off her desk as though someone was angry with her. There were no drafts and her feeling was that the spirits wanted her to go home and so she did.

All in all, this whole area is very interesting and really has wonderful places to visit as well. Just make sure you are prepared for something to happen when you least expect it. Also be prepared for others to tell you that what you saw didn't happen, and that you were just imagining it! Because after all, the mining offices oversee a graveyard long neglected and forgotten and beyond this an ancient Indian burial ground looks down upon it. Although at present the graveyard is being spruced up with a white picket fence and the movement of an old log cabin near it, so that one day soon we may drive into it and see what the first cemetery looked like. Above are the mining offices where all manner of things took place. All this is on only one side of the little valley the Jordan River has made, a valley once full of smelters, mills and workers, and other people who came and went, exposed to tailings and things that go bump in the night!

HAUNTED OLD GRANITE PAPER MILL

BUTLER--LITTLE COTTONWOOD CANYON

Construction of the Old Mill, or Granite Paper Mill, was begun in 1861 under the supervision of Willard Richards. Two of the masons were James H. Hoyle and James Muir. Machinery for the mill was hauled across the country and according to Brigham Young, would be 'The best to be obtained and will cost 20,000 thousand dollars." It was built of granite blocks from the temple quarry in Little Cottonwood Canyon. In 1863, operators of the mill announced that there could be no edition of *The Desert News* until the wheel was repaired. Part of the wheel had broken off and floated down stream. "Mill wheel gone again. While locking up this issue we have no hope of being able to issue the paper next week, we are told that a portion of the water wheel of the paper mill has gone down stream and left us without paper. We trust the wheel will shortly be repaired and we thereby again be enabled to accommodate our readers with the promptness so customary with us when not hindered by circumstances beyond our control." ("Paper Mills," *Heart Throbs of the West*, Kate B. Carter, editor, Daughters of the Pioneers, Volume 3, 1941, page 31.)

People were asked to save and gather rags to be turned in to the paper mill for 5 cents a pound. White rags produced a very high quality paper but these were rare because there were no bleaching agents then, so most of the paper was gray from the colored rags that had to be used. When any article of clothing became lost someone was sure to make the comment that a nickel was being made at the paper mill. During the first fifteen months of operation, 35,024 pounds of rags produced 28,997 pounds of paper of various qualities at the Granite Paper Mill.

In 1881, the Granite Mill burned for the first time, though the cause of this first fire has never been determined. The first mill burned to the ground and a new mill was built on the site in 1882-1883. This mill operated for about ten years and then a second fire severely damaged this building on April 1, 1893. This fire supposedly started from a night watchman's lantern being turned over. The roof and all of the interior were burned, but a few renovations were made after this. Still paper was never made again at the mill. By then the process of making paper from wood pulp was perfected and paper could be shipped from the east. The Granite Paper Mill was never fully re-built after that and Utah was no longer a high ranking paper mill state again. Thomas Howard was the father of papermaking in Utah. He came from Oxfordshire, England, converted to Mormonism while still a young man and married in 1838, but his first wife died only 6 years later. He married a Martha Savage and emigrated to the United States with his 7 member family and then came across the plains from Council Bluffs. The family first ran a tollgate in Red Butte Canyon and then eventually Howard and his partner Thomas Hollis started a small papermaking concern on the Temple Block. He eventually helped to plan and run the first Granite Paper Mill at the mouth of Big Cottonwood Canyon.

The huge four story building sat abandoned and vandalized until about 1928, when J.B. Walker bought and rebuilt it into a club. It became a locally famous dance and dinner resort. There had always been a brewery near by operated by Philander Butler which added to the allure of the place. As far as is known, the dinner and dance resort operated until the early fifties, when another fire burned the inside. Business had already begun to drop off. After this the Old Mill had a series of promoters trying various things such as a disco dance floor in the 70s; and in the 80s there was the Dickens Festival, the Folk Dancing Festival, various fairs, and finally of late, an annual spook alley. But there has never been a solid renovation and steady business since the dinner resort which my parents remember going to in 1938. There were a series of fires which started the curse part of its legend and those who want to try a venture of one kind or another there seemed to run into one kind of problem or another. The hauntings at the Old Mill have caused many an adventurer to leave the premises earlier than planned and the curse on the place seems to ruin any owner's good intentions.

When the rebuilt paper mill burned for the second time in 1893, two employees died in the fire. Another version of this story is that the two were caretakers who started arguing and in the course of this one of them knocked over a lantern. Each of them had a dog but only one of the dogs was killed. The dog that died can be heard barking inside the mill at night. The second big fire involved two vagrants who started a small fire to keep warm. They also had a dog with them and were camping on the third floor. One of them swore that he heard a voice telling him to wake up and he did escape the fire while the other fellow was found in the fireplace wrapped around his dog after the fire was put out. Both fires, though years apart, are said to have happened around the same time of year. There is also at least one story of a young girl committing suicide there over an unrequited love when it was a dinner and dance resort. The Old Mill has several steep staircases and she apparently jumped from the top floor into the atrium below. This story is one which circulated in the 1960s and may or may not be true.

Another story is told of a much more recent incident when another caretaker committed suicide there. This was after the only activity in the old mill was the annual spook alley. The caretaker and his wife lived in an apartment on the grounds. He had apparently been upset in his personal life as well as having difficulties maintaining the mill like he felt it should be. He played Russian roulette with his revolver in front of his wife. So it is possible that there are at least seven ghosts, if not more, haunting the Old Mill, two of them dogs! It is also true that a famous parapsychologist slept over night there once and wrote up his report of shadowy figures, lights, sounds, footsteps, and voices recorded on tape. People who have tried to sleep overnight in the old mill have been frightened out of their wits or at least could never stay the entire night, especially on the third floor where the cold spot is.

The south end of the building has a large open room with a balcony above it which leads to a tower and this end is locked. The north end is three stories with a sort of atrium and outside pavilion or deck at the top of the hill. The north end is where all the more current groups hold their events. On the third story of the north end is where most of the ghosts have been sighted or heard or felt. The large brick wall on that floor can really put on a moving shadow play at sunset. It is rumored that underneath the mill are several tunnels which were used to carry water into the original old mill. When I was there, not only the third floor but the outside patio and the tower which one can only view from a distance, gave off those familiar eerie feelings, coldness and the feeling of being touched on the hand or the back of the neck. But I have never been to the spook alley; the real ones are enough for me!

In the 1970s, the Old Mill was surrounded by a beautiful valley of cottonwood trees and oak scrub brush; we went to several events at the old mill during that time. There was a small country and western bar up the road and the old brewery still stood next to the mill. The bar is still in place, and has become a quaint little place called The Hog Wallow Inn with flowers all around it. The old brewery is now long gone and a huge subdivision of quite expensive and large houses, called The Old Mill Estates, has swallowed up this whole little valley and the old haunted mill is completely engulfed by it all. A high wire fence encircles the mill and lots of small pieces of equipment and junk sit around it. The beautiful natural surroundings that so many enjoyed on their romantic dates to the club are all but forgotten. Many keep hoping that someone will try again to go against the curse on the place before it is too late and try to bring it back to its former glory days.

The Old Mill could be replaced at any time by another home or two, and so another wonderful old building that carries a lot of the history of this valley with it would be lost. The irony being that while all the huge corporate buildings, offices, subdivisions, restaurants and even a golf course have their names linked to that of the old Mill's, the old mill sits in the middle of all this abandoned, used privately as a storehouse for large equipment behind chain linked fences. It is crumbling into disrepair in the middle of all of its namesakes. Its ghosts occupying the premises and its curse continuing to discourage others from restoring it.

FIVE OLD PIONEER MILLS

BENSON GRIST MILL - CHASE MILL
KNUDSEN - BICKNELL - WOLVERTON MILLS

GENERAL MILL HISTORY

Studying all the mills around, even just in the Salt Lake Valley, can become as overwhelming as searching for the lost gold and silver mines in Utah. The so called "Old Mill" which is famous for its ghosts and hauntings and the Gardner Historic Village, now a wonderful memorial to these mills in many ways, were easy to write about, but not so, the hundreds of mills throughout the state, both extant and now gone forever. So I felt some relief in deciding to write up a general introduction to those mills which Brigham Young sanctioned and oversaw in the early days. Then, it will be interesting to personalize stories about them by selecting several mills which represent important perspectives on or aspects of all the mills, or even just a personal intuitive interest in them.

Visiting two of the still-standing mills has resulted in some intuitive impressions. The Chase mill is considered the first mill in the valley of any importance and is located in Liberty Park which is a large city park similar to Central Park in New York City but not so huge. The Benson Grist Mill is the last standing mill which not only informs one about all of the workings of a mill with all of the original parts still inside the old building, but also shows how a community spirit of renovation has brought about a successful and lucrative set of projects for the community of Stansbury Park. It was somewhat easy to select the Knudsen Mill, which no longer exists and is covered by modern homes, as a representative of efforts on the part of ancestral families and historic preservationists to personalize a history of mills and milling by putting up markers. Last are a couple of mills found in or near small towns around the state.

Many of the first pioneers in Utah had come from the leading milling areas and were acquainted with the most advanced technology which the industry offered at the time. Some of them brought milling equipment with them, though without access to good transportation and hard cash, milling in Utah was much more difficult. Millstones for grinding came first, and then bolting machines which had to be turned by hand. Back east great improvements in milling had taken place between 1790 and 1870, such as the conveyor, the elevator, the "hopper-boy" which spread the flour for cooling, the drill, and the kiln drier. The pioneers had none of these conveniences at first. The plan for building mills was, on the other hand, very well-organized and planned by Brigham Young. Councils of local citizens were formed which regulated in each area the building of mills, dams and canals. Crop rotations very quickly raised the demand for more and more mills of all kinds: sawmills, grist mills, flour mills, woolen mills, sugar, carding, dye, and cotton mills.

As already noted, the first grist mill in the valley was begun by Charles Crimson in 1847 in City Creek Canyon where Memory Grove Park is now located. The first sawmill was built in the same year in Warm Springs and was soon relocated to Milicreek Canyon by Archibald Gardner. The second gristmill was built by John Neff in Millcreek Canyon, becoming the first flour mill as well; he was selling flour by the following year. Then Archibald built a second flour mill in the same canyon in 1848. Isaac Chase's grist mill is considered the fourth mill to be built though technically, with Archibald having two mills, it was actually the fifth one. From there, mills of all sorts began to be built all over the valley and eventually throughout the state, as groups were sent out to settle certain areas. The Benson-Grist mill, which was both a saw and grist mill right next to a tannery, was built in 1850 by Ezra Taft Benson. Several other operators erected a similar structure on the Mill Pond or Twin Creek which flowed north of Tooele.

Mills began with hand-powered millstones or horse-powered mills. They were crude and makeshift until the first water-powered mills were built. Eventually multiple-use mills were developed, in which, for example, rough hewn logs and flour could be produced in the same mill. Automated mills were introduced when an Easterner, Oliver Evans received patents on various inventions which ushered in a new age of milling back east and eventually in Utah. Then came the turbine mills which by 1880 powered at least 75 percent of the mills in Utah. Finally, metal roller mills came into use, powering nearly all the mills by the turn of the century.

CHASE MILL - LIBERTY PARK

The Chase sawmill was operating by December 1847 and the flour mill was being built by the fall of 1848. During the grasshopper invasion and famine of that winter, flour was given out to those who knocked at their door, even when the Chase family themselves were low on flour. Brigham Young obtained permission from his own council to build this flour mill and construction began on the second Chase Mill in February of 1849. Isaac Chase was part owner and manager of the mill which took three years to build and opened in 1852. In the meantime, from the lumber from his sawmill, Isaac Chase built a temporary shanty for his family to live in. Soon after this he built a log cabin and eventually by 1856 completed the two-story adobe house which stands today in Liberty Park perhaps only a block or two from the mill. During these years the Chase family continued to supply free flour to those in need. In 1859, Brigham Young Jr. took over the management of the mill and moved his family into the Chase home while Isaac Chase sold his half to Brigham Young to pay off bills. In 1861, Isaac Chase died in his second adobe home located just across from the old Salt Lake Theater.

The mill continued to operate until 1877 when Brigham Young died and his heirs sold it to the city of Salt Lake in order to establish a city park. During these years from 1877 to 1899, the mill was used as a barn for zoo animals housed in Liberty Park and the home was used for park management offices. In 1899 after a year of bickering as to whether to tear both buildings down or not, citizens won out and a building contractor took on the task of restoring both the home and mill for the city. In 1914, a huge newspaper article appeared concerning the mill and home which garnered some renewed interest in the mill. But it was not until 1933 when the Daughters of the Pioneers began their own campaign to preserve these two buildings that some positive changes took place. By 1935, the Chase home and mill and certain historic articles were dedicated, commemorating their 85 year existence with the city, state and LDS church participating in the ceremony. In 1952, renewed interest came when several publications about the mill appeared, and in 1964, the Chase home was designated as a museum by the City Parks Commissioner for the DUP. Recent visitors had been sorely disappointed when they find the place and observe that it is no longer a museum and is all locked up. In 1978, three separate archeological excavations took place at the mill and the DUP published a wonderful small book on its history.

The home was sadly in need of repairs when I first saw it, apparently rented out to various groups such as the Arts Council with a big banner promising a reopening in 2002 for the Olympics as an arts center. Later it had scaffolding and plastic all over it. Now the 147-year-old mansion has been totally renovated at a cost of $900,000 from monies supplied by the state, city and LDS church. Rewired, shored up, refurbished with new plumbing, heating and air conditioning, it is now the home of the Utah Folk Arts Foundation and displays quilts, blankets, saddles, origami and other pieces from different cultures around the state. It is quite an attractive art gallery and made the news recently, only because it is not yet handicapped accessible and someone complained. The second floor can only be reached by climbing steep stairs and there is no room for an elevator. A video of the exhibits is planned for the upstairs, so that those who can't climb the stairs can view it comfortably from the first floor. Admission is free and it will be interesting to see if the spirits who live there decide to visit.

Isaac Chase and his wife Phoebe moved into their home in 1856. Their daughter Louisa drove an ox team across the plains with her wagon loaded down by the millstones and mill irons for their flour mill. Their home has 8 rooms, a large kitchen with a built-in Dutch oven and glass window panes which were freighted across the plains. Park employees used the home until 1964 when the DUP began their museum and until about two years ago park employees and Arts Council employees occupied a portion of the building. As one walks around the outside of the home, one may receive personal spectral impressions. There are reports that a spectral young woman often looks outside the second story window towards the mill waiting for someone to come home from a day's work. She is a wife and mother who is upset about the disarray in her home now. She wants the home repaired and all the park visitors to go away. She lost her favorite child and mourns this loss and cannot leave the upper floor for some reason, though she occasionally makes a foray or two down to the kitchen. She had 3 more children and did not spend her last days in the house, and this was also upsetting to her.

Other strange goings-on that I intuited include something down the well with valuable historical information that needs to be retrieved or perhaps already has been. There are voices and activity on the second story front porch where parties and summer time activities formerly took place but none on the ground level porch. People sat out there, had good times and can't forget them. The upper left hand window in the front and the back storage room have constant activity. The female resident ghost changes things around when she wants attention. The woman seems to have been a daughter who loved the mill and did not want to leave and it is possible that she is not a Chase, but a Young.

In the mill itself, information is sketchy about outside activities, just as it is from the home. One man was injured and almost died there. In another incident, three men ran out from the mill either to avoid injury or to protest something that was unsafe. They stood outside the mill and two of them argued with the other one quite heatedly. In still another story, a man had a millstone break his arm. There is a general impression that old memories or pictures are stored in the mill's walls, which have yet to show us many more interesting and marvelous things. But beyond these sorts of private impressions, some believe that there is an actual spirit in the Chase home to this day.

BENSON GRIST MILL - STANSBURY PARK

The Benson Grist Mill in Stansbury Park, on the other hand, has very little out-of-this-world activity in it except for the feeling that there is one old man who might hang around deep in the bowels of the multi-storied mill and the unrestored tannery next door, which apparently has strange activity in it. However, there is one story about the mill which involves a small group of ghost hunters who got permission from the owners to stay overnight in the mill. The mill is several stories high and it would take very high ladders for someone to climb up to where the windows are in the mill. It would also take several people to get all the windows at such height all around the mill. Since it was in the summer time the mill was very hot, and so the ghost hunters asked the owners if they can open all the windows on the top floors. The owners gave them permission to do this and in the middle of the night as the ghost hunters slept away peacefully, they were all suddenly awakened to the sharp sound of every single window in the place slamming shut at the same instant. This was enough to get the ghost hunters to pack up and leave for the night. If pranksters have been involved, it would have taken a massive amount of planning, equipment, and amazing stealth and quiet, to carry off this trick. In my opinion, it is more likely that the old apparition who ran the mill didn't think his building was secure enough with the windows wide-open.

What makes this mill so interesting is the fact that its entire interior has survived intact to the present and one can actually see the whole process step by step as those who manage the mill have spent time making exhibits of each step of the process. The other thing is that the whole community worked together not only to save it, preserve it, and to build a historic tourist town of transplanted log houses and even a blacksmith's shop, but they also began a small museum and various seasonal events built around the theme of the mill. There is now an ever-growing pioneer pageant every year in late summer with its own local cast and musical score which is really pretty good. A resident ghost entertains the kids. There is a great build-up story by the tour guide, and then when the children are told to look down a particular shaft, only a plastic glow-in-the-dark cookie-cutter ghost smiles back up at them through the darkness!

A sawmill had already been built up the canyon when plans for the grist mill were begun in 1850. There were many snowbound Gentile immigrants that winter stranded in Salt Lake City and one of them, Lorenzo D. Custer, took on the job of building the grist mill and impounding the water of the Mill Pond for Ezra T. Benson and his partners. There are two accounts of Custer's death, one of which seems more plausible. The first is that the Goshute Indians in the area were blamed for stealing oxen and horses from Custer and that a posse had arrested some of the Indians. On his way back with the posse, Custer was killed by the Indians. The real story is probably that Lorenzo had brought suit against Ezra Taft Benson for non-payment of services and that friends of Benson's offered to help Custer recover his horses and oxen and on the way back in the darkness, he was shot in the back. Legend even links Orrin Porter Rockwell to this event, and those interested may want to read the later Skull Valley section to learn more about these rumors. Suffice to say that here is another spirit who is perhaps roaming this area, seeking a bit of retribution for his unfortunate demise.

In 1851, the grist mill was in partial operation when three Lee brothers arrived in Tooele County. They were the artisans who completed the complex woodwork of mortised timbers and wooden pegs and green leather, which led to the mills completion in 1854. The mill was known for its honesty and produced 200 bushels per day. By 1860, the mill had one male employee and one run of millstones producing 1200 barrels of flour, 7200 pounds of bran, and 56,000 pounds of corn meal. By 1862, Benson was called to settle Cache Valley and Lorenzo D. Young and John Rowberry took ownership of the mill. In the 1870s, three men acquired the mill. The tannery next door came into existence in 1857. It became the Summerhays Wool Pullery with a very potent smell. After several fires, the tannery closed in the 1940s. The two foot thick stone wall foundations exist today and it is a pity that the town cannot find a way to restore at least some of this huge complex of buildings as well. But then there is nothing very romantic about a house of death like a tannery. One can be both drawn to and repelled by the tannery which has a strong sense of a man, and not a very pleasent man, standing in the middle of its ruins gazing back up as one stands in the high back windows of the mill. He seems to be from a more distant time and his tattered clothes smell of the tannery. Walking down through the place exposes one to whatever it is he wants one to see in the mind's eye - things most people have absolutely no desire to see or smell!

By 1900 only a few families resided at the mill and in 1919, ownership changed again from the Richville Milling Company to Joshua Reuben Clark. J. Reuben was an attorney who owned lots of property in Tooele County and a Mease Houtz ran the mill for him. The flour was sold under the title of the Bonneville Grain and Milling Company. In 1928, two brothers leased the mill from J. Reuben and ran it for ten years with Oscar Jones as the miller brother. The mill ceased flour production in 1939 and Samuel Clark, J. Reuben's brother, turned it into a feed and poultry mill that began operations in 1946. In 1955, the machinery stopped for the final time and the building sat idle until 1970 when the Clarks sold it to the Terracor Corporation. The community of Stansbury Park was built and the mill was placed on the historic register in 1972. It was not until 1983 that the community banded together to do something about the mill before it too was gone forever. It was an 8 year restoration project but in 1985 Terracor donated the mill and 7 acres of land around it to the restoration committee via Tooele County.

An interesting tale associated with the mill - another one of those unsolved mysteries of Utah - is yet another story of lost gold. The first man who operated the mill liked to graze his cattle just east of it. One day when he went looking for his wandering livestock and looked up one of the draws he saw an outcropping of pure gold. He marked the spot and waited to tell the Prophet about it. Brigham Young told him not to tell anyone about it and that God would let people find it when the Mormons really needed the money. On his deathbed he told his family about its location southeast of the mill. The news spread like it does in small towns around the area and people began looking for it. Many men at the local smelter spent their weekends looking for it. Another story is that two young men looking for their cattle in the area went up a particular draw in the canyon and their horses started acting up so that they could not seem to control them. So they turned around and came back out but could find no evidence of rattlers or a mountain lion, etc. They believed that it had been a supernatural warning not to look for cattle in that area because maybe it wasn't time for anyone to find the gold. A visit to the old Benson Grist Mill is well worth anyone's time, even though the spirits there seem to have left for higher ground!

BICKNELL GRISTMILL - BICKNELL

Just outside the town of Bicknell in Wayne County, one can see the Bicknell Gristmill. It was one of four such mills built in the area but it is the only one left standing. It was built in 1890 by Niels Hansen who was a Danish carpenter. Hans Peter Nielson was the first miller. It has two stories above the ground with a sandstone foundation. Like the Benson mill it still has much of its original equipment such as stone burrmills, a turbine, gears and shafts, wooden flumes, roller and bolting machinery, etc. and it is in the same style as the Benson mill though a bit smaller. It is the only other mill in Utah today which still has all of its original machinery intact. The mill was in operation until Nielson died in 1909 and then three brothers ran it. After a series of other owners for shorter periods of time, the mill ceased operation in 1935. Unlike the Benson mill it has not been restored, which makes for more of a chance of sensing the feelings of the place since there are usually not a lot of others around. (*The History Of Wayne County* by Miriam B. Murphy Utah State Historical Society 1999, pp. 193-94.)

In Cynthia Larsen Bennett's *Roadside History of Utah*, put out by Mountain Press Publishing from Missoula, Montana, she is quoted on page 229 as saying that the old mill was "Not just a place to grind wheat for flour and animal feeds, it also had an old fireplace adjacent to it that was an ideal spot for socializing, roasting hot dogs, and occasional romancing." In other words even though the mill is on private land, many a teen or young adult got to the place anyway to enjoy both its benefits and its apparitions with friends.

KNUDSEN MILL - KNUDSEN'S CORNER - THE COTTON BOTTOM

I came across the Knudsen Millstone marker on my way home one day. Just about anyone in the Salt Lake Valley can find such a marker or such a history in their area of town if they wish to notice them. Our entire state is riddled not only with the whispers of lost mines but also with the real ruins of all sorts of mills, some only a memory, others with a bit of foundation left and a very few whose buildings are at least preserved, even though their interiors have been vandalized greatly. The Benson Grist Mill may have survived vandals because it was in an isolated area and once the town was there the citizens were pretty vigilant about protecting it. The old miller, Oscar Jones, visited it in 1985 and said he could see many things that had been taken anyway, including the water wheel which he knew to be in Grantsville and also lumber and metal tools which he knew for a fact had furnished a few basements in the area. A crew of men about 12 years ago went out to this mill in the evening hoping to get some things and found instead a whole group of locals working on its restoration.

It seems necessary to mention what the Knudsen Mill says on its plaque, only because there ought to be a lot more plaques, and people ought to be aware of just where all these mills might have been. The Knudsen Flour Mill was established in 1878 by Rasmus Christian Knudsen who was a millwright and master joiner from Alborg, Denmark. He walked across the plains so that his wife and two small children could ride. He first built the Mork Jeff Flour Mill in Heber City, sawmills in Big Cottonwood Canyon and several other mills around the state. He also loved to build windmills. But the Knudsen Mill was his and where his family lived.

The huge millstone, believed to be the largest and first pearing stone west of the Mississippi, has been cemented upright into a stone fence under which is buried the foundation of the old mill. In the center of the millstone is the plaque about his life and a poem written by his grandson entitled "The Millstead Grove" by Darwin Knudsen, 1977. Rasmus carved the millstone from a large piece of hard quarzite hauled from Farmington by six yoke of oxen. A second millstone stood on top of the first which caused a scissoring action through which the barley was ground in curved furrows called "sickle dressing" that removed the husks from the barley. The mill operated for 30 years, grinding white and graham flour, cornmeal, pearled barley, cracked wheat and steel-cut oats, and winning awards for excellence. The DUP put this plaque up in 1996 with a picture of the old mill, mentioning that both Knudsen's Grove (established in 1912) and Knudsen's Corner (established in 1919) would not have been named as such, but for the old mill.

In the poem, a 5 year old grandson remembers visiting his grandfather at the mill and watching his grandfather carry buckets of water from the stream to water the pines which he had planted there. The pines have outlived father and son and possibly even grandson and now make a most pleasant grove to drive through between subdivisions and freeways. "All that is left of the barn and the mill is the grove," the grandson says. The millrace spring and pond and perhaps an old square nail or two remain, though it is in an old summer home area for the rich, now toned down a bit by slightly smaller homes with less land around them but still quite a ritzy area and on private land. One really can't go nail hunting now. But the pines are still there and a man's memory of his grandfather watering them. "...And yet to those who pass this way, these aging pines are mine - they say."

Passing by the mill location, one may wonder about the old house across the street and east a bit of this plaque. Is it anywhere near as old as the mill? Could it possibly have been there as part of the mill and its properties? Is there anyone near who still remembers? Did Knudsen's Corner have a market? What once was The Heather or Scottish restaurant, is now The Tuscany an Italian restaurant just southeast of the mill site. Next door to the restaurant on the same side of the street is The Cottonbottom which has catered for years to the skiers coming down from the mountains at the end of the day, as well as locals and college kids. All of these buildings are interesting and quaint, and must surely have histories of their own. People who have eaten at the

Tuscany mention ghostly happenings around there, though the employees say no such things have been observed. One customer claimed to have seen a golden arm coming up through the table towards him right in the middle of his dinner. Others say that things have been moved on the tables by unseen hands. Of course it could all be made-up nonsense to get more people to go there for a meal. This story needs to be investigated further!

What can be visualized quite well, is old Mr. Knudsen with his hard ways and stubborn Danish roots, out in those little woods watering pines that will live on without him. As we of another and faster time, drive by him unseeing and oblivious to his spirit in these woods, we should remember that they stand now as a monument to him and his love of a forest that he literally created. His ghost wears an old broad brimmed but tightly woven straw hat, unusual cover-alls perhaps somehow made or altered by his wife, and he has a little white beard. He is thin and stooped over, perhaps from arthritis, which has given him a bit of a rounded back, and he likes to whistle, though he isn't very good at it. This is how some see him anyway, a representative of his time. Most of all, he is as silent as his trees and speaks only when necessary. In one's mind's eye he can be seen walking through this area, caring for his trees, even though decades have passed.

WOLVERTON WOLLEN MILL - HANKSVILLE

Down in Southern Utah there is a little town called Hanksville. Once a large woolen mill stood on the outskirts of town. The mill is one of very few fortunate enough to get restored rather than perishing. It was moved to assure its safety, so there is no log saw or ore grinder about and not even a running stream. Instead it sits next to a parking lot and a BLM brick building. A man named Edwin Thatcher Wolverton, who came from Maine to mine in the hills, ended up building this mill in 1921 with the help of his two sons. Thatcher had been in the Henry Mountains for quite a few years looking for gold before he gave up and built a mill instead. He probably never did give up his search for that lost Spanish mine, though he did settle down to mill. It took him 12 years to secure the land and mining rights and he built the saw and then the ore grinder. The original cabin was built near a stream in a beautiful protected but narrow canyon. Two things make this mill unique, one being the way it was built without notches and overlapping timbers. Instead, Wolverton built it by stacking up the logs and then bracing them together. Second, the mill had two separate functions both to cut the timber and to crush ore.

When the mill began to deteriorate and was being destroyed by vandals in its isolated location; the BLM decided that the only way to save it was to move it. "Some of the old mill house is still on the mountain. So, too, is the old cabin, a shanty in the side of the hill." BLM employees used a helicopter to move the mill into Hanksville in 1974 and then spent fourteen years restoring it. They felt that this way they could at least preserve a bit of the history of the Henry Mountains, which are quite famous for being spooky and fraught with legends of lost mines and ghostly miners.

A most interesting fact about this mill is the legend of an Indian curse being placed upon it. Anyone who opened the old gold diggings from ancient times on Mount Pennell, would have all sorts of sufferings and hardships, with death even being an option. While Wolverton did not mine the gold, it is known that gold ore from the mountain was run through the mill for a short time. No one ever knew if Wolverton found his lost gold mine, but from time to time he would come into town with a little gold in his possession. It is said that no one ever did get anything out of that mountain but hardship and suffering. Wolverton was 67 when he was thrown from a spooked horse. He survived the surgery and then died from pneumonia shortly after. He died in 1929 when there was still a hospital in Fruita, Colorado where he had his surgery. This is personally interesting to me as I lived there when I was in the VISTA program and worked at a Headstart program. I remember a little old lady who wandered the town with her bible under her arm, muttering to herself all the while. I treasure the remembrance of the best cherry limeades I have ever had served at the old drugstore. It seems the curse got him after all, and personally, Fruita, Colorado always seemed a bit haunted to me as well!

Wolverton died there but was buried in the Elgin Cemetery near Green River, another place for an intuitive visit in the near future. Apparently the spirits felt very strongly about not allowing anyone to find gold in the Henry Mountains, even for a very short period of time.

200 CO-OPS

THE BRIGHAM CITY MODEL PROGRAM - MILLS & FACTORIES

MERRELL PLANING MILL

BARON WOOLEN MILL

BOTT MONUMENT FACTORY

CHRISTENSEN ACADEMY OF MUSIC AND DANCE

The planing mill can be found at 547 East Forest Street in the middle of a residential area in Brigham City not far from the other mills, all of them just waiting for some preservation group to pick them up en mass. I chose Brigham City to represent such milling plans all over the state because it turned out to be the model for all the others because of its short lived success. The early pioneers were directed to found and operate these Co-ops by Brigham Young. Brigham City was very successful at being both a cooperative community in its time, but even more important, somehow preserving the most mills of any other small town in the state. The Co-op plan was a dream of Brigham Young's and was successful for only a very short span of time. It was started in Brigham City under the direction of Lorenzo Snow. The Merrell Planing Mill was built in 1864 as part of Brigham Young's plan to build a network of over 200 co-operative mills and businesses around the state. It was a communal effort to encourage the saints to buy only at their own church run stores and thus share this wealth. From 1868 to 1884, this was the plan, and though eventually most communities failed in their efforts, to this day in Brigham City alone, there stands remnants of a flour mill, granary, woolen mill, mercantile store and the planing mill. All three mills still have much of the original materials and equipment inside, though all of them have been altered over the years by their various private owners. While the woolen mill has a Friends of the Mill group, the old grist mill has been owned by the Bott family for four generations. The old planing mill is still awaiting an interest group of its own, though present owners have plans for a country furniture store inside and have carpenters working on it as this is being written.

Lorenzo Snow who had first built the mill under Brigham Young's direction, sold it to John Finley Merrell in the late 1890's. It was run as a lumber mill with hundreds of workers who hoisted the timbers from the first floor planing room through a hole in the ceiling to the second floor. The carpenters and gluers then created cabinets, doors, window sashes and furniture and then these pieces were lowered by pulleys to be loaded onto wagons. Merrell owned several farms in the area and thought this mill might employ some of his dozen children. He made several improvements, including replacing the water wheel with a gravity pipeline which brought water directly from the Bear River. He renamed the place, The Merrell Lumber and Salt Company, producing salt from the Salt Creek near there. The pulpit in the Brigham City Tabernacle is stamped with the Merrell Planing Mill mark and several relatives ran the mill in succession, including one mayor of Brigham City. John Merrell was even charged with cutting down 17,000 trees on federal land, fined and condemned to serve three months in jail. But he escaped from the federal marshal and never served his sentence. John Merrell even died wild, when at the age of 80 he crashed his car; he loved to drive at high speeds out in the country.

The third generation of Merrells finally shut their doors in 1983 but it is still owned by members of the family who are struggling to make improvements. They have put on a new roof, restored some of the antique machinery and are working to stabilize some of the walls. The additions built in 1947 are within the block and hidden from view; they are several lean-to structures and a one-story addition. Its first level is built of quartzite and the second level is adobe brick; the building houses many treasured pieces of machinery such as a woodworking machine, a molder, a drum sander, and big leather belts and pulleys. It is in good sturdy shape for all of its 123 years of existence. Perhaps the Merrells will find other preservationists who wish to help in this project just because they want to preserve it and not because there is money to be gained. ("Brigham Coop Is Anything But Run-of-the-Mill" by Jack Goodman, *The Salt Lake Tribune*, Sunday October 24, 1999, p.E2.)

The Baron Woolen Mill was built on the banks of Box Elder Creek in 1870 as part of the same cooperative LDS plan. It is no longer powered by creek water but has much of the original machinery intact from 70 to a 100 years ago. It is also the last mill in the county with every part of the manufacturing process housed under one roof. The Barons bought it once again from Lorenzo Snow when the communal cooperative failed. James Baron bought it and moved to Hyrum to operate another mill for 25 years, but his son Thomas went back to Brigham City in 1915 to rebuild the woolen mill. It had had several owners and a series of fires in between. His sons and grandsons ran the mill for 73 years. They sold the business in 1988 to a Cache county businessman but within 3 years the mill was bankrupt. In 1992, Bob and Marva Sadler fell in love with the mill and spent the next 6 years trying to revive a blanket and rug business at the mill. But in 1998, they too had to declare bankruptcy because of very old and faulty equipment failures such as when the boiler exploded in 1994 and when rubber rollers in the wash box also left black marks all over blankets destined for their Christmas sales in another year. Mr. Baron was quoted as saying that even though they could not keep their business going, they would both be happy to hear that the old mill might be preserved and that they might be a part of its history.

A woman who often drove by the mill, though she was from Salt Lake City, organized a Friends of the Mill group who want to raise the money to buy the mill from impatient creditors. They want to turn it into a living history park and hope to form a non-profit foundation. The mill could show not only traditional methods of washing, drying, dyeing, spinning and weaving the wool, but could also become a retreat for fiber artists, painters and photographers. Near the woolen mill are a tannery and the planing shop, which could also be restored if interest in the project increases. According to sources all around the country, what is now called "heritage tourism" is growing so fast that it is incredible. Friends of the Mill membership is growing and the Utah Open Lands Conservation Association which is in the market for sheep growers, is doing its own campaign to save such mills and will donate to this project as well. Undoubtedly we will hear about both of these places in the near future, and the future life of these buildings looks bright. ("Spinning History Into Gold?" by Kristen Moulton, *The Salt Lake Tribune*, October 24, 1999, front page of Utah and B5.)

The Co-op project included the woolen mill, the planing mill, the saw mill, grist mill, a boot and shoe shop, harness shop, carpentry shop, butchery, adobe and brick yards, and of course dairy and crop farms. Brigham City became a model for other Mormon settlements with 29 cooperative departments displayed in 1875 during Pioneer Days. Crop failures, the burning down of the woolen mill, attachment by the federal government of the saw mill and federal taxing all contributed to the downfall of the Co-ops by the early 1880s. In 1884, some of these tax monies were returned, which enabled the town to build the new Brigham City Mercantile and Manufacturing store in 1891. The store continued to operate after the Co-op system closed down completely in 1895. Private businessmen took over most of these mills and businesses. J. F. Merrell bought the planing mill, the Baron family bought the new woolen mill in 1916 and Christian Hansen purchased the big diary farm outside of Logan. Two other men continued to use the saw mill for various logging ventures and new mills began: a cement plant, knitting mill and Jensen Brothers Milling and Elevator Mill or the Big J Mill. On a drive to photograph some other sites, we took the back road to Logan through Deweyville and Honeyville and as we headed down into the Cache Valley, we found the old dairy farm totally by chance. It is privately owned but an old historic marker identified the place and it is a mystery as to why it was so far outside Brigham City!

Brigham City offers the following historic sites, which have not been torn down, though in most cases, changed very much from their original functions: the Davis and Box Elder Fort locations, an old log cabin, the Union Pacific Train Depot, old city hall and fire station, old county courthouse, tabernacle and ward house, and most interesting, the Box Elder Academy of Music and Dancing. The Academy opened in 1903 at 64 North Main. Christian and Peter Christensen learned music from their father Lars Christensen who was the original pioneer settler from Denmark. They were already members of a popular orchestra which performed all over Utah and Idaho. The second floor of this building was used for dance instruction and dances, while the first floor had an open air pavilion, refreshment stand and music instruction rooms. Christian and Elizabeth Christensen had four sons who were raised in this background of music, including their uncle Peter's ballet instruction, as he had once studied ballet in New York City. "Three of these four sons became national figures in the ballet world: William as founder of the Portland Ballet and Utah's Ballet West, Harold as director of the San Francisco Ballet School and Lew as director of the San Francisco Ballet." The academy building was sold in 1909 and was then used as a roller skating rink, bowling alley, office space, a clothing store, and is now completely surrounded by other buildings and various businesses which either use its interior or surround the vacant building entirely. One can just imagine the spirits which inhabit this place! ("Brigham City Historic Tour" by Kathleen Bradford, Brigham City Museum-Gallery: Brigham City Corporation, 1995, p.26.)

Of interest to these mill stories are the following and still standing buildings: the Tithing Office, Relief Society Granary, Brigham City Co-op Store, Grist Mill, Woolen Mill, and of course the Planing Mill, already mentioned. The two-story brick Tithing Office had ground level storage rooms for the ten percent tithing from Mormons for their church, a rock wall outside to house all the animals tithed to the church with offices for church officials on the second floor, and a baptismal font in the basement for children and converts. A family moved in in 1937, but the place is presently divided into apartments. The Relief Society (LDS women's organization) Granary distributed grain to the needy. It was built in 1877 and the women and children gleaned in the fields after the men had harvested the grain. "Children collected old glass which was crushed and mixed with the mortar used in the building to discourage mice from making holes in the walls and entering the building." (ibid, p. 28). The granary is now owned by the Box Elder School District which used it as a food storage place from 1913 to 1987. It is now vacant and up for sale, though in danger of being torn down. However it is on a main thoroughfare and would make a really nice little antique or boutique shop with a little fixing up!

The old Brigham City Co-op Store at 5 North Main still stands where it was completed in January of 1891. In December of 1894 a fire destroyed some of the interior and the store never fully recovered from its losses. Several businesses have occupied the building since, though the main floor has always belonged to one bank or another. Interestingly, the north end of the building was once a furniture store where the owners included selling coffins as part of their business and eventually expanded into offering mortuary services including embalming which was offered in the west annex. The second floor had a variety of tenants; the U.S. Post Office was once housed there as well as various businesses such as real estate, insurance, lawyers, dentists, etc. The third floor was used by the Chamber of Commerce in the 1920s, and as a theater for high school drama productions from 1972 to 1995. First Security Bank, now Wells Fargo Bank, bought the building and it is still being used as a bank to this day.

The Grist or Flour Mill was originally intended to form the northeast corner of a rock wall around the town and Frederick Kesler designed this one too. It began operation in 1857 and Lorenzo Snow was the owner. John H. Bott purchased it when the Co-ops failed. He was a stone cutter and so he opened a stone cutting and gravestone monument business when he purchased the entire block for $300 in 1890. The mill became a monument factory and he ran it until his death in 1914. Four generations of the Bott family have run it ever since and it is the oldest monument company in Utah. It is still the best preserved Kesler Mill in the state and has been on the National Historic Register since 1990. Though privately owned and very well protected by the family, stories of ghosts there have circulated around town for quite some time.

The Woolen Mill was completed in 1870 and began operating in February of 1871. The owners also operated a large sheep herding concern as well as a cotton farm in southern Utah. The building was destroyed in a fire in 1877 and rebuilt one year later on the same spot. James Baron continued to operate it as a mill after the Co-ops failed. It was then sold to another private businessman and a second fire destroyed it in 1907. Baron's two sons returned to Brigham City and bought and rebuilt the Woolen Mill in 1923. Sherwood Hirschi bought the business from the Barons in 1988 and he operated it under the Baron name until 1992. In 1993 the Sadiers bought it and ran it as the Baron Woolen Mill. The Planing Mill right next door along the Box Elder Creek, was run by the Merrell family for several generations until 1983.

The most spectacular is the old Baron Woolen Mill. In front is a little red brick store added to the building, and one has to visit by appointment only. As you round the corner, there spread out for hundreds and hundreds of feet is the huge old mill with lots of broken windows and quite an eerie effect. Fortunately, the mill is well-hidden and the present owner can keep an eye on it to prevent the vandalism that occurred when it was abandoned. A visitor doesn't even have to go in the place to sense the presence of quite a few who linger there. It is also exciting to see how the three mills are laid out along the creek. There is an open area near the middle school and one can see all three of the mills in a sort of triangle. One can easily visualize the town really taking an interest in restoring all three and adding a park. They are all three privately owned which is probably the main reason why they have been as well preserved as they are and have as much character as they do.

Within the town as a whole, it is the monument factory which houses ghosts, but it is closely guarded by the very private family who live on the premises, and does give off a strong energy of such things. However, both the planing mill and the monument factory are small and not quite so dramatic as the Woolen Mill. The huge old Academy of Music and Dance is surrounded by some sort of business on all sides and so the beauty of the original building is quite hidden. The bank building lost the south side wing some time ago and looks a bit odd with only two thirds of it left standing. The Relief Society Granary somehow lost its second story as the years rolled by. So while all the buildings are still standing, they are in entirely different shape than the old photographs showed them to be in their glory days. They have fortunately been preserved because private families kept or bought and preserved them, and yet on the other hand, only recently has a group effort apparently begun to try to restore them. What a spectacular preservation project that would be, as the old Bushnell Hospital and Intermountain Indian School is being torn down now just around the corner.

The most active areas are the Academy on Main Street and the Woolen Mill, though the planing mill and the monument factory are a close second. I may get a chance in the future to enter them and have a look around, though not everyone wants to talk about this aspect of such old buildings. But here are my own intuitive impressions anyway, as I stood near them and jotted them down. At the Woolen Mill I felt the presence of a woman in a long skirt from a really long time ago when she ran or managed the place. She is still around putting equipment back where it belongs and locking things up and organizing them. Her husband apparently ran the place in name only and she was the real business woman behind it all. A child drowned in the creek behind the mill a very long time ago. There were two boys playing together. Although it was an accident, the boy who survived, even though there was really nothing that he could have done, had to live with the memory of it all of his life. The boy's spirit still lingers there and played little tricks on people working in the mill. One not so good spirit is a former caretaker from a much later era who patrols the inside and is a bit ambivalent in his feelings towards the place. On the one hand he is overly protective, slamming doors and such, while on the other hand he is angry about something; perhaps he was fired? He apparently has contributed to the various runs of bad luck at the place, including the fires and flooding. In a much more recent period, a group of teenage boys really vandalized the building. Many of them became pillars of the community later and must have had a twinge of conscience about what they did there.

One man contemplated suicide at the planing mill a very long time ago but did not go through with it or was saved and energy from this event still lingers. Another man had a real interest and hobby in all of the old antique equipment at the mill and he is still around guarding and taking care of all these objects, sometimes moving them around or rearranging them so people who come in the next morning cannot find them.

Doors seem to slam a lot around the place and visitors are really not welcomed. At the monument factory, stone cutters can still be heard at night when no one is there, working, chipping away with their ancient tools. Lights dim or go off entirely too often and they also go on when left off. A grandfather in the family worked quite diligently to keep his family separate from the community and apparently succeeded within his generation. His energy can be felt around the place not wanting strangers to enter his mill. Certain areas of the building apparently have a strong guarded feeling still to this day and people feel very uncomfortable inside the structure.

The Academy of Music and Dance still offers up its music in the middle of the night. People claim that they have heard the music along with voices and dining sounds like the clinking of glasses. The evening dances and a place to sit outside and dine must still carry a strong energy. Peter Christensen seems to be the primary ghost and I don't know if the next thing I felt is connected to him at all, or if it is just another passing thought as I stood by the place. Anyway, someone in the family went off to war and was shot down in a plane and did not return. Whoever this is, it is his spirit who is also in the building now. I felt the most activity in town and had a strong feeling that at one time ancestors and family members contemplated buying and restoring the place back to its original purposes, but the plan was abandoned. Lots of residual sounds and music can be heard by some and the main spirit is waiting for the building to return to its former glory days, which is of course unlikely at this point in time. It was a very different looking building in its time anyway, and now is totally surrounded by big ugly cement block buildings. Someone with a lot of money and time on his hands would have to take it over and devote his life to its restoration.

It does remind one of the little Granite church where family members are still trying to restore it as a gallery and memorial to their ancestor, Avard Fairbanks, the famous Mormon sculpture and painter. What a monument this could be to the Christensen family and the legacy that they will leave behind them, if it were turned into a ballet museum in this little town. But then I am a visionary dreamer with no funds to back up my dreams. However, these images linger in my second sight, sometimes wrong or misinterpreted; though they often prove to be true. So like always I advise others to take all of these impressions with a grain of salt. Those who are willing to research these things or perhaps know about them already, will have to separate out the truth from the fiction and the interpretations from the facts.

FRANKLIN RICHARDS MILL

NORTH COTTONWOOD CREEK, FARMINGTON

Mormons settled the Farmington area in the fall of 1848. In 1850, Willard Richards built a grist mill there and later a sawmill. Samuel Richards asked the local designer of mills, Frederick Kesler, to design and then construct a carding mill in 1856 in the same area. A few years after this, Kesler was asked to make improvements on the grist mill. Willard's son Franklin inherited the mill and asked Kesler to design and build a larger and more modern mill and by March of 1862, the new three story stone mill with a Penstock 40 feet high, was operating successfully. Kesler had designed one of his more modern grist mills which he did after 1860, with an enormous inside water wheel. The overshot wheel was 22 feet in diameter and was inside a stone lean-to built against the east wall of the mill. The new mill was dedicated on June 19th, 1862. By 1866, the water wheel required extensive repairs however.

Over the years, this mill was first converted into a roller mill and then at the turn-of-the-century was converted to the electrical generator building for the city of Farmington. In the early 1960s it was converted again into a popular restaurant, The Heidelberg. The Heidelberg put in a big kitchen and brought in relics from other Salt Lake City mansions as well as Tiffany windows and lamps. It was during The Heidelberg period that ghostly happenings were reported in the old mill. But by the 1990s, the restaurant had gone out of business and the state of Utah ended up with the property. During this time vandals did thousands of dollars worth of damage including smashing every Tiffany window but one. They had also had late night bonfires inside the building which had reduced many of the original hand-hewn posts and beams to ashes. Utah decided to put the 8 acre place on the auction block and a former engineer, Tom Owens, who had worked on the Apollo moon landing project and was now a wealthy entrepreneur, saw the ad for it and bought it.

Tom Owens is a Utah native from the Weber area who after a successful career as as TV producer in Hollywood, a manufacturer of private planes in Los Angeles, a graphic designer in New York and a successful advertising agency, wanted to return to his home state to take care of his mother. He saw the ad for the old mill in the paper, showed up at the auction and in 1992, the mill became his. When he saw the mill and all of the out-buildings he was appalled at the mess. It took him a year to clean up the property, 21 dump trucks to haul off the debris and the local fire department to burn a huge pile he had hauled off into an open pasture. Owens renovated the out-buildings first, making them into office space for his advertising agency which he recently sold. He is semi-retired now, but he does keep a video and editing center in one studio. He then began working on his home and the mill, and he figures at present that he has about 20 percent more to go to full completion.

He found a designer who came up with what he wanted - a craftsman-style house that would mirror the old mill. Owens was able to obtain old railroad ties from the Lucin Cutoff to decorate the ceilings and Montana Douglas fir for the wood floors. He even has cherry cabinetry in the kitchen where he can look out on the 100 year old cherry orchard, a 3acre pasture and 2-acres of lawn and gardens. All of the original hand-hewn posts and beams are exposed with the authentic wooden dowels and iron nails. A master bath was been added, as well as a huge picture window designed in the profile of the mill. Much of the rest of the mill is still being worked on in one way or another and it has become Mr. Owens full time work and passion. He says that he shares his mill with "one dog, two cats, two chickens, two ducks, two horses and a grundle of fish." His ultimate goal is to make the place into a museum so that others can enjoy it after he is gone. ("Mill Make over: Once derelict Farmington building is transformed into a stylish home" by Jeanie Van Amen, *The Salt Lake Tribune*, Utah Living, Section F, November 14, 1999.)

There are no ghost stories that I know of in the present, although all the usual ghostly signs were reported when the place was a restaurant. The Heidelberg was a fancy exclusive place to dine in the evening and doors and lights and windows all performed for some of the employees that worked there. Perhaps when Mr. Owens reads this he will provide me with a few stories of his own or say that any ghosts that were there have now left the building for good. I have learned on this particular journey, that ghosts are everywhere, and that most old buildings contain the remnants of recorded pictures and sounds, and even aromas and movements, which people often mistake for illusions or even delusions of one kind or another. If they are not ghosts, then as some believe, they are the cellular memory which we all hold within us of places from the past. The undiscovered countries of the brain apparently can take us anywhere, though I may not live to see this proved. Perhaps I will encounter such spirits in some other form or place. The heart can give us the faith to believe in such things, as one man's obsession has done to preserve a place that one day all of us might enjoy.

WASHINGTON COTTON FACTORY & NURSERY

WASHINGTON CITY

Located at 385 West Telegraph Street in Washington, Utah, this old factory was built in 1865. Cotton production in Utah's Dixie was an important part of Brigham Young's plan to industrialize Zion. But cotton production turned out to be an unsuccessful venture in Utah and the old factory spent about a hundred years with a series of owners who did not take care of the building. It also stood idle on several occasions and vandals got into it. An out of state woman, Norma Cannizzarro, saw the place and fell in love with it. She purchased the building and began an eight-year effort to renovate the place with a vision of it becoming some sort of community center. She ended up saving one of Utah's earliest and must unique industrial businesses. The old cotton mill is now a successful nursery called the Star Nursery.

Washington county is in the southwest corner of the state and is most famous for St. George which is less than ten miles away from Washington City. St. George is now a huge retirement center and much of the old town has been preserved as an historic district which includes Brigham Young's Winter House, the old courthouse, opera house, school, and of course, LDS temple and tabernacle. The Mountain Meadows massacre took place close to Washington City and many ancestors of those who participated have their names in the local cemeteries. The massacre is still shrouded in secrecy to this day; at least one woman who was an infant survivor of this tragedy became an indentured servant and eventually ran away from her husband after they went to live up north. This woman, claiming to be a survivor of the massacre, would never know that one of her grandchildren would become the great silent screen star, John Gilbert. Many descendants of participants still hold evidence of the events in journals and letters and talk among themselves, but never to outsiders. Descendants of those massacred are still looking for ancestors and information on those who were murdered.

Washington City is also not far from Zion Canyon and the little town of Grafton where several western movies have been filmed. There is a lot of history in the area where this little town is located. Both Washington City and County were named for George Washington and the County was formed in March of 1852. People who had left the South to join the Mormon Church, continued their trek to "Utah's Dixie" in hopes of growing cotton in the warmer climates of Southern Utah. However, the Southern families who lived in wagon boxes or dugouts on the side of a hill their first winter, found life in this area extremely difficult. There were epidemics of various diseases and quite a few of the children died. There was a constant lack of water, and it was difficult to grow food in these "starving times." The first settlers really suffered and eventually only those who were too poor to leave stayed. Both the cotton industry and the silkworm industry did poorly. There were also several floods which forced many settlers to leave the area. Brigham Young tried to help his "Cotton Mission" by providing finances for the Cotton Factory as well as the Tabernacle and Temple in nearby St. George, Utah. Without this Cotton Factory, the Cotton Mission would not have endured as long as it did.

Expecting to see the little city of Washington and then the little city of St. George, I was shocked at the changes. I had heard about how St. George was popular now and how many people go there for the weekend to golf and enjoy the sun. I knew that it had become a retirement area with lots of rich people moving in from California particularly, but I was not prepared for the changes since I had seen the area as a little girl. Shocked and a little saddened by the loss of its small town atmosphere, I found St. George now to be just another metropolis with fast food joints and food marts, gas stations, crowded streets and expensive motels and houses. On the other hand, because of the money pouring into the area, the city is using much of it wisely and city officials have restored and preserved many, many buildings in the old part of the city.

Washington City was settled in 1857 by Mormon converts from the South just before the Civil War. These settlers christened the place "Dixie" after being sent down there to settle and grow cotton. The granary, the cotton mill and the old LDS Relief Society Meeting Hall are all well preserved and the meeting hall is the oldest of its kind in the entire country. Both locals and visitors say the old granary and the cotton factory are haunted. For decades now, there has been a vague reference to the lady who haunts the old mill. She has never been given a name, like the White, Black or Gray Lady, and yet past and present employees and bosses, as well as others in town, say that her presence is always there. Individuals have claimed over the years to have sensed her presence, caught a fleeting glimpse of her, and even seen a light or wisp of something, but no one has ever come forward and claimed to have seen an actual apparition. What is consistently reported however, is that you can hear her singing in the old mill. People over time have reported hearing her beautiful voice and also her humming in the empty building, as the last occupants close down the place in the evening or as the first employees open up in the morning. They will even hear her as a group and ask each other if anyone of them has been singing and no one has.

At closing time, as employees log out, voices can be heard in the empty building and windows left locked will be found opened just a crack in the morning. There is a tremendous amount of watering that must be done in the nursery every day and on many an occasion, an employee will be in the midst of watering and the water will just shut down on its own. The person then goes over and finds the water turned off and has to turn it on again. Like most mills, fires occurred in the mill a lot, though the rumor goes that there was a huge one long ago during which one or two people died, though no one seems to know just when or if anyone was injured. The most interesting incident reported happened one night while an employee was locking up alone. The employee heard a voice and then a humming sound and finally a huge moaning sound which frightened the individual as he knew he was the sole occupant of the building. The current owners always have a cat or two living inside the mill and at this time there were two such felines. The minute the sounds start the cats scatter and hide as fast as they can and will not come out for hours. Today there is a little black cat named Waddles who is the watch kitty for the Star Nursery and for any ladies who sing or hum or moan, late into the night.

The old cotton factory as it came to be called, is a massive three-story stone structure which served as a 50-year symbol of hope and industry for those Dixie pioneers. Construction on the building began in 1865; it took a good two years of hard work to build it. The factory only ran for a very few years locally and was not productive enough for locals to run it on their own. The United Order, founded by Brigham Young, took over operation of the mill in 1871 and ran the mill until 1890, but even with help from the Mormon Church, it was not very profitable. It was then leased to Thomas Judd of St. George, who operated the mill until 1898. It then stood idle for a few years although all of the machinery was sold off by 1910. Later, it was sold to the Rio Virgen Manufacturing Company and for the next thirty years the factory continued to operate through a series of crises, any one of which might have closed the place down. There were fires and floods, along with financial and material disasters, and yet the the mill still managed to continue to produce cotton and wool for batting, as well as textiles and manufactured goods such as clothing and blankets. Consistent operation of the cotton factory ceased around the turn of the century because there were no longer raw materials for the factory. Various sporadic operations were attempted at the old factory, but none were consistent, nor did they succeed. All the machinery in the place was sold by 1910, and the building was used for storage. Still the factory remained through various uses, a credit to its original builders and a community which did not let it be destroyed. It is now listed on the National Register of Historic Places.

The pioneers of the Dixie area endured more difficulties than any other group in Utah because of the hot desert climate and years and years of unbelievable catastrophes. There were frequent floods which washed out dams and irrigation works, alkali, heat, outbreaks of malaria, typhoid fever, dysentery and near starvation at various times in those early years. It was a hard life for most and perhaps the apparitions are just a reminder of this period in history when the early pioneers lost so much of what they worked so hard for. The most precious being all those young ones who did not make it to adulthood and many residents were left so weak from malaria that they could not endure the hardships in so desolate a land and they left, even if they were poor.

John D. Lee of Mountain Meadows Massacre infamy, lived there part-time in a huge old mansion which was torn down due to rumors of a little girl ghost living in the deserted mansion who had come from the massacre site. After Lee's execution some family members even changed the spelling of their last name to Leigh. Lee had over 19 wives and so there are many descendants still very touchy about his reputation to this day. The story goes that Lee had brought one little immigrant girl home from the massacre and murdered her and buried her either under or near the old home. This particular story was probably entirely untrue but it scared the town's people so that they sold it to the Presbyterian Church who added a bell tower to it. Then, because the minister was only there one day a week as he rode his circuit, a bunch of teenage boys would sneak into the church and ring the bell in the middle of the night making everyone think that the little girl ghost was ringing it. A sort of guilt by association for all the town's people one would think, or at least a kind of terrorism to keep people quiet. Anyway, the town council decided to have it torn down in the 1890s to rid themselves of both the tales, the mischief and any ghosts that might really be about.

Brigham's cotton project was a very rapid failure financially and the first settlers took the brunt of this failure. All of these various events contributed to the history held within the stone walls of this imposing structure, although just how many fires, floods and other catastrophes took place within it are lost to history. The Washington Cotton Factory certainly had enough events take place within it or near it, to have more than one ghost on the premises. One day, while all those interested in the building were standing around talking, somewhere in the conversation the subject of the lady ghost came up. When these people left, one of the employees heard humming while she was the only one left in the building. It is said that talking about ghosts will bring these apparitions out, so that perhaps it was a woman employee of the old factory who hummed while she worked alone.

EPHRAIM CO-OP MERCANTILE & GRANARY

"LITTLE DENMARK", SANPETE

Ephraim is one of four Mormon Utah villages along with Mt. Pleasant, Gunnison and Manti, which form a sort of area of totally LDS settlements in Utah. While Ephraim did not get a temple or a county seat, it has managed over the years to gain the most in population. Fort Ephraim was founded in 1854 and was the biggest and most important fort in the area. This fort also sat parallel to one of the largest Indian settlements in the valley at the time. The first white settlers were Danish converts to the LDS church in the 1860s and this is why even today one can find all sorts of stories from the Danish sense of humor floating about. A Norwegian named Canute Petersen was appointed by Brigham Young to the Sanpete Stake and he brought peace with the Indians to the area, as well as incorporating the town and building two very unique structures on main street: a co-op store and a tabernacle. The forerunner of Snow College in Mt. Pleasant was located first in the second floor of the Co-op and then in the huge storefront with the look of a tabernacle.

By 1880 the town was ninety percent Scandinavian and one of the most interesting things about Ephraim were the various nicknames which these residents gave to each other. For example, a milliner Stean Christiansen was called "Hat Stenie" or a farmer named Jorgen Jorgensen was called "Yern Dragoon." These were names which indicated a person's trade or position in town, etc. Then there were such names as "Old Swensen" or "Hannar White," where a person's name might just be changed slightly so that every person in town had his or her very own signature name. To this day there is a Scandinavian festival each year in Ephraim, honoring their especially Danish ancestry, which is one half of my own ancestry as well. Judging from my own father's family, these Danish Americans are hard working, down to earth, full of good humor and mirth, and often musically inclined. They love their coffee and their beer and had a hard time giving these things up when they became LDS; many of them did not. They can also be stubborn in their habits and are often strong believers in "what you see is what you get" or if it isn't visible then it does not exist. They are often warm, friendly people with a word of good cheer and comforting ways when their friends and neighbors need a helping hand. Carpentry was a master trade among the Danes; it's interesting that my Danish-ancestry grandfather, all of his sons and some of his grandsons became carpenters.

In 1869 the railroad came to Utah and the Zions Cooperative Mercantile Institution was formed, with branches in 100 locations all over the state, one of which was in Ephraim. "The stores took in farm produce, hand-crafted items, products of home industry, and all manner of goods to be sold or exchanged for needed materials by the local pioneers. Metal ZCMI coins, sometimes called 'tin money', were also used occasionally." (*"A Brief History of the Ephraim Cooperative Mercantile,"* Sanpete Trade Association, 96 North Main, Ephraim, Utah.) A lot of Danish carpenters made Greek Revival-style buildings, very imposing structures and unique in the area as well. Like all ZCMI mercantile stores it had "Holiness to the Lord" painted on the front, arched over the All Seeing Eye of Jehovah and a beehive symbolizing the theme of industry in Utah. People for the first time were able to get items never before available in a small frontier town.

The original mercantile building had a "Society Hall" upstairs and Relief Society meetings were held there along with dances, receptions, city meetings and local plays and dramatic productions. The first Snow College classes, then known as The Sanpete Academy, were also held there from 1883 to 1909. The college expanded during this time and had to use rooms in the tabernacle, until a campus was built one block east of the store. The Co-op system eventually began collapsing in smaller towns all over the state due to all the unpaid bills and most of these enterprises were taken over privately and continued to run as stores for many years. "From 1883 to 1969 legal documents show at least one dozen owners, from general store merchants, to a farm implement store, to an auto garage, to a milling company, which used this beautiful building for grain storage." (Ibid) The granary next door was originally the Relief Society Granary but was converted to be used in an expanding milling operation later on. It was originally built for the Relief Society sisters to feed the needy not only locally but overseas as well. This grain was sent as far away as China during various conflicts overseas or even closer to home in the United States.

In 1969, the Sanpete Development Corporation was formed to save several of these formidable buildings which were in danger of being razed. Originally the members hoped to make the old mercantile into a community theatre but this dream never materialized. However, local money and funding from grants got the buildings repaired and preserved from further decay. When this group ran out of money two local citizens assumed the payments and saved the buildings from demolition, thus preserving the buildings though there were still many who wished that the "old eyesore" be torn down. In the mid 1980s, the Sperry Univac Company closed and many of their employees went back to Snow College to change careers. They formed a support group called "Second Time Around" and eventually decided that they also needed to form their own business to bring in extra income to their families. They organized the Sanpete Trade Association and formed an arts and crafts cooperative hoping to house this in the old mercantile store in Ephraim.

Snow College, USU Extension Service, six county commissions and some private citizens pitched in with grants and then the city of Ephraim became involved. The store, the granary and the grounds were fully restored. The other still-standing and very imposing building just down the street, the Social Hall, is privately owned but well taken care of at present. It was built in 1911 by six local business men and is a three story, two level brick building. It housed a general store on the first floor and a wagon and machine company in the rear. A grand social hall on the second floor contained a 22 foot high ceiling, tall windows, full length mirrors, a ticket/coat room and ladies and gents parlors. The huge dance floor was made of maple hardwood and all the big events and parties were hosted there from 1911 to the late 1950s. During this time the main floor became a variety store and the second floor was a roller rink. In 1960 a sewing factory took over the entire building and in 1987 it was purchased to be used as a pizza parlor which it still is today. However the second floor is still used as a social hall for events in town.

The granary is closed to the public but I did manage to spend time in the upper floors of both the social hall and the mercantile, which is a wonderful store to visit. So many people pass through these two areas that it was quite confusing to pick up on anything specific, or to tell which time period I was in, but I did manage to garner some general impressions of both places anyway. In the Relief Society Hall, used mainly for wedding receptions now, the most startling effect was the acoustics. One could hear a pin drop from across the entire length of the building and it echoed wonderfully around the hall. Active spirit areas seemed to be around the kitchen and the back entrance and one could feel the dancers moving about. I had a tingling sensation all the time I was in there which tells me that it always has an active movement of other-worldly goings-on, unlike the downstairs which had no feeling to it at all, except of course a warm and friendly Danish one!

I did hear little children and a teacher and since they were little children, I wondered if the second floor was ever used as a substitute school at one time for elementary-aged students. I also had a strong feeling that the stairs to the second floor were not the original ones, though the store clerk was pretty sure that they were. I felt that the original stairs were located quite a ways away from these. A young girl got her heart broken in that upstairs room by a young man who left her and a lot of people are still in that Society Hall, for the buzzing sound in my ears was intense wherever I wandered in the room. I wanted to spend more time there but we were at the end of a long day and I was tired from traveling and even more tired from "listening." However, I did feel that many, many people were waiting there to tell me things that they needed to pass on to others, eager to do so, in fact. I felt as though I would need an army of sensitives to get it all down. In the grand Social Hall, it was a similar fate - lots of activity, lots of noise in my head, lots of energy floating around.

It was a very active place.

I shall probably have to go back there next summer with a couple of friends, compare notes, and then add more to this story. But for the time being, for those of you who love history and wonderful small towns and who care about preserving them, Ephraim is the place to go! Do not miss the Witch's Knoll where bones which many believe belong to an ancient Indian mound were discovered where people were always searching for gold. Archeologists made their excavations there in the 1920s and disturbed the unearthly atmosphere. Or visit the old pioneer cemetery and the jail which is now a physical therapist's business and was the original town hall with a two-cell jail downstairs. Old timers claim there were more rooms than can be seen today in the old social hall. Also look at several of the mansions which have been turned into museums. In short, Ephraim, like Spring City, is quite an historical place with townspeople who have worked to preserve a great deal of it. As for the apparitions, they dance in the early morning hours, still enjoying a turn around the room from time to time at the old Social Hall, as well as wander about through the various older homes in town. Stories abound of black shadows in their backyards, especially near the local elementary school. Strange noises can be heard, bells don't work and in short, the entire little town of Ephraim certainly has its share of ghosts.

DEATH OF THE MURRAY SMOKESTACKS

MURRAY BRASSWORKS

South Cottonwood was located 8 miles south of Salt Lake City and settled in 1849. It became Murray City when Eli Murray became the territorial governor from 1880 to 1886. The town incorporated in 1902 and evolved from an agricultural area to an industrial one when smelters were needed for all of the mining being done. The Woodhill Brother's smelter was constructed in 1869 and produced the first silver bars smelted in Utah in 1870. Smelters were the main business in Murray until the ASARCO smelter closed its doors in 1950. Murray City has always been proud of its independence from the city of Salt Lake. The residents have their own water plant, lighting system, school district, and even their library is not part of the Salt Lake County Library System. In the old days the people of the city had their own smelters, canning factory, flour mills, and brick yards.

The depression hit Murray hard and its smelters began to close one by one, until in 1941 only one smelter remained. But the city took advantage of federal projects and created a 22-acre park, buildings, and housed the Salt Lake County Fair for many years. Its present population is around 32,000 by the 1990 census and it continues to enjoy its independence, as opposed to the cities around it who are slowly being absorbed by the metropolis around them. One thing that represented the city of Murray the most was the pair of smokestacks at the old American Smelting and Refining Company at 5100 South State. The 295 foot south stack was built in the 1870s and the 455 foot north tower was built in the early 1900s. When the company folded, nobody knew just how to topple them. While adjoining Midvale had a big party on the Fourth of July in 1948 to celebrate the toppling of the Big Bear and Little Bear smokestacks, Murray City's smokestacks have been eulogized throughout the city in drawings and paintings everywhere. They had always stood as a strange sort of monument to the people in Murray.

In June of 1999, talk of toppling them brought on a fight between Murray City and the Boyer Co. which was planning on building Chimney Ridge, a 45-acre commercial theater complex on the old smelter site. Company representatives told preservationists that the expense and potential liability of the stacks warranted demolition. It is ironic that developers often name their developments after the very sites that they intend to raze to the ground. The company at first tried to think of a way to keep them but could not so they finally demolished the old smelter buildings (alas all those hauntings!) and just hoped that the preservationists and citizens of Murray would understand. Not so!

People trying to save the smokestacks realized that the smaller south chimney was unsafe and older and would probably have to come down, but they fought to save the taller one. "It ain't over until it's over," they said. After a year of study and negotiation meetings, the company suddenly announced that the smokestacks would come down. They were an albatross that would scare off tenants, the company said. Even though the stack could have been retrofitted to withstand a strong quake and had its toxins removed, the company wanted it down. Locals offered to provide the money needed to transform the smokestack into a tourist attraction and were saddened by the company's decision. They kept fighting to the end, while others were happy to see them go. Unlike some beautiful old home or theater, two old smelter smokestacks hardly seemed worth the fight, many said.

However, observant visitors can notice just how proud Murray is of their smokestack symbols. Everywhere one goes in Murray, one sees photographs or lithographs or even paintings of them in businesses, in the library, the schools and even the parks. They have always represented the independence of this city from the County or Salt Lake City governments, by having their own separate school district and library system, etc. But unless you live in Murray you might not know this. They are not just smokestacks but a symbol of this small taste of freedom we all yearn for. Too bad that the big corporation didn't understand this, though as developers, they did worry about safety concerns.

Stories I have heard from people who ventured to the stack site on their own to determine for themselves if they could bring one down, or simply to do something daring and different, have said that the insides were coated with so many layers of soot that one could hardly breathe, let alone find a way to tumble them. They said that it was indeed eerie all around the place. Even as I write this, the buildings are being torn apart and hauled off for scrap. There is little chance of ever knowing what might have been there, unless one went in the dead of night and avoided the guard dogs and company night watchmen. Perhaps someone who lived there before the stacks came down could tell us more. But it doesn't matter now, because the whole city of Murray has lost them in a much safer manner.

Yet every time I turned around the demolition of these smokestacks got delayed again. There was something quite mystical about it to me, though others would say that it is just all those left-brained people who want to be better safe than sorry. First they delayed it until school was out for the summer, because Murray High School was right across a busy street from where the smokestacks were. Then the EPA's plan came under fire from the Murray City Council who wanted them to rethink their plan just a little. This was nothing like when the smokestacks in Midvale came down in the forties and everyone watched it happen with fireworks and applause. More and more critics of the implosion surfaced while the EPA pushed back the date to the end of June, 2000.

Five of the Murray councilmen had written their state senators asking for alternative methods for bringing the smokestacks down. The Chimney Ridge project, a $100 million development, was tied up in negotiations about the stacks, while the EPA, having been brought into the fray, ordered the stacks down after determining them to be unsound. The first date was April 30, 1999, then it was mid-May and then the day school got out in June, and then the end of June. The plan was to implode and collapse the two towers northward into 5-foot deep trenches bordered by 5-foot beams. Water jets would soak the site before and after to minimize dust and no one would be allowed within 1,000 feet of the site except those involved in the demolition. Critics say that the plan never addressed the high levels of asbestos concentrated near the top of the taller stack, and that both towers contained high concentrates of both lead and arsenic. The councilmen wanted the asbestos removed before the demolition and said that they had a company who could do it safely, while the EPA said that no one could do this safely. They wanted the towers taken down brick by brick, which would have been much more time consuming and expensive, but certainly safer. The trailer park residents near the stacks hired lawyers to represent them and they wanted to know where they would go and who would pay for their inconvenience. They got an injunction to halt the whole thing, but in the end, this failed too.

The mayor of Murray was on the EPA's side and thought the plan very safe. The American Smelting and Refining Company owned the property at this point and was footing most of the bill. Local homeowners became concerned and hired their own lawyer as well. The EPA planned to monitor the local TRAX station and had back-up plans in case the stacks missed the trenches or the wind was blowing the wrong way on demolition day. The Idaho-based Engineered Demolition Technology which was hired for the job, had previously taken down four stacks also contaminated with arsenic and lead at the Bunker Hill Mine in Kellogg, Idaho in 1996. They ranged in height from 310 feet to a whopping 715 feet tall. The demolition took place on a Sunday when everyone was at home. A crowd of around 50,000 people and at least 80 security officers were expected on demolition day. The police chief had his own opinion about how to handle the demolition; have it at 6 a.m. on Sunday and don't tell anyone to come.

By July, 2000, the smokestacks were still standing. The EPA approved the plan at last, the long ditches were dug, the high barbed wire fences were placed and the watering system was ready. The "dust suppression system" was tested before the demolition took place. Security was beefed up, just in case people tried something strange. On August 2, 2000, Citizens for a Healthy Environment filed a complaint in federal court to stop the demolition. These were mainly people who lived in the area where the smokestacks were. Demotion was scheduled for the following Sunday and experts were drilling holes at the bases to insert the explosives. Concern about the arsenic and lead contents in the stacks continued. August 5, 2000, people gathered to say goodbye to something that had stood as a monument to their city for over a hundred years. A federal judge overruled the complaint filed by local citizens, paving the way for the demolition. "We're taking history and we're tearing it down. You can't replace history. Those stacks speak to you. It's going to be a sad day," says Murray City councilman John Christensen. ("Blasting the Past: Farewell to Stacks," by Joe Baird, *The Salt Lake Tribune*, Saturday, August 5, 2000, front page.)

Sunday was D-Day. The whole thing took only 10 seconds after the base was weakened by removing material on all sides so that the towers stood only on smaller legs. Then 70 pounds of Magnum 75 dynamite were loaded in bore holes, primed with blasting caps and secured with clay stemming. There were around 35 bore holes on each stack. The base was then wrapped with number nine gauge chain link fence and a geotextile wrap. Mounds of earth were piled up against this to reduce flying debris. The small stack was detonated about three seconds after the taller one. "The stacks are our marker, our identity, here in the city of Murray, and now we will just be another part of the urban sprawl", citizens of Murray said.

The shorter stack was built in 1902 and the taller one in 1918, after the first smelter appeared there in 1869. The stacks saw many an historical event as they stood towering over this rough mining and smeltering town. For example, in one year a riot broke out between smelter workers and the local cowboys which resulted in the burning of both a brewery and a dance hall. Smelter workers worked ten hours a day, six days a week and on the seventh day and in the evenings they played hard as well. Most of them were single, though the married ones lived in the surrounding areas such as West Jordan and Sandy City. All this time they risked being crushed, being hit by flying shrapnel, being burned by chemicals and were exposed to high levels of arsenic, lead and mercury as they worked. Lawsuits by local farmers whose crops were being killed by the chimney emissions forced the construction of the higher stack, and finally the smelter closed in 1949, when even the second, higher stack did not stop the uproar against the place by the local crop growers and others.

Many old timers remember the stacks with bitterness, for while they provided a good living for many, they also killed. People who lived nearby ingested arsenic from the ponds and their lungs and eyes would burn. When the wind blew from the Great Salt Lake, there was not only a foul smell, but an increase in these symptoms in the whole town of Murray. Even with these thoughts about their past, many Murray citizens wanted the chimneys preserved, but not from their own pocketbooks. Murray residents voted overwhelmingly against a $3.4 million bond that would have paid for the purchase, restoration and preservation of the smokestacks. The fight between the preservationists and the Murray City Council continued right up to the demolition day. The mayor put it succinctly when he said, "I love the chimneys ... But right now it's blighted. It's an eye sore. Let's get on with life and build something that brings people there. In 1949, they made a tough decision to close the smelter, because it wasn't feasible to stay in business. And guess what? It's not feasible to save the stacks today. It's time to move on." (ibid, p.A6.) On the other hand, Murray's cultural programs specialist said the loss of the stacks will leave a gaping hole in the city's soul. "The sad thing is, we never really articulated what the smelter meant to the nation .... People of Murray were being sent by the president of the United States to open smelters in other countries. During World War II, we produced all the lead for our bullets here. We've done a poor job of telling our story. And now Murray is losing an opportunity to communicate its history to its children." (Ibid, p.A6.)

Jim Ure, a Salt Lake City resident, remembers working as a high school student in the fifties when he was part of the Disney film crew using some of the vacant smelter buildings to film the movie *Perry*. "In the heat of the day we'd go over to the stacks because it was cool in there .... The fun thing was singing inside those things. It was like the sound would swirl around you, head up the stack and then rain back down on you. It was a reverb chamber. And from the inside you could see light touch the edge of the bricks. It was a beautiful design." One does have to think about all the young kids and older vandals who visited the place over the years, some perhaps even to sleep there in the summer. One could also think of the men who launched their own plan to blow up the stacks unbeknownst to anyone, and then found that their plan did not work, injuring them or at least their pride. The stacks and the city continued to stand where they were; the symbolic nature of these two great beasts continued on.

On Monday, August 7th in the year 2000, *The Salt Lake Tribune* headlines read "Murray Blows Its Stack." (by Rebecca Walsh and John Keahey.) They did not topple northward as planned and only about 10,000 people came to watch. But they did fall into the trenches dug for them and the cloud of smoke, even with the watering system, caused the spectators to scramble for cover. Some Murray residents stood nearby crying, as the symbol of their town disappeared into a cloud of dust., while others cheered the stacks' destruction. People found their spots early and waited a long time. News helicopters hovered overhead while the ground and the stacks were dampened. At exactly 9 a.m., the 455 foot tower toppled after the first boom, followed by the second boom 3 seconds later, when the 295 foot south tower toppled as well. The EPA announced at almost the same time that the arsenic levels around the area had exceeded the monitoring criteria and people living right next to them had already been evacuated. Cleaning crews went into the housing complexes and did extra clean up as a result of this announcement. All twelve of the monitoring stations reported zero asbestos levels at the same time. The huge dust cloud went further east than anticipated and so even more monitoring and clean-up was expected for several days after the event. The stacks had fooled everybody by not falling like a tree, but rather simply collapsing downward. People had to run for their cars to escape the dust, though others had worn their own "just In case" dust masks while watching the event. Residents who lived close by took some supplies with them as they watched from their roof tops, wearing gauze masks. "Did you see *Titanic*?", they asked. "The ones with the life jackets were okay." The biggest complaint was: "How will I find my way home now?"

The best comment however, came from a 72 year old resident of Murray, Harold Unander. He had climbed to the top of the taller north stack in 1952 to help install a Harman's Kentucky Fried Chicken sign. He had to do it five times and each time it took him 35 minutes to do it. The sign was removed in the mid-1990s, but Colonel Sander's head alone was 30 feet high and the letters were 12 feet tall. "It's too bad the stacks have to go," he said, "but maybe it was time. It was pretty crumbly up there even in 1952." The mayor had to have the last say in things. It's too bad they have to go, he said, but, "today marks the birth of a new beginning. We're going to put something beautiful here." The "something beautiful" was to be called "Chimney Ridge" without the chimneys.

Sometimes when I drove past the old Murray stacks, not far from the tiny laundry and dry cleaning stack that still stands in an abandoned field in the area, I would stop my car just to look at them. For a long time, all the old smelter buildings were still there and some people actually lived there too. I would think about the huge slag heap that I drove by each day on my way to work in West Jordan along 7800 South just a little southeast of the Gardner Historic Village. Over time I watched them cover the place with a field so that nowadays, people who didn't live there would not know what dangers lie beneath this place. I would imagine what that whole area must have looked like at one time, a huge industrial complex of smelters and mills that stretched from West Jordan through Midvale and Murray, and on into Sandy City where the workers lived in the area surrounding this chemical toxins wasteland. I thought about what I was being exposed to each day as I passed through the area, and how much worse it must be for those who worked there each day or lived there or grew up in the area. I also thought that when they toppled the smokestacks in Midvale on a Fourth of July celebration in 1948, it was back in a time when not so much was known about toxins terrorists and exposures.

The whole vast area is haunted by the ghosts and happenings of this era, and has been for over a hundred years. The stories are being told and retold, for all the people who wish that they would go away and never come back. My own experiences there are always heavy with visions and images and touchings which I just can't imagine that others do not feel or hear or see. The only thing I can think of to express all this is the tone and inflection that the Wicked Witch of the West uses upon capturing Dorothy in *The Wizard of Oz*, "What a world! What a world!" Later, when the twin towers in New York City collapsed surprisingly downward, the world changed forever. I realized that events can echo each other either afterwards or as a foreshadowing before a much more tragic event takes place. One sees the after image behind closed eyes or even in the mind's eye of a spacecraft exploding in a trail of white smoke or two towers, hit by what seems to be a fireball explosion and then collapsing straight down to the ground one after the other. These are the sorts of ghosts or haunting images that change the entire world forever. The irony being that now in front of Chimney Ridge they are building on top of all those supposedly cleaned up tailings and toxins, a brand new IHC hospital where once the smelter stood.

MURRAY BRASSWORKS - ARE THEY IN MURRAY?

Murray City also houses, I think, the old Murray Brassworks building which has been used in the past few years for a haunted house at Halloween. I don't even know if residents know what I am talking about. In 1998, eight workers building structures for the haunted house, suddenly quit their jobs en mass, because in the area where they had been setting up things, objects were being thrown at them by invisible hands - big objects, like some 2 by 4s which were propelled across the room by an unseen force. Lights went out and there were mysterious power outages. Tools disappeared and then reappeared in very odd and hard to reach places. Every time a worker was entirely alone in a room or space, things would fly at him from around the room. In fact, one worker was so frightened by it all, he hurt himself while running from the area. The Murray Brassworks had had trouble before at Halloween but not in this proportion. I drove around Murray everywhere and could not find this place. Can anyone confirm that this place once existed or still exists today? And if it does, let me know where it is? Did these events really happen or are they just urban legends that aren't really tied to a specific place? IS there a Murray Brassworks building? Although rumors have it that THE INSTITUTE OF TERROR on State Street, might be this building, even the people I asked in Murray said they didn't know what I was talking about. I left feeling as if this story at least, was pure fiction.

THE STAR FLOUR MILL

A PLACE WHERE DREAMS COME TRUE
KEEP LOOKING AND YOU'LL FIND IT! - AMERICAN FORK

What is it that people search for? Some sort of Shangri-La or even a Brigadoon? A place where every hundred years or even every thousand, someone has a chance to get off this mad merry-go-round called life, and escape to a time and place, though imprisoned, where one can be happy forever? There is such a place, right here in Utah. It is called the Star Flour Mill. If you spend an afternoon there, you will come to understand its rich history. It's a great place for every person who loves to hunt through giant junk and antique places. The Star Flour Mill has spirits who love the place. Watch townspeople and total strangers intermingle there and see the history of the place in the red brick floor display where the names of every owner or person involved in its history are carefully engraved on a brick. The present owner will tell you its story if you have time and the inclination to stand and listen to his narration, for he has it memorized. It is even possible buy a brick with your name on it to add to one of his future projects, a front patio of people's names intertwined with the various historical owner's names.

One can pick up a spoon from Wake Island or an old antique book or a piece of furniture or sheet music from an old song of the 30s. Downstairs in the "kitchen" are all sorts of things to improve one. Daniel Copper, the owner, plans to open up the basement door and install a bakery and cafe. Beyond the original mill are rooms and rooms - endless rooms - full of things that everyone brings to him. He bought all the stuff that was already there and his family collects for the store. Beyond the buildings is an outdoor yard with larger objects, an old log cabin and of course, the stream which contributed the power for the mill to do its work. Some people say that the owner will never accomplish his projected dreams. It is even fewer people who realize that he already has. One can see clearly what is essential to the heart, and like the Little Prince, someone very small and simple shows you the way.

A good example is the group of little children from the neighborhood who come into the store to buy something just about every day, especially in the summertime. They will have a quarter or seventy five cents and ask Daniel what they can buy with it. Knowing which children actually have the money and which do not, he will drop whatever he is doing and take them around the store and show them. Then when it comes time to select something and pay for it, he pretends that they really do have the money. When some of them don't, he gets out his book. It is not a very big book, but it is his "I.O.U." book. Inside are the names of many children who owe Daniel money. He will patiently have a talk with them each time about the importance of paying off one's debts, and they in turn will carefully sign their name in the book, each and every time. After they have signed he will then tell them that when they reach a million dollars to "pay it forward". This makes sense because if they ever do have a million dollars, they just might.

There is an old Hollywood movie called *Good Sam*. Gary Cooper plays the lead. He is always helping others and giving away possessions and savings, you name it. His wife, Ann Sheridan, has the best part because she gets to strut around being very sarcastic and as a result, very funny. After giving away their money for a house twice, having their borrowed car wrecked and losing his job over all this, he decides to end it all. Then out of the blue one of the young couples that he has helped comes back and pays him everything plus interest. I believe that someday Daniel will have the same thing happen to him. But then I am a believer and many people are not.

Daniel Copper is a 43-year-old transplant from Hood River, Oregon and spent a few years in Boston, Massachusetts working at an architectural firm after graduating from U.C.L.A. He was already interested in antiques because he used to go with his mother to antique shows and auctions when he was a child. He bought the Star Flour Mill in American Fork from Nancy Long, who had her own vision one day. Ms. Long or Mrs. Christiansen, bought the Gardner Mill and its surrounding property after watching some beautiful birds near the river there and realizing that this was what she wanted to do. People thought she was crazy for doing it, but she took out a loan, rebuilt, and eventually made a great success of the venture, and has been building and adding on ever since. Ms. Long doesn't really like to emphasize the ghosts and spirits in her many buildings, though you really can't fight city hall as is often said, for the apparitions at the various Gardner mills have been talked about and written about for over a hundred years. Mr. Copper, on the other hand, talks freely about them, accepts their guidance, and is willing to take the ridicule that often accompanies belief in such things. Even the title of the article about him in *The Salt Lake Tribune* was a gentle reminder that one man's (or woman's) dream is another man's folley. ("'Spirits' Help Architect Make Project A Reality," by Mark Eddington, *The Salt Lake Tribune*, March 6, 2000, Section B, front page.) Still, the newspaper managed to tell his story quite nicely.

The first pioneer flour mills, just like the other types of mills built in Utah, were part of a well-organized effort on the part of the first Mormon settlers guided by Brigham Young, to create a systematic and extremely well planned network of industries and supplies for all Utah people. Four of them were built in the Salt Lake Valley first, but then others soon followed as LDS church members were sent out to settle various areas around the state. The land on which the mill now stands was originally homesteaded by Daniel and Eliza Allen. James Chipman, who was both American Fork's mayor and the state of Utah's first treasurer, established his mill in 1888. Four men - William Grant, Josiah Smith, Darius Allen and James Chipman - had gone in to business together and bought the land. James then turned right around and bought out all of his partners.

An interesting story about James Chipman's mother, Stephen Chipman's first wife, showing her strong will and independent streak, recounts that she, "...warned her husband that if he ever brought a polygamous wife in the front door she would leave out the back." (ibid, p.B3.) Amanda Chipman remained true to her word and left her husband when he did, divorcing him. Stephen's second wife was Phoebe Davis Chipman. But Amanda never could or would abandon her seven children, and when her new second husband wanted her to move out of state with him, she left him and returned to her children. It is interesting that when we went to the graveyard, it was Phoebe's side of the monument that I walked directly to without even knowing just where it was. It took me several minutes to discover Amanda's name on the other side, because being a stranger to all of this, left me rather confused as to who was married to whom. Then I read the phrase: "Mourn not for me my rest is sweet," and decided that I would have liked her a lot.

Amanda's son, James Chipman, rebuilt the mill in 1908 adding the newest mill machinery, after the original mill burned down the year before. He also had two wives; his first wife was Sarah Annadelia Green and his second was Selena Huntsman. He had married Sarah Annadelia quite young, as she had 4 children by the time she was 21. She was also hauntingly beautiful. A rumored story is that one night she wanted to go to a dance in town and James could not or would not take her. So she went by herself in the dead of winter walking into town and back. James' new wife, Salena was quite jealous of Sarah and took this opportunity to lock her out of the house as it was quite late. By the time Sarah got into the house later that night she was ill. She caught pneumonia and died shortly after that. Others say that there is not so dramatic a story as this surrounding Sarah's tragic early demise, and even that Sarah never came west with her husband but stayed back east, or passed away there. But then why would she be buried in the American Fork cemetery? These are questions that perhaps some day may be answered.

It is possible, either way, that it was her husband James who had a huge statue of her put in the American Fork Cemetery on a high pedestal, but no one knows for sure. It was not until we left the cemetery and drove down the hill to the mill that I realized that he had also had her statue placed so that it was looking directly across to where the mill was, so that she would gaze down upon it eternally. Over the decades, the statue which was the biggest and most unusual in the cemetery, attracted kids who began to vandalize it. Eventually it was completely destroyed and thrown away.

Daniel Copper wanted to get a new statue put up for Sarah Annadella in the cemetery. Right now an artist is creating the miniature version of the statue. It will look just like the old one with two important changes. It will be in bronze to assure a long existence, and the face on it will be Sarah's, something that was rarely done in those days. It will be one of a kind in a way, because of this, though Daniel and his partners will have to raise the $45,000 dollars it will take for the bronze statue to be completed and placed in the cemetery. The town has an annual Living History presentation each summer where people go to the graveyard and stand by someone's grave while someone else tells the story of this person's life. This summer, Sarah's story will be added to the list and people are hopeful that others will join in the fund raising for Sarah's statue to be returned to the graveyard.

The artist was a bit frustrated because he did not know what the back of the statue looked like, how her long hair draped or how the folds of the long gown looked from behind. Just a few days later an older woman came into the store with pictures. She said that she had heard about what was going on and that she had taken pictures of the back of the statue some years before and handed them to him. Daniel looked at me and said, "Now whom do you know that takes pictures of the backs of statues in cemeteries?"

James and Selena Chipman ran the mill along with his brother Henry. The Chipmans ran it as the Peoples Mill and Elevator for a while. But then in 1924, Sanford Walker bought it from them. In 1931, Sanford traded it to August Purduhn who operated it with other family members, his wife Augusta, and later, his sons Ernest and Herman Purduhn. It became a family affair when Henry and Mabel Parduhn, Don and Marion Parduhn, Leon and Laura Parduhn and Jay and Molly Parduhn all ran the mill together. Two of these grandsons, Leon and Jay, operated the flour mill officially, but some people thought that it was the four women who really ran it. On September 21, 1979, after almost 50 years of family operation, the Parduhns shut down and ceased operating the mill. It stood idle for only a few months and then Bill and Tammy Adams bought it and turned the old main mill into a craft store. They operated this store for about two years, had some difficulty and the Parduhns got it back. So for about ten years the mill stood idle and empty. If you go there you will understand what an immense job it would be to maintain it, and how it could easily become the town's scariest site, standing empty.

Teens and others vandalized the place, carried on strange explorations and clubs, and otherwise gave it a reputation that it really did not need. Nancy Long saw the mill one day and decided to buy it in 1990, probably both to preserve it and perhaps to start a second venture there like her other successful one in West Jordan. Then Daniel Copper came along in 1993 and bought it from her. The Star Flour Mill is considered by the experts to be one of the best preserved mills in the state. "It is extremely rare to find so much original milling equipment still intact," Smithsonian Institution milling expert Robert Johnson is quoted as saying." (Ibid, p.B3.) Mr. Copper, following his dream to convert the whole place into a hotel, restaurant and convention center, has worked tirelessly as a one-man team to bring this event about. According to him, he has had a lot of help, from the "spirits" in residence.

Copper says he has had a great deal of help and guidance from those who built, worked at and maintained the mill long before he became the owner. If everyone believed this, they might just find out that there is more help provided in this arena than most people are certainly aware of. Many great philosophers, inventors, scientists, mathematicians, artists and writers, just to name a few, were considered dreamers in their own time. Many of them had "aha" experiences which provided them with information that they vitally needed for this plan or that invention, this great poem or that great philosophical idea. Each went to bed one night or maybe for many nights, puzzling over a theorem or a problem or some detail in their plans that made them incomplete and had the answer come to them either in a dream or a vision or even in words spoken out of thin air. The next morning an answer came or was written or drawn on the bedroom walls. If this is difficult to believe, study a bit; this has happened over and over again in every field of endeavor, where a person considered a dreamer, made his dream come true through the help of the "spirits."

Copper was obviously drawn to the old place like most intuitive people are. He knew that he had seen it before, perhaps even many times before, with every detail in its right place just as he had envisioned it. He first built his general store to support his work on the mill, which has been in operation since 1997. He began right away to hear footsteps walking around on the second floor when no one was there but him. He feels that the mill founder James Chipman and his mother, Amanda Chipman have helped him out on many an occasion, including saving his own life at one point.

In December of 1993, he fell 45 feet while working on the mill. He landed on his head, which sent him into convulsions; he also broke his ribs and right elbow. It took him about two years to recuperate from this mishap. After this, he consulted a psychic, to help understand what had happened. He also might have wondered if he had done the right thing in purchasing the mill, and if the residual energies and apparitions there perhaps did not want him to change anything or maybe that he was simply an unwelcome visitor. The psychic told Mr. Copper that his injuries would have been worse if he had not been helped by two angels, whom he says are James and Amanda Chipman. The psychic did call them by name after saying that they were "'...the eternal father of a big project I was doing,' he recalls. 'The psychic said that the woman angel was a very independent woman who does whatever she damn well pleases. She told me her name was Amanda." (ibid, p.B3.)

Other things have happened to guide him that cannot be explained away, such as finding Amanda Chipman's grave site. During the time that he was recuperating from what was a near-death experience, Copper read anything and everything he could find on the history of the mill, its founders and their families and even the town of American Fork and the history of flour milling itself. He hoped to gain a better understanding of the mill and its various previous owners. He also drew architectural plans of it from various angles, both of the mill now and then what he hoped that it would someday look like. A near-death experience, as many know, can set a man or woman on an entirely new path, as well as make him or her more of a humanitarian, and certainly more in touch with his own intuitive gifts and abilities. Copper visiting a psychic is a perfect clue that he was beginning his personal spiritual quest and gaining an understanding of his own innate intuition, though Copper was apparently already on his path long before. Eventually a person does not need others to use their intuition to tell him what he needs to know, because he slowly comes to realize that we all have these gifts to one degree or another.

He feels the presences and the changes of atmosphere in the building and wants to get more specific information using his intuition, because he now understands that he can. This may be the first step in understanding both the path of least resistance, and going with the flow of the river. He does his research in the world which we can see, and now he continues his explorations in the world which we cannot see so clearly, nor so chronologically. He has found out that all those "no trespassing" signs he sometimes runs into, mean that he has to travel these particular paths by himself. He also realizes that, no matter how much he works to fit into the world which we think of as the real one, he will, sooner or later, be a target for those who cannot not follow him. There are those who shake their heads and say that he will never get "it" all done. But the mill is only one of a thousand other such places where people go to find refuge of one kind or another. In the end, those of us who go there, cannot explain where we have gone, nor when we might be coming back for another visit.

Copper says that "...the spirits proved to be invaluable tutors. Historical photos of the mill, unavailable anywhere else, suddenly turned up on the doorstep of the former miller's house next door to where Copper now lives. Whisperings, he says, have helped him uncover documents and to fill in other parts of the historical puzzle ever since." (ibid, p. B3.) "Whisperings" is a kinder, gentler way of saying that Mr. Copper is hearing voices. It seems to be all right for the intellectual professional who abandons his lucrative career in the city, to follow his dream in the country. It is a legitimate thing to do, perhaps even the "in" thing to do. Unless of course this same professional, having had a serious fall and possibly head injury from this fall, begins to hear voices and follows the advice of apparitions from the past, while believing a psychic who tells him that they are his guiding angels. Being a member of the local culture which once accepted such things, he must sometimes be frustrated by both his neighbors and his on-going rehabilitation. Of course he is lucky to be a man and not a woman, because women intuitives who do this sort of dreaming are of course giving into their emotions or even worse, claiming an extra-natural power in the world. Perhaps it was fortunate that Daniel fell, and though he still struggles with the aftermath of his injuries, it gives meaning and reason for seeing things that others cannot.

"Gradually, Copper's vision is taking shape. The 3-year-old general store specializes in antiques. He plans to convert the mill, miller's house and several log cabins on the site into hotel rooms. The mill's basement will become a bakery and cafe. The warehouse behind the mill will see double duty as a conference center for family reunions and other small gatherings. An 1872 barn he is disassembling in Salt Lake City and moving to American Fork also could be used for meeting space. He is confident the investors and finances necessary to finish the project will come. 'The spirits will help out once the time is right." (ibid, p.B3.) When I was there, I felt as though I was one of these several "helpers" yet to come. People will just show up to help out on the mill. It is my job to write about it, while another person might choose to capture photographs, and still others will come with ways to build and finance the project. The fact is that Copper is not going to find them or seek them out, they are just going to "come when the time is right".

Sometimes, I marvel at the state and culture from which I sprang. The mysticism and spiritualism made very strong individuals take flight from other places to come here and build a kingdom of their very own. It is interesting how time and the need for power has changed all that. Where once there were wide open spaces, clean air and non-polluted water, there now stand highway construction roadblocks, fences, wires and no trespassing signs. Once, communities of families and friends, of both male and female persuasion, blessed and cared for each other in a world they thought magical. People now scurry about in fear and separations from those things which they love. Where once power, though compartmentalized, was still a shared commodity for all to enjoy, there are now power centers, telling the rest of us what to do and how and where to live, whether we are aware of these centers or not. Some of them have names, while others are hidden from view. Some of these power centers are hidden under the guise of religion or benevolence, while others show us outright that they do indeed mean us harm. Worse, a man marching to the beat of his own drum, may be somehow suspect.

The first time I visited the mill and surroundings, I knew nothing about the mill except for the article that I had read in the paper. I immediately knew that I wanted to write about the place, to try and tell its story as accurately and precisely as possible after meeting Daniel. The place is just full of feeling and mostly a loving one at that. After I had walked around a while, I was passing a door to the other attached rooms when it suddenly swung open, not a few inches like the wind does to it all the time, but at least a foot and a half. Then it just stood there suspended as if it was making sure that it had my full attention and then when it did, it swung ever so gently shut again. I'd had doors slam in my face before but never such an inviting "come in." I went back and asked Daniel if I could go into the part that was off-limits to customers; he answered that it would be all right. I started in and went through room after room, feeling as if I would really get lost, even though one could only really walk in a straight line to the north with little aisles running east and west in each room. With so many items to be observed, the feeling was really overwhelming. When I got to the last room I didn't want to go in and turned around and went back. Then suddenly there was Daniel standing before me, showing where he had fallen not far from where this door was located.

When I came back out I asked Daniel who Charles, Amanda, Sarah and Jim were. I told him that there were 6 men and 8 women and possibly two little children who had been involved with this mill at one time or another and that all of them were still around from time to time in spirit form. But the four mentioned above were the guardians of the mill and they were quite often. The little children would come up and tap on my legs to get my attention, but the others were just smells and feelings and images which I saw in my mind. Without hesitation, and this was long before I knew a single thing about this mill, he told me who he thought each of them were. Charles was James's middle name and Amanda was his mother. These were the two "angels" who had saved him he said. Sarah, who seemed to draw me into her story more than the others did, was James's first wife, though there was another Sarah, his second wife Selena's oldest child. Jim is a mystery; either I misunderstood and it was really James, or they called him or his oldest son James Jr., "Jim." Then there is always the possibility that "Jim" is someone else who came along later. Though I am really sure that Sarah Annadelia is who I felt around me as I walked about.

When I went back a week or so later, with two other people with intuitive abilities, to walk about and compare what we felt, the most interesting thing was how we all agreed on three areas in the building's rooms. One area was the heart of the house and was warm and tingly. It was close to where Daniel fell. Another area had people in it - an old man who was sick and in bed a lot and a little girl who had a favorite spot by a window that was no longer there and a kitchen. This turned out to be the area where an old re-located log cabin had once stood and where some of the first settlers had lived. Back in the far northwest corner all three of us felt sick and could not breathe very well and did not like what we were sensing - danger and death. We learned afterwards that this area had been where dead animals had been kept for a side business. When we all sat down later, Daniel took out one of the maps of the place that he had drawn and we went through it room by room describing to him what we had felt, sensed, heard or seen. Then he talked about the healing that the mill has done for people who come there. We went off to explore the outside too. Later we visited the cemetery and without any directions walked straight to Sarah's grave, and then Arza Adam's grave, the first miller in the area, and finally to Stephen Chipman's grave with Amanda's name on one side of the monument and Phoebe's on the other.

Daniel Copper's mill has special good luck. One day while cleaning out an area on the second floor, he found in a piece of equipment something soft that he could feel with his hands and pulled it out. He realized at once that it was a petrified white owl. Before he was finished he had found three of them. They had apparently crawled in together and had somehow gotten caught. No one knows just how long they had been in there. He has them in a basket hidden in a drawer and jokes about one of them saluting like a cub scout. I guess they sort of symbolize the whole place, both frozen in time and yet so beautiful. They also represent two entirely different beliefs. In the tribal cultures, white owls can represent protection and good luck or wisdom and spiritualism. On the other hand they can represent a death that is coming soon or solitude and mourning. One can always hear the owl calling one's name, for good or for ill. They shelter one's home from the death of a community, or welcome its end.

Buildings have their own energy and soul it is said. They create communities of people and have a life span all their own. Sometimes after the death of a building, the community bands together to bring the building back to life. Or someone, usually a stranger from out of town, comes along with a vision or a plan, and with a little help and money, infuses the place with a new life and a new reason to be. Sometimes it is a brand new building and not like the old one. Sometimes, which may be even better, the people try to return it to its original use or at least capture the flavor of it in what disposition is made of it. When the community is behind the project, or when someone from outside the community introduces a new vision, others catch on and join in. The building then has a chance once more to be considered a part of the community which breathes life back into the building's own soul and in turn, that of the community.

If you go to the Star Flour Mill, be prepared for more than just a walk through a wonderland of things from the past, or even the spirits that reside there. Be prepared to meet yourself and your own dreams and failures and successes. Look in the mirrors inside and see what it means to be successful as a human being. There may be a little boy sitting on the steps examining his new purchase for the day or a housewife, weary from her day of children and family, wandering in her own memories about the store and feeling better about things when she leaves. Then there are the people who just seem to plain love these types of places, becoming all excited about the bargains that they have just found. Or perhaps one will see a mother and daughter sharing time together. There are men who stop in for a few minutes from a busy day looking for something specific, but really just loving the atmosphere and the chance to be themselves if only for a few minutes. Old folks also join in, loving to reminisce and tell their stories. Perhaps even an intuitive person or two, may be drawn to Daniel's "angels." Everyone is welcomed at the Star Flour Mill.

(Courtesy Daniel Copper)

- BIBLIOGRAPHY -

BOOKS:

Abbot, Delila. DAYS OF OUR FATHER. Delila M. Abbot: Salt Lake City, Utah, 1981

Alexander, Thomas G. UTAH, THE RIGHT PLACE: THE OFFICIAL CENTENNIAL HISTORY. Utah Division of State History & Gibbs -Smith Publisher: Salt Lake City, Utah, 1996.

Angus, Mark. SALT LAKE CITY UNDERFOOT: SELF-GUIDED TOURS OF HISTORIC NEIGHBORHOODS. Signature Books: Salt Lake City, Utah, 1996.

Arrington, Leonard and Swinton, Heidi S. THE HOTEL: UTAH'S CLASSY LADY 1911 - 1986. The Westin Hotel Utah 75th Anniversary Edition: Salt Lake City, Utah, 1986.

Barton, William G., Chairman, Centennial Committee. OUR YESTERDAYS: A HISTORY OF EPHRAIM, UTAH 1854 - 1979. Centennial Book Committee: Ephraim City Corporation, 1981.

Bateman, Noel, et. al. WALKING TOUR OF HISTORIC SANDY. Sandy Museum Foundation: Sandy City, 1997.

Bennett, Cynthia Larsen. ROADSIDE HISTORY OF UTAH. Mountain Press Publishing: Missoula, Montana, 1999.

Benson Grist Mill. MEMORIES OF THE MILL. Historical Publication Committee: Stansbury Park, Utah, 1999.

Brackenridge, R. Douglas. WESTMINSTER COLLEGE OF SALT LAKE CITY. Utah State University Press: Logan, Utah, 1998.

Bradford, Kathleen. BRIGHAM CITY HISTORIC TOUR. Brigham City Museum Gallery: Brigham City Corporation, 1995.

Bradley, Martha Sonntag. SANDY: THE FIRST 100 YEARS. Centennial Committee: Sandy City, 1993.

Bradley, Martha Sonntag. A HISTORY OF KANE COUNTY. Utah State Historical Society: Kane County Commission, 1999.

Cannon, Kenneth L. A VERY ELIGIBLE PLACE: PROVO AND OREM: AN ILLUSTRATED HISTORY. Windsor Publications, Inc., 1987.

Carter, Kate B., editor, et. al. THE CHASE MILL AND PIONEER MILLS AND MILLING. Daughters of the Pioneers: Salt Lake City, Utah, no date provided.

C&W, Kate B., editor, et. al. HEART THROBS OF THE WEST. Volume 1, 1939, Volume 2,1940, Volume 3,1941, Volume 6,1945. Daughters of the Pioneers, Salt Lake City, Utah.

Crawford, D. Boyd. HISTORY OF OGDEN, UTAH IN OLD POST CARDS. Maury Grimm, Publishing: Ogden, Utah, 1996.

Daughters of the Utah Pioneers. PIONEER BUILDINGS OF EARLY UTAH. Pamphlet, 1991.

Dixon, Madoline C. PETEETNEET TOWN- A HISTORY OF PAYSON. Press Publishing, Limited: Provo, Utah, 1974.

Garn, Russ, et. al. BOX ELDER COUNTY HISTORICAL PHOTO TOUR- UTAH STATE CENTENNIAL EDITION. West Wind Litho, West Valley City, 1996.

Goodman, Jack. AS YOU PASS BY: ARCHITECTURAL MUSINGS ON SALT LAKE CITY. Kearns - Tribune Corporation, 1995.

Haglund, Karl T. and Notarianni, Philip F. THE AVENUES OF SALT LAKE CITY. Utah State Historical Society, 1980.

Hauck, Dennis William. THE NATIONAL DIRECTORY OF HAUNTED PLACES. Penguin Books, 1996.

Huchel, Frederick M. A HISTORY OF BOX ELDER COUNTY. Utah State Historical Society, Box Elder County Commission, 1999.

Holzapfel, Richard Neitzel. A HISTORY OF UTAH COUNTY. Utah State Historical Society: Utah County Commission, 1999.

Hunter, Milton R., et. al. BENEATH BEN LOMOND'S PEAK. Daughters of the Pioneers, Weber County Chapter, Quality Press, Salt Lake City, Utah, 1995.

Intermediate Grades. COMMUNITIES OF THE JORDAN SCHOOL DISTRICT VOLUMES I & II. Jordan School District, 1945-46.
Jensen, Maurine C. MIDVALE HISTORY 1851 - 1079. Midvale Historical Society, 1979.
Kanab Heritage Council. PRESERVING THE PAST FOR THE FUTURE. Kanab Heritage Council, third edition, 1996.
Lester, Margaret D. BRIGHAM STREET. Utah State Historical Society:Salt Lake City, Utah, 1979.
Long, Nancy and Mills, Argene. ARCHIBALD GARDNER 'HIS LIFE AND HIS LEGACY.' Gardner Historic Village:Salt Lake City, Utah, 1933.
Lowe, Doug, editor. WINDOWS ON SCIENCE. Hansen Planetarium Publication, 1990.
Miller, Alta, editor, the boys and girls of the intermediate grades in Jordan School District. SANDY VOLUME 1 1. Jordan School District, 1945-46.
Mooney, Bernice Mahler. SALT OF THE EARTH: THE HISTORY OF THE CATHOLIC CHURCH IN UTAH 1776 - 1987. Catholic Diocese of Salt Lake City: Salt Lake City, Utah, 1992.
Myers, Arthur. GHOSTLY AMERICAN PLACES: A GHOSTLY GUIDE TO AMERICA'S MOST FASCINATING HAUNTED LANDMARKS. Chapter 36, "The Ghost of Brigham Young's Nineteenth Wife," Wings Books: New York, 1990.
Neff, Andrew Lowe. HISTORY OF UTAH, 1847 - 1899. The Deseret News Press, Salt Lake City, Utah, 1940.
Olpin, Robert. ARTISTS OF UTAH. Gibbs - Smith Publisher: Layton, Utah, 1999.
Petersen, F. Ross. A HISTORY OF CACHE COUNTY. Utah State Historical Society, Cache County Commission, 1997.
Powell, Allan Kent. UTAH HISTORY ENCYCLOPEDIA. University of Utah Press: Utah Centennial Commission 1896 - 1996: Salt Lake City, Utah, 1994.
Powell, Allan Kent and Murphy, Miriam B. UTAH TRIVIA. Rutledge Hill Press: Nashville, Tennessee, 1997.
Provo Landmarks Commission. HISTORIC PROVO: A SELF-GUIDED TOUR OF HISTORIC ARCHITECTURE IN PROVO. Provo Landmarks Commission: Provo, Utah, no date given.
Ringholtz, Raye Carleson. HISTORIC BUILDINGS ON CAPITOL HILL. Utah Heritage Foundation: Moench Printing, 1981.
Roberts, Richard C. and Sadler, Richard W. OGDEN-JUNCTION CITY. Windsor Publications, Inc., 1985.
Robinson, Adonis Findlay. HISTORY OF KANE COUNTY. The Utah Printing Company, Salt Lake City, Utah, 1970.
Ross, Soren. EPHRAIM UTAH. Copyquest of Ephraim, Utah, 1998.
Roylance, Ward J. UTAH, A GUIDE TO THE STATE. Utah Arts Council, Salt Lake City, Utah, 1982.
Sanpete Trade Association. EPHRAIM HISTORICAL AUTOMOBILE TOUR. Pamphlet, no dates or authors given.
Seagraves, Anne. HIGH-SPIRITED WOMEN OF THE WEST. Weanne Publications: Hayden, Idaho, 1992.
Seagraves, Anne. SOILED DOVES: PROSTITUTION IN THE EARLY WEST. Wesanne Publications: Hayden, Idaho, 1994.
Shelley, George F. EARLY HISTORY OF AMERICAN FORK: WITH SOME HISTORY OF A LATER DAY. American Fork City, 1993.
Sillitoe, Linda. A HISTORY OF SALT LAKE COUNTY. Utah State Historical Society: Salt Lake County Commission, 1996.
Smith, Barbara. GHOST STORIES OF THE ROCKY MOUNTAINS. Lone Pine Publishing: Renton, Washington, 1999.
Tobler, Douglas F. and Wadsworth, Nelson B. THE HISTORY OF MORMONS IN PHOTOGRAPHS AND TEXT: 1830 TO THE PRESENT. St. Martin's Press: New York, 1989.
Van Wagoner, Richard S. LEHI: PORTRAITS OF A UTAH TOWN. Lehi City Corporation, 1990.
Wharton, Gayen and Tom Wharton. IT HAPPENED IN UTAH. Twodot: Falcon Publishing Company: Helena, Montana, 1998.

Whitley, Colleen, editor, et al. WORTH THEIR SALT: NOTABLE BUT OFTEN UNNOTED WOMEN OF UTAH. Utah State University Press: Logan, Utah, 1996.
Woodward, Don C., editor. THROUGH OUR EYES: 150 YEARS OF HISTORY AS SEEN THROUGH THE EYES OF THE WRITERS AND EDITORS OF THE DESERET NEWS. DESERET NEWS PUBLISHING COMPANY, 1999

ARTICLES:

Adams, Brooke. "Library Writes New Chapter For Academy Square", THE SALT LAKE TRIBUNE, October 19,1999, Sec-D.
Amen, Jeanie. "Mill Make Over", THE SALT LAKE TRIBUNE, Sunday, November 14,1999, Sec-F.
Arnold, Sharon S. 'The First Large Factory in Utah", BEEHIVE HISTORY 6, Utah State Historical Society, 1980, pp.22-23.
Bagley, Will. 'Facts Often Get Lost In Pageantry", THE SALT LAKE TRIBUNE, September 2, 2001,Sec-B-2.
Baird, Joe. "Arsenic Exceeds Limits Near Stacks", THE SALT LAKE TRIBUNE, Monday, August 17, 2000, Sec-A.
Baird, Joe. "Blasting the Past: Farewell to Stacks", THE SALT LAKE TRIBUNE, Saturday, August 5, 2000, front page.
Baird, Joe. "EPA's Smokestack Plane Under Fire", THE SALT LAKE TRIBUNE, Monday, April 24, 2000, Sec-A.
Baird, Joe. "Groups Sues to Stop Demolition", THE SALT LAKE TRIBUNE, Wednesday, August 2, 2000, Sec-B.
Baird, Joe. "Murray Stacks Set for Demolition", THE SALT LAKE TRIBUNE, July 19, 2000, Sec-D.
Berrett, Bernie. "Ghosts For All Seasons", MOUNTAIN TIMES, October 29,1998, cover story, pp. 1 - 3.
Bradley, Martha Sonntag. "Foundation Honors Those Who Preserve The Past", THE SALT LAKE TRIBUNE, Sunday, November 21, 1999, Sec-D.
Broschinsky. Korral. "Salt Lake Tenth Ward: Neighborhood of Industry and Diversity", UTAH PRESERVATION, Volume 6, Spring 2002, pp. 38-42.
Brown, Larry. "Wasatch Academy: A Lesson in History, Longevity, and Quality", UTAH PRESERVATION, Volume 6, Spring 2002, pp. 32-35.
Buttars, Lori. "Fair Future: Expand Scope, But Retain Historic Flavor", THE SALT LAKE TRIBUNE, January 14, 2000, Sec-B.
Cantera, Kevin. "Fire Ravages Historic Dorm at Academy", THE SALT LAKE TRIBUNE, D4.
Christian, Patrick. "NEIGHBORS: Custodian turns wall into art creation," PROVO HERALD, May 30, 1989.
Eddington, Mark. "'Spirits' Help Architect Make Project A Reality", THE SALT LAKE TRIBUNE, March 6,2000, Sec-B.
Egan, Dan. "Park Becomes Home for Indian Remains", THE SALT LAKE TRIBUNE, Saturday, May 12, 2001.
Estes, Ashley. "Ex-Students Return to Bid Adieu to Whittier Elementary", THE SALT LAKE TRIBUNE, Thursday, November 16, 2000, Sec-B.
Evans, Max J. "William Staines: English Gentleman of Refinement and Culture", UTAH HISTORICAL QUARTERLY, Volume 34, Number 4, Fall 1975, pp.410-420.
Fattah, Geoffrey. "In a search for the supernatural- members of the Utah Ghost Hunters Society have different hobby", OGDEN STANDARD-EXAMINER, Sunday, August 30, 1999.
Fife, Austin E. "Popular Legends of the Mormons", CALIFORNIA FOLKLORE QUARTERLY, Volume 1, April, 1942.
Fleming, Paul. "Law Enforcement: Ghosts at Trolley Square", THE SALT LAKE TRIBUNE, Monday, October 19, 1999, Sec-B2.
Goodman, Jack. "A Feast For Railroad Buffs", THE SALT LAKE TRIBUNE, Sunday, February , 2001.

Goodman, Jack. "A Fine Face Lift for South Temple Mansion", THE SALT LAKE TRIBUNE, Sunday, January 9, 2000, Sec-D.
Goodman, Jack. "Big Red House And Area Near Trolley Square On Right Track", THE SALT LAKE TRIBUNE,May 17, 1998, Sec-D2.
Goodman, Jack. "Bingham Co-op ts-Anything But Run-Of-The-Mill,'THE SALT LAKE TRIBUNE, Sunday, October 24, 1999, D2.
Goodman, Jack. "Handsome Hostelry In Kanab", THE SALT LAKE TRIBUNE, Sunday February 25, 2001, D.
Goodman, Jack. 'Logan Weighs the Fate of Stately Whittier School", THE SALT LAKE TRIBUNE, Sunday, October 22, 2000, Sec-D.
Goodman, Jack. "New Tower Won't Squash 2 Old-Timers in Salt Lake, THE SALT LAKE TRIBUNE, Sunday, September 26,1999, Sec-D.
Goodman, Jack. "Old Main Looks New Again at USU", THE SALT LAKE TRIBUNE, Sunday, August 15, 1999, Sec-D.
Goodman, Jack. "Painted Ladies In Utah Are Scarce, Pricey", THE SALT LAKE TRIBUNE, Sunday, January 2, 2000, Sec-D.
Goodman, Jack. "S.L.'s Venerable Alta Club Keeps Changin", THE SALT LAKE TRIBUNE, November 14, 1993, Sec-D2.
Goodman, Jack. "School Days In Magna", THE SALT LAKE TRIBUNE, Sunday, March 4, 2001, D.
Goodman, Jack. "Snow Building Owes It All to Eggs", THE SALT LAKE TRIBUNE, Sunday, December 5, 1999, Sec-D.
Goodman, Jack. "Spanish-Style Columbus School", THE SALT LAKE TRIBUNE, August 9, 1987.
Goodman, Jack. "St. Mark's School Students To Inaugurate Arts Center", THE SALT LAKE TRIBUNE, October 11, 1992, Sec-E6.
Goodman, Jack. "Tenth Ward Square Gets Its Chance to Shine", THE SALT LAKE TRIBUNE, Sunday, November 28, 1999, Sec-D.
Goodman, Jack. "Victorian Finery Makes Its Mark Amid Kanab's Western Icons", THE SALT LAKE TRIBUNE, Sunday, August 1, 1999, Sec-D.
Goodman, Jack. "Wall Falls May Signal A Rebirth On Main Street", THE SALT LAKE TRIBUNE, Sunday, September 9,1999, Sec-D.
Goodman, Jack. "Westminster Work Yields Surprises In Attic", THE SALT LAKE TRIBUNE, Sunday, June 19,1994, E2.
Goodman, Jack. "At Wheeler, City Kids Get View", THE SALT LAKE TRIBUNE, October 20, 1996, Sec-D2.
Gruenwaid, Kim M. "American Indians and the Public School System: A Case Study -of the Northern Utes", UTAH HISTORICAL QUARTERLY, Volume 64, Number 3, Summer 1996, pp.246-263.
Haddock, Sharon M. "What will become of historic Maeser School?" DESERET NEWS, Wednesday P.M./ Thursday, April 16-17, 1997.
Havnes, Mark. "Preservation Efforts Thrive in Southern Utah", THE SALT LAKE TRIBUNE, April, 1999.
Henning, Elizabeth. "Heritage Foundation Not Consulted on Arcade", THE SALT LAKE TRIBUNE, Sunday, February 11, 2001, AA5.
Israelsen, Brent. "Ghosts? Hauntings? It's Not Halloween, It's the Parapsychology Course at WSU-Course Peers Into the Paranormai", THE SALT LAKE TRIBUNE, October 29, 1996, Bl.
Keahey, John. "Before Sunrise, There Was Copperton", THE SALT LAKE TRIBUNE, Tuesday, January 23, 2001, B3.
Keahey, John. "Historic School Won't House S. Jordan Museum", THE SALT LAKE TRIBUNE, December, 2000.
Keahey, John. "New Day Dawning in S. Jordan", THE SALT LAKE TRIBUNE, January 23, 2001, B.
Keahey, John. "'Little House on the Park, Cemetery Getting New Life", THE SALT LAKE TRIBUNE, November 25,1999, F6.
Keahey, John. "Slag Heap to Showplace: Midvale Has Hopes for Bingham Junction", THE SALT LAKE

TRIBUNE, Saturday, June 3, 2000, Sec-B.
Keahey, John. "West Jordan May Restore Meeting Hall", THE SALT LAKE TRIBUNE, Tuesday May 7, 2002, Sec-B2.
KSL Eyewitness News. "Ghost Hunters", November 8, 1999.
Loomis, Brandon. "With Plans for Urban Neighborhood, Brigham City Hopes To See 'Indian School' Reincarnated: 'Indian School' Redevelopment Is In The Works, THE SALT LAKE TRIBUNE, February 16,1999, Nation/World Section.
Lund, Herbert Z. "The Skeleton In Grandpa's Barn", UTAH HISTORICAL QUARTERLY, Volume 35, Number 1, Winter 1967, pp. 31-36.
McLish, Carrie. "Relics of St. Therese of Lisieux to Visit Oakland This Week", THE CATHOLIC VOICE, January 10, 2000, p.3.
Magid, Judy. "Haven On The Hill", THE SALT LAKE TRIBUNE, Sunday, August 1, 1999, Sec-F.
Martin, Wilson; Holt, Susan; Pett, Rob and Sonntag, Ellis. 'The Governor's Mansion: Ready For Utah's Second Century", UTAH PRESERVATION, Volume 1, pp.10-19.
Masonic Temple. Reprint from "Masonic Temple Dedication Edition", supplement to THE SALT LAKE TRIBUNE, November 20, 1927, reprinted by the Grand Lodge, F. & A.M. of Utah, Masonic Temple, 60 East South Temple.
Masonic Temple. "Masonic Temple", pamphlet provided by the Grand Lodge of the Utah Masonic Temple, 650 East South Temple.
May, Heather. "Last Walks in the Hallways", THE SALT LAKE TRIBUNE, Saturday, June 1, 2002, Sec B.
McHenry, W.C. "Bill and Nada's Cafe Namesake, W.C. McHenry, Is Dead at 82", THE SALT LAKE TRIBUNE, Friday, August 1999, B3. (No author listed)
Miller, Layne. "Students Sift for Belongings After Fire", THE SALT LAKE TRIBUNE, Friday, December 1, 2000.
Mims, Bob. "Living Legacy of St. Ann's", THE SALT LAKE TRIBUNE, 1999, front page.
Mims, Bob. "The Relics of 'the Little Flower of Jesus'", THE SALT LAKE TRIBUNE, Saturday, January 1, 2000, Sec-C.
Mims, Bob. "Utah's Catholics Throng To See St. Therese's Relics", THE SALT LAKE TRIBUNE, Wednesday, January 26, 2000, D2.
Moulton, Kristen. "N.M. Foundation Wants Indian School Mural Saved", THE SALT LAKE TRIBUNE, Wednesday, March 28, 2001, D3.
Moulton, Kristen. "Renovation Makes Way for Demolition at Intermountain Indian School", THE SALT LAKE TRIBUNE, January 31, 2001.
Moulton, Kristen. "Spinning History Into Gold", THE SALT LAKE TRIBUNE, Sunday, October 2, 1999, Sec B.
Moulton, Kristen. "With Memories Painful and Sweet, Indian School Heads for Demolition", THE SALT LAKE TRIBUNE, Monday, March 19, 2001.
Murvosh, Marta. "Utah's Oldest School In Use Faces Razing, Needs Funding", THE SALT LAKE TRIBUNE, Tuesday, March 26, 2002, Sec-B2.
Oberbeck, Steven. "Avenues Residents Ask Leavitt to Put a Stop to 'Bureaucratic Madness", THE SALT LAKE TRIBUNE, Sunday, August 8,1999, Sec-C.
Ogden City Landmarks Commission. "Historic 25th Street", O.C.L.C., 1973.
Ogden, Utah. "Haunted Hotel Offers More Than a Great Rate", NATIONAL HAUNTED PLACES MAGAZINE, Volume 1, Number 2, August 1, 2001. (http://powow.com/ghostmag/aug01/page5.html)
Petheram, Susan. "Neighborhood Schools: Kearns - St. Ann and Columbus", PRESERVATION MAGAZINE, Volume 6, Spring 2002, pp. 74-79.
Pray, Amy. "Local legends and spooky stories", OGDEN STANDARD-EXAMINER, Sunday, Ocotober 31, 1999.
Pray, Amy. "Stubborn spirits refuse to show off: Ogden tour provides ghost hunters with a few chilling experiences", OGDEN STANDARD-EXAMINER, Sunday, October 31, 1999.

Rolly, Paul. "Female Alta Club Members Agree: Fewer Barriers For Everyone", THE SALT LAKE TRIBUNE, May 31, 1993, Sec-Al.
Roper, Roger. "Hotels Revisited: Retracing a 1919 Utah Road Trip", UTAH PRESERVATION, Volume 2, pp. 38-43.
Sandy Museum Foundation. "Sandy Co-op/ Fire Station", SANDY HISTORICAL GAZETTE, Sandy Museum Foundation: October, 1987, p.2.
Schvaneveldt, Kathy. "Hail to the Hermitage", and "Great Man's Elaborate Planning Created a Grand Resort", OGDEN STANDARD-EXAMINER, May 5,1996.
Scott, Carl W. "Symbolism In The Masonic Temple At Salt Lake City, Utah", Record presented in Wasatch Lodge No. 1, F.& A.M., March 10, 1944.
Seethaler, Karl. "Old Rock Church & Providence Inn Bed & Breakfast, private papers, March 25, 2001.
Smith, Christopher. "Alta Club Reveals What's Behind Closed Doors", THE SALT LAKE TRIBUNE, April 14, 2002, Sec-Al.
Smith, Jason Matthew. "True Ghost Stories: Ten Haunted Locations", THE EVENT, October 28, 1999, p.6-7.
Smith, Max J. "Restoring Health To This Arcade Requires Promise", THE SALT LAKE TRIBUNE, Sunday, February 11, 2001, AA5.
Snyder, Susan. "Utah Legends Could Have You on Pins and Needles", and "Authors Seek to Spin a Good Yarn, Not Analyze Historical Events", OGDEN STANDARD-EXAMINER, no dates given.
Kapaloski, Gayle. "Ghost Stories," UTAH HOLIDAY, Volume 14, Number 1, October 1984, pp.70-76 and 78.
Stack, Peggy Fletcher, "Rowland Hall-St. Mark's to Turn Over Building in Ceremony", THE SALT LAKE TRIBUNE, Wednesday, May 15, 2002, Sec-D-2.
Stettler, Jeremiah. "Owner Refuses to Give Up on Old Woolen Mill", THE SALT LAKE TRIBUNE, Monday, January 21, 2002, Sec-B.
Tebbs, Irene Henrie. "Panguitch Brick", Panguitch Carnegie Library, May, 2000.
Thompson, Lisa. "Renovating Memorial House; The Power of Partnerships", UTAH PRESERVATION, Volume 3, pp.46-49.
Vinateri, Joseph A. "The Growing Years: Westminster College From Birth To Adolescence", UTAH HISTORICAL QUARTERLY, Volume 75, Number 4, Fall 1975, pp.344-361.
Walsh, Rebecca. "Historic House Is Rapidly Crumbling", THE SALT LAKE TRIBUNE, Monday, May 27, 2000.
Walsh, Rebecca. "Home Improvement", THE SALT LAKE TRIBUNE, April 15, 2001.
Walsh, Rebecca and Keahey, John. "Murray Blows It Stacks", THE SALT LAKE TRIBUNE, Monday, August 7, front page.
Walsh, Rebecca. "Plan to Save Brooks Arcade Is Just a Facade, Critics Say", THE SALT LAKE TRIBUNE, Friday, February 2, 2001.
Walsh, Rebecca. "Renovation Makes Way for Demolition at Intermountain Indian School", THE SALT LAKE TRIBUNE, January 31, 2001.
Walsh, Rebecca. "Sugar House Neighbors Seek to Save Old Chapel", THE SALT LAKE TRIBUNE, Tuesday, January 23, 2001, 1 OA.
Walsh, Rebecca. "Wrecking Ball May Yet Swing For Building Next To Mansion", THE SALT LAKE TRIBUNE, July 16,1999, Sec-E.
Wharton, Tom. "Kanab Women Are Used To Making History", THE SALT LAKE TRIBUNE, October 30,1999, Sec-D.
Wharton, Tom. "Mill a Reminder of Legend's Curse", THE SALT LAKE TRIBUNE, Saturday, February 24, 2001, B.
Wolfson, Hannah. "A Longing For The Days of Close-Knit Communities", Associated Press, THE SALT LAKE TRIBUNE, Sunday, November 28,1999, A25.
Young, S. Dilworth. "The Beehive House", UTAH HISTORICAL QUARTERLY, Volume 50, Number 2, Spring, (1 960). 1982.

WEB SITES:

GHOSTS OF THE PRAIRIE:
www.ghostprairie.com

HAUNTED AMERICA:
http:hauntedamerica.com/wphw/attractions.phtml?State=Utah
http:hauntedamerica.com/storyghost.utah/ut-mill.htm#title.

http://www.maeserelementaryschool.com

PROVIDENCE INN: BED & BREAKFAST:
http://www.providenceinn.com

SALT LAKE CITY GHOSTS AND HAUNTINGS RESEARCH SOCIETY:
www.ghrs.org/slc

THE SHADOWLANDS - GHOST STORIES BY STATE:
http://theshadowlands.net/places/utah.htm

UTAH GHOST HUNTER'S SOCIETY:
www.ghostwave.com

UTAH GHOST HUNTERS RESEARCH SOCIETY:
www.ghostpix.com

UTAH GHOST TOWNS:
www.inconnect.com/-ghostown/haunts.htm

- ABOUT THE AUTHOR -

Linda Dunning has always been aware of spirit. She was accused of daydreaming too much all during childhood, when she flew over places in her dreams. She knew things about other people and thought at the time that this was just an artist-writer's vivid imagination. It never occurred to her in those days that what she was seeing and hearing might be real. She attributed such "knowingness" to her creativity and first began drawing and painting them, eventually abandoning this past time for writing.

With a learning disability, it became clear that foreign languages and mathematics would be beyond her reach and so she became a special education teacher after seeing a film on the deaf-blind that highlighted Helen Keller and her teacher, Annie Sullivan. She began her travels as a teacher in this nonverbal, sightless world, with children who often could not move much of their bodies. It was in this world that she discovered her ability to "hear" in the dark and to often "see" in it as well. When others seemed not able to "talk" with these children, she was at first angry and frustrated, thinking that they were refusing to try, but eventually began to understand that not everyone could walk in the spirit lodges of others, even though everyone has it within themselves to do so.

For twelve years with the severely multi-handicapped and another twelve spent in special education resource rooms, Mrs. Dunning continued to write. After several books of poetry and two collections of short stories entitled THE SUEDE-LIKE PETALS OF A GIANT CRIMSON GLORY and A YEAR FOR THE DAYROOM CHILD about her experiences with the multi-handicapped, she began to write novels. THE NIGHT RAINBOW is a science-fiction ghost story taking place on two parallel planes with two separate sets of characters that eventually converge together into one story. SOYALA, is a very long western Gothic, mystical romance, set in southern Colorado, involving several female characters in the late 1800s and their lives, loves, and mystical ties to the land and Hopi beliefs. Turning to nonfiction, she began writing books on a variety of subjects including her life as the wife of a Vietnam Hospital Corpsman combat veteran entitled SHADOW WIFE and her awakenings as an intuitive in her mother-daughter memoir, LIGHT ON A SENSITIVE SURFACE. Several of these unpublished works have received awards over the years.

About the time she began to do intuitive readings for others and jumped from special education into gifted education for the last part of her career as a teacher, Mrs. Dunning, with a master's degree and 60 hours beyond this, also began collecting her ghost stories. She had about 65 ghost stories collected when she moved to Utah from Colorado to care for her ailing mother. Seven years later, with a lot of research, summer traveling about her home state and a newfound interest in history and preservation, her book was just too big to be one book. She divided the stories by theme and suddenly had five books instead of one. Overwhelmed by the ghosts she found in every nook and cranny, she has now become the historical preservation "ghost story lady" who tells these wonderful and sometimes scary tales to those who will listen!

Printed in the United States
1177000003B/102

9 781892 523334